GOLD-HALL AND EARTH-DRAGON:
BEOWULF AS METAPHOR

ALVIN A. LEE

Gold-Hall and Earth-Dragon:
Beowulf as Metaphor

UNIVERSITY OF TORONTO PRESS
Toronto Buffalo London

© University of Toronto Press Incorporated 1998
Toronto Buffalo London
Printed in Canada

ISBN 0-8020-4378-x (cloth)
ISBN 978-1-4426-1312-6 (paper)

Printed on acid-free paper

Canadian Cataloguing in Publication Data

Lee, Alvin A., 1930–
  Gold-Hall and earth-dragon : Beowulf as metaphor

  Includes bibliographical references and index.
  ISBN 0-8020-4378-x

  1. Beowulf.   I. Title.

PR1585.L4 1998   829'.3   c98-931674-2

University of Toronto Press acknowledges the financial assistance to its publishing program of the Canada Council for the Arts and the Ontario Arts Council.

This book has been published with the help of a grant from the Humanities and Social Sciences Federation of Canada, using funds provided by the Social Sciences and Humanities Research Council of Canada.

TO MY FATHER, NORMAN LEE

Contents

PREFACE ix

INTRODUCTION 3

Part I: Modes of Imagining and the Workings of Words 7
1 *Wunder æfter Wundre*: Modes of Imagining 9
2 *Word Oðer Fand*: The Inwardness of Kennings 53
3 *Þryðword Sprecen*: The Language of Myth and Metaphor 84
4 *Ealdgesegena Worn Gemunde:* Memory and Identity 114

Part II: Structure and Meaning 139
5 *Fyr on Flode*: War against the Creation 141
6 *Swa Sceal Man Don*: Germanic Tales and Christian Myths 177
7 *Heold on Heahgesceap*: The Structure of the Poem, the Heroic Theme, and the Shape of the Hero's Life 205
8 *Nu Is Wilgeofa ... Deaðbedde Fæst*: Tragedy and the Limits of Heroism 232

CONCLUSION 252
NOTES 255
BIBLIOGRAPHY 263
INDEX 271

Preface

I have written about *Beowulf* before and some repetition of an earlier understanding of the poem is unavoidable. But the main course of the argument of this book is quite different from that in essay 4 of *The Guest-Hall of Eden: Four Essays on the Design of Old English Poetry* (1972). Much of the close reading of *Beowulf* that lay behind that earlier discussion has been intensified, extended, and brought into the foreground. Where the earlier account of *Beowulf* was primarily concerned with structural contours, recurrent patterns of imagery, and major themes – in relation to those of other poetic texts from the Anglo-Saxon period – this present study goes much more deeply into the actual figurative workings of the words of the poem. It also returns to questions of structure and meaning, but probes these subjects from a wider range of literary and cultural perspectives, even while staying close to the text and taking detailed instruction from it.

In 1998, a broader and more fully articulated theoretical inquiry seems more necessary than it did in the relative critical innocence of the early 1970s. We begin by reading *Beowulf* as we read other poems, with due regard to the cultural and linguistic conditions and limitations of its own time; also to our own cultural and personal limitations as readers in receiving and understanding this old text. We conclude with a sense of powerful metaphors and myths breaking through the cultural obstacles and scholarly biases that would hamper our responses. We start out with certain notions of what the poem might be thought to mean, and end seeing that what it actually does mean far exceeds our initial fumblings with the words of this enigmatic text.

During the years that I have been working on *Beowulf*, two main contexts have surrounded the poem in my mind: that of the rest of Old English literature, particularly the extant poetry, and a broad, what used to be called comprehensive reading and thinking about other literature, mainly of the Western world.

Early on in my experience, two very different scholars, Laurence K. Shook and Northrop Frye, taught me: the first of these was a historically inclined philologian and close scrutineer of the words of Old English poems; the second was a major literary critic who produced *Anatomy of Criticism: Four Esssays* (1957) and numerous other works, and went on to become one of the twentieth century's most cited and influential cultural philosophers. These men pointed to paths which, in a general way, I am still following: Shook taught me the necessity of puzzling over the polysemous functioning of the actual words in Old English poems; Frye helped make me a theoretically and critically conscious participant in a wide range of literary and other cultural expressions. Neither scholar can be held accountable, of course, for my many divergences since, in which more often than not I have been doing things with literary texts quite distinct from anything they would have done. Nonetheless my obligation to them is real, including in the present book.

As this study of *Beowulf* was taking shape, I was appointed general editor of a scholarly, annotated edition of the collected works of Frye. Three of an estimated thirty or more volumes have now appeared from the University of Toronto Press. This major editorial project involves preparing for publication both the extensive Frye writings printed during his lifetime and a large body of carefully written but never before published notebooks, diaries, and other papers. It has become clear to those of us in the project that the thinker who wrote *Anatomy of Criticism*, by which book he is still mainly known, went well beyond that epochal text in his later explorations of language and culture. This present book, inevitably and, I think, for the better, shows the influence not only of *Anatomy* but also of Frye's still relatively unknown recent work.

Beowulf studies is a much-worked field, and those of us active in it owe large debts to those scholars who have gone before. Some of these are acknowledged in the following pages. There are many more whose influence is real, though not direct enough in relation to this book to surface here. But I am grateful to them and have recently discussed the work of many of them in chapter 12 of *A 'Beowulf' Handbook* (Bjork/Niles 1997). Among current Anglo-Saxonists who have written about *Beowulf* in recent years and who do appear in this book, I acknowledge in particular the work of Robert E. Bjork, James W. Earl, Roberta Frank, Edward B. Irving Jr, John D. Niles, and Fred C. Robinson. No one of them can be blamed for this book's shortcomings or its main argument, but I have found their scholarship particularly useful in helping formulate what follows.

Over the years colleagues and students in the Department of English at McMaster University have been invaluable, not only for the usual reason of academic stimulus but because, had they not been there with their lively minds and demanding energies, my senior administrative responsibilities could have completely supplanted serious literary work. I particularly thank Harry Thode (recently deceased) and Arthur Bourns, my predecessors as presidents of McMaster. Even while they were encouraging me to take on ever more demanding administrative challenges, they also valued and facilitated my scholarly work. At the Press, Suzanne Rancourt, Kristen Pederson, Barb Porter, Amanda Foubister, Judy Williams, and others have provided excellent professional assistance in bringing this book to its published form. In the private world, Hope, my wife, has been loyal beyond reason, balancing her own and my public duties with our good family life. Our five daughters, their husbands, and our grandchildren are splendid company as we all proceed together.

A.L.
McMaster University
1998

GOLD-HALL AND EARTH-DRAGON

Introduction

The aim of this book is to help re-create as fully as possible for modern-day readers the original metaphorical force of the poetic language of *Beowulf*. By thorough immersion in the words of the poem, its internal verbal patternings, and its narratives, and by articulation of the *ars poetica* used in doing this work of critical renovation, I offer an intensive verbal and imaginative experience of *Beowulf* and a theoretical explanation of how that experience is made possible. The book provides a new way of reading and understanding the poem. It is an invitation to others to think about this strong, sinewy text from a thousand or more years ago in ways that recognize and respond to its highly figurative language. It is this language, in my view, that does the main work of the poem.

Beowulf is 3182 lines of Old English poetry. As the still-relevant New Criticism would have put it, the poem is a thing in itself, a unique verbal structure with multiple internal subtleties and meanings. It is also a large and important part of the thirty thousand extant lines of poetry from the Anglo-Saxon period. Less immediately but also important, it belongs to the wider verbal and non-verbal culture of Anglo-Saxon England. While writing the following chapters I have kept centrally in mind the fact that *Beowulf* – first, last, and foremost – is a poem and a fictional narrative. It is not a doctrinal treatise, as some would have it, or a documentary guide to any actual situations or events in history. Despite the intractable problems of the dating of *Beowulf*, I have tried to understand how Anglo-Saxons, particularly in the light of what we know of their other poems, might have experienced and interpreted this one.

A good deal of the content of this book has been derived from within the verbal processes of the poem itself, in a sustained attempt on my part to experience and imaginatively confront what *Beowulf* is, and what it is doing, word by word and part by part. At times this work of deliberate immersion has required me to adopt an evocative, even incantatory style of writing. Much of the time, however, for critical balance as well as for variety of tone, the text is being identified and described objectively, from outside it, with the help of a range of critical perspectives. One of these, which follows logically from the immersion experience, is the critical task of giving an overall account of *Beowulf* as a total, interrelated, complex verbal structure. Another perspective, in which the poem is placed in the middle distance, involves recognition of other cultural facts of the Anglo-Saxon period, most especially the uses in other Old English poems of biblical mythology. There are still other contexts brought into focus, which permit a realization of further illuminating phases of meaning in *Beowulf*: imaginative literature from times and places other than Anglo-Saxon England; certain theologies and philosophies of the Western world relevant to the critical model fashioned and used here; and finally, some of the principal lines of theoretical and critical thought about language and literature in recent decades.

Particularly useful in relation to this last, in addition to Frye (acknowledged in the Preface), are Walter Ong's ideas about language and verbal expression in oral and residually oral cultures (*Orality and Literacy*, 1982); also what Paul Ricœur says about the creation of meaning in language (*The Rule of Metaphor*, 1977, published first in 1975 under the French title, *La métaphore vive*, which I prefer). Ong, Ricœur, and Frye (and other critics cited throughout) have provided valuable ideas and insights which I have adapted, fused together, and used both in the theoretical argument and in the practical exploration that follow. Many of us who study Old English poems are well aware of the concrete physicality of the poetic language encountered in *Beowulf*, and some of us recognize that, despite this concreteness, the resultant poem is not really mimetic or descriptive literature, as we know these terms in relation to historically later writings. I think our scholarship and criticism so far have failed to come to terms with the concrete non-realism of *Beowulf*. It is that gap in understanding that I hope this book begins to fill. I do not know of any study which focuses on the metaphorical power of the language and verbal imagining of *Beowulf* with the thoroughness that this book does, while at the same time providing a theory that is wide-ranging and supple enough not to be a critical straitjacket for the poem.

The critical path for *Gold-Hall and Earth-Dragon* began to appear because of a hunch that came to me when I was a graduate student reading for the first time the Old English text of *Beowulf*. Something similar to this hunch will be known to others who have been similarly initiated, though I sensed at the time that my problem was not bothering other members of the seminar the way it was me, except for one individual in the group who was and still is an accomplished poet. The problem was this. The class time was taken up mainly by translation of the text, followed by commentary about historical background (Northumbrian culture in the time of Bede, that being thought by the professor to be the likely context out of which the poem had come). In preparing for class I regularly got fairly deep into wrestling with the possible meanings of the Old English words on the pages of Klaeber's edition, as they occurred and, usually, recurred. Since I had recently come out of a fairly sustained study of the Hebrew Old Testament and the Greek New Testament, and had been intensely interested in the highly concrete imagery and figurative language of much of the Bible, I was sensitized to these features when I found them in *Beowulf*. When Klaeber's Glossary and Bosworth-Toller (*An Anglo-Saxon Dictionary*) provided, as often they did, a literal, even etymological, meaning for a word, along with more thoroughly translated ones (that is, culturally, historically, and linguistically removed ones), I found myself opting for the former, if the poetic context seemed at all to allow it. My intention was to stay as close as possible to the Old English text. It seemed to me then, and still does, that that was what the poem itself invites. Often the literal meaning is the literary or poetic meaning. If one opts for the more thoroughly translated senses of the words, the concrete Old English images and figurative expressions are severely diluted or disappear completely, and one is no longer reading the poem *Beowulf* at all. The professor, back then, described one of my oral translations as 'rather William Morrisy,' and no doubt it was. He might also have mentioned Sir Thopas. But the early intuition has stayed with me, and this book is the long-term result.

Gold-Hall and Earth-Dragon: 'Beowulf' as Metaphor has by design both a figurative and a literary critical title. It is organized in two parts, each with four chapters. Part one of the book is concentrated on the modes of imagining in the poem, broadly characterized, and on the intricate workings of the poetic language and narrative art used in that imagining. Chapter 1 develops the thesis that *Beowulf* is composed predominantly in the mode of romance but with a marked tendency to move into myth, with a consequent minimal involvement in mimetic art. Chapter 2 explores the centripetal or inward-turning nature of some of the verbal workings of the poem, especially the ones that take the form of kennings. Chapter 3 introduces and uses Frye's concept of 'first phase' language to account for and help explore the concrete, corporeal, and non-abstract nature of the poem's metaphorical language, as this is used pervasively to characterize and present (but not represent) physical and mental things and processes, in ways quite distinct from what we find in mimetic or in allegorical writing. Chapter 4 continues the centripetal exploration, this time in relation to the narrative art of remembering and associating that is extensively at work throughout the text, establishing the poem's metaphorical identities for places, people, things, and events. This chapter also includes a brief centrifugal inquiry into certain other early texts that help us understand particular poetic identities established in this poem.

6   Gold-Hall and Earth-Dragon

Part two of the book is a sustained scrutiny of the overall structure of *Beowulf* and of some of the many meanings, the polysemy, of that structure. Chapters 5 and 6 construct a theory of interpretation, which I hope is clear, flexible, and wide-ranging. It is meant to help us accommodate in our understandings of *Beowulf* both original Anglo-Saxon meanings and modern or postmodern ones, all the while staying under the guidance of the text itself. This theoretical construction involves a specifically non-doctrinal, non-theological use of the ancient and medieval exegetical theory of four levels. The old mode of interpretation is recast in the light of Frye's post-Hegelian transformation of it, and then adapted and used in reading and interpreting *Beowulf*. Chapters 7 and 8 continue the polysemous inquiry while simultaneously examining closely the relationship between romance and tragedy which is at the structural and metaphorical core of the poem. Here the developing argument invites readers to consider the poem's widest and deepest levels of meaning.

PART ONE

MODES OF IMAGINING AND THE WORKINGS OF WORDS

1

Wunder æfter Wundre: Modes of Imagining

When the hero is first mentioned in *Beowulf*, the *Scyldingas* 'Sons [or 'Men'] of Shield' are at the nadir of their experience. In complete contrast with their earlier happy condition when the great hall Heorot first was ready for guests, these noble ones have now endured twelve years of Grendel's slaughters. Some of them are caught in devil worship (175–88) and are honouring the very power that is destroying them.[1] Hroðgar 'Glory Spear,' who broods endlessly on the time of trouble, is completely powerless to uphold the former dynastic glory of the house of the Scyldings (189–93). Having earlier achieved great power, culminating in the construction of Heorot, he now is an aged king who can no longer effectively exercise his will: 'the wise warrior could not / turn aside woe' (*ne mihte snotor hæleð / wean onwendan*). The conflict which has come upon the Danish people is 'too harsh, hateful and long-lasting' (*to swyð, / lað ond longsum*). It is *nydwracu niþgrim* 'a cruel, unavoidable violence,' *nihtbealwa mæst* 'the greatest of night-evils,' as Grendel continues his relentless oppression. The condition of the Danish court could hardly be worse and their protector-lord is powerless. Evil and destruction are in control.

Across the sea in Geatland, the hero learns of the Scyldings' disastrous situation. When he first appears in the narrative he is not named: he is 'Hygelac's thane / good among the Geats' (*Higelaces þegn / god mid Geatum*, 194b–5a). The rhetorical buildup of his stature is immediate and uses a sinewy hyperbole: *se wæs moncynnes mægenes strengest / on þæm dæge þysses lifes, / æþele ond eacen* 'of mankind he was the strongest of might / in the day of this life, / noble and powerful' (196–7a). 'Powerful' is an inadequate translation of *eacen*. The Old English word connotes the strength that comes from extraordinary physical size; the related noun *eaca* means 'addition, increase' and the verb *eacan* means 'to be increased' or 'added to, augmented, enlarged.' This protagonist, in his being made, has been 'added to,' compared to other men. In him we have humanity writ large. He is the poem's answer to Grendel, the monster who a few lines earlier has been called *feond mancynnes* 'enemy of mankind' (164) and *gastbona* 'the slayer of souls' (177). This is a work of literature in which the hero's physical powers of action and his moral fibre are closely identified. In both aspects Beowulf is *god* 'good,' to use the poem's own understatement. The adjective simultaneously characterizes and indicates approval of him, and also recalls the formula *þæt wæs god cyning*, applied a little earlier to Scyld (11). It leads aurally as well to the 'good' ship ordered by Beowulf as he prepares to go to Denmark. A couple of moments later, the hero again is referred to as *se goda*, as he chooses the *cenoste* 'keenest' or 'boldest' champions to go with him. In case the moral and physical resonances are not yet strong enough, the narrator shortly adds to his own assessment of the protagonist that of someone else (247b–51a). The vigilant Danish coast-guard has no knowledge of Beowulf beyond what can readily be seen on first observation but he recognizes at once the hero's unique excellence: *Næfre ic maran geseah / eorla ofer eorþan,   ðonne is eower sum, / secg on searwum* 'Never have I seen a greater nobleman on earth than one of you is, a man in his armour.' He concludes that Beowulf is no 'hall-man' or 'retainer' (*seldguma*) 'unless his appearance, his unique form, is lying' (*næfne him his wlite leoge, / ænlic ansyn*).

The men closest to Beowulf, his own troop of companions, are part of the strength rapidly being mobilized at this stage of the narrative. Like their leader they are eager for the coming adventure (*weras on wilsiþ* 'men on a desired voyage,' 216a), as they load the boat and push its well-braced timbers away from the shore. Even the ship itself, in a subtle touch of prosopopeia, is *winde gefysed* 'made eager by the wind,' as *famiheals* 'foamy-necked' and *fugle gelicost* 'most like a bird' its *wundenstefna* 'curving prow' moves across the *wægholm* 'wave-tossed sea' (217–20). The brief but animated account of the Geatish seafarers' approach to the broad sea-nesses, gleaming cliffs, and high hills of the Danish coast (222–3a), and of the arrival on shore, conveys a pronounced sense of purpose and rapidity of movement. As the Geats disembark on to the *wang* 'land' and fasten their *sæwudu* 'sea-wood, ship,' their mail-coats and battle-dress rattling, they thank God that for them the 'wave-farings were easy' (*Gode þancedon / þæs þe him yþlade   eaðe wurdon*, 228).

The poet's presentation of Beowulf's decision to go to Denmark and of the voyage itself is done with economy and just enough featural information to shape a vivid narrative. The main focus is on the extraordinary figure of the protagonist. Everything mentioned – his thanes, other Geats in Hygelac's court, the ship, the weather and the waves, God himself – favours the heroic action. The mood is one of exuberant energy on every level, mobilized and purposeful, meeting no obstacle as it moves towards its goal. All this is in sharp contrast to the situation of paralysed impotence in Heorot. A sense of openness, of spaciousness and freedom of movement, replaces the claustrophobia, darkness, and death that envelop the great hall in Denmark. The mood of brooding and desperate sacrifice to 'the slayer of souls' (*gastbona*) has given way, for the moment, to a sense of buoyant, confident power made possible by the united force of the hero, his personal dryht,[2] his people, the heroic world's weapons and ship, natural forces, and heaven itself.

In recent decades, many scholars and critics have come to see that *Beowulf* is an unreliable guide to history, including to its own time and place in literary history.[3] Its modes of imagining are not directly representational of people, things, and events in the actual world. It is easy for most of us now, much later in the culture, to see that the poem is primarily imaginative fiction, however many bits of history and actuality it may have drawn into itself. But among the thousands of fictions in our literature, where does this one sit? Put differently, what, in the wider context of the universe of our literature, *is* this poem, from sometime in the early medieval period? How fictional or imaginative is it, when compared with other works, either from approximately the same period of history or from other periods? If we take up these questions in the light of the thirty-four lines just scrutinized, an answer starts to emerge.

In the figure of Beowulf, strongest of mankind, we are dealing with what Walter J. Ong (1982, 69–70) has called a 'heavy' figure and with what Northrop Frye (1957, 33–67) has called a relatively 'weighty' one. In Ong's penetrating description of the 'heroic tradition of primary oral culture and of early literate culture, with its massive oral residue,' he points out that human memory in these kinds of cultures works effectively with 'heavy' or 'outsize' figures, 'persons whose deeds are monumental, memorable and commonly public.' These are all apt terms for Beowulf. Around such main figures, says Ong, there are groupings of other easily remembered type characters and of bizarre or monstrous forms. Even in the short passage of *Beowulf* just discussed, there are examples of each of these two kinds of figures: in the first group, the type characters, there are the loyal companions of the hero, the fourteen eager thanes who accompany Beowulf to Denmark, and, beyond these, the supportive Geatish community; in the second group, that of the bizarre, we have in the background the weird, monstrous Grendel, devourer of bodies and slayer of souls. The fundamental contrast immediately evident between the two groups pervades the poem and gives it much of its central meaning.

Ong emphasizes the memorability or 'mnemonic serviceability' of such sharply contrasting figures in the verbalizations of oral or residually oral cultures, to the point of saying that these contrasts are there 'not for romantic reasons or reflectively didactic reasons but for much more basic reasons: to organize experience in some sort of permanently memorable form.' Apparently realizing that this statement is too exclusionary, he adds the comment that 'other forces besides mere mnemonic serviceability produce heroic figures and groupings.' He mentions psychoanalytic theory as one modern explanation of such forces. But it is clear that he thinks the main cause of outsizing is orality's necessity to preserve and organize human experience in memorable ways, so that it will not be entirely lost. This is because there is no written or other means, at least in the primary oral culture, of preserving the experiences that need to be remembered.

But it is difficult to see why the functional, mnemonic demands of preserving certain kinds of experience need be set in any way, exclusionary or otherwise, against 'romantic reasons' or 'reflectively didactic' ones, as Ong does. The mnemonic compulsion is a credible, partial explanation of 'outsize' antithetical imagery, but we know that romance is a perennial mode of imagining, especially on a popular level. It is found in many times and places, including those in which its production is dominantly literary and, increasingly in our time, electronic. We cannot rule out the romance impulse as a force in itself, when for whatever reason the human imagination moves emphatically away from actuality and creates something notably fictional. This happens in each kind of culture defined by Ong: oral, residually oral, literate, and electronic. Nor, in the same vein, is there any need to exclude didacticism. In the case of *Beowulf*, it seems clear that all three elements – the mnemonic, the romantic or heroic, and the didactic – are working together. It would be difficult to establish that any one of the three is more basic to the poem than the others. It needs to be observed as well that the conventions of romance, like those of didacticism, are more enduring than those of orality's mnemonics, since both survive in countless formulations into both the literary and the electronic cultures.

When Ong speaks of 'romance' and the 'romantic,' it is clear that he means something much more comprehensive than the formal genre of romance familiar from later medieval literature and from the tales told or written in other periods, of swashbuckling adventure or erotic quests, or both. He is discussing a mode of imagining that is particularly congenial to what he describes as 'the old oral, mobile, warm, personally interactive lifeworld of oral culture' (80), in which thought processes of human beings grow out of simply natural powers (78) and verbal discourses are not, as they are in print, cut off from the one who speaks them. They are closely connected to the oral poet or teller of tales in his role as the mouthpiece or channel for something held to be communally important, and so in need of being expressed and remembered by a particular live audience. In *Beowulf*, for example, the communal formula *we gefrunon* 'we have heard' in the first few words of the text is one of many illustrations of the special relationship Ong thinks exists between the narrator of heroic romance and the live audience who are brought, by his spoken words, into closely knit unity both with him as story-teller and with some remembered, interpreted, and adapted (that is, fictionalized) part of their communal past. The *we* at the beginning of *Beowulf*, although for us it is part of a readable, written, printed text, or even of an electronically reproduced or live oral performance, needs to be understood as part of what Ong calls the large oral residue that survived long into the age of literacy. This communal formula is in fact a vital part of the 'situational thinking' within which romantic tales were told and out of which such works as *Beowulf*, in some form, seem to have emerged. Ong speaks as well of 'the agonistic lifestyle' (69–70), the 'Enthusiastic description of physical violence' (44), the encouragement of 'triumphalism' (49), and the way 'orality situates knowledge within a context of struggle' (44). These are all suggestive, descriptive phrases when brought to *Beowulf* in its fuller dimensions, and they are well worth bearing in mind as we proceed.

Further broad theoretical understanding of the kind of imagining found in *Beowulf* is possible on the basis of Frye's account of five major fictional modes historically discernible in European literature. The term 'fictions' is used here in a multi-generic sense to designate all literary works that have plots or narratives. Although Frye's now-classical modern statement of modes was published in 1957 and has been used and discussed in many contexts since, it has not to my knowledge been brought in any sustained way to *Beowulf*.[4] With one important correction in its application to medieval literature, the theory can serve as an excellent preliminary means of locating *Beowulf* in a broad literary context and of laying the groundwork for more intensive analysis of its poetic language, including how this language creates meanings, Old English and modern; and of how the poem takes finally the overall structure of a unique tragic romance. Frye took his cue for the theory of modes from the second paragraph of Aristotle's *On the Art of Poetry*, where differences in works of fiction are said to be caused by the different elevations of the characters in them. Aristotle wrote:

Since the objects of imitation are men in action, and these must be either of a higher or a lower type (for moral character mainly answers to these divisions, goodness and badness being the distinguishing marks of moral difference), it follows that we must represent men either as better than in real life, or as worse, or as they are. (4)

In literature, and in painting, says Aristotle, men are depicted as nobler than they are, as less noble, or as true to life. Homer makes men better than they are, and tragedy does the same. In contrast to tragedy, comedy 'aims at representing men as worse ... than in actual life' (5).

Frye noted that because of its apparently moralistic view of literature this passage had been little regarded in modern times, but he saw in it a potentially useful critical insight in need of development. For good reason he decided to move the matter from the moralistic to a different level, by reading Aristotle's two key terms for good and bad (*spoudaios* and *phaulos*) in their figurative senses of 'weighty' and 'light.' On this basis he was able to articulate an unusually illuminating idea: 'In literary fictions the plot consists of somebody doing something. The somebody, if an individual, is the hero, and the something he does or fails to do is what he can do, or could have done (1957, 33). What he can do or could have done is determined by 'the level of the postulates made about him by the author and the consequent expectations of the audience.' In this way, a broad, general scheme for classifying fictions becomes possible, according to 'the hero's power of action, which may be greater than ours, less, or roughly the same.'

The resultant theory is a description of five modes, all of which in varying degrees are useful in trying to understand *Beowulf* but two of which are particularly important. Frye begins with what he sees as the boundary of literature, *myth*. Here the protagonist who acts is a god or divine being, superior in *kind* both to human beings and to the environment within which he functions. If, however, the protagonist is superior only in *degree* to other human beings and their environment, he is the typical hero of romance. His actions are marvellous but he is identified as a human being. At this point Beowulf begins to come into focus. The romance hero 'moves in a world in which the ordinary laws of nature are slightly suspended' (1957, 33). The word 'slightly' is too qualifying in the case of *Beowulf*, whose protagonist performs prodigiously unnatural actions, despite numerous nineteenth- and twentieth-century attempts to explain these exploits naturalistically or to marginalize them while concentrating on other elements of the poem.[5] What we, as heirs since the eighteenth century of a geophysical cosmology, see in the poem as suspension of the laws of nature would not have been thought of as such in Anglo-Saxon times, but it nonetheless is what makes possible in this old fiction extraordinary acts of courage and endurance. Beowulf is an exuberantly active being who through free acceptance and vigorous use of his God-given powers takes on superhuman challenges. In doing so he realizes his great *wyrd* 'destiny' and wins a favourable *dom* 'judgment' both in heaven and middle earth. In his youth he begins his *mærða fela* 'many glorious deeds' (408b–9a) by binding and crushing five of the *eotena cyn* 'race of giants' and by enduring *nearoþearf* 'great distress' in the waves at night so that he may slay *niceras* 'water monsters' (419b–24a). Also in another episode in his youth (530–81a), with his friend and rival Breca he performs the second of four extraordinary feats of sea-craft. (The other two are in Grendel's mere and in the return to Geatland after Hygelac's defeat and death.)[6] By his own account he spends five nights battling sea-creatures and helping Breca, followed by another two nights alone in the stormy waters, where he engages in ferocious sword-fighting with mighty sea-beasts who try unsuccessfully to destroy him. Many years later when he is an aged warrior-king fighting his last battle, against a fire-dragon, his hand is still so strong that it breaks the venerable old sword *Nægling* 'Nailing,' which bursts apart and provides no help when needed (2677b–87). For the hero of romance, the kind of extraordinary powers and actions demonstrated by Beowulf are 'natural,' part of the imaginative hypothesis of the particular fiction. For us, culturally conditioned human beings of modern and postmodern times, they are profoundly 'unnatural.' We of course have developed our own broad array of unnatural technological devices for doing far more extraordinary things than ever occurred to the *Beowulf* poet.

The ancient, medieval, and early Renaissance cosmology assumed a fixed physical and moral order in the universe, based on divinely shaped laws and designs. In the eighteenth century and after, this cosmology was shown to be a human projection, literally a human creation. This major cultural transposition from a theological to a geophysical focus led to the realization that nature, including human beings, was engaged in a trial-and-error process of self-generation, and was not acting out some predetermined script that began with the war in heaven when Lucifer first rebelled against the Deity. The protagonist Beowulf is part of the old order, before this radical reconfiguration. In that old order he is praxis, an embodiment of ethical codes and powers of action radically linked to a divine plan for rescuing and preserving the 'given' created world itself, including certain social and political structures in that world.

Beyond the protagonist's relative abilities, other characteristics of fiction in the romance mode are equally unnatural (to us). To illustrate again from *Beowulf*, with at this stage of our discussion only a few of the more obvious examples, there is the marvellous appearance from the sea of the boy Scyld (46), who is destined to become king of the Danes. There are the omens consulted by the Geats in connection with Beowulf's proposed journey to Denmark (204). There is the springing open of the door of Heorot at a mere touch from the hand of Grendel (720–4a), who on his first foray into the gold-hall has seized thirty thanes (123a). There is also the monster's imperviousness to weapons: 'not any of the choicest of irons on earth, of war-bills, was willing to touch [or greet] him' (*ænig ofer eorþan irenna cyst, / guðbilla nan gretan nolde*, 802–3). There is the marvellous sword provided for Beowulf by God at the crucial, agonistic moment in the depths of the mere, when Grendel's mother would have killed the hero if this miraculous intervention had not taken place (1557–69). There is also the mysterious *glof* 'glove,' 'wide and strange, fast

16 Modes of Imagining and the Workings of Words

with cunning clasps' (*sid ond syllic, searobendum fæst*) and made of 'dragons' skins by devil's craft' (*deofles cræftum on dracan fellum*), into which Grendel apparently tries to put his victims (2085b–92). Above all, and central to any definition of the modes of imagining in the poem, we have the hero, superior in degree to all other men, with *þritiges / manna mægencræft on his mundgripe* 'the strength of thirty men in his hand-grasp' (379b–81a), pitted during his lifetime against numerous monsters, including the three major ones around which the primary tale is composed. Frye's main point about the romance mode is that 'once the postulates of romance have been established,' all such contraventions of what we think of as the natural or the normal 'violate no rule of probability.' They simply belong in this mode of fiction and, in fact, they define its essence.

Repeatedly in *Beowulf* the narrator tells us that we are hearing about marvels, things strange and wonderful. The two key words that draw attention to this fact are *wunder* and *sellic,* studded throughout the poem. Normally these expressions occur as part of the direct narration, but sometimes they are used by other speakers – Hrothgar, Beowulf, Wiglaf – to articulate a sense of wonder or awe about what they and others are experiencing. When for example Beowulf and Grendel, both of them 'furious' (*Yrre*), are fighting for the guardianship of the 'fair life-dwelling' Heorot (*fæger feorgbold*), the narrator marvels at the strength and durability of the great hall, and says, *Þa wæs wundor micel, þæt se winsele / wiðhæfde heaþodeorum, þæt he on hrusan ne feol* 'Then was a great wonder, that the wine-hall withstood the battle-fierce ones, that it did not fall on the ground' (769b–73a). By the morning after, word of what has happened in Heorot has spread, and there are many warriors around the gift-hall, including folk-leaders come from far and near 'to gaze on the wonder' (*wundor sceawian*) of the loathsome Grendel's footprint (837–41a). Again the same morning (916–31), after the Danes and Geats have followed Grendel's tracks and celebrated his defeat, we are told that 'many a strong-hearted man' (*scealc monig / swiðhicgende*) goes to the high hall 'to see the strange wonder' (*searowundor seon*) that is Grendel's hand. Hrothgar too, 'guardian of ring-hoards' (*beahhorda weard*) and 'fast in glory' (*tirfæst*), comes in stately manner with his queen and a large retinue to look up at 'the high roof shining with gold, and at Grendel's hand' (*steapne hrof / golde fahne ond Grendles hond*). The sight of the juxtaposed golden roof and the remnant of the monster causes the king to call for a prayer of thanksgiving to be raised to the 'One Ruler' (*Anwealdan*), the 'Keeper of glory' (*wuldres Hyrde*), who 'can always work wonder after wonder' (*a ... mæg wyrcan / wunder æfter wundre*). The first wonder brought about by God in the poem has been the mysterious appearance and almost equally mysterious funeral voyage of Scyld Scefing. Heorot is the

Modes of Imagining 17

second, called into existence by Hrothgar's words after the idea has come into his mind. The emergence of the hero is the third. And so on. Now that Beowulf with his own mighty hand-grip has torn off the hand of the enemy for all to see, many other human hands, both men's and women's, go to work making the hall ready again for guests: *Goldfag scinon / web æfter wægum,   wundorsiona fela / secga gehwylcum   þara þe on swylc starað* 'Gold-decorated weavings shone on the walls, many wondrous sights for each man who gazes on such things' (991–6). On the evening of this same day on which Hrothgar's creation is restored and celebrated in its renewal, cupbearers once more pour out wine from *wunderfatum* 'wondrous vessels,' and the golden-diademed Wealtheow comes forth to perform her ritual tasks (1161b–3a).

In addition to the hall and its beautiful objects, other important works of human hands or voices are explicitly singled out for wonderment. We are told that the bright helmet worn by Beowulf (1448–54) when he goes 'to stir up the mere-depths' (*meregrundas mengan*) was long ago so 'wondrously fashioned by weapon smiths' (*wæpna smið,   wundrum teode*) and so 'made worthy with treasure, grasped round with princely bands, ... set with boar-likenesses' (*since geweorðad, / befongen freawrasnum, ... besette swinlicum*) 'that never afterward could any blade or battle-sword bite into it' (*þæt hine syðþan no / brond ne beadomecas   bitan ne meahton*). When Beowulf has returned to Geatland and is giving gifts in Hygelac's court, these include an 'artful wonderful treasure' (*wrætlicne wundurmaððum*, 2173a), the neck-ring that Wealtheow has earlier given him which now will do honour to the breast of Queen Hygd. Also among the wonderful things Beowulf brings to Geatland is his memory of the *syllic spell* 'strange tales' told by the *rumheort cyning* 'roomy hearted king,' Hrothgar, on the Geats' last full day in the Danish court (2109b–10). The sense of wondrous human artifacts continues in part II with *Nægling* 'Nailing,' *wæpen wundrum heard* 'a weapon wondrously hard' or 'a weapon brave (and strong) with wounds' (2687),[7] and with the fabulous hoard that Wiglaf sees when he enters the dragon's barrow (2756–71). Among the long-hidden treasures are many precious jewels, glittering gold lying on the ground, and unidentified 'wonders on the wall' (*wundur on wealle*). High above the hoard hangs (*seomian*) 'a standard all-golden' (*segn eallgylden*), 'the greatest of hand-wonders, linked with fingers' skill' (*hondwundra mæst / gelocen leoðocræftum*).

There is another important motif in the poem in which each of the images is characterized as marvellous by one or another of the speakers. But this set of images, like Grendel's hand and glove, is demonic, in sharp contrast to most of those just noted. There is the fire which can be seen each night on the mere, called a *niðwundor* 'hateful wonder' by Hrothgar, who has been told about it by others (1345–6a; 1365–6a). There are the *sellic sædracan* 'strange sea-dragons' exploring the blood-stained waters when the Geats and the Scyldings arrive there (1426). From among the curious mélange of the race of serpents (*wyrmcynnes fela*) in and around the mere, one is singled out for special attention: a *wundorlic wægbora* 'wondrous wave-bearer' wounded by one of the Geats is tugged up on to the shore with barbed boar-spears and exposed there as a *gryrelicne gist* 'horrible stranger' for men to stare at (1437–41a). Another vivid example of the wondrous demonic takes us close to the mind of the slayer of souls, who moves in when human vigilance lapses and pride takes over. In Hrothgar's sermon the workings of this *bona* 'murderer' are described as *wom wundorbebodum wergan gastes* 'crooked strange urgings of the accursed spirit' (1747). The exemplum of the prosperous proud man who exhibits 'folly' (*unsnyttrum*, 1734) instead of 'wisdom' (*snyttre*, 1726) and so falls into damnation is introduced in words that indicate Hrothgar's own sense of wonder or awe at the divine power which he sees as the real determiner of human fates: *Wundor is to secganne, / hu mihtig God manna cynne / þurh sidne sefan snyttru bryttað, / eard ond eorlscipe; he ah ealra geweald* 'It is a wonder to tell how mighty God through his large spirit gives out wisdom to mankind, land and earlship; he possesses power over all things' (1724b–7). Death too is characterized as a wonder. Late in the poem (3028 ff.) after the Geatish messenger has spoken one of the most ominous, fear-filled speeches in the whole text, the unhappy company of Geats go beneath Eagles' Ness and 'with welling tears gaze on a wonder' (*wollenteare wundur sceawian*): the body of the lifeless hero, holding its 'bed of death ... on the sand' (*on sande ... hlimbed healdan*).⁸ Apparently expressing the Geats' reaction to the sight of their dead lord, the narrator tells us that the war-king, prince of the Weather-Geats, has died 'a wonder-death' (*wundordeaðe*). On the shore there is as well something even more awesome: *hi þær gesegan syllicran wiht, / wyrm on wonge* 'they saw there a stranger creature, a worm [or 'dragon'] in the place.' The fire-dragon, scorched by flames and lying fifty feet in length, is *grimlic gryrefah* 'grim and terrible in his shining.' Pondering the mystery of this strange scene (3058–75) of the two wondrous deaths, and also the curse that lasts till Doomsday, the narrator expresses his own wonderment in a generalizing maxim: *Wundur hwar þonne / eorl ellenrof ende gefere / lifgesceafta, þonne leng ne mæg / mon mid his magum meduseld buan* 'It is a wonder where then a warrior famed for courage should fare to the end of his fated life; then no longer may a man dwell with his kinsmen in the mead-hall.' *Swa wæs Biowulfe* 'So it was for Beowulf.' The hero and his life have been part of the wonders of God's Creation. This was first obvious long ago to the guardian of the Danish shore. Now too at the end of his life, Beowulf's death and the manner of his dying are a marvel, made known to the Geats who gaze at him with his mysterious dead companion on another shore.

In these ways and others still to be considered, *Beowulf* announces itself as imagined and composed in the romance mode. It repeatedly invites us to respond accordingly. The extensive use of marvels and wonders and of extraordinary beings, places, and events not encountered in the actual world signals a kind of fiction known from other areas of our literary experience: from the ancient classical world, in the stories of Achilles, Hector, Odysseus, Hercules, Alexander, and Aeneas; from the biblical world, in the tales of Noah, Moses, Deborah, Gideon, Samson, Elijah, Elisha, David, Judith, Daniel, Jonah, the Maccabees, Jesus, and the apostles; and from the northern Teutonic world, in the narrative fictions about Athils, Atli, Bjar, Grettir, Günnar, and Sigurd (Sigmund). There are many others, in other traditions. As a mode of imagining, romance is perennial and widespread. Its broad characteristics are easily recognized.

The third mode delineated by Frye has a protagonist who is superior in degree to other human beings but not to the natural environment. The male embodiment of this protagonist is found in Shakespeare's Henry V, Macbeth, Lear, Antony, and Hamlet, in Marlowe's Tamurlaine and Faustus, in Corneille's Le Cid, Horace, and Polyeucte, and in Racine's Britannicus. The female embodiment is in Shakespeare's Juliet, Rosalind, Portia, Cordelia, and Cleopatra, Webster's Duchess of Malfi, and Racine's Andromaque, Phèdre, and Esther.[9] The protagonist in this mode, female or male, is a leader and has authority, passions, and powers of expression that exceed those of ordinary human beings. Even so, what this figure does is 'subject both to social criticism and to the order of nature' (1957, 33–4). Frye calls this mode *high mimetic* and includes in it most epic and tragedy, pointing out that the still relatively weighty protagonist of these high mimetic fictions 'is primarily the kind of hero that Aristotle had in mind.' It will be necessary to consider *Beowulf* to some extent in relation to this mode because, although this is a poem and fiction imagined primarily in the romance mode, it is also a memorable account of the limitations placed on the effectiveness of heroic leadership by the societies within which that leadership is expressed. In almost high mimetic fashion, *Beowulf* probes deeply into the forces, social and 'natural,' that hold together the court-centred dryht world and those that tear it apart.

The fourth mode centres on a principal figure who is superior neither to other human beings nor to the physical environment. He or she is 'one of us.' We respond to a sense of his or her common humanity and 'demand from the poet the same canons of probability that we find in our own experience' (34). This kind of imagining provides literature with the protagonist of the *low mimetic* mode, of most comedy and of realistic fiction. On this level and with this mode, the words 'hero' and 'heroine' should be abandoned because they are not strictly applicable to realistic literature and because to use them in this connection would render them less functional in relation to the three previous modes.

The fifth and last historical mode of imagining identified by Frye includes those fictions or literary works in which the protagonists are 'inferior in power or intelligence to ourselves, so that we have a sense of looking down on a scene of bondage, frustration, or absurdity' (34). This protagonist and this perspective give the ironic mode. If we were to read *Beowulf* as if it were in the mode of irony, we would put into the back of our minds the elements of romance and myth and concentrate instead on all those features that pull the tale towards what Byron called 'the devil's scripture' (Byron, 339), the record of what human beings actually have done, to what Joyce's Stephen Dedalus called the nightmare of history from which he was trying to waken (Joyce, 35). We would set aside, as many modern interpreters have preferred to do, the markedly fictional parts, what Klaeber in his edition calls the 'fabulous' elements compared to the 'historical' ones. We would emphasize instead such things as the final disaster looming over Heorot from the moment of its beginning (82b–5) and Beowulf's sober prediction to Hygelac that however good the Princess Freawaru is as a bride she will fail at peace-weaving between the Scyldings and the Heathobards (2024b–30). Especially we would emphasize the increasingly ironic vision of human existence in part II of the poem, where wars, feuds, treacheries, usurpation, accidental death, ruined halls, rusted treasure, trapped victims, broken vows, cowardice, and general disintegration build to a climax of destruction and death. There are many ironies in the poem to think about. Where in part I Grendel's mere is the main expression of hell in middle earth, in part II there is something very close to a man-made hell on earth. But importantly the central figure is still the warrior hero with the powerful hand, now doing battle with the fire-dragon who has hoarded a treasure for three hundred years. These figures are unambiguously part of romance and myth and the poem is not in any sustained way in the ironic mode.

If we were to read the vision of life in part II as one of unrelieved human failure and misery, we could see in it the same archetypal ironic *mythos* that we find in Baudelaire's *Les fleurs du mal*, Kafka's *In the Penal Colony*, Hardy's *Jude the Obscure*, and Goya's war paintings. Such transhistorical comparison of narratives can be critically illuminating, provided we recognize that it involves modal displacement as well as substantial cultural translation. But to read *Beowulf* this way, all the way, we have to argue that the hero, at least in part II, is not finally a hero after all but a prideful, avaricious, and foolish old king, part of the general human failure and misery, and that the dragon is not an evil monster but a creature just doing his job of guarding a treasure. In other words, we have to sever the ironic, all-too-ordinary parts of the poem from its overall ways of imagining.

Looking back over the table of the five modes, Frye points out, first, that 'European fiction, during the last fifteen centuries, has steadily moved its centre of gravity down the list' and that for the last hundred years or so, longer in French literature, 'most serious fiction has tended increasingly to be ironic in mode' (1957, 34–5). The general progression, not progress, has been from a literature lacking in naturalistic realism, which gives to the protagonist the greatest freedom, to a literature of verisimilitude and lack of freedom. Finally, the dominant fictional mode in the modern world turns back through irony to myth. This Viconian *ricorso* described four decades ago by Frye has now been in process for about a century in Western literature. Recognition of it – even in the broad-brush characterizing manner of the modes thesis – can help in seeing part of what *Beowulf* is as literature; also, particularly valuable with a work for whose composition we have no sure knowledge, something of where the poem sits in the overall sequence of literary history. It can do this if we practise a kind of criticism that goes beyond objectifying analysis. By that I mean that if we are to understand the free imaginative play of myth and metaphor in *Beowulf*, and in most other Old English poems, we shall need not only the discipline and rigour that are part of the best literary historical scholarship but also a critical *theoria* not itself confined by the dying gasps of modern and postmodern ironic assumptions. We shall need a criticism capable of embracing and at least partly experiencing through imaginative re-creation an early stage of our literary past in which cultural productions, including the making of poems, were part of a 'world-making' enterprise. When Hrothgar and the Old Testament patriarchs in the *Genesis* poem of the Junius manuscript are shown building great gold-halls, this is one part of a human community in Anglo-Saxon England which is being imagined into existence by fusing biblical myth and Germanic cultural experience. The legacy of that kind of imagining in its numerous iterations in Anglo-Saxon culture can still have value, but if we are to reclaim it we shall have to combine the study of literature as an object of knowledge with the study of literature as experience. It will be necessary to recognize that the mind-set in Cædmon, the *Beowulf* poet, Cynewulf, and the anonymous poets behind the Anglo-Saxon poetic records was one of creation and re-creation, not of mimesis, of working (*wyrcan, gewyrcan*) skilfully with traditional words and stories to see what curiously inwrought patterns they would shape themselves into. Another way of putting this is to say that we need both an objectifying poetics of Old English poetry, focused on its structures and themes, and an ethics of participation in its metaphorical processes, if we would know it as it once was. If we can do that, we can then help release its energies into new times and places.

Frye's essay on the historical modes of fiction was thought out in the 1950s and published in 1957. The 'modern' period has since given way, at least in fiction, architecture, and some literary theory, to the 'postmodern,' with its heavy emphasis on 'situating' each work in more than one historical or cultural context, as in historiographic metafictions like *The Name of the Rose* and *Foucault's Pendulum* (Umberto Eco), *The French Lieutenant's Woman* (John Fowles), *The Tin Drum* (Günter Grass), *One Hundred Years of Solitude* (Garcia Marquez), *Midnight's Children* and *The Satanic Verses* (Salman Rushdie), *Flaubert's Parrot* and *The History of* the *the World in 10½ Chapters* (Julian Barnes), and, of special interest for Anglo-Saxonists, the brilliant fusion of modern and Old English perspectives and epistemologies in *Grendel* (John Gardner).

In 1987 there appeared an interesting and unpretentious novel, *The Legacy of Heorot*, which helps illustrate some of the modal, non-Anglo-Saxon possibilities in the *Beowulf* fiction. This book's three authors – Larry Niven, Jerry Pournelle, and Steven Barnes – have realized, as have many others in the twentieth century, that one of the main imaginative areas now available for the expression of romance is science fiction. Their subject is a human colony in outer space. In a place called Tau Ceti Four, two hundred men and women sponsored by the National Geographic Society create a paradisal world called Avalon. Here initially they live as easygoing, peaceable farmers, engineers, and scientists. So that there will be narrative conflict appropriate to the romance mode, the authors give the place a terrible secret in the form of an ancient monster which threatens to destroy Avalon. The principal characters are Cadmann Weyland, a physically powerful Englishman who by nature is a warrior as well as a loner, also a lover, and a leader (he is chief of security); Sylvia, a physically attractive biologist, highly intelligent and responsible, and the only one who at first listens to Cadmann's warnings; Zack Moscowitz, the administrator and head of the expedition, who is not up to dealing with the growing crisis; Carlos, the good friend of the hero Cadmann, who is a womanizer and a fighter, and is key to the colony's possible survival; Mary, who is Cadmann's wife and the mother of his child, and is loyal and brave; and Terry, Sylvia's husband, who is fiercely opposed to Cadmann's ideas and actions and is jealous of him, and becomes a quadriplegic. Then there are the monsters and other strange creatures, variously called Grendels, pterodons, samlons, and joes.

Structurally the book is narrative romance, with its sequential tale of adventure, its hero, the hero's faithful friend, a love interest, monsters, a beleaguered society, and various at first incomprehensible natural phenomena. Modally as well as structurally, because of the science fiction hypothesis, the overall contour of the imagining is romance. But, in inverse proportion to the modes of imagining in *Beowulf*, it is the low mimetic and ironic modes that predominate in *The Legacy of Heorot* as the authors provide us with plenty of detailed description of natural phenomena and physical circumstances, including numerous plausible technological and scientific explanations of things. Towards the end of the narrative even the monsters have all been explained empirically and it has become clear that the basic problem facing the space colony is that its establishment has been an unwitting disturbance of the ecosystems previously in place. The resolution of the plot turns on the question of whether the Darwinian struggle of the fittest to survive is to be won by the human beings or the monsters. If it is to be the former, the human disruptions in nature will have to be corrected.

In what Frye called the 'pre-medieval' period – meaning by that the patristic and early medieval centuries up to the time of the Norman Conquest – he saw literature as 'closely attached to Christian, late Classical, Celtic, or Teutonic myths.' He then commented, provocatively for Anglo-Saxonists, 'If Christianity had not been both an imported myth and a devourer of rival ones, this phase of Western literature would be easier to isolate. In the form in which we possess it, most of it has already moved into the category of romance' (1957, 34). Frye, it should be noted, did not claim to have a thorough knowledge or understanding of the literature of the Anglo-Saxon period, but he was partly accurate in this observation. A significant portion of Old English literature and much of Middle English, broadly speaking, is in the romance mode, although the Old English texts are seldom characterized in this way by the historically minded scholars who favour this field of literary studies.

Most Old English poetry is markedly non-representational and takes shape within what to us moderns or postmoderns are very wide canons of plausibility. The surviving poetic records include numerous accounts of miracles and other marvellous happenings so that what we, thinking from within the perspectives of a scientific culture, might call 'the laws of nature' are suspended most of the time. This is true to such an extent that Frye's perception of Old and Middle English literature as being mainly in the romance mode needs substantial correction: a large portion of Old English poetry is *myth*, within the broad classificatory terms of the theory of modes just outlined, as well as in other senses that I come to in the course of this book. Figures from heaven and hell move throughout the three-tiered universe of Old English poetry, often directly impinging on human life as they do so. Human figures go into hell and heaven. Human existence in the 'middle dwelling' normally is imagined as situated in the midst of the ongoing war between heaven and hell which for the Anglo-

Saxons is human history. Many times in Old English poems the reader confronts directly the apocalyptic imagery of heaven and the demonic imagery of hell, when either the narrative or the theme of a particular poem moves at these outer limits of the human imagination, or they both do. This kind of metaphorical thought has implications for the identity and role of the poet. The semi-legendary Cædmon, for example, is a spokesman for heaven. He miraculously receives the gift of song, and his repertoire, by means of its several individual stories and overall narrative conception (what we might call its metanarrative), presents the biblical account of God and the angels, humankind, Satan and the host of hell, and the numerous episodes of sacred history (Bede, 419). Although it is not now accepted that any of the extant Old English poetry beyond the nine-line *Hymn* is directly attributable to Hild's cowherd, the poetic records that we have do provide the same complete story, what literary criticism should now call the biblical mythology in its first 'Englished' poetic form. It was a wish to come to terms with that large literary historical fact that, in part, led me to write *The Guest-Hall of Eden: Four Essays on the Design of Old English Poetry* (1972).

The first essay of that earlier book sets out at some length the ways in which a large and central body of Old English poems is in fact an Anglo-Saxon poetic reworking of biblical and hexaemeral myth. The poetry that has come down to us provides ample evidence of the comprehensiveness and power of the Christian mythology as it took hold of the imaginations of the largely anonymous poets who succeeded Cædmon. Each major Christian myth receives one or more poetic reshapings in the heroic language of the Old English word-hoard. The group of poems in which this can be seen happening directly, in intricate and often powerfully poetic ways, are *Genesis A*, *Genesis B*, *Christ and Satan*, *Exodus*, *Judith*, *Daniel*, *Christ I*, *The Dream of the Rood*, *The Descent into Hell*, *Christ II*, *The Fates of the Apostles*, *Christ III*, *The Judgment Day I*, and *The Judgment Day II*. This first-ever vernacular poetic reworking of Christian myth provides a context, though not always a detailed guide, for the sometimes difficult work of interpreting other less 'mythical' Old English poems. Some readers of this literature apparently still have difficulty accepting or using terms like 'myth' and 'mythology' in connection with the images, symbols, and narratives of Christianity. My use of the words was and is confessionally neutral. But I do recognize that there is still a good deal of residual canonicity or sense of true versus false myth surrounding these cultural expressions even in our postmodern world. It is one of the intentions of this present book to reduce anxiety about such things and to make clearer the use of such terminology. Such vocabulary is necessary if we are not to trap ourselves in largely unconscious ideological biases, and if we are to recognize what I would call the most important imaginative fact about Old English poetry, the centrality in it of Christian myth. So far

Modes of Imagining 25

as literary criticism is concerned, this is not primarily a matter of doctrine or theology, of the religious ideas pondered in exegetical commentaries, although at some points parts of that ideological complex are relevant. Nor is it a question any more of finding 'history' reflected or described in Old English poems. There have been many modern attempts to do this latter, to see circumstantial history in the extant poems, but most of the time the specifics of history are not there in any other than the most speculative scholarly ways. In poetry there is no such thing as a fact – that is, a fact from the actual external world outside the poem – because metaphorical imagining destablilizes such things. As with the Bible itself, the actual people, places, and events that are in the poems have been swallowed and absorbed into imaginative verbal structures and made to serve poetic and fictional purposes. The Anglo-Saxon poetic records are largely emanations from a controlling mythology, not a collection of phenomenological data worked into descriptive documents. These literary records are thoroughly logocentric. In the case of *Beowulf,* the poem's exuberant repudiation of everything we normally consider to be historical evidence should lead us to try other categories and modes of reading.

If the presence of the mythical mode in Old English poetry is too little regarded and thought about, the importance of the romance mode is almost equally so. There has been an overall tendency among scholars and critics to proceed as if romance is a later medieval and post-medieval development, or, for those who look to the classical past, as something also found extensively in ancient Greek and Latin literature. A selective bibliography illustrating this general point would include the following: W.P. Ker, *Epic and Romance: Essays on Medieval Literature,* 2nd ed. (1908); Eric Auerbach, *Mimesis: The Representation of Reality in Western Literature,* trans. Willard Trask (1953); Rosemond Tuve, *Allegorical Imagery: Some Medieval Books and Their Posterity* (1966); Gillian Beer, *Romance* (1970); Christopher Caudwell, *Romance and Realism: A Study in English Bourgeois Literature,* ed. Samuel Hynes (1970); Eugene Vinaver, *The Rise of Romance* (1971); William W. Ryding, *Structure in Medieval Romance* (1971); Paul Zumthor, *Essai de poétique médiévale* (1972); John Stevens, *Medieval Romance* (1973); Patricia A. Parker, *Inescapable Romance: Studies in the Poetics of a Mode* (1979): Jay Macpherson, *The Spirit of Solitude: Conventions and Continuities in Late Romance* (1982). Of particular interest for this present book, in addition to the discussion of romance (both mode and structural *mythos*) in Frye's *Anatomy,* are his *The Secular Scripture: A Study of the Structure of Romance* (1976); also another study of what its author, Daniel T. O'Hara, calls the 'antinatural' aesthetics of critical theorists Pater, Nietzsche, Frye, Bloom, Hartman, and de Man, *The Romance of Interpretation: Visionary Criticism from Pater to de Man* (1985).

As long as much of the serious thinking about *Beowulf* was done by historians and literary historians intent on mining the text for actual historical events, places, and people, its romance character tended to be seen as inconvenient or embarassing and so was pushed aside. Almost a century ago, W.P. Ker expressed a once-famous view, that the story of *Beowulf* is thin and of little consequence, centred as it is around a hero fighting three monsters (Ker, 1897). What made the poem 'really interesting' for him 'and different from the later romances, is that it is full of all sorts of references and allusions to great events, to the fortunes of kings and nations'; 'the story is not in the air, or in a fabulous country' but is buttressed 'all round with historical tradition and references to historical fact.' The poet, said Ker, did not 'let it go forth as pure romance.' This view appeared first in *The Dark Ages* (1897, 252–3) and again later, somewhat revised – my quotations come from this version – in *Medieval English Literature* (1912, 23–8). In J.R.R. Tolkien's landmark lecture to the British Academy in 1936, he set out to demolish Ker's historicist bias, not by denying the presence and importance of cultural references to the ancient Northern world in *Beowulf* but by showing that the dragons and other monsters are 'no idle fancy,' that in fact they are central to a poem that is a blend of myth and heroic legend (Tolkien 1936, 245–95). A great deal has happened in the criticism of *Beowulf* since Tolkien helped persuade large numbers of students, critics, and scholars to treat it as a poem, of a very distinctive kind. But it is one of the contentions of this book that we have not yet faced up fully and squarely to this poem's special character as a unique product of the romance and mythical modes of imagining, to the ways in which the poet presents his myth 'incarnate in the world of history and geography,' to use Tolkien's words, without being bound or circumscribed by that world.

Whoever composed *Beowulf* and however this was done, it is clear that it is presented as a tale of wonders. It could even fittingly be called *The Wonders of the North*. Whoever compiled or issued instructions for the compilation of the second of the two parts of MS Cotton Vitellius A.xv. recognized the poem's preoccupation with wondrous things and, appropriately enough, placed it with others also filled with marvels: *The Wonders of the East*, *The Letter to Alexander*, and *The Life of St. Christopher*. To recognize the fictional mode common to these four texts is not to slight at all the far greater imaginative and verbal powers evident in *Beowulf* than in the other works. It is interesting to realize that if whoever planned the compilation had not realized that *Beowulf* belongs in the romance mode, we very likely would never have seen or heard of the poem.[10]

Walter Ong and Northrop Frye have signalled something fundamental when they bring the terms 'romance' and 'romantic' to *Beowulf*, something that needs to be probed at length in relation to this particular Old English work and to much of the rest of the Anglo-Saxon poetic records, especially the saints' lives. In critical terms, the Bible for the Old English poets was the epic of the Creator, with the *Scyppend* 'Shaper' as its protagonist and the dryhts of heaven, middle earth, and hell as the settings for his battles on behalf of his human thanes who wander as exiles among the ruined guest-halls, waste places, and stormy seas of this world. In comparison, *Beowulf* and the hagiographic narrative poems are epics of the creature, the beginnings of heroic romance fiction in the English language. They all draw on folk-tales and legendary materials and they all provide clear examples of what a series of modern critics have now recognized, that romance is the structural, inescapable core of all fiction. It is the mode of verbal imagining which gives a sense of fiction as such, by presenting within a narrative form a combination of events, characters, and things that could not ever come together that way in actuality, in which human life is presented as a quest because a shaping imagination has imposed a pattern where there was none. Romance is not one narrative structure or genre among others but the paradigm, however displaced or modulated, of all fiction.

Because the Old English poetic narratives *Andreas, Juliana, Elene, Guthlac A, Guthlac B, Judith*, and to some extent *Beowulf* proceed in close alignment metaphorically and symbolically with biblical myth, their protagonists as heroes and heroines are identified imaginatively, that is, in the imagery of the poems themselves, with the Creator or the Dryhten Christ. They are identified *with* not *as* this divine figure. The particular heroic quest or mission or challenge in whatever situation the central figure finds herself or himself is to emulate one or more of the mythological acts of the divine protagonist in the biblical story. At the same time, because the dominant mode is romance, the myth is somewhat displaced in the direction of realism, though it needs to be noted that in literary criticism the words 'romantic' and 'realistic' are absolutely relative terms referring only to other modes and to modulations within the modes.

The history of romance shows that, however much this kind of imagining uses description of nature and the actual world, its primary driving force is not that of representational art, and its canons of plausibility are wide. The fictional context includes varying amounts of 'unnatural' or 'unreal' elements. While still alive in middle earth, for example, Guthlac in *Guthlac A* is taken bodily by a troop of devils to the door of hell itself and told by his tormentors that he must enter and suffer with other hell-dwellers. Even at this the lowest point in his temptations the sorely tried holy man does not give way to *orwennysse* 'despair' (*ASPR* 3,66:575) but instead sings a hymn of praise and thanksgiving to God for all the gifts God has created for angels and for earth-dwellers, and then proceeds to lecture the devils on their fatal error long ago when they forsook 'the fair Creation' (*þa fægran gesceaft*) and rejected the Lord (629–31). As a reward for his marvellous endurance, Guthlac is rescued from hell's gate by an angel from heaven (684b ff.) who is one of the twelve apostles. He then is returned 'whole of body' (*limhalne*, 688) to 'that pleasant spot of earth' (*to þam onwillan eorðan dæle*, 728) which, 'exulting in victory' (*Sigehreðig*, 732), he has turned into a paradisal barrow in the midst of the Crowland wastes. Similarly Saint Andrew in *Andreas* is subjected to three days of grotesque physical tortures and mutilation but is miraculously made whole again. Saint Juliana, caught up in the same war between heaven and hell as Guthlac and Andrew, has her body mutilated and boiled in hot lead but also is marvellously restored. Beowulf, already gifted with the strength of thirty men in his hand-grasp, is provided as well with a miraculous sword at a moment of crisis so that the monstrous mother of Grendel cannot kill him, in the depths of the mere.

As in the account of Guthlac's ability to avoid despair, so in *Beowulf*, the two references to this spiritual condition are at points in the narrative at which the heroic forces and their demonic assailants are in decisive confrontations, as a result of which the theme of paradise regained, or the order of the world as God meant it to be, emerges. Beowulf in the depths of the mere, his and Heorot's hell, has been almost defeated by the monster who has dragged him there (1550 ff.) and is *aldres orwena* 'despairing of his life' as he seizes the ornamented hilt of the marvellous *ealdsweord eotenisc* 'giantish old sword.' But with this help his despair gives way to joy (*secg weorce gefeh* 'the man rejoiced at his work'), he utterly defeats the Grendel kin, and then he experiences another 'wonder' (*wundra sum*). The sword-blade melts, even as the bonds of frost and ice do when the *soþ Metod* 'true Measurer' who controls the times and seasons 'unwinds the ropes of the deep pools' (*onwindeð wælrapas*). The other *Beowulf* reference to despair concerns Grendel, but this reference moves in the opposite narrative direction, not to hope and a heaven-assisted victory but to death and damnation. After the tumultuous fight between Beowulf and Grendel, when the Scyldings set about restoring the *beorhte bold* 'bright dwelling' Heorot, the narrator refers again to the *aglæca* Grendel 'shining in his wicked deeds' (*fyrendædum fag*) as 'in his flight he wound away, despairing of life' (*on fleam gewand, / aldres orwean*, 1000b–2a).

There are many indications of the ways in which *Beowulf* eludes what Frye calls 'the ordinary laws of nature' and so places itself predominantly in the romance mode, even as from time to time it brings into focus the mythical mode and to a lesser degree the high mimetic one; also, minimally, the more realistic ones. Again to illustrate, in the first line of the poem the phrase *in geardagum* – which means literally 'in days of years' and is perhaps best understood as 'in former days, in days of yore' – in the context is a romance formula. Like 'once upon a time' or 'long ago' or 'in the olden days,' these two Old English words are instrumental in creating in the audience or reader a willingness to imagine far back to an indefinite and perhaps more ideal past when *þrym* 'glory, greatness, splendour' was achieved and *ellen* 'brave deeds' were done by the 'Spear-Danes' (*Gar-Dena*), 'the kings of the people' (*ðeodcyninga*), by 'those nobles' (*ða æþelingas*, 3) the origins of whose dynasty are now about to be told. The phrase may well connote a mythical time, *in illo tempore*, that exists only in the imagination and in poetry.

The second word of *Beowulf* is *we*. Who is implied by this pronoun? Whose memory and imagination are being appealed to when the poet says, 'We ... have heard ... how ... in the olden days ...'? Most immediately the word indicates the one who is a teller of the tale and his audience. The whole formula *we ... gefrunon* seems to imply either a live audience in a dryht hall or refectory setting or a literary harking back to an oral or *epos* tradition that had such an audience and setting. It is the people of this original audience of the poem that many scholars have tried to describe or imagine. But the unsolved problems of dating and geographically locating the composition of *Beowulf* make this a very hypothetical exercise. From the perspective of a modern or postmodern scholar and critic, the first person plural pronoun *we* could mean, respectively, an oral poet or poets and an original audience or audiences, or a literary poet or poets and readership, or some combination of the two.[11] The pronoun could also embrace the two scribes and their overseer(s) who saw to the writing or copying of the manuscript we have and their intended readership, or their intended live audience for readings from their manuscript text. The possibilities are numerous and they reach on through the centuries, in many modern printed editions and other forms of production. As the process continues, more and more people are included in the pronoun 'we,' and each is involved in some way in receiving and reacting to the traditional tale which begins by saying 'Yes, we have heard of the glory ...'

More specifically still, how does the actual verbal art of the beginning of *Beowulf* take us into its modes of imagining? If we expose our senses and our minds to the first fifty-two lines, the much-studied exordium, a great deal begins to happen. We experience an extraordinarily rich pattern of sound and rhetorical texture, as the traditional four-stress variously alliterating lines tell a hieratic, dignified tale of the origins of a royal dynasty. The imaginative focus is on the original appearance, life, and funeral of the first king of the Scyldings. Scyld Scefing mysteriously emerges out of the sea as a desolate foundling child. After his death many years later he is sent back into the mystery of the sea and dispatched by his lamenting followers towards a destination unknown to them. We are not actually told anything about the birth or even the death of

Scyld. What is pointed to briefly and suggestively is the Scyldings' sense of the unknown at both ends of the life of this shadowy figure, and something of the glory in between. With this passage, moreover, the poem introduces a sense of revolving cycles, of the rise and fall of heroes, kings, and their peoples, of the perennial movement of the sea, of birth, growth, and dying, and of heaven's generous intervention in the affairs of one formerly lordless but now favoured people. As the verbal fabric takes on increased meanings, interlocking motifs of rings and circles begin to fill the listener's or reader's imagination: a ring-giver, a ring-prowed ship, ringed byrnies, shields, a life from the sea going back into the sea, tribute required and paid across the sea, the coming and going of men loading the funeral ship, the ebb and flow of the waves, and the closed circle of fate as seen by the hall-counsellors who exist 'under the clouds' (*under wolcnum*, 8a), 'under the heavens' (*under heofenum*, 52a).

Imaginatively and poetically the passage is intensely alive and includes numerous rhetorical devices and tropes. The metaphorical names *Scyld Scefing* 'Shield, son of Sheaf' have martial and fertility significance, both connotations being expressed immediately in what follows: Scyld triumphs in war, produces a son, and founds a dynasty and prosperous kingdom, thus gaining great honour from 'the men [or 'sons'] of Shield.' There is a stark contrast between his widespread conquests, which are told about first, and his unpromising beginning as a foundling. The compound *meodosetla* 'mead-seats' is a kind of two-phase synecdoche by which a terrified people's experience of being conquered and losing their political independence is summed up as having their mead-seats, their halls, seized. In *hronrad* 'riding-place of the whale' we have a traditional kenning for the sea across which all the neigbouring peoples have to pay tribute to Scyld. The word *frofor* 'consolation, comfort' is used to indicate God's provision of prosperity for Scyld (7b) and is repeated soon after to mean a second gift of God, this time the birth of Beowulf I, who becomes the second Scylding ruler (14a). In the rapid accumulation of words for growing and prospering, the listener or reader enters into the midst of the Old English poetic device of variation: *weox* 'grew' (8a); *þah* 'thrived' (8b); *wæs ... cenned* 'was ... born' (12); *woroldare* 'honour in the world' (17b); *wæs breme* 'was renowned' (18a); *blæd wide sprang* 'his glory, prosperity, abundance, success, honour burst forth far and wide' (18b); *gode gewyrccean, / fromum feohgiftum* 'bring it about by goodness, abundant gifts of property' (20a–1b); *lofdædum sceal ... geþeon* 'by praiseworthy deeds will ... prosper' (24b; 25b).

There may be metaphor in *blæd wide sprang* 'his glory burst forth' (a rapidly growing plant? 18b). The phrase *on fæder bearme* 'in his father's bosom' (21b) is an imaginative figure for caring and protection. The euphemism for dying, 'At the fated time he set out to go ... into the keeping of the Prince' (*Him ða ...*

gewat   to gescæphwile / ... feran   on Frean wære, 26–7), accords perfectly with the patterned, evocative manner in which the poet tells his tale. So also does the phrase *þenden wordum weold*; this too is a figure, another synecdoche, for saying 'while he was still alive and ruling,' but it is also specific and literal, 'while he was wielding words' or 'ruling with words' and giving instructions for his funeral. In the description of the funeral ship there is prosopopoeia, but it is subtly done. The ship is *utfus* 'eager to be out,' many treasures are laid on its bosom (the figure of the ship's bosom occurs twice), and, like a living, eager warrior about to render loyal service, the physical body of the ship is decked with weapons and armour. Before the vessel and its rich trappings are given to the ocean, a standard is placed above the dead king (49a). There is another hint of prosopopoeia in the way the sea is said now to take Scyld into its possession (*on flodes æht*, 42a), he himself having previously possessed the country for a long time (31): 'they let the sea bear him, gave him to the spear-man' (*leton holm beran, / geafon on garsecg*, 48b–9a).[12] The Prince of life long ago has given Scyld to a lordless people, to whom in turn Scyld has given many gifts. Now in a final ritual act of gift-giving, the nobles who have received gifts from the king sadly hand him back to the ocean, which will take him far away (42b). As they do so they do not know who will receive that cargo (50b–2).

The narrator comments directly in this passage and frequently throughout the poem on the character and actions of the people described. His assessment of Scyld – *þæt wæs god cyning* 'that was a good king' – is followed shortly by a maxim assessing Beowulf I in equally positive terms as a prince who met the conventional expectation of royal gift-givers: 'Among all peoples / By praiseworthy deeds a man will prosper' (*lofdædum sceal / in mægþa gehwære   man geþeon*, 24b–5). After the exordium the brief panoramic account of the Danish kings who follow Scyld continues the related themes of martial prowess and of the Scyldings as a heaven-favoured people. The diction again is noble and elevated, the language of encomium: 'dear king of the nation' (*leof leodcyning*), 'famous among peoples' (*folcum gefræge*), 'the High Healfdene' (*heah Healfdene*), 'the gracious Scyldings' (*glæde Scyldingas*), 'leaders of armies' (*weoroda ræswan*), 'Halga the Good' (*Halga til*), 'the War Scylfings' (*Heaðo-Scylfingas*). The names *Heorogar* 'Sword Spear'[13] and *Hroðgar* 'Glory Spear' are part of the encomiastic heroic pattern. Such apparently unqualified praise may well trigger something in the modern reader's mind, and quite possibly in Anglo-Saxon ones as well, raising the question of whether these preliminary definitions of human worth and good kingship – they are idealizing and romantic – will be borne out by the whole poem. Or are they a kind of foreshadowing of something whose fuller, more ambiguous meaning will emerge only gradually?

While there seems at this point in the narrative to be no suggestion of irony, the larger tale told in parts I and II increasingly reveals the destructive results of wars, bloodshed, and feuding, just the kind of actions carried out early in the story by both Scyld and Hrothgar, and praised by the narrator. *Gar-Dena* 'Spear Danes' is a metaphorical compound identifying a people as a weapon. The poem never moves away from this heroic warrior code to a pacifist ethic, although it subjects the results of the code to intense scrutiny. Even as the mad savagery of blood-feuding increasingly is exposed as monstrous, both the narrator and the central character in the poem accept that protector lords must fight to defend those for whom they are responsible, though it is a large fact that most of the fighting in which we see Beowulf directly involved is with monsters, not other human beings. The striking exception to this is his killing of the Huga champion *Dæghrefn,* in a crushing bear hug (2501–8a). Many years after the beginnings of the Scylding dynasty, Beowulf is shown as an aged king preparing for his last battle and we hear him at length taking stock of his life. He describes himself as the 'old guardian of the people' (*frod folces weard,* 2513) with an obligation to fight their enemies to the end: 'and so through life I am to do battle' (*ond swa to aldre sceall / sæcce fremman,* 2498b–9a). But it is important to note that this paramount duty of a warrior-king is qualified, so that it does not include unprovoked aggression. A little later in the narrative, after Beowulf is mortally wounded, he looks back (2732b–43a) with satisfaction on the fact that he has not been the instigator of wars or a slayer of kinsmen: *Ic on earde bad / mælgesceafta* 'In my dwelling I waited for what was shaped for me in time ...'

In a similar vein, with the benefit of the hindsight that goes with having read the whole story – or from the perspective of someone in an Anglo-Saxon audience who has already heard the poem – there is irony in the reference early in the text to generous gift-giving by a young prince so that his *wilgesiþas* 'willing comrades' (23a) will remain by him when war or crisis comes. Many years later in his fight with the dragon, Beowulf experiences the fragility in practice of the ideal set out here. Hrothgar also, by the anticipated end of his story, has apparently been betrayed by his nephew Hrothulf, to whom he has been generous (this is discussed further in chapter 6). The last word of the poem, *lofgeornost* 'most eager for fame,' ironically echoes the early occurrence of *lofdædum sceal / in mægþa gehwære man geþeon.* Both at the beginning and the end of *Beowulf* the dryht ideal of mutual loyalty to the death between lord and thanes is clear, but by the conclusion of the tale the rarity of its embodiment or actualization in someone like Beowulf or Wiglaf has been massively and tragically demonstrated. Even well before that point, the romantic mode has modulated somewhat, to include a greater measure of the ironic mode of fiction and a sense of how things actually are in a very imperfect world, even though a fire-breathing dragon looms large throughout part II and keeps us firmly and predominantly within the mode of romance.

There are several descriptive epithets in the exordium, all of them helping establish the close connections between heaven, the Scylding rulers, and the Scylding people themselves. Following Scyld's marvellous arrival and rise to power, God, who has earlier perceived the distress of the lordless Danes, now sends a son for the king and as the *Liffrea* 'Prince of life' and *wuldres Wealdend* 'Wielder of glory' grants *woroldare* 'world-grace' to Beowulf I. When Scyld dies 'at the fated time' (*to gescæphwile*), he goes 'into the keeping of the Prince' (*on Frean wære*, 26b–7). The epithets describing Scyld – *wine Scyldinga* 'friend of Shield's sons' (30b), *leof landfruma* 'dear land prince' (31a), *æþelinges* 'of the noble one' (33b), *beaga bryttan* 'dispenser of rings' (35a), *mærne be mæste* 'the famous one by the mast' (36a) – are all appropriate to the situation; because Scyld has been given the role of protector-lord by divine favour, he is in a position to give gifts. The Prince of life who has sent Scyld to the land of the Danes is, in turn, his Protector-Lord, and, as the narrator (though not the Scyldings) knows (26, 50b–2), it is into the keeping of that Prince that he goes after death, having been honoured greatly by the people whose well-being has depended both on the grace of heaven and on that of the powerful lord sent them by heaven.

Who, then, in the actual language and thought of the poem, are the principal actors in this passage and what are their relative powers of action? Clearly the setting is in the middle dwelling. Within this setting, despite Scyld's followers' sense of mystery surrounding his origin and final destination, natural processes of living and dying are at work, and human disasters, fears, needs, happiness, and affections are in evidence. Scyld and his successors act in certain ways and their people respond, but the overall action is presented as initiated and controlled by the *wuldres Wealdend* 'Wielder of Glory' (17). Nor is this mere ornament. It is, as we shall see, part of the fabric of the language and meaning of the poem. *Beowulf* begins at the upper bound of the romance mode, close to myth. The poem is about *hæleð under heofonum* 'heroes [or 'men, warriors'] under heaven' (52), but the influence of heaven is not something remote, merely to be piously referred to as background by a traditional poet. God is a personified, immediate power shaping human lives. We might even say, accurately, that the exordium to *Beowulf* functions in the modes of romance and myth simultaneously, with the actions of heaven and of the heroic world closely intertwined. There are suggestions as well here of high mimetic tragic and epic poetry surrounding the great king and leader Scyld Scefing, who is presented as subject to the laws of nature and to social judgment, despite his heroic stature. But these suggestions are not developed in relation to the strange figure of Scyld, who remains obscure even while commanding central attention. They are left germinally present, waiting for fuller expression in connection with the royal courts of Denmark and Geatland in the main narrative that is to follow.

When Beowulf and his men arrive in Denmark, they are challenged by an alert coast-guard who senses immediately that something extraordinary is happening and that the hero is different from other men (229–57). From the vantage point on the sea-cliff 'the guardian of Shield's sons' (*weard Scildinga*) sees 'bright shield bosses' (*beorhta randas*) and 'war-trappings eager-like' [or 'ready'] (*fyrdsearu fuslicu*) crossing the gangway of the ship. If we understand *fuslicu* literally (literarily) as 'eager-like,' the metaphorical force of the personification is heightened. Even taking it as 'ready,' there is still metaphor at work. The coast-guard is intensely curious (*hine fyrwyt bræc* 'curiosity tormented him') about the identity of these unexpected intruders who have brought their tall ship across the sea-highway and now in full armour and broad daylight have come ashore in Danish territory. The figure of the hero in particular draws the coast-guard's attention and his admiration. Beowulf is immediately recognizable as superior in degree to other men.

It is in the encounter with the coast-guard that the protagonist makes his first speech in the poem. Just before the hero speaks, the narrator identifies him in terms of his social role, as a 'chieftain' (*yldesta*, 260) and 'leader of a troop' (*werodes wisa*, 261). Still unnamed, this leader of men now unlocks his word-hoard and as he does so it is his people the Geats, his lord Hygelac, and the high-born chieftain Ecgtheow, his father, who are presented as the further indicators of his own identity. Following this formal introduction, the extraordinary visitor states openly that he and his troop have 'a mighty errand' (*micel ærende*) to the great prince of the Danes. They have heard of the mysterious being who shows hatred by his deeds and they have come 'in friendly [or 'loyal'] spirit' (*þurh holdne hige*) to offer Hrothgar 'counsel' or 'help' (*ræd*) in overpowering the *feond* 'fiend, enemy.' After further deliberation the coast-guard permits them to proceed. The whole scene is charged with acute observation and an electric awareness of details. It is not only the human beings who are shown to be intensely conscious and animated; as the Geats set forth again towards Heorot we are told that 'warlike' (*guþmod*) boar figures shine above the cheek-guards of gold-adorned helmets, keeping 'life-watch over the fierce ones' (*ferhwearde ... grimmon*), while in the background 'the floating vessel' (*flota*) waits quietly (301–3a). As the Geats move through the carefully choreographed ritual of approach to the royal court, we see their byrnies shining and hear their iron armour-rings singing out. The newcomers are guided along 'a road gleaming with bright stones' (*Strǣt ... stanfah*) to 'the timbered hall, splendid and shining with gold' (*sæl timbred / geatolic ond goldfah*), 'the most celebrated of buildings beneath the heavens' (*foremǣrost ... receda under roderum*). As they are about to enter the hall (395 ff.) they are told by the herald to leave their 'battle-shields' (*hildebord*) and 'deadly shafts of wood' (*wudu wælsceaftas*) outside, to wait 'for the result of the talks' (*worda geþinges*, 397-8).

As the hero approaches the Danish court, Heorot is no longer presented as the humiliated, corpse-strewn place enslaved by Grendel told about earlier. At least for the moment it is luminous again, the idealized guest-hall linked in its origins and purpose with the Creation of all living things, and of the world itself (89b-98). However briefly, and perhaps only in the narrator's and his audience's imaginations, once more it is the hall whose 'light shone over many lands' (*lixte se leoma   ofer landa fela*) and in which 'the mighty one dwelt' (*on þæm se rica bad*, 310b-11). We know, and Beowulf and his troop know, that 'the best of houses' (*husa selest*, 146, 285) is still in dire straits, because of the furtive night-time attacks of the envious, malicious monster who slaughters and then flees under the cover of darkness back into his underwater lair. The land of the Scyldings is in a state of siege and of wary, apprehensive vigilance, but it is as if the very presence in Denmark of the unmistakably unique (*ænlic*, 251) man who has just arrived has restored something of Heorot's former glory. In complete contrast to Grendel, the unexpected guest from across the seas has come in a spirit of magnanimity, confidently and in broad daylight, and has already made it possible to think again about Heorot as God meant it to be, as 'the bright dwelling of brave men' (*hof modigra / torht*, 312b-13).

When Hrothgar learns who is seeking permission to speak with him, he shows immediately that he is well aware of who and what kind of man Beowulf is, both in his lineage and in his powers of action (371-84a). He knew Beowulf when he was a boy and so is also aware that the newcomer's father was Ecgtheow, to whom King Hrethel of the Geats had given his only daughter in marriage. Equally or even more important, Hrothgar has been told by Danes who have taken rich gifts from him to the Geatish court that Beowulf is 'famed in battle' (*heaþorof*) and 'has the strength of thirty men in his hand-grasp' (*þritiges / manna mægencræft   on his mundgripe*). In the light of this previous knowledge, the king of the Danes now understands that Beowulf has been sent by 'the holy God in his grace' (*halig God / for arstafum*) and so hopes or expects (383b) that the visitor will help them 'against the Grendel terror' (*wið Grendles gryre*). Hrothgar recognizes Beowulf, so to speak, as the typical protagonist of romance: as someone socially high born (son of a princess, grandson of the former king of the Geats); as a man having powers of action far beyond those normal in the order of nature (his *mundgripe*); and as a potential deliverer and agent of divine grace (*for arstafum*, 382a). For very good reasons the hero and his men are welcome guests for the Danish people.

Like several of the grand, ceremonial scenes in Heorot, the one in which Beowulf actually arrives 'under Heorot's roof' (*under Heorotes hrof*) and presents his credentials to Hrothgar (399–455) is both heroic romance and high mimetic epic, a fusion of the marvels of romance and the rituals of a royal court presided over by 'the Lord of the bright Danes, protector of the Scyldings' (*brego Beorht-Dena ... eodor Scyldinga*, 427–8). In this particular scene, Beowulf is absolutely the centre of attention. He is presented in a cumulative series of strong idealizing epithets, words, and phrases: *se rica* 'the powerful one,' *se hearda* 'the hardy one,' *secg* 'man,' *heaþorinc* 'warrior,' *heard under helme* 'hardy under his helmet,' *on him byrne scan* 'on him his byrny shone,' *Ic eom Higelaces mæg ond magoðegn* 'I am Hygelac's kinsman and retainer.' His actions are those of an exuberant, confident leader who moves decisively and quickly. He shines. As he stands *heard under helme* on the hearth before Hrothgar and begins to speak, his words take the form of a *beot* 'boasting speech' about the 'many glorious deeds' (*mærða fela*) undertaken in his youth. He has heard from seafarers about Grendel and the fate of the hall which now each night stands *idel ond unnyt* 'empty and not useful.' Wise counsellors in Geatland have advised him to go to Denmark because they know the *mægenes cræft* 'power of his strength' and that he has already proven himself a successful champion of a bedevilled kingdom, Geatland itself. They know of his marvellous exploits and have looked on as he extricated himself from his armour, all blood-stained after the battles in which he bound and destroyed five giants, killed water-monsters in the sea at night, and ground down the enemies who were afflicting the Geats. Both his countrymen and he himself know that he is ready to take on Grendel, the 'monster' (*aglæca*) and 'demon' (*þyrs*). His heroic purpose is 'to cleanse Heorot' (*Heorot fælsian*), which has become 'a war-hall' (*guðsele*). Since he has learned that Grendel despises weapons, he too will do without them and will trust in a combination of his hand-grip and 'the Lord's judgment' (*Dryhtnes dom*).

In this account by Beowulf of his previous monster-quelling, with the evident suspension of the laws of nature explicit in it, the poem is clearly continuing in the romance mode of imagining. The hero's powers of action cannot be fitted into the ordinary historical world of courts, tribes, and their wars. Although the Geats and Danes were historical peoples outside the text, their fictional analogues within the poem move in a world of romance. Similarly, the enemies Beowulf fights as their champion do not accommodate themselves to the plausible confines of what we call history. Even so, and this is one of the main differences between *Beowulf* and the other longer narrative poems in Old English,

Modes of Imagining 37

there is much in the presentation of the court-centred world in which Beowulf lives and moves, especially as it is represented by Heorot with its gracious king and queen, its gift-throne and treasures, and its splendid rituals, that would be imaginatively at home in a high mimetic fiction. But, equally important, Grendel and Beowulf do not fit there. Neither finally does Heorot. When we are told by Beowulf in this his first speech to Hrothgar about Grendel's contempt for the weapons of the aristocratic, heroic world, it is a reminder, as if this were necessary, that any rescue of that world from such an assailant will require powers greater than those contained within 'history' or even within the ostensibly high mimetic dimensions of the Danish court.

As if to consolidate just such a realization, Beowulf concludes his address to Hrothgar (442 ff.) with several grisly images about how Heorot, now 'the war-hall' (*guðsele*) in which no 'broad shield' (*sidne scyld*) or 'sword' (*sweord*) will serve, may well become the scene of a ferocious cannibalistic banquet. If this happens the monster will eat without fear both the Geatish warriors and Beowulf himself, as Grendel often has done with the Danes, 'the might of the Glory-men' (*mægen Hreðmanna*, 444b–5a). Even as the Scyldings' splendid attempts at civilization and human joy embodied in Heorot have been devastated for twelve years, so now it is the Geatish warriors and their venerable trappings which the fiend from hell will tear at. If Grendel devours him, says Beowulf (in the first of several uses in the poem of the decapitation metaphor), Hrothgar will not need to hide the hero's head or worry about his body, because Grendel, 'the one who goes alone' (*angenga*) 'without regret (*unmurnlice*) will have carried the hero's body parts, dripping blood, into the moorland retreats. What may remain afterward for Hrothgar's attention will be one of the heirlooms of the heroic world, a piece of Weland's work, the 'best of corslets' (*hrægla selest*), which has come to the hero through King Hrethel himself, and was to have protected Beowulf's chest. If things have gone wrong, the corslet should go back to the king of the Geats.

Late on the evening of Beowulf's arrival in Heorot, after further speeches and a great banquet, Hrothgar for the first time in his life assigns 'the best of houses' (*husa selest*) to another man for protection, and retires for the night (655–61). It is interesting to note that his brief seven-line speech giving the hero protective custody of the great hall includes two uses of the word *ellen*. This is a key word, heard first in the poem at the very beginning when the narrator introduced his primary theme of bravery and great deeds in connection with those 'noble ones' (*ða æþelingas*) of the Spear-Danes who in days long ago performed valiantly. As the new protector of the Scyldings, Beowulf is being urged by their now-powerless fifth king to make known his *mægenellen* 'mighty strength,' in the promise that if he survives this 'brave work' (*ellenweorc*) there will be no lack for him of anything he desires. What Denmark needs now if Scylding well-being is to be restored is more of the same *ellenweorc* on which their dynasty was founded. But there is heavy, unmistakable narrative irony in the words 'Then Hrothgar, protector of the Scyldings, with his *hæleþa gedryht* went out of the hall' (662–3), whether we translate *hæleþa* fairly neutrally as 'men' or 'warriors,' or more ironically as 'heroes.'

In the poet's description of the situation in the hall after the Danes have left, he reminds us that Beowulf is what he is and does what he does because God wills it: 'The King of Glory, so men have heard, had established a hall-guard against Grendel' (*Hæfde Kyningwuldor / Grendle togeanes, swa guman gefrungon, / seleweard*, 665b–7a). Beowulf has become the *seleweard* 'hall-guard' who is to provide *eotonweard* 'guard against a giant' (668b) because he *georne* 'eagerly, willingly' trusts 'in his brave [or 'high-spirited'] might, the Measurer's favour' (*modgan mægnes, Metodes hyldo*, 669b–70). The two sources of Beowulf's confidence, his own exuberant *mægen* and the measure of favour he has from God, are in close apposition without even a coordinating word, because in fact, as the hero himself knows and says repeatedly throughout his life, they are inextricably connected (227b–8, 440b–1, 555b, 569b–75a, 669–70, 686b–7, 963–70a, 977b–9, 1270–4a, 1655–66a, 2327b–32, 2352a, 2524b–8, 2736b–43a, 2794–2801). Without the gift of his powers from God he can do nothing, and in the coming encounter with Grendel it is 'the holy Lord' (*halig Dryhten*) who 'will decree the glory to one side or the other' (*on swa hwæþere hond ... mærðo deme*) 'as to him seems fitting' (*swa him gemet þince*, 685b–7). Even though the young Geatish warriors who are with Beowulf are frightened and expect never again to see their homes and loved ones, the poet makes clear before the battle that the result will be good: 'to them, the people of the Weather Men' [or 'Weather-Geats'], the Lord had granted that the web of their fate was woven with war-success' (*him Dryhten forgeaf / wigspeda gewiofu, Wedera leodum*, 696b–7). In case there is any doubt about who is the ultimate actor in this agonistic, heroic tale with its powerful mythic resonances, the narrator ends the passage leading up to Grendel's arrival with these words: 'The truth is known that mighty God rules over mankind for ever' (*Soð is gecyþed, / þæt mihtig God manna cynnes / weold wideferhþ*, 700b–2a). And – the audience are meant to realize – is ruling over the Danes and Geats at this moment.

The battle does go well, for everyone except the unfortunate Hondscio, who is swallowed whole, as we learn much later (2080b), by 'the one who goes in shadows' (*sceadugenga*, 703a). The following morning, crowds of warriors and chieftains from near and far gather around the gift-hall to see two marvels. Above the doorway hangs 'Grendel's grip' (*Grendles grape*, 836a) – his hand, arm, and shoulder – put there by the hero whose own mighty grip has brought about the long-awaited deliverance of Heorot. Away from the hall stretches the second marvel, Grendel's bloody tracks, leading right to the waters of the mere with their 'horrid surging of waves, all mixed with hot gore' (*atol yða geswing eal gemenged, / haton heolfre*, 847–9); it is into these threatening waters that the fatally wounded monster has fled. In the depths of the mere the 'death-doomed one' (*deaðfæge*), 'the joyless one' (*dreama leas*), has given up his 'life ... and heathen soul' (*feorh ... hæþene sawle*). At this point the poet underlines the thematic meaning of his account of the defeat of Grendel in an unequivocal half-line: 'There hell received him' (*þær him hel onfeng*, 852b). The myth that structures this heroic, marvel-filled tale is clear. With full support from the heavenly Gift-Dispenser, Hrothgar has created a great hall in which human beings are meant to live in joy and happiness, but a monster from hell has for a time destroyed that possibility. Now the reversal brought about by the heaven-sent hero has restored the primal joy. The mere, hell, has received back its evil monster even as he dies.

Within the foreground narrative of the poem, Beowulf's exploit becomes an instant legend (853 ff.). As comrades old and young turn away from the 'happy journey' (*gomenwaþe*) along Grendel's tracks to the mere's edge, they ride in high spirits on their glossy horses back to the hall, reciting Beowulf's 'glorious deed' (*mærþo*) as they go. Repeatedly, the narrator tells us, it was said by many 'that nowhere, south or north between the seas, across the broad world under heaven's expanse' (*þætte suð ne norð be sæm tweonum / ofer eormengrund oþer nænig / under swegles begong*, 858–60), was there any warrior or potential ruler equal to Beowulf: there is no 'better shield-bearer or one more worthy of a kingdom' (*selra nære / rondhæbbendra, rices wyrðra*, 857b–61). Just the night before, the man who had already been recognized as extraordinary because of his killing of giants and sea-monsters in Geatland has triumphed over Grendel, in a wild, ferocious wrestling match. Now in the light of morning the warrior society who celebrate this exuberant use of prodigious powers display a complementary release of pent-up energies, both in their words and actions. After the first verbal recognition of Beowulf's achievement, including also praise for Hrothgar (862–3), there is pure unbridled play in the form of horse-racing: 'At times these famous fighters let their dusky horses gallop, go in competition together, wherever the country trails seemed fair to them and were known to be excellent' (*Hwilum heaþorofe hleapan leton, / on geflit faran fealwe mearas, / ðær him foldwegas fægere þuhton, / cystum cuðe*, 864–7a). The countryside is theirs again and they race about in uninhibited delight. The joyless spirit who could not tolerate the sounds of human happiness from the newly created Heorot is gone.

It is not only horses and riders that spread out to enjoy being alive in the world freed from hell's grasp. In the mind of 'a thane of the king, a praise-laden man full of songs who could recall many, many stories' (*cyninges þegn, / guma gilphlæden, gidda gemyndig, / se ðe ealfela ealdgesegena / worn gemunde*), there is an imaginative reaching out in space and time paralleling the athletic actions of the warriors on their horses. This *gilphlæden* man, accustomed to singing praises, draws from his memory store words with which to work on the imaginations of his hearers and to identify Beowulf's exploit by *telling* it into its rightful place with others of the community's ancestral memories. In a fascinating description of oral poetry in process, we are told how in this man's mouth one word now finds another and is 'truly' or 'fittingly' bound (*soðe gebunden*) into a poetic structure which is at once old and new, a skilful tale about 'Beowulf's exploit' (*sið Beowulfes*) linking it with the heroic deeds of the legendary dragon-slayer Sigmund. The expression *word oþer fand* 'a word found another' is a telling personification metaphor both for the actual way in which words come together in the process of poetic composition and for the living oral tradition now reaching out to take into itself this latest hero. The alternative (favoured) translation of *word oþer fand* is 'he found other words.' This equally possible translation, if we consider grammar alone, is probably favoured because it excises figurative content. With the first reading we can see here, as well, a metaphor for the creation of the poem *Beowulf* itself. In this extraordinary work as each event is put into poetic language it evokes other metaphorically related words and events, to provide cumulatively one of the most associatively rich verbal fabrics in English literature.

From the four passages examined so far in this chapter – the introduction of the hero in Geatland and his voyage to Denmark, the exordium, the account of the Geats' arrival in Denmark, the celebrations the morning after the defeat of Grendel – it can readily be seen that the poem does work predominantly within the broad, flexible boundaries of the fictional mode of romance. Its hero is manifestly superior in degree to other human beings and to his physical environment. The enemies he fights are monstrous, coming from well beyond what we think of as the limits of the natural or the ordinary world. Even though there is a degree of mimetic art in the poem, giving at several points a vivid sense of the places and trappings of antique Germanic life, the laws of nature are easily suspended. The fiction moves without strain or incongruity across the imprecise boundaries of the romance mode, in two directions: towards the imagery of an actual, palpable world of people, places, and things, in which human beings of a kind known to have lived in history also function in the poem; towards the undisplaced mythical imagery of heaven and hell, in the midst of which both the Prince of Life and the inhabitants of hell exert major direct influences on people and events in the middle dwelling. This is poetic art that makes natural the supernatural, that integrates unnatural and marvellous elements so well into its fiction that they are at once central to the mode of imagining involved and, within the canons of plausibility characteristic of that mode, completely acceptable and functional there.

One of the realizations that emerges from this kind of preliminary critical analysis is that settings in *Beowulf* are symbolic: beings, human and other, inhabit the places appropriate to their natures, and external locales are poetic or mythical expressions or projections of what in more modern literature would be psychologically conceived inner states. In all mythologies, including the ones working in this poem, earth is middle earth, because of an imagined psychological/cosmological correspondence. In this respect *Beowulf* is very much part of the Old English poetic corpus. As one would expect on the basis of what we know of both pagan Germanic and Christian beliefs, Old English poetry functions in accordance with the prevailing cosmological sense of a three-tiered universe composed of heaven, middle earth, and hell. Primary narrative actions proceed on any one, two, or three of these levels, depending on the particular blend of myth, romance, and mimetic art appropriate to the purposes and themes of the poem concerned. The action in *Christ and Satan*, for example, takes place mainly at the polarities of the imagined cosmos, beginning in heaven with the myth of the fall of the angels and then proceeding for the most part in hell, but including also numerous references to the impact that the war between heaven and hell has on existence in the middle dwelling. *Genesis*, both *A* and *B*, moves freely throughout all levels of the cosmos. The narrative line of *The Dream of the Rood* functions mainly on the level of this world, but the cosmic significance of the crucial events of Christ's life and death in the world of the earthly dryht is powerfully present throughout. In *The Battle of Maldon*, a poem sufficiently involved in mimetic representation to have generated in modern times a whole scholarly industry of historical sleuthing, the main action proceeds on a 'this world' level. But even here the traditional imaginative sense of the three-tiered universe is operative and the heavenly determination of human affairs makes itself known. As Byrhtnoth dies he gives thanks to 'the Ruler of peoples' (*ðeoda waldend, ASPR* 6, 11:173) for all the joys he has known in the world and asks God to ensure that 'hell-sent enemies' (*helsceaðan*, 180) not be permitted to harm his soul as it ascends to heaven. The heroic task that he has carried out on behalf of his prince and people against the *hæðene* 'heathen' foes (55, 181) was a God-given one, and he now goes to his heavenly reward.

Recognition of the pervasive presence of the three-tiered universe in Old English poetry is basic to any understanding of symbolic settings in the poems; also to an understanding of the beings that inhabit these settings and the narrative actions that take place in and among them. The reader of other bodies of literature who comes to Old English poetry with extensive literary experience will have encountered elsewhere numerous versions of the three-tiered cosmos, whether in Northern mythological texts, later medieval and Renaissance English or other European literatures, in classical texts, or in any one of several Asian, African, and Amerindian literatures in which human existence is imagined as located between an upper and a lower world. That kind of structuring of verbal art is familiar, archetypal. At the same time, the new reader of Old English poetry will encounter a highly distinctive use of this structure. The particular poetic language of myth and metaphor deployed here is unique to this poetry. So also, as in other Germanic texts from the early medieval period, the 'social content' is distinctive. By social content I mean primarily the sociopolitical organization which has its centre in the two principal human figures in the poetry of this particular culture, the *dryhtguma* or noble thane and his *dryhten* or lord. This relationship provides the basic unit of a social and political order that sometimes includes but normally goes beyond tribal or kinship loyalties. It appears in one form or another in the great majority of the Old English poetic texts that we have and it takes on a broad range of meanings, to the point that it characterizes or affects in some way the presentation of virtually all relationships between human beings themselves, between non-human beings, and between non-human and human beings, on any level of the cosmos or between the levels.

As the Germanic social ethos meets the Christian mythology, with the latter's rich profusion of narrative patterns and structures of images, the order of the dryht in numerous poems comes to mean the Christian community or *ecclesia*: specific Christian communities, the whole church on earth, the community of the blessed in heaven, or all of these in mystical harmony. Frequently in Old English poetry an earthly dryht is given an added dimension of meaning through its metaphorical identification with the heaven of Christian mythology. At other times the mutual loyalties of the dryht are parodied and made demonic through their identification with the society of hell, even though they are still described by the same conventional images and word patterns. The term 'dryht' may indicate the most ordinary human society, it may signify a society in the grip of devil worship, it may point to an idealized or romanticized *goldsele* 'gold-hall' world wrapped in nostalgia, it may connote the utter perversion of all true loyalty and love that is the Anglo-Saxon hell, and it may symbolize the perfect, unchanging society of the heavenly *Dryhten* 'Lord' and his angels.

In accord with the pervasive sense of a three-tiered universe, this complex pattern of images may function in a particular poem on any one, two, or all levels of the cosmos. Because human and supernatural beings inhabit or move towards the level appropriate to their natures, narrative patterns are, in this sense, predetermined. The actions or events described are the results of the kinds of beings that interact in the particular poem. Individual human beings like Guthlac or Juliana, aspiring to inclusion in the dryht of heaven, are assailed by demonic foes who would pull them instead into the dryht of hell. But in such narratives of the romance mode, with this mode's strong wish-fulfilment character, the strenuous efforts of Satan's thanes regularly are thwarted through an indivisible combination of prodigious saintly courage and heavenly assistance, by the mutual loyalty, that is, of Lord and thane to the point of death and beyond.

On the uppermost level of the imagined cosmos, we find the dryht of heaven centred round the Dryhten and his troop of angel thanes. Originally and ideally this society, as described for example in *Genesis A*, 1–14, is the perfect, eternal order of being which precedes, transcends, and succeeds any action pertaining to any other part of the cosmos. In poem after poem, including *Beowulf*, because the dryht of heaven is treated as a mythical 'given,' it is the perfect society which is the ultimate frame of reference for every action and relationship in middle earth or hell. It serves, moreover, as a palpable and immediate influence on the course of events in each poetic narrative. Part of what this means is that, according to the main narrative line of the Christian mythology which shapes Old English poetry, all narrative begins with the account of the war within the dryht of heaven, presented in *Genesis A*, 22–77; *Genesis B*, 246–441a; and *Christ and Satan*, 22–364. It is Lucifer's radically divisive act of rebellion that introduces conflict into the universe, by breaking the unitary *dream* 'joy' of the order of eternity. As long as there is only one indivisible reality, one totally harmonious heavenly society, the only possible activity is doxology: *þegnas þrymfæste   þeoden heredon, / sægdon lustum lof,   heora liffrean* 'Thanes firm in glory lauded the King, joyfully told their Life-Prince's praise' (*Genesis A*, 15–16). But whatever strengths wholehearted hymns of praise may have – and there are many such utterances in the Old English poetic corpus, starting with Cædmon's *Hymn* – doxologies are not rich repositories of interesting stories. In the biblical and hexaemeral metanarrative it is, so to speak, thanks to the arch-rebel Lucifer that story or narrative as such becomes possible, even necessary. Once the archangel through a mixture of envy and pride and 'thirsting for malice' (*niþes ofþyrsted*, 32a) turns traitor to his Lord and leads a troop of thanes into error, the cosmic stage is set not only for the account of the first war ever but for the stories of all those other conflicts that will follow from it, including the ones precipitated from Grendel's mere and the fire-dragon's lair. But even though in this tradition Lucifer is mythologically the first cause of human story-telling, and in his second role as lord of hell plays major parts throughout the overall story of the human race caught between heaven and hell, he is – when we follow the myth to its conclusion – far from being the power that determines how the story ends.

It is of course on the level of middle earth, the middle dwelling, that the Old English poetic accounts of human existence have their primary settings. Here the intermediate area of the three-tiered cosmos divides and we find two main levels or versions of the world of the dryht: in the upper level is the paradisal or idealized gift-hall of the Creation as the *Scyppend* 'Creator' means it to be and as human desire would want it to be, symbolized by Eden (*Genesis A*, 92–234; *Christ and Satan*, 1–21); on the lower level is the ruined *dryhtsele* 'dryht-hall' found when alienation from heaven, exile, social disintegration, destruction, and death hold sway in middle earth. Old English poetry is ideologically very clear, and the loyalty of any being on any level is usually not hard to see. But occasionally, as for example in *Beowulf* at the time of the hero's arrival in Denmark, we find an ambiguous mixture of the two earthly societies caught in the war between heaven and hell. Hrothgar welcomes Beowulf as a man sent by God, but the poet has already told us how at least some of the Danes are engaging in devil worship. The mythological explanations of the condition of human blessedness symbolized by the guest-hall of Eden and of the second, ruined world under demonic influence are set out clearly in *Genesis A* (22–77, 92–234, 852–964), *Genesis B* (246–441a, 442–851), and *Christ and Satan* (1–21, 22–364), in three closely related stories: the account of the way in which the fall of the angels leads to the creation of the dryht of hell; the way the war in heaven prompts the Prince of the celestial dryht to replace the fallen angels, now become exiles, by creating the world; and, finally, the story of the fall of man, described in *Genesis A* and *B* in the heroic diction of Old English poetry as the disloyalty of God's thane Adam when he takes from Eve's hand *hell and hinnsið* 'hell and a journey hence' (718), and so comes to know himself (927–30a) as an exile from Eden 'deprived of the joys of paradise' (*neorxnawanges / dugeðum bedæled*) and doomed to become a wanderer (*on wræc hweorfan*) seeking 'another homeland' (*oðerne eðel*).

Close examination of the myth of the Creation of the world in these poems reveals a structural metaphor which also plays a major role in *Beowulf*, in the particular fusion of myth, romance, and limited realism that is the subject of this chapter. It has just been shown how in *Genesis A* the Creation of the world is imagined as both a restoration of an original divine pattern and an extension of the dryht of heaven into another part of the universe, this latter logically being called 'the middle dwelling,' since it is located between the halls of heaven and the dryht of hell. As 'the Measurer' or 'Ordainer of angels ... and Giver of life' (*Metod engla ... lifes brytta*, 121b–2a) is about to create the *mid-*

dangeard, so goes the narrative, he looks out on 'a wide land, deep and dark, alien to himself as Dryhten, empty and not useful' (*wida grund / ... deop and dim, drihtne fremde, / idel and unnyt*, 104b–6a). These last formulaic words, *idel and unnyt*, characterizing the emptiness and uselessness of the uncreated world, are the same words applied to Heorot by Beowulf as he stands for the first time before Hrothgar and announces why he has come to Denmark. In his homeland, he says, 'the Grendel thing' [or 'business'] (*Grendles þing*) has been made known to him, 'not secretly' (*undyrne*), and he has been told by seafarers that 'after evening's light becomes hidden under heaven's vault' (*siððan æfenleoht / under heofenes hador beholen weorþeþ*), the best of halls 'for every man stands empty and not useful' (*rinca gehwylcum / idel ond unnyt*, 409b–14).

The connections between the accounts of Creation in the poems of the Junius manuscript and *Beowulf* go well beyond repetition of a verbal formula. It is not surprising that both the mere in *Beowulf* and the hell formed to house the dryht of rebel angels are located 'down under the headlands in the lower depths' (*Christ and Satan*, 31; cf. *Beowulf*, 1360–1, 1411), and that there are numerous other parallels between the two versions of hell. What is perhaps unexpected is the way the imagery of the uncreated state in *Genesis* also shows close symbolic parallels with the two major settings of part 1 of *Beowulf*: first, with the desolate state to which Heorot is reduced by Grendel (Hrothgar's creation has in a sense been 'uncreated' because its essential purpose as a place for the experience of *dream* has been frustrated); secondly, with the joyless, mist-shrouded world of darkness and hell from which this *feond on helle* (101b) comes, and which receives him back after he has been fatally wounded by a champion favoured by heaven.

In the Cædmonian *Genesis* it is said (106b ff.) that the uncreated waste which meets the eyes of 'the strong minded King' (*stiðfrihþ cining*) is a place 'deprived of joys' (*dreama lease*) and covered by dark mist that broods over it in endless night, 'black beneath the heavens' (*sweart under roderum*). The word for 'endless night' (*synnihte*) is repeated (109, 118). We recall that after Grendel's first attack on the newly created Heorot he is described as one of those beings who are *helrunan* 'skilled in the mysteries of hell' and that he holds the misty moors in *sinnihte* 'endless night' (161b–2a). As the *wuldorcyning* 'King of glory' in *Genesis* by his word calls 'the created world' (*woruldgesceaft*) into being, his spirit moves over the black waters, carrying out (before the lacuna in the manuscript) three actions on three successive days: the bringing of light into the primordial darkness (119b ff.); the formation in the midst of the 'mere-flood' (*mereflod*) of a 'joyous heavenly structure' (*hyhtlic heofontimber*) whose roof, says the poet, still remains above peoples (144b ff.);

and finally, as in the biblical Genesis 1, the quelling and separating of the waters from the land (155b ff.).

The key metaphor functioning in the *Genesis A* account of the Creation of the world for human beings is that of the newly fashioned *middangeard* 'middle dwelling' as a radiant, wonder-filled place in an 'all-green earth' (*eorðan ælgrene*, 197) surrounded by a 'mere-flood' (*mereflod*, 145). It is a dwelling whose roof (as in Cædmon's *Hymn*) is the firmament, a 'joyous heaven-timber' (*hyhtlic heofontimber*, 146), its Dryhten is the Creator, and its inhabitants, now to be brought into being, are the human race composed of Adam and Eve and their descendants. Initially the human pair are the high point of Creation – 'They were like angels' (*Heo wæron englum gelice*, 185b) – and they are filled with burning love for their Dryhten, who blesses them as he gives all living things into their hands: *Inc hyraþ eall* 'All belongs to you two' (205b). Paradise (*Neorxnawong*, 208b) is 'excellent and ready for guests, filled with gifts, with lasting benefits' (*god and gastlic, gifen gefylled / fremum forðweardum*, 209–10a). This newly created world is the perfect place for gift-giving, and its treasures symbolize the lasting love of God for his Creation. Like Heorot in its pristine state, built by a glorious king who has wide power through his word (*Beowulf*, 79), the middle dwelling of Eden is characterized by two features above all others: the joy that comes from perfect loyalty between Lord and followers; the giving and receiving of gifts, the visible form of that mutual bond.

We have, then, in Old English poetry a basic structure of metaphorical images: the eternal halls of the heavenly dryht above the clouds, filled with radiant brightness and songs of praise; the paradisal dwelling-place on earth, in a light-filled green plain, bordering on waters where the sea-paths are easy; the ruined hall in the midst of a wasteland of cold and darkness, encircled by stormy seas inhabited by monsters; the wind-swept halls of the dryht of hell, down under the headlands in the lower depths. These are the four major symbolic settings of Old English poetry, spread over a three-tiered mythological universe, in which the middle level is precariously placed and capable of being moved into a higher or a lower division of itself. There are accordingly four primary narrative movements: descent from a higher world, descent to a lower world, ascent from a lower world, and ascent to a higher world. The particular, individual stories spread throughout the Anglo-Saxon poetic records are complications and adaptations of these four 'narrative radicals' (Frye 1976, 97), metaphorical derivatives from them.

As noted earlier, the narratives of a substantial body of Old English poems are developed largely on the level of pure myth. This can be seen without difficulty in the parts of *Genesis A* and *B* just considered, in most of *Christ and Satan*, in *Christ I, II,* and *III*, in parts of *The Dream of the Rood*, in *The Descent into Hell*, and in *The Judgment Day I* and *II*. Perhaps the most vivid example of narrative as pure unimpeded myth, in what I have called the epic of the Creator, is the account in *Christ II* (712–43) of the great 'leaping' acts of the cosmic Christ as he moves through all levels of the universe on behalf of lost humanity. But in many other poems as well, mythical outlines appear, less continuously but at key thematic points, when the poet decides to indicate the didactic (often theological) purpose or larger frame of reference of the story being told. In the hagiographic romances and in many of the shorter lyric poems, the levels are there to provide a larger context of meaning and to enable greater or lesser degrees of narrative development and elaboration. The imagination, individual and collective, that brought *Beowulf* into verbal form works primarily with the imagery of the middle dwelling, but it uses all four levels, to whatever extent is appropriate at each particular point. In the romance mode of literature there is often a god or supernatural being behind the fictional action, and *Beowulf*, in this respect, is no exception. In the passages already discussed and in many other parts of the poem, both the narrator and those characters who are presented as seeing or understanding each situation recognize that the *Alwalda* 'All-ruler' is the final determiner of how each major event will turn out, and the ultimate judge of human worthiness. From the perspective of the Scyldings, Scyld Scefing appears mysteriously from across the sea and disappears back into the unknown. But both the narrator and, through him, the audience know that Scyld has gone 'into the keeping of the Prince' (*on Frean wære*, 27b) who is above the middle dwelling.

Since *Beowulf* is predominantly romance not myth, but with myth clearly in sight much of the time, the radical narrative movements are somewhat displaced. The protagonist in the three *Christ* poems descends from a higher world in the Advent, descends to a lower world in the Harrowing of hell, ascends from a lower world in the Resurrection, and ascends bodily to a higher world in the Ascension. Beowulf too is sent by God, but he comes across the sea from Geatland, not down from heaven. He descends into the lower world when he seeks out Grendel's mother in the depths of the mere and he is miraculously permitted to survive a gigantic struggle there, one that requires more than even his enormous strength. He must directly experience divine power and depend on it absolutely. It is almost as if he must lose his own heroic identity, symbolized by his mighty hand-grip and the weaponry of the *dryht* world, in order to reemerge from the mere as triumphant champion and deliverer of the middle dwelling. The recovery of that identity in the eyes of others involves an elaborate three-stage reintegration of the protagonist back into the world of the *dryht*. First, carrying the head of Grendel and the hilt of the giantish sword, Beowulf swims to the top of the mere and rejoins his Geatish comrades who are 'sick at heart' (*modes seoce*) and do not expect to see their lord again (1602b–5a). Earlier, the 'wise men' (*snottre ceorlas*) of the Danes who counsel Hrothgar have looked at the mere waters shining with blood and concluded that Beowulf is dead. At 'the ninth hour of the day' (*non dæges*, 1600) they and their 'gold friend' (*goldwine*) Hrothgar have abandoned the headland and gone home (1591–1602a). The second stage of heroic reintegration comes with the triumphant return to Heorot and the elaborate rituals of recognition and thanksgiving that take place there. The third stage is the return of the hero to his own lord Hygelac and to his Geatish homeland, where further recognition ceremonies take place.

The mere from which Beowulf ascends is one of the most richly symbolic locales in Old English poetry. Metaphorically and literally it is hell and is so named by the narrator several times in the poem (101, 163, 788, 852, 1274).[14] The monsters that inhabit this not pleasant place (*nis þæt heoru stow*, 1372b) are repeatedly described as demonic enemies of God and man. But the fact that the mere is hell does not mean that it is remote or in any way abstract; in relation to Heorot, as Hrothgar knows all too well, the distance to the mere is 'not far as measured in miles' (*Nis þæt feor ... milgemearces*, 1361b–2). In another passage earlier in the poem (164–88), hell is even nearer than the space of the short journey indicated by Hrothgar. After the Grendel terror has started and it has become clear that in the dark nights the 'enemy of mankind' (*feond mancynnes*) has taken possession of Heorot (*Heorot eardode*), it is said that the tormented Scyldings offer sacrifices at heathen shrines and pray for help to the 'soul-slayer' (*gastbona*). At this point of desperation, hell is right inside the great hall. It is, in fact and literally, inside the Danes themselves: 'Such was their custom, the hope of heathens; they remembered hell in their hearts' (*Swylc wæs þeaw hyra, / hæþenra hyht;   helle gemundon / in modsefan*). This almost psychological, modern-sounding spatial metaphor might seem an extraordinary displacement in an Old English poem, but it is another reminder that the imagining of the world in *Beowulf* knows nothing of either the vast Copernican spaces described in later literature, in Milton's account of hell's assault on paradise, for example, or of the galactic immensities of modern astronomy and astrophysics. Heaven and hell in the lifeworld of this poem are immediate to human experience. Finally, to complete the narrative pattern, when Beowulf dies his soul but not his body ascends to the upper world, 'goes from his breast to seek out the judgment of those fast in truth' (*him of hræðre gewat / sawol secean   soðfæstra dom*, 2819b–20). Since he has been a *spoudaios* 'weighty' hero not a god, his body is cremated and the ashes are consigned to a great barrow whose mnemonic function is to remind seafarers of the one 'who of mankind was strongest in might in the day of this life' (*se wæs mon-*

cynnes   mægenes strengest / on þæm dæge   þysses lifes. 196–7; see also 789–90), and who has now given his life for his people.

There are many more metaphorical resonances in the locales of the poem than those just outlined, and it will be necessary to return to some of them later. At this point it is sufficient to recognize how, in the romance mode in which *Beowulf* is imagined and composed, narrative patterns of descent and ascent are foregrounded. At times, as in the account of the hero's voyage from Geatland and his arrival in Denmark, we are carried along by a linear narrative whose settings and actions could almost belong to the actual world. But then, because the demands of romance require a departure from the world of ordinary experience, some form of break in consciousness, we are taken (up) into the idealized realm of the greatest of halls beneath the heavens or down into a nightmarish hell-world. Only some of nature's laws are suspended in *Beowulf*, and they are in abeyance only part of the time; but when they are, a superabundant imaginative energy is released. The swimming, wrestling, sword-fighting Beowulf does not have quite the range or powers of action of the 'leaping' man-God Christ who in the epic of the Creator carries out completely all four narrative radicals of descent and ascent. But at the height of his God-given powers he is presented as truly the greatest of human beings and he fully enacts two of these narratives while approximating the other two.

The romance mode of literature is not the same thing as romance narrative or plot (*mythos*). As has been shown, the former can be identified broadly, but clearly and usefully, on the basis of the powers of action of its protagonists, relative to those in more mythical or in more realistic modes. 'Mode' is a large, approximate designation of a fictional area within the world of words. The boundaries of romance, as in *Beowulf*, are flexible enough to allow it to reach into or combine with other modes, for greater complexity and imaginative range. It is this mode that dominates much of medieval European literature, including, as we have seen, a considerable number of the texts in the Old English poetic records. In these texts from Anglo-Saxon England, romance imagining is usually closely aligned with Christian myth.

Romance as narrative structure or plot, as distinct from mode, is a more formal designation. The essential element of plot in romance is adventure, which means that the story takes a sequential form, as in long poems or other sustained fictions. According to Frye (1957, 186–206), the sequence tends to develop in three stages: the perilous journey and preliminary minor adventures (the *agon*); the crucial struggle, usually some kind of battle in which either the hero or his foe, or both, must die (the *pathos*); and the exaltation of the hero (the *anagnorisis*), the recognition that he has proved himself to be a hero even if he does not survive. This three-stage narrative structure is of course a theoretical construct, derived by Frye from massive reading of many texts from different times and places.[15] It is not to be supposed that the three stages constitute a rigid determining pattern fully adhered to in slavish fashion by anyone who would write a romance. The theoretical construct is rather an attempt to account for one of those large, pre-generic narrative structures which give shape and meaning to a very large and diverse body of literature. If we bring to *Beowulf* these terms pertaining to the structure of romance, as distinct from those to do with the mode of romance, we find that there are preliminary minor adventures, the youthful hero's early battles with sea-monsters that are harassing the Geats and the exuberant contest with Breca. These are preliminary and minor only relatively, in relation to the three major battles later. A modern ironic consciousness might say of the high-spirited contest with Breca that the two young men brandishing their naked swords and struggling with the stormy sea-waters are simply experiencing an excess of testosterone and are engaging in macho displays of masculinity that lead them to risk their lives by recklessly pressing the boundaries of their developing physical powers. But in the non-mimetic terms of the poem itself both this episode and Beowulf's other preliminary acts of monster-quelling are presented as prodigious feats of strength and endurance and are clearly seen by the narrator as establishing Beowulf's credentials for even greater actions, on behalf of others.

One part in particular of these preliminary adventures serves the foreshadowing purpose. When Beowulf tells his own richly detailed account of the contest with Breca in order to rebut Unferth's insulting version of the same adventure, he states that the escapade was the result of a vow between him and Breca made when they were boys (535–8). But the larger purpose and the result of this early demonstration of 'strength in the mere' (*merestrengo*, 533a) also are made clear. After five nights of battling the stormy seas together, during which Beowulf protects his comrade, the two young men are separated, and Beowulf finds himself beset by fierce 'beasts of the mere' (*meredeor*, 558) and by darkness, icy winds, and waves. One of the monsters pulls him to the sea-bottom, as Grendel's mother also does later; like her, this hostile aggressor early in the hero's career is killed by him. In this preliminary episode, he also destroys nine sea-monsters in all and so, as he tells us, denies these 'evil-doers' (*manfordædlan*) 'the joy' (*gefean*) of sitting about eating him at a banquet near the sea-bottom' (*symbel ... sægrunde neah*, 564). The result of Beowulf's victory (565 ff.) is more than a matter of his individual conquest and survival: 'never again' (*syðþan na ... ne*) did these enemies 'hinder the passage of seafarers over the high seas' (*ymb brontne ford   brimliðende / lade ne letton*, 568–9a). Appropriately enough, then, as also happens later in the depths of Grendel's mere,

'God's bright beacon shines' (*beorht beacen Godes*, 570a) as the exhausted young man comes ashore at sunrise.

One of the numerous complexities of the poem comes into focus when we address the structural question of where the *agon* leaves off and the *pathos* begins. There is no problem in seeing the passages just discussed as preliminary and in connection with what follows relatively minor, though still significant. But the sequence in the main narrative includes three major battles for the hero, not one, two of them in Denmark and the other more than fifty years afterward in Geatland. Late in the poem in the old king's retrospections before his death, we get glimpses of still further battles he has been involved in. Each of the three main conflicts is a gigantic struggle and in each of them Beowulf is severely tested. In each situation he knows that he must rely both on his own powers and on whatever outcome God and *wyrd* 'fate' decide for him. In the sense that all these episodes are enormous challenges, they are all integral parts of the hero's *pathos*. But in another sense the fight with Grendel is preliminary and less severe than the one with Grendel's mother, and the second battle clearly is not the ordeal *in extremis* that the mutually fatal conflict with the fire-dragon is. Going even further in recognizing structural complications, we observe that the element of *anagnorisis* or recognition of Beowulf is not a one-time-only occurrence. Rather this structural feature is elaborately, even lavishly, expressed at several points, after the conquest of Grendel, then again after the killing of his mother, and finally at the end of the poem. There are in fact several big scenes of recognition for Beowulf's Danish achievements, including the one back in Geatland in which he is rewarded by Hygelac. The memorial barrow on the promontory by the sea at the end of the poem is the final internal expression of this theme. The poem itself is a sustained act of *anagnorisis*.

Beowulf both belongs to the mode of romance and bursts the boundaries of the mode. Similarly, in its structure, it uses, complicates, and goes beyond the fairly simple three-stage shape of archetypal romance narrative. Because among other things *Beowulf* is both a product of residual orality and a symbolic poem, telling and alluding to many stories and having multiple meanings attached to its one main story, it does not move along in a strict sequential way. It deals extensively in the simplifications and exaggerations of imagining which are appropriate to the romance mode, and to the telling of what on one level is a simple-minded and naïve folkloric tale. But *Beowulf* is also a work of art whose language and primary plot constantly point beyond themselves, in richly connotative, often subtle ways. It is metaphorically conceived. Its imagery and its narrative voice invite us in passage after passage to inhabit a world of metaphor and in that world to feel, imagine, and make important connections – and to think long and hard about large and serious matters to do with what creates and sustains human communities, and what destroys them.

Much of the discussion in this introductory chapter has been focused on passages that occur early in the poem and are concerned with the hero's adventures in Denmark. But that of course is only part of the story, the part that first takes the audience or reader into both the plot and the modes of imagining. Consideration of structure – I return to this in part two of this book, especially in chapters 7 and 8 – must by definition embrace the whole work. *Beowulf* as a whole is a particular example of archetypal romance narrative in several phases with increasingly tragic cadences. Because these darker elements are present throughout, held in check in part I but becoming almost omnipresent in part II, the splendid heroic achievements of the protagonist in Denmark are set against an ominous backdrop that prevents even part I of the poem being the account of a completely successful heroic quest. Romance is about the rhythm of life, and in one of its expressions, as in *Beowulf*, it joins forces with the imagery and narrative structure of tragedy.

2

Word Oðer Fand:
The Inwardness of Kennings

Words used in the grammatical formulations that we think of as sentences are always to some degree self-referential. They turn away from externals into the world of word-ordering itself. This tendency is pronounced in Old English poetry, where syntactical considerations are strongly influenced by dependence on the formulaic resources of the word-hoard and by compliance with the auditory and semantic demands of alliteration and markedly accentual rhythm. These strong centripetal or internal poetic pressures ensure that whatever empirical observation lies behind the words being used it will have been imaginatively displaced and fitted to poetic needs and purposes. Old English poems are pervaded with corporeal images – these are fundamental to whatever power and beauty the poetry has – but the presentation of these images does not show any sustained sense of an obligation to describe the external world in a representational way. We can get help in understanding this strongly centripetal, non-mimetic character of Old English poetry by consideration of what has become one of the major intellectual preoccupations of literary criticism in our time, the alleged inability of verbal language to do more than turn back on itself.

Much has been written and said in recent decades about the difficulty or impossibility of language escaping its own subjectivity. In the intellectual worlds of science and social science, numerical language or mathematics is known to be essentially a hypothetical language of the imagination. However many applications it is given, it can never be made to coincide precisely and comprehensively with physical or social facts. Similarly in the verbal disciplines, it has been accepted by many thinkers that words cannot reliably tell or describe anything so that the words connect, other than asymmetrically, with any reality in the non-verbal world. What has been called the principle of negation or non-coincidence runs through a great deal of recent critical discourse, and has generated a climate, healthy in some ways, of *aporesis* and scepticism about the power of words as acts, because of the delusions words can foster, and also because there is no direct way from literature to action.

Paul de Man, for example, studied and wrote at length about the self-referentiality of language, about the ways in which language is concerned with its own activity (1979, 1984, 1986, 1989). Northrop Frye, a very different kind of thinker, also emphasized as one of his main themes throughout his career the centripetal ways in which verbal discourses operate. In the last period of his life, his two main concerns were the inwardness of the workings of words and, equally important, the external impact in human culture and the existential lives of men and women of that inwardness. In *The Great Code: The Bible and Literature* (1982) he explored the centripetal ways in which words interconnect within the Bible itself, and in doing so provided a brilliant post-Hegelian account of verbal language. In *Words with Power, Being a Second Study of the Bible and Literature* (1990), he turned his attention to the centrifugal outreach of the Bible in Western culture and probed deeply into the different ways in which verbal language functions in the world, including in non-biblical literature.

Where Frye displayed on every page a mind that is a synthesis of intellect and feeling engaged in creative construction, de Man's deconstructive mind was schooled in rigorous, ascetic analysis and was intent on the philosophical task of stripping away epistemological delusions. As early as 1953, for example, in de Man's essay on 'Montaigne and Transcendence' (1989, 3–11), we find him functioning as a very late post-Cartesian explorer of German idealistic philosophy, pointing out that human rational faculties have their mainspring in 'an entirely subjective intentionality' and that 'rational construction does not conceal an objective truth, but is merely the expression of our pleasure in constructing it' (5–6). De Man was intent on showing the unreliability of language and in demonstrating how all writing tells a story of its own inability to tell a story which connects, other than very inadequately, with the world of event and action. Because all writing concerns itself with its own activity as language, it is the task of criticism to point out 'the discrepancy between the power of words as acts and their power to produce other words' (1984, 101). It is this principle of non-coincidence that led de Man to develop the concept of allegory that informs his influential theory of rhetoric, a theory that is paralleled in Derrida (1967a, 1967b, 1972a, 1972b, 1984) and other theorists and has done much to create an awareness of what deconstructionist thought considers the traps of language and the problematics of reading.

My studies of language and literature, including Old English poetry, lead me also increasingly to an awareness of how words in a literary work find, and work on, each other, how they pursue their own internal patterning activities in relational, dynamic ways which ensure that their connections with the nonverbal world can never be more than oblique. Such obliquity is not a negative limitation. It is precisely what gives imaginative literature its peculiar powers, including its abilities to cast light on, influence, and even remake the external world, for good or for ill, by projecting into that external world things that it itself is not. Recognition of the obliquity of verbal art need not lead, I think, to an impasse in lengthy aporias and turgid ruminations about the performative failures of words or the prison house of language. It is literature and myth with their endless plurality and their ability to set up a counter-environment to the nightmare of history that provide real power to liberate human beings, through the creating of visions or models of what we really do want and need, in the midst of what so far we have had to tolerate; or models of what we really do not want but need to be shown by powerful artists in fictional form in order to know how repugnant it is. Obliquity is the fundamental core of whatever revelation literature offers. In the case of Old English poetry generally, and *Beowulf* in particular, I see at work an enormous confidence in the power of words to act creatively, to inform and reshape human existence in ways better than those that would otherwise have held dominance, and to do these things by letting poetic language carry out its own metaphorical work. This confidence implies, I suggest, not a principle of negation focused on language as an epistemological trap, as in de Man, but a principle of identity, by which the very inwardness itself, the self-referentiality, of the poetic language demonstrates a powerful, creative force which expresses extraordinary insights, knowledge, and wisdom, in ways that only poetry can. It is this inwardness in *Beowulf* and the metaphorical identities revealed by it that are the main concern in this chapter and the next.

There is nothing Cartesian about *Beowulf*. By that I mean that there is no rationalist distrust in this poem of the kind of human imagining that relies massively on a combination of sense experience and poetic, highly figured language. Surprisingly perhaps, given the period of Western cultural history in which *Beowulf* appeared, there is no sustained feeling in the poem that the gross, the physical, or the particular is a contamination of some purer and more abstract reality that is assumed to be more important and more real than the corporeal elements themselves. On the contrary, in this text figuration and recurrence of images assist thought, and help sustain whatever moral or rational teaching is involved. By constructing a verbally intricate and suggestive pattern, the poet invites the listener/reader to experience certain effects and to reach certain perceptions through his or her own mental play. The language is inventive, exploratory, and daring, however traditional and formulaic. Although some of the invention and initial verbal exploration would have taken place decades, even centuries, before the poem itself came into being, that does not mean that the power of the words to address the feelings and imaginations of listeners and readers would have been diminished by the time of composition. On the contrary, time, tradition, and cultural experience may well have ensured that only the most powerful verbal materials, the most durable metaphors and myths, would have continued to resonate and so bring their semantic and poetic force into this poem. One of the things this tried and true quality in the poetry should mean for criticism and scholarship is that, instead of simply saying that the language of *Beowulf* is formulaic and traditional, and then doing the arithmetic about how often the extant poetic records include the formula in question, we need to dismantle and take apart the compounds and the other words and phrases which are actually doing the poetic work, in order to see how they do it and to experience for ourselves the verbal elements as words of power. Whenever it is possible to do so, and it won't always be, we need to recognize and expose the original physical and conceptual impact of the actual material language of the poem.

Friedrich Klaeber's introductory essay on 'Tone, Style, Meter' in his edition of *Beowulf* (lviii–lxxi) includes a statement about the diction of the poem that has led many readers astray on the important matter of metaphor: 'On the whole, we note a scarcity of conscious poetic metaphors, by the side of the more numerous ones of faded and only dimly felt metaphorical quality' (lxiv). In a note he lists six 'conscious' metaphors, one of which occurs twice in the poem. He does not translate any of these six to demonstrate or analyse what it is that makes them metaphors, let alone why he thinks they are conscious as compared with the 'faded' and 'dimly felt' ones that get passed over without being cited. As for the related figure of speech, the simile, which he also discusses, we now know that a simile is a diluted metaphor, a poetic identification displaced somewhat in the direction of empirical realism (the ship *is very like* a bird rather than the ship *is* a bird). Klaeber does not show that he recognizes the relationship between the two kinds of figure or the important distinction between them. He is accurate nonetheless when he points out that in *Beowulf* similes are 'few,' 'brief' (he means in comparison to the similes in Homer), and 'formula-like,' and that they are 'scattered through the first part' of the poem. In a note (lxiv–lxv, n. 5) he lists nine similes, making an unappreciative comment on one of them: 'The pretty lines 1570 ff.: *Lixte se leoma ... efne swa of hefene hadre scineð / rodores candel* can hardly be said to contain an imaginative comparison.'

Klaeber was a superb 'history'-minded scholar writing in a period of our culture in which literary tastes, including those of scholars, were still largely the product of low mimetic or representational expectations and biases, and in which similes and metaphors often were thought of, at best, as vivid ornaments and, at worst, as pathetic fallacies or mimetic failures. Klaeber makes a large assumption when he says which metaphors would have been 'conscious' (presumably he means for the poet, perhaps also for the original readers or listeners), and we would make an equally large assumption if we tried to distinguish in this way among the figurative expressions in the poem. We know virtually nothing about the poet or poets involved in shaping *Beowulf*, certainly nothing about the relative degrees of consciousness he or they were experiencing when using particular words or expressions in the genesis of the poem. But we do have the words, all of them in contexts within the poem, and we do have the poem in the context of other Old English poems. If these words and this poem are to do their work for us, we have to become as conscious as we possibly can of what the words and the poem literally are and what they are doing. If we are at least partly successful, we may even come to understand something essential of what *Beowulf* once meant, before we brought to it meanings and expectations from other places and times.[1]

It is a main contention of this book that *Beowulf* belongs to an area or mode of language in which metaphor is both functional and pervasive, and that in this important matter Klaeber was radically wrong. What he failed to realize is that there is a large difference between explicit metaphor, which announces its presence by a 'this is that' predication ('the ship *is* a bird'), and implicit metaphor, which is based on juxtaposition, association, and intensified uses of language. Whatever imagination fashioned *Beowulf*, it is clear that it did not feel a need to spell out or grammatically announce for prosaic, analytic, descriptive minds the host of metaphorical identities that are established by the interconnections which exist in the verbal patterns of this text. The world of the poem is intensely alive emotionally. A radically anthropocentric ontology informs its mode of language. It is pervaded by an animism that finds numerous interconnections between the human and the non-human, both within created nature (*winter ybe beleac / isgebinde* 'winter locked the waves in ice-bonds,' 1132b–3a; *Heofon rece swealg* 'Heaven swallowed the smoke,' 3155b) and in human actions (*oþ þæt wordes ord / breosthord þurhbræc* 'until a word's point [or 'front'] broke through a breast-hoard,' 2791b–2a).

The contents of the poem are not objectified by a seeing, observing, and describing mind separate from those contents. Rather, the narrator presents and characterizes the contents. Often he identifies with and comments sympathetically or negatively on the things, people, places, and events within the story: *Swa sceal geong guma   gode gewyrcean* 'So a young man should,' literally, 'perform by good', that is, do good deeds (20); *ne gefrægn ic freondlicor   feower madmas / golde gegyred   gummanna fela / in ealobence   oðrum gesellan* 'I have not heard of many men who in a more friendly way gave four treasures, gold adorned, to another on the ale-bench' (1027–9); *Sinc eaðe mæg, / gold on grunde   gumcynnes gehwone / oferhigian,   hyde se ðe wylle!* 'Treasure, gold in the ground, easily may overpower each one of mankind, hide it who will!' (2764b–6). Even though the poem apparently is told by someone from a later time to people of a later time, there is in it no epistemological separation of subject and object. *Beowulf* is, in this sense, psychologically primitive. Its psychology is founded on a model of knowledge that is stored in the metaphorical powers of the word-hoard. The deeply traditional, radical metaphors found in abundance throughout the text have been forged by wordsmiths into fusions of identities, between things or beings in the world shaped by God and the human (and other) beings in that world, and between all these and the narrator. This is an identity – actually a complex pattern of many identities – in which, by the poem's welcoming rhetoric, we too are invited to participate.

Among the hundreds of compounds in *Beowulf*, one on average in every other line and a different one in every third line (Klaeber, lxiv), I conservatively identify as kennings between sixty and seventy.[2] There are many more *kend heiti*. In saying this I follow the usual distinction made between *kend heiti* and *kennings*, although like others I recognize that the dividing line between the two is often impossible to draw with any confidence. A *kent heiti*, as usually understood, is a somewhat oblique or indirect way of characterizing something and referring to it by one of its attributes: a *winsele*, for example, is a hall in which one of the activities is wine drinking; a *hronrad* 'whale-riding' is the sea referred to in terms of one of the many creatures and activities associated with it. Such compounds are metonymic in that a part is made to stand for a whole. They are also figurative and imaginative, but they are not as oblique in their references as *kennings* are. Kennings in an important sense are almost entirely verbal. They are imagined realities that do not exist in the actual physical nonverbal world, until material language puts them there. From an empirical perspective, they are more circuitous than *kend heiti*. They are more completely products of the order of words, largely detached from the givens of nature but still somewhat connected with them, both in residual and potential ways. Though *kend heiti* are far from being naturalistic or mimetic uses of language either, the distinction between the two kinds of figurative device depends on the degree of abstraction from what is being alluded to: alluded to, not described. Where the *kend heiti* go part way, the kennings go all the way imaginatively. That is why they have special centripetal force in the poem. That is why I have chosen in the remainder of this chapter to concentrate on them as a good means of access into the curiously inwrought, metaphorical imagining that pervades the text. Many of the *kend heiti*, only a few of which are mentioned in this chapter, come into focus in the rest of the book.

The largest group of kennings in *Beowulf* has to do with weapons and war,[3] the next largest with the sea, seafaring, water, and ships. A third group is related to the human body and, by parodic extension, to the bodies of monsters. A fourth group is used to characterize thoughts and emotions. A few additional kennings not included in any of these groups are also associated with the monsters but are not concerned with their physical bodies. Finally there are a few miscellaneous kennings that do not fall into any of these categories. In what follows I list the kennings according to these groupings and then translate and comment on them, giving special sustained attention to a few. In this last critical activity I am treating the few as exemplary or typical. For each kenning cited I provide, on the one hand, a literal, almost etymological translation, and, on the other, one or more somewhat more abstract or prosaic translations. The translations and commentary are meant to be illuminating and illustrative and make no claim to being a definitive statement about all that these kennings are and do in *Beowulf*. As will quickly become clear, a full commentary on that subject would require an extensive treatise and would usurp the role of readers who are perfectly able to continue these explorations for themselves if so inclined. I know from years of conducting this kind of critical reading with students that there is no better way to help them get their minds and imaginations inside the Old English poem.

In the first and largest group of kennings, those to do with weapons and war, we find several associated with shields: *bordweall* 'board-wall, shield-wall, phalanx of shield-bearing warriors' (2980); *lindplega* 'linden-play, shield-play, battle' (1073, 2039); *scildweall* 'shield-wall, phalanx of shield-bearing warriors' (3118). In the case of *scildweall*, and this is typical of what kennings are and do, it is the first part of the compound that seems to be literal and the second that is metaphorical. At least this is how it appears if we look at the word in isolation as a lexical item. This kenning occurs only this once in the extant Anglo-Saxon poetic corpus and its most immediate imaginative content is easily perceived. But if we take into account that the compound is being used by a poet skilled in letting one word find another in curiously intricate and suggestive ways, we can see that the word as a whole, with both its parts, is metaphorical, and has a figurative impact in the entire context in which it occurs. Let us examine this one striking use of *scildweall* in *Beowulf*. It comes in the brief, vivid speech by Wiglaf just after he has issued a command for wood to be gathered for Beowulf's pyre (3114b–19). As the profoundly unhappy thane anticipates the flames and smoke of his lord's funeral fire, he recalls how, often in the past, the warrior-king whose body now is about to be consumed has 'lived through the iron-shower, when the storm of arrows, forced from bowstrings, hurried quivering over the shield-wall' (*gebad   isernscure, / þonne stræla storm   strengum bebæded / scoc ofer scildweall*, 3116–18a). In those battles, says Wiglaf, 'the shaft held to its task, made eager by its feather-gear, helped on the arrow-tip' (*sceft nytte heold, / fæðergearwum fus   flane fulleode*, 3118b–19). We can hear and see what is happening verbally. The arrows moving through the air metaphorically become first a shower, then a storm, and, finally, by the sheer force of narrative context and the association of images, the flames of the pyre about to devour or eat (*fretan*) the body of the hero, which always previously has survived the onslaughts of arrows. The shields on the former battlefields of Beowulf's life have formed phalanxes of warriors and metaphorically, almost actually, according to the kenning, have become a wall. The wall now, in Wiglaf's words, becomes the pyre over which the weapons/flames move (he does not say it here, but we know that in the battle with the dragon there was no shield-wall, no phalanx of dryht men). The eager arrow-shaft, personified, carries out its appointed task, as does Beowulf – and as the speaker, Wiglaf, has been doing and will continue to do.

Arrows are alluded to in the kenning *isernscur* 'iron-shower, volley of arrows' (3116), and spears in *wælsceaft* 'slaughter-shaft, death-shaft, spear' (398) and *wælsteng* 'slaughter-pole, spear-shaft, spear' (1638). The visually arresting kenning *wigheafola* 'war-head, helmet' is almost a catachresis and is used in connection with *Wiglaf* (his name 'War-leaving' itself is probably a kenning, and certainly a metaphor), as the young Waegmunding alone plunges through the deadly flame to help Beowulf. There are two occurrences of *hringnet* 'ring-net, mail coat' (1889, 2754) and one of *herenet* 'war-net, battle-net, corslet' (1553).[4] The kenning *hondgemot* 'hand-meeting, battle' refers to the many conflicts in which Hrunting has excelled (1526) and to the one in which Hygelac dies (2355); the similar compound *hondræs* 'hand-rush, hand-fight, attack' is used by Beowulf to describe to Hygelac the struggle between himself and Grendel (2072). *Wealaf* 'woe-leaving, those left after calamity' is used twice of the few survivors among Finn's thanes after the fight against Hengest (1084, 1098). *Wælfyllo* 'slaughter-fill, fill of those slain in battle, abundance of those killed in battle' is applied to Grendel just after he has seized thirty thanes in Heorot and made his way back to the mere (125). Since *wæl* by itself means either 'those slaughtered in battle' or a more general sense of carnage, *wælrest* 'slaughter resting-place' is a metaphor for the place in which slain warriors 'rest,' that is, lie dead. It is used, along with the kenning *deaðbed* 'deathbed,' of the place in which Beowulf's body lies 'by the deeds of the serpent' (*wyrmes dædum*, 2901–2). Similar to *wælrest* and *deaðbed* are *morþorbed* 'murder-bed, bed of death by violence' (Herebeald's, 2436); *legerbed* 'bed for lying, bed of death, grave' (that of humankind in general, 1007); and *wælbed* 'slaughter-bed, bed for the slaughtered.' This last is the deathbed on which Beowulf had hoped to bind Grendel in Heorot before the monster fled, fatally wounded (964). One of the most potent kennings in this set that have to do with weapons, war, and battle-death is the stark oxymoron *hreawic* 'corpse-dwelling, dwelling-place of corpses, place of death.' It is used in association with the kenning *guðscear* 'war-shearing, war-harvest, carnage' to characterize the battlefield strewn with dead Geats in the land of the Franks at the end of Hygelac's disastrous expedition. The two kennings together call up obliquely but clearly enough a gory field of mown-down corpses (1213–14a).

The kennings associated with swords provide a rich pattern that takes us deep into the poetic thought of the poem. Two closely related kennings for 'sword,' *beadoleoma* and *hildeleoma*, apparently are unique to *Beowulf*. Both are translatable as 'battle-light,' as in 'flashing sword.' The single occurrence of the compound *beadoleoma* comes in the account of the battle in the mere, in connection with the famous sword Hrunting 'Thrusting,' which Unferth has given to Beowulf. The use of the kenning is ironic in the context. Beowulf, confronting Grendel's mother, does thrust powerfully with Hrunting, causing its etched blade to sing out 'a fierce war-song on her head' (*hire on hafelan   hringmæl agol / grædig guðleoð*, 1521–2a), but he then finds that for the first time ever 'the precious treasure' (*deorum madme*, 1528) will not 'bite' (*bitan*) effectively enough to harm the monster's life.

Like *beadoleoma*, the kenning *hildeleoma* 'battle-light' or 'flashing sword' occurs only once with that meaning, but it does so with deadly poetic accuracy, in the Finnsburg episode. It comes at the end of the narrator's brief account of how the long winter endured by the inmates in Finn's fortress has been stained with the thought of further slaughters in revenge for those that have taken place earlier (1125 ff.). The Jutish king, Finn, and the Scylding leader, Hengest, bitter enemies, have been holding to a tensely precarious truce, after Hengest's Danish king, Hnæf, Hildeburh's brother, has been killed by the Jutes. The seasons change. Winter, with its stormy seas in surging conflict with the wind and its waves locked in ice-bonds, is gone. A new year with gloriously bright weather has come to men's dwellings. The 'earth's lap' again is 'fair' (*fæger foldan bearm*), and the exiled Hengest is eager to go, 'the guest from the dwelling' (*gist of geardum*). But he is even more intent on vengeance, so that when someone (the narrative details are not clear) ignites the situation, by placing a well-known 'battle-light' in his lap (*hildeleoman, / billa selest   on bearm*, 1143b–4), bloody slaughter breaks out again. The scene on which this sword shines its light is not one of joy-filled life returning in the spring to the order of Creation.

There is another use in the poem, subtle and imaginatively apt, of the word *hildeleoma*, though in this case the referential significance of the compound is not 'sword' and the figurative association is not with the light that is given off by a moving sword. The associative metaphor is with 'battle-flames' themselves (2583). Again, as with the *beadoleoma* Hrunting in the encounter in the mere, the hero is at the beginning of a crucial battle, but this time it is his last one, with the fire-dragon. At this almost apocalyptic point in the narrative action (2538 ff.), 'the man of the Weather-Geats' (*Weder-Geata leod*), 'bulged, enraged' (*gebolgen*) and 'stout-hearted' (*stearcheort*), has 'stormed' (*styrmde*) 'in under the gray stone' (*under harne stan*) his human challenge and hatred to the 'guardian of the hoard' (*hordweard*). The monster recognizes 'the voice of a man' (*mannes reorde*) and, 'burning and twisted' (*byrnende gebogen*), comes slithering and hurrying to his fate. Again here, as in the battle with Grendel's mother, the emphasis turns to the theme of the inadequacy of a sword. Beowulf has just raised his ancestral weapon *Nægling* 'Nailing' and struck 'the shining horror' (*gryrefahne*) of the dragon, but the sword's edge fails to bite deeply enough to kill. In fact, the sword-blow serves only further to enrage the serpent, so that he throws out 'murder-fire' (*wælfyre*), causing 'battle-flames' (*hildeleoman*) to spring far and wide. The meaning of *hildeleoma*, by this point in the poem, has shifted. Now it is fire, not a flashing sword. It is as if some linkage in the poet's imagination has led him, this time, to transfer the earlier metaphorical association of the kenning 'battle-light' away from the sword itself to the result of its failure, to the answering flames from the dragon which has been struck by the sword. The 'battle-flame' sword, literarily, metaphorically, has reignited the dragon, who, terrified of Beowulf, as Beowulf is of him, has coiled himself together and is waiting in his armour, after belching the 'hot battle-sweat' (*hat hildeswat*) of his flames from inside the barrow.

The motif of shining swords being expected to serve effectively in battle but not doing so also appears, not surprisingly, in connection with the impotent Unferth. Towards the end of Beowulf's rebuttal of the thule's invidious insults, he says that he has never heard, in connection with Unferth, 'of any such skilful battles, of such sword-terror' (*swylcra searoniða ... billa brogan*, 581b–3a) as he himself has demonstrated in the sea, when with his sword he slew nine sea-monsters and then swam ashore as 'Light came from the east, God's bright sign' (*Leoht eastan com, / beorht beacen Godes*, 569b–70a). Nor ever yet 'in the games of war' (*æt heaðolace*, 584a), Beowulf continues, has either Breca or Unferth 'achieved so bold a deed with bright swords' (*swa deorlice dæd gefremede / fagum sweordum*, 585–6a). This pattern of light and sword imagery leads Beowulf to a kenning which occurs only once in the poem and only in this poem, *ecgþracu* 'sword-storm' or 'sword-power' (596a). In using this particular figure of speech to help demolish Unferth verbally, Beowulf comes as close

The Inwardness of Kennings 63

as he ever does to insulting the whole Danish people. He tells the 'son of Edge-leaving' (*sunu Ecglafes*) that the awful monster Grendel would never have humiliated Heorot so badly if Unferth's heart and spirit were really as fierce in fighting as he pretends. But Grendel has noticed that he need not fear very much 'the terrible sword-storm' (*atole ecgþræce*) of Unferth's people, 'the Victory Scyldings' (*Sige-Scyldinga*). Because the Danish sword-edges, in fact, have no power, Grendel in his role as cannibalistic banqueter happily 'puts to sleep' (kills) and 'cuts' or 'carves up' (*swefeð ond snedeþ*, 600) the Danes for his feasting.[5] But now there will be a change. Beowulf soon will demonstrate 'the strength and courage ... of the Geats' (*Geata ... eafoð ond ellen*) so that afterwards anyone who wishes will be able to walk in high spirits to the mead, 'when the morning-light of another day, the sun clothed with sky light, shines from the south on the children of men' (*siþþan morgen leoht / ofer ylda bearn   oþres dogores, / sunne sweglwered   suþan scineð*, 604b–6). A great deal is happening metaphorically in this passage, as the poet lets the right words find each other. What we have as a verbal fabric – surrounding the ironic phrase *atole ecgþræce*, applied to Unferth and the Danes – is the juxtaposing of imagery of the sunrise and heaven with both the sword-victory that Beowulf has already achieved over sea-monsters and the situation that Heorot will find itself in after he has defeated Grendel. Skilfully, obliquely, but clearly, the imagery poetically identifies the source of real 'sword-power' and tells – in the terms in which this poem understands and presents human existence – what it is fundamentally (God-given power) that enables a sword to shine effectively in use. The imagery also, periphrastically but again clearly, explains the absence of power and why the force required to deal with monsters is not with Unferth's bright sword or with Breca's.

Another kenning, related to but distinct from *ecgþracu*, occurs twice and may be exerting some of the subtle, riddling quality found in many kennings as metaphorical figures. The word *ecghete* is usually understood as 'war' or 'hostility.' Perhaps this has some slight legitimacy as a translation, on some level well removed from the poem, but it is prosaic and far abstracted from Old English. The poetic word *ecghete* is at once concrete and oblique. The first half of it, *ecg*, normally understood and read as 'sword,' is itself a conventional figure found in other texts, a synecdoche in which the edge of a sword-blade, perhaps especially its sharpness, is taken to signify the whole weapon. This in turn combines with the apparently straightforward Old English word for the intense emotion 'hatred.' But how straightforward or literal is this word for hatred? What does the Old English compound, by itself, mean? Most obviously it seems to refer to hatred that leads to or shows itself in sword-fighting. But whose hatred? The obvious answer would seem to be the hatred of the human enemies who in a particular situation are using the swords. But kennings being what they are, and the connotative art of the *Beowulf* poet being what it is, there may well also be another metaphorical sense at work in the figure, by which swords – like other animate, feeling things in the poem – are being imagined as living embodiments of hatred, as live beings who hate and kill.

It is exactly this kind of poetic resonance that surrounds the first use of *ecghete* in *Beowulf* (84). I accept the usual editorial emendation of the manuscript *secg hete* to *ecghete* (Klaeber, 4). The word is heard, ominously, immediately before the first mention of the *ellengæst* 'bold demon' Grendel, who is still unnamed, but the kenning does not in any direct sense refer to the hostility Grendel is about to show towards Heorot. Rather the reference is to events far in the future. The context in which the kenning is embedded is instructive. Hrothgar's great dwelling-place has just been created, named, and given its first use. The king, keeping his earlier promise, has dispensed rings and other gifts. We are told that 'the hall towered upward, high and horn-gabled' (*Sele hlifade / heah ond horngeap*, 81b–2a), indicating a large, upward-thrusting architectural structure with stag-antlered projections. Then at this climactic moment of great human achievement comes an allusive foreshadowing, apparently assumed to be meaningful to the audience, of the disaster that is to come years later, when a war will break out between Hrothgar and Ingeld, the Heathobard husband of the king's daughter Freawaru. In that conflict the 'greatest of hall-dwellings' (*healærna mæst*, 78) will be destroyed. For now, we are told, Heorot 'was waiting for battle-wellings, hostile flames' (*heaðowylma bad, / laðan liges*), but the time was not yet at hand 'for *sword-hate* between son-in-law and father-in-law to be born [or to awaken] after slaughter-rage' (*ðæt se ecghete aþumsweoran / æfter wælniðe wæcnan*, 84–5). The verb *wæcnan* 'to be born' or 'to awaken' used with *ecghete* 'sword-hate' further animates or personifies both the sword in the kenning and the compound *wælniðe* 'slaughter-rage,' in a context in which the great hall itself has already taken on a towering, animated character as it stands waiting, even at the moment of its inception, for the 'hostile' (*laðan*) flames that will be its doom.

The other occurrence of *ecghete* (1738) is in a quite different context, that of Hrothgar's sermon against pride delivered on the Geats' last night in Denmark, after Beowulf has defeated both Grendel and his mother. Here as well the kenning 'edge-hate' is still fully alive. As in the other occurrence, it is heard along with a group of figuratively active nouns and verbs. But this time it has relatively less narrative intensity. Again context determines much of the meaning. Hrothgar has described the joyless, stingy king Heremod, who brought slaughter and destruction to the Danish people, and has now moved on to describe another kind of ruler, one who prospers so much that he forgets that for him as for all men an end will come to his well-being. This heedless figure lives 'in feasting' (*on wiste*); 'sickness and age do not at all dwell in his way' (*no hine wiht dweleð / adl ne yldo*); 'malicious sorrow does not become dark in his heart' (*ne him inwitsorh / on sefan sweorceþ*); 'strife nowhere shows sword-hate' (*ne gesacu ohwær / ecghete eoweð*). For now, as Hrothgar puts it, 'the whole world turns to his desire' (*him eal worold / wendeð on willan*). The passage, as well as the use of the kenning *ecghete*, reveals something centrally important about language in *Beowulf*. There are no true abstractions. For the *Beowulf* poet, language operates metaphorically, not conceptually. Even here in the midst of an early medieval sermon about pride, in which one might expect to find allegorical abstractions, the concepts of sickness, age, sorrow, and strife all have concrete, animate associations and identities. Sickness and age are beings that take up their dwelling in a body. Sorrow is a malicious force that can enter a human heart or spirit and darken there. Strife or contention is not something abstract or remote but an active energy that expresses sword-hate. Even the 'whole world' (*eal worold*) is something sentient that for a time will turn itself to accommodate human desire. Such conceptions are intensely physical, anchored in concrete images connected with bodily and material processes. We are still, even in the homily, in the midst of a poetic language in which subject and object are not separated.

The many hundreds of language events and word characters in *Beowulf* demonstrate a sense of energy common both to human beings and the world they move in. What this seems to mean, from the perspective of criticism now, is that although the *Beowulf* poet's metaphorical conceptions may not have been thought out as such in a rational, conscious way, or responded to on that level by an audience, still they are the poetic product of a mind and imagination acutely aware of verbal sound and sense, and willing to let metaphors do their own peculiar work. Klaeber may have been partly right when he spoke of 'a scarcity of conscious poetic metaphors,' if he meant by that metaphors being inserted according to some deliberate plan, but he was wrong when he spoke of 'the more numerous ones of faded and only dimly felt metaphorical quality' (lxiv). In passage after passage the metaphorical language is anything but faded and dim, however traditional and formulaic much of the word-stock is. It regularly exerts vivid figurative and imaginative energy, if through our translation filters we do not drain it of its power and in so doing show our contempt for the poetic thought involved. Although the people who originally experienced the energy in the poem's language may have had no conscious analytical or intellectual conception of metaphor *per se*, that is no reason to assume that the language was faded or dim for them. On the contrary, the very composition of a poem like *Beowulf* is credible only on the assumption that its words were words with power. It has to be 'metaphorical' for us because as we think of words it is only metaphors that can express in language the sense of an energy common to subject and object. Most of us, we need to remember, do not not know ourselves to be living *in* the 'middle dwelling,' closely interconnected with heaven and hell, in the immediate way the human beings in the poem do.

Two other kennings associated with swords extend further the range of figurative associations surrounding this weapon which plays such key roles in the agonistic encounters of the poem. One of the two occurs in connection with an important battle in one of the background narratives and refers to the death of Beowulf's lord, Hygelac. The other is important in one of the major events in the primary narrative, in relation to the *eotenisc* 'giantish' sword found in the mere. The first is in the narrator's explanation of why Beowulf, when he first learns of the destruction of his hall by 'the far-flyer' (*widflogan*, 2346), is not worried about his own life. He has come through many battles since crushing Grendel's 'loathsome race' (*laðan cynnes*, 2354), not the least of his hand-combats being the one in that 'rush of war' (*guðe ræsum*, 2356) in which 'Hrethel's son died of sword-drinks' (*Hreðles eafora   hiorodryncum swealt*, 2358) – that is, according to the kenning applied to Hygelac's death, of having a sword drink his blood, and, equally figuratively, of being 'beaten down' or 'trampled' by this not at all inanimate weapon (*bille gebeaten*, 2359) that kills him.

Of the several instruments of war turned into words and characterized metaphorically in *Beowulf*, the one that is miraculously made available to the hero to save him from Grendel's mother has the widest range of imaginative meanings, all compressed into a series of figurative expressions. These include the kenning *hildegicelum* 'battle-icicles' (1606b), to suggest the appearance of the huge sword as its patterned blade melts in the poisonous blood of Grendel and his mother. She has just been killed by this sword, but the blood that melts the blade includes as well the blood of her son, who, although dead earlier, has just been beheaded with it. In the immediate context the reason for the inclusion of Grendel's blood is not entirely clear, but it becomes so later when Beowulf, back in Heorot, tells about the strange event (1665 ff.). In isolation, the kenning *hildegicelum* would seem bizarre and far-fetched. In the verbal and narrative context in which it occurs it is singularly effective. To see how this is so we have to engage, as the poet frequently does, in circumlocution; we have to let the verbal patterns move around in our heads so that the kenning, a device for surrounding a meaning but not stating it, itself becomes surrounded by connotations. If we do this here, the identification of melting blade and melting icicles does a significant piece of strong poetic work.

Beowulf, we recall, is at the bottom of the mere, having taken a good part of a day to swim that far down and having been obstructed as he went by a variety of water-monsters (1495b ff.). Grendel's mother – the weird being who has been holding this domain for the same hundred half-years that Hrothgar has been ruling Denmark – has seen while Beowulf was descending that 'some man from above' (*gumena sum ... ufan*) is exploring the 'dwelling of alien creatures' (*ælwihta eard*), and so has dragged him to the bottom and into her 'hostile hall' (*niðsele*). It is here that the fierce struggle between them takes place and it is during this encounter that the famous Hrunting fails. Even the hero's 'hand-grip of power' (*mundgripe mægenes*, 1534) proves inadequate. As 'the mighty mere-wife' (*merewif mihtig*) sits on him (or sits opposite him) and prepares to avenge her son by stabbing him with her knife, he is partly protected by his battle-shirt. Even so, he is on the verge of being killed when 'holy God' (*halig God*), 'the wise Lord, Ruler of the heavens' (*witig Drihten, / rodera Rædend*) decides to wield the war-victory in his favour (1554b–6). It is at this point that the poet is ready to unbind more of the mystery associated with the poem's most significant sword.

In a highly figurative passage (1557 ff.) replete with adjectival compounds, *kend heiti*, simple adjectives, defining genitives, kennings, and other metaphors, the poet variously describes the strange instrument now provided, by which heroism and the will of heaven are shown combining to wreak vengeance on the Grendel kin. It is 'a victory-blessed blade' (*sigeeadig bil*), 'a giantish old-sword strong in its edges, the glory of warriors' (*ealdsweord eotenisc   ecgum þyhtig, / wigena weorðmynd*), and 'the best of weapons' (*wæpna cyst*), 'good and adorned' (*god ond geatolic*). It is 'giantish' in two senses, 'larger than any other man could bear to war-play' (*mare ðonne ænig mon oðer / to beadulace   ætberan meahte*) and made by giants (*giganta geweorc*). It has an ornamented hilt (*fetelhilt*) and it is 'ring-marked' (*hringmæl*). When Beowulf wields this formidable weapon, it grasps hard against the monster's neck and breaks her 'bone-rings' (*banhringas*). As it cuts through the 'fated flesh-covering' (*fægne flæschoman*) and Grendel's mother falls dead, the sword is described as 'sweaty' or 'bloody' (*swatig*) while 'the man rejoiced at his work' (*secg weorce gefeh*).[6] Once the female monster is dead, a blaze of light shines from within the underwater hall, 'just as from the sky heaven's candle shines brightly' (*efne swa of hefen   hadre scineð / rodores candel*). We note here how the venerable kenning for the sun emerges from the word-hoard at the propitious narrative moment to mark the joint triumph by Beowulf and God.

But the vengeance being taken on the Grendel race is not yet complete. As the hero looks around the hall, he is still holding the giant sword-hilt, and he is still angry and determined to repay Grendel further for his many crimes against the Danes. When he finds Grendel's body 'lying lifeless with the wounds he had got earlier in the fight at Heorot' (*licgan, / aldorleasne, swa him ær gescod / hild æt Heorote*), he administers 'a hard sword-swing' (*heorosweng heardne*) and cuts off the head. This provides the immediate context of meaning for the kenning *hildegicelum* 'battle-icicles,' but again the poet proceeds periphrastically. Instead of immediately telling about the melting sword, he switches attention, almost cinematically (1591 ff.), from the underwater scene to the one up above on the shore of the mere where the Scyldings and Geats are waiting. It is on that level that the blood of the monsters first gets attention, as the thanes see it staining the surging mere waters and are led to conclude, wrongly, that it is Beowulf's blood and that the 'she-wolf of the sea' (*brymwylf*) has destroyed him. Hrothgar and his people wait until the ninth hour of the day and then go back to Heorot, leaving 'the strangers ... sick at heart' (*Gistas ... modes seoce*) staring at the mere.

This is an important juncture in the story and in the metaphorical meanings of the poem. The poet does not waste it. He shows how, from the perspective of those up on the level of middle earth, the story of Hrothgar's kingdom has sunk to the same low point of its existence to which Grendel had brought it earlier. Heorot's twelve years of misery and gloom were thought to have been ended with the defeat of Grendel. When that hope was dashed by the unexpected revenge taken by his mother, Beowulf had again buoyed up the Danish hopes with his decision to try for another victory. But now, it seems, the monsters have won and Beowulf himself is dead. Both Scyldings and Geats abandon all hope and give way to despair, the former going back to their fated hall, the latter remaining to look at the blood-stained hell waters. But Beowulf, the narrator, and we the listeners or readers all know that this reading of events is a delusion based on incomplete knowledge. We have been right down in the hall of hell and so know that God's champion who descended into the depths has already defeated there the two monsters who were preying on the bodies and souls of those trying to live in Heorot.

In the kenning *hildegicelum* 'battle-icicles' a major pattern of meaning comes to its climax. The poet shows clearly how he would have his listeners or readers understand the 'wondrous thing' (*wundra sum*, 1607) of the disappearing sword-blade. As the blade melts entirely away, the narrator says, it is 'most like the ice when the Father loosens the bond of frost, unwinds the fetters [or 'ropes'] of the deep pools [or 'of the deep waters'] – he who has power over times and seasons. That is the true Measurer' (*ise gelicost, / ðonne forstes bend Fæder onlæteð / onwindeð wælrapas, se geweald hafað / sæla ond mæla; þæt is soð Metod*). The highly figurative language here is not mere ornamentation, to be passed over quickly en route back to the main narrative. The melting is being linked closely, through one of the poem's rare similes, with the coming of spring. The figure that expresses this particular, highly suggestive analogy is surrounded closely by two kennings, a *kent heiti*, a verb used metaphorically, and then two more kennings, each of them also used with a verb that has metaphorical meaning: *heaþoswate* 'war-' or 'battle-sweat and blood' and *hildegicelum* 'battle-icicles'; *wigbil* 'war-bill, war-sword'; *wanian* 'to wane, waste away, lessen'; *forstes bend* 'frost's bond' with the verb *onlæteð* 'loosens' and *wælrapas* 'fetters of the deep pools' [or 'of the deep waters'] with the verb *onwindeþ* 'unwinds.'

The kenning *heaþoswat* 'war-' or 'battle-sweat and blood' is perhaps not in itself a particularly startling metaphor, though again it is found only in this one Old English poem. In the exertion of physical fighting a warrior obviously sweats. When the fight results in his also being wounded and bleeding, the sweat and blood mix. One interesting naturalistic aspect of this is that the 'battle-sweat' on a sword at a particular moment can belong to the one wielding the weapon, to his opponent or opponents who have been wounded by it, or to all of these. The figure may be somewhat oblique, as any metaphor is, but its main metaphorical meaning is also apt and easily perceived. In the context in which it occurs here, however, it takes on three additional specific associations, and a wider one as well. Just after the sword has cut into the 'fated flesh-covering' (*fægne flæschoman*) of Grendel's mother, it is described (1569) as 'sweaty and bloody,' that is, as having a living, corporeal identity of its own. To the sword's own 'battle-sweat and blood' is added first that of the female monster just killed by this weapon and then Grendel's. It is important to remember that however grounded in physical images the poem is at this point, it is still proceeding in the romance mode of imagining, and it is romance, moreover, that here is pressing hard across the boundaries into myth. It is this modal stretching that brings us to the wider meaning of the kenning *heaþoswat*, one arising from the myth of the war between God and the giants in Genesis to which the poet returns in some detail in the next section of his story, when he again (1668) uses the kenning, just before Hrothgar examines the sword-hilt.

At first encounter, the compound *hildegicelum* 'battle-icicles,' as a figurative expression or trope, is puzzling. It is so enigmatically compressed as to give up little of its meaning. Why compare a melting sword at the end of a sword-fight with icicles melting, even in this bizarre conflict far below the surface of the water between a monster and an extraordinarily 'weighty' protagonist? Why would a sword-blade melting because it has been covered with sweat and blood, even including venomous blood, be like icicles? Granted, there is a kind of visual accuracy in the notion of the melting metal looking like melting ice, but there is more to the figure than that. The first half of the kenning is readily understandable. There has just been a major battle, two of them in fact – when we take into account the hero's consolidation of his victory over Grendel – but where in the imagined space of the poem do the icicles come from? This I think is quintessential kenning art, and the poet makes it work, by things told of earlier, by piling up further connotations here, and by pointing out the direction of the main meaning of the kenning.

When Heorot was first constructed and named, in accord with Hrothgar's words of power (*se þe his wordes geweald   wide hæfde*, 79), the great hall was explicitly associated with God's Creation of the world and with the Almighty's ornamenting of the regions of the earth 'with branches and leaves' (*leomum ond leafum*) and all living things (89b ff.). Even at the moment of this association, however, as the harp music and the song of the scop were being heard, we were also being introduced to the *ellengæst* 'bold demon' who lived in darkness and could not tolerate the sounds of human happiness coming from the new creation. Then followed for the Scyldings twelve winters of misery (147a), during every night of which the monster worked his ravages in the hall. When not engaged in destruction in Heorot, this 'dark death-shadow' (*deorc deaþscua*) Grendel 'held the misty moors in the endless night' (*sinnihte heold / mistige moras*, 161b–2a), and throughout his existence as a being familiar with hell's runes (*helrunan*, 163) has inhabited, as we are told later, 'a secret land (*dygel lond*) and 'windswept nesses' (1357b ff.). At the centre of this demonic place, now penetrated and mastered by Beowulf, is the storm-tossed mere over which hang frost-covered woods and above which 'the heavens weep' (*roderas reotað*). Beowulf's other main association with the poem's imagery of piercing cold, winds, ice, and winter is in the contest in the sea with Breca, during which he has proven himself superior both to the wintry waters and to the monsters that inhabit them.[7] All this background, I suggest, prepares for the kenning *hildegicelum*. The battle fought by Beowulf on behalf of Heorot is a battle for life, living things, freedom of movement, and human joy against death, shadowy demonic beings, enslavement by powers of darkness, and the joylessness of a frozen world locked in wintry bonds. The sword whose blade is now described as melting in the poisonous blood of the monsters is about to have its ancient and its contemporary mythological meaning recognized, as Hrothgar reads the runes on its hilt.

The other figurative words and phrases immediately surrounding the image of the melting blade fit well into the interlacing pattern of associations just described. *Wigbill* 'battle-sword' is a *kent heiti* serving here as a synonym for sword and alliterating with the metaphorically used verb *wanian* 'to wane.' The simile comparing the melting sword, which looks like icicles, with ice and frost being melted in the springtime by the benevolent Father God, who is Lord of the times and seasons, links the triumph over the monsters by 'the prince of the

Weather-Geats' (*Weder-Geata leod*, 1612b) with the power of life and Creation itself. The two remaining kennings in the passage about the melting illustrate this power by identifying him even more closely with it; just as God frees life from death by releasing frost's bonds and unwinding the ropes of the deep pools, so Beowulf has freed Heorot from the grip of the Grendel race by going into the depths down under the nesses.

The tale of the two swords, Hrunting and the 'giantish' one, is brought to its conclusion in the account of Beowulf's return to Heorot and his reception there. (The giant sword receives only passing mention later, in line 2140, when Beowulf back in Geatland tells Hygelac about his Danish experiences.) The language of myth and metaphor, firmly based in physical imagery, is still much in evidence as the narrator tells of the sword-hilt 'bright with jewels' (*since fage*, 1615) being taken by Beowulf, along with the huge head of Grendel, as the hero swims up through the 'cleansed' (*gefælsod*, 1620) waters of the mere to rejoin his comrades. Together the two macabre objects, 'the head and the hilt' (*þone hafelan ond þa hilt*, 1614), form 'a mighty burden' (*mægenbyrþenne*, 1625) or 'sea-booty' (*sælace*, another kenning, 1624) in which the 'stout hearted helm or protector of seamen' (*lidmanna helm / swiðmod*, 1623b–4a) rejoices after his success in battle. As on the morning following the defeat of Grendel, so now after the victory in the mere, the imagery is of open spaces and exuberant energies unleashed. Beowulf's 'strong band of thanes' (*ðryðlic þegna heap*) thank God that again they are seeing their chief and they quickly loosen his *helm* and war-shirt (1626–30). It takes four of these 'very exuberant ones' (*felamodigra*, 1637) to carry Grendel's head on their 'killing-poles' or 'spear-shafts' (*wælstenge*) as they and their companions – in all 'fourteen bold, battle-keen ones of the Geats' (*from fyrdhwate feowertyne / Geata*), along with their *modig* lord – now go striding across the *meodowongas* 'mead-fields' to the hall. (We note in passing the presence here of two more kennings, 'killing-poles' and 'mead-fields.') In contrast to the animated human figures, the waters of the mere, which now are left behind and earlier were described as turbulent and teeming with monsters, are characterized by the verb *drusian* 'to drowse' (1630). Modern descriptive or representational language, as for example in Klaeber's Glossary (317), translates this as 'stagnate' and so loses the metaphor.

In his report to Hrothgar (1651 ff.) Beowulf emphasizes, initially by understatement, the difficulty he experienced in the 'war under the water' (*wigge under wætere*). He has escaped with his life *unsofte* 'unsoftly' and only because God 'shielded' (*scylde*) him. Hrunting could not do anything in the fight even though it is a good weapon. The kenning for God used by Beowulf at this point tells something important. The 'Wielder of men' (*ylda Waldend*) granted him that he should see hanging on the wall 'a fair ... huge old-sword' (*wlitig ... eald-sweord eacen*) and that he should wield it to make flow 'the hottest of battle-sweats' (*hatost heaþoswata*, 1668a), and so slay the 'keepers of the house' (*huses hyrdas*). The metaphorical meanings suggested by the kenning *ylda Waldend* are clear. As the 'Wielder of men' God in a real sense has himself been an invisible warrior fighting and shielding the hero, and Beowulf has been the instrument or weapon wielded by him. In some part of the art of the kenning there has been another fusion of warrior and sword of the kind we have seen at work in other kennings. But this time the metaphorical identities have pushed into pure myth where divine and heroic human actions are totally interwoven. It makes no sense in logic or to a prosaic mind, but it goes some way in suggesting why Weland's great sword Hrunting is useless and why the miraculous sword, 'the work of wonder-smiths' (*wundorsmiþa geweorc*, 1681), associated with the divine power and vengeance revealed in the myth of Noah, has been necessary to bring about this latest 'fall of devils' (*deofla hryre*, 1680).

If any doubt were to remain that this in fact is what is happening poetically and imaginatively, Hrothgar's reading of the runes on the sword-hilt of the ancient heirloom should prove both the effectiveness of the poet's art and the direction of the meaning. The poem never spells out that the flood Beowulf has just quelled *is* metaphorically identifiable with the ancient biblical Flood by which the 'eternal Dryhten' (*ecean Dryhtne*, 1692a) quelled the race of giants, that race who were 'alien' (*fremde*, 1691b) to him and were 'the origin ... of ancient strife' (*or ... fyrngewinnes*, 1688b–9a), or that the 'battle-sweat' of the Grendel race metaphorically *is* the same demonic blood as that shed in the destruction in the ancient Deluge, but the parallel between those ancient enemies and the monsters who have tried to destroy the splendid creation Heorot is clear enough. The poem provides all the riddling clues and kennings necessary to lead us to these identities. The great sword that appears on the wall of the hostile hall beneath the waters is the runic and metaphoric guide.

Before concluding this exploration of sword-related kennings it may be illuminating briefly to summarize the changing metaphorical identities that this weapon takes on in *Beowulf*. A sword is a flashing light, something that bites into flesh, a being with power, a thing of terror, a physical object or toy used in 'war-play,' and an instrument for cutting or carving at a feast. It is a being that sings a 'war-song' on a monster's head and a creature that hates or kills or drinks blood or tramples down an enemy. It is the hatred and killing that break out when kinship relations are perverted. It is a warrior who sweats and bleeds, an instrument of both divine grace and divine vengeance, and it is a world locked in winter needing to be released. It is a rare 'victory-blessed' treasure fashioned by giants who were 'wonder-smiths' when they made this instrument which tells of the clash of heavenly and demonic powers. Now obviously not all these identities are functioning simultaneously whenever we encounter the particular words *hildeleoma, beadoleoma, ecgþracu, ecghete, hiorodrync, hildegicel,* or *heaþoswat,* because each compound has its particular characterizing and imaginative force and its own context in the poem. But they all function connotatively not denotatively and they all are capable of exercising their particular poetic power as the poet deploys and surrounds them with other figures and by so doing establishes rich, intricate but strong, and often surprising patterns of meaning.

Kennings for the sea include *garsecg* 'spear-man, ocean, sea' (49, 515, 537); *merestræt* 'sea-street, sea-path' (514); *seglrad* 'sail-riding, sail-road, sea' (1429); *lagustræt* 'sea-street, sea-road' (239); *hronrad* 'whale-riding, riding-place of the whale, sea' (10); *swanrad* 'swan-riding, riding-place of the swan, sea' (200); and *windgeard* 'wind-yard, wind-dwelling, dwelling-place of the winds, sea' (1224). The kenning *wælrapas* 'deep pool ropes, deep pool fetters, fetters of the deep pools, ice' (1610), unique to *Beowulf,* applies equally well to sea and inland waters. The metaphor *sæweall* 'sea-wall, high shore' (1924) seems to refer to a seacoast with hills or cliffs. There are two compounds for ships in which a part of the vessel is taken as a kenning-like allusion to the whole vessel: *bundenstefna* 'bound stem, bound prow, ship' (1910); *hringedstefna* 'ringed stem, ringed prow, ship' (32, 1131, 1897). The kenning *merehrægl* 'sea-garment, sail' contains a suggestion of personification of a ship as someone wearing a garment (1905). The compounds *sæwudu* 'sea-wood' (226) and *sundwudu* 'sea-wood' or 'swimming-wood' (208, 1906) probably should be designated as *kend heiti* rather than kennings, since they identify a ship as something that it is, wood, but the reference of the figures themselves is circuitous and indefinite enough almost to make the words function as kennings. In any case, as already recognized, the line between kennings and *kend heiti* is sometimes unclear.

The first half of a kenning has a double function. It carries some measure of referential meaning and normally is a recognizable image of something in the physical world. At the same time it is often so oblique or highly selective, as a means of indicating the external referent, that it has some of the character of a poetic conceit. The second half of the kenning is even more figurative. It is a metaphor establishing an imaginative identification of the referent with something that logically it is not but poetically it has become. One familiar example is *swanrad* 'swan-road,' referring, probably we should say alluding, to the 'sea.' It appears in *Andreas* as well (*ASPR* 2, 8:196). From among the many possible ways of indicating or pointing to the idea of the sea, the image of a swan is a highly selective, even fanciful one. Also by itself this first noun of the compound simply puzzles the mind, invites it to place the swan in some kind of spatial or otherwise meaningful, identifying context, and by so doing leads into the metaphor of the road or 'riding' along which the swan or the birdlike ship moves. This is as far as the figure needs to go in providing clues to the identity of the referent. There is of course a great deal of arbitrariness in such a figure. The one *Beowulf* occurrence of *swanrad* comes, interestingly, in the midst of the first reference in the poem to the hero, along with what is probably an equally worthy *kent heiti* for 'ship.' Beowulf has just been described as 'of mankind the greatest in strength in the day of this life' (*se wæs moncynnes mægenes strengest / on þæm dæge þysses lifes*), and he now commands 'a good wave-crosser to be made ready' (*yðlidan godne gegyrwan*) so that he may go 'over the swan-road' (*ofer swanrade*) to the famous prince Hrothgar, who has need of men (196–201). *Hronrad* also occurs once in an equally heroic context at the beginning of the poem, indicating the sea across which Scyld Scefing's conquered neighbours were obliged to yield tribute (9–11a).

The kenning *garsecg* 'spear-man' for 'sea' or 'ocean' is found in fourteen other Old English poems. It may or may not carry into its three occurrences in *Beowulf* (49, 515, 537) some resonance of a mythological kind to do with Oceanus or Woden or the figure of an armed man who, with the instrument he carries, is the imaginative result of someone – somewhere, sometime – observing wave formations and thinking about them in the visual metaphor of a 'spear-man.' Although on the surface it may seem improbable that the literal, that is the literary or figurative, meaning is working in *Beowulf*, the question may be worth rethinking.[8]

As a general principle in reading this poem, it is unwise prematurely to rule out active metaphorical functioning in the figures encountered, even when such meaning is not immediately clear. We modern readers, after all, are historically and linguistically remote from the verbal resonances of the contents of the Old English word-hoard. Most of what we know about the world as a result of scientific observation or representational art comes long after the Anglo-Saxons. The compound noun *garsecg* is notably metaphorical in and by itself, simply as an isolated lexical item. It occurs of course only in particular contexts and in juxtaposition with other images. We, like the original listeners or readers, are not free to choose arbitrarily and without regard to context whether or not to let its figurative and etymological meaning of 'spear-man' work on our imaginations. The important question is whether the three *Beowulf* contexts in which it occurs actively invite or insist on its functioning metaphorically, in ways that suggest meaning beyond that of the sea broadly indicated, and beyond the particular auditory impact required by the metre and alliteration. The first use of *garsecg* in *Beowulf* is in connection with the shadowy figure of Scyld Scefing as he is sent on his funeral voyage by his followers: 'they let the water bear him, gave him to the spear-man' (*leton holm beran,   geafon on garsecg*, 48b–9a), or to 'the ocean,' if we assume as is regularly done in modern translations that a more abstract term should replace the literal, corporeal metaphor that the word clearly is. In this particular instance in *Beowulf*, perhaps it is the option of the listener or reader whether the metaphorical sense of the two images 'spear' and 'man' in the kenning is to work.

The other uses of *garsecg* occur in the accounts, by Unferth and Beowulf respectively, of the hero's swimming (rowing?) match with Breca. Their flyting-like interchange of verbal aggression and vigorous response takes place in a context carefully created by the poet, not in a narrative vacuum. The battle of words occurs part-way through the sequence of events on the hero's first day and night in Denmark. This period of time within the overall story of the poem involves a series of actions in which Beowulf is shown revealing his identity, establishing his credentials, and making known his purpose in coming to the land of the Scyldings. Hrothgar has just been talking about events in his kingdom, including his settlement years ago of a feud involving Beowulf's father, and also about the more recent disasters that have overtaken his people because of Grendel. The king has concluded his talk by inviting Beowulf to sit down at the feast and 'untie' or 'loosen' his thoughts (*onsæl meoto*) as his 'heart whets' or 'inclines' or 'urges' him (*swa þin sefa hwette*, 489–90). As a bench is cleared and the 'stout-hearted' (*swiðferhþe*) Geats take their places, a thane carries round an ale-cup, pouring a sweet drink, and a scop sings *hador in Heorote* 'clear-voiced in Heorot.' Then the poet uses a line and a half, the last word of which sounds an anticipative note for something that is about to happen poetically: *Þær wæs hæleða dream, / duguð unlytel   Dena ond Wedera* ('There was joy of warriors, a not-little troop of Danes and Weather-Geats,' 497b–8). Why *Wedera* at this point, from among the several identifying epithets for Beowulf's people that are used in the poem – *Geatas, Guð-Geatas, Sæ-Geatas, Geat-mæcgas, Hreðlingas* – any of which could have been used here? The medial *d* in *Wederas* works well in the sound pattern, though it is not strictly required by the alliteration. Something else is happening. If we take into account, as the poet seems to be doing, that both Unferth's and Beowulf's descriptions of the swimming contest emphasize the wintry, stormy weather in which the young men's struggles take place, in what the Weder chieftain Beowulf himself, a few lines later, calls *wedera cealdost* 'coldest of weathers' (546), it seems that again on the level of auditory appropriateness, and of metaphorical meaning, the developing pattern of words has found the poetically right word. *Wederas* comes just before the conflicting accounts of how the hero did or did not establish himself as a brave seafarer who achieved glory under the heavens by mastering wind, weather, darkness, and sea-monsters to make safe the passage of other seafarers over the high seas, and then finally swims ashore exhausted, as 'God's bright sign' (*beorht beacen Godes*, 570) brings light from the east.

At the beginning of the flyting itself as the invidious Unferth is about to speak, his character is obliquely but effectively alluded to when the narrator says of him that 'he unbound a battle-rune' (*onband beadurune*, 501a). The purpose of the rune is clear. The poet's ordering of the words which he puts in Unferth's mouth (506–28), like the words themselves and the situation in which they are spoken, is sharply antagonistic: 'Are you that Beowulf who struggled with Breca on the wide sea, competed in swimming' (*Eart þu se Beowulf,   se þe wið Brecan wunne, / on sidne sæ   ymb sund flite ...*), he rudely asks, 'when the two of you out of arrogance explored the waters and out of foolish boasting risked your lives on the deep water?" (*ðær git for wlence   wada cunnedon / ond for dolgilpe   on deop wæter / aldrum neþdon?*) As Unferth continues his insults, alleging that both friends and enemies tried to talk the young fools out of their exploit, he uses figured, metaphorical language, including the kenning *merestræt*, to suggest the intense effort and struggle of the movements of the two young men in the turbulent waters: 'there the two of you embraced the water-streams with your arms, measured the sea-paths, flung forward with your hands' (*Þær git eagorstream   earmum þehton, / mæton merestræta,   mundum brugdon*). Unferth says that 'the sea was surging with waves, winter's wellings' (*geofon yþum weol, / wintrys wylmum*) and then states that the contestants laboured 'for seven nights in the water's possession' (*on wæteres æht / seofon niht*). At the end of all this, he alleges, Breca 'overcame' (*oferflat*) Beowulf because he was more powerful.

Does this context answer our question? Could or does the phrase *glidon ofer garsecg* (515a), which occurs in the midst of Unferth's figured account of the movements of the young men while they were in the 'possession of the water' (*on wæteres æht*) for seven nights, include any mythological or metaphorical sense of the stormy waters as 'spear-man'? Does the connotative way in which words are functioning in the passage make possible or likely that the old kenning is performing as more than a faded metaphor from far back in the prehistory of the word-hoard? An answer has not yet come clear. It seems that a little more periphrastic thinking is wanted. Before engaging in it, we recall that Old English kennings, like Old English riddles, are not all fully understandable or solvable by us moderns and postmoderns: consider for example the long scholarly discussion of *ealuscerwen* 'dispensing of ale,' a kenning that occurs during the uproar caused by Grendel and Beowulf wrestling (769).[9] But those kennings which do finally divulge their meanings do so only when all the clues provided by the poetic context come together and point to one, or more, possible solutions.

There remains the third occurrence of *garsecg* in *Beowulf*, in another context to be puzzled over. The use of the word that we have just looked at above is Unferth's, and it is possible, after all, as Beowulf himself says, that Unferth is so 'drunk with beer' (*beore druncne*, 531) that he does not know what went on in the stormy seas, or even what the seas were, poetically or in any other way. But that is a consideration of a different order. Unferth wasn't there. Beowulf was. In contrast to what Unferth has just done, says the hero, he will tell the truth. The first truth he tells is that in the swimming contest he showed that he had 'greater mere-strength' (*merestrengo maran*) than any other man (533–4). The second is that the whole exploit was the fulfilment of a boast and agreement made between him and Breca when they were still boys (535–8). Third (537b–43), as they went out risking their lives *on garsecg*, carrying their naked swords to guard them against *hronfixas* 'whale-fishes,' it was he, Beowulf, who looked after Breca, because Breca '*could* not float away' (*No ... fleotan meahte*) and he, Beowulf, '*would* not' abandon his companion (*no ic fram him wolde*). Finally, Beowulf explains, after five nights they were driven apart in the darkness by the growing storm, by the flood and welling waters (544–5). These points as stated by Beowulf are, so to speak, the narrative facts about the episode as presented so far, improbable and fictional as the whole adventure obviously is from a modern perspective.

But then Beowulf begins to use language that is even more figurative and curiously inwrought than Unferth's was, more removed from any naturalistic sense of what could ever happen to any human being in any 'real world' sea. The imagery is vivid and very physical, but it is clear that the stormy night-waters in which the hero is struggling belong to an area of the imagination not confined or contained by descriptive or referential language which relates in a direct way to the actual physical world. The forces of nature have now obviously taken on malign intelligence: the 'battle-grim north wind' (*norþanwind heaþogrim*) turns against the swimmers; the waves are 'fierce' or 'savage' (*hreo*); the 'spirit' or 'heart' (*mod*) of the sea-fishes is aroused; a 'hostile, deadly foe' (*fah feondscaða*) drags Beowulf to the sea-bottom; the sea-beasts are 'workers of malice' (*manfordædlan*) who try to enjoy a banquet with the hero as their food.

Our question about *garsecg* still sits before us. Is the 'spear-man' of the literal kenning present and functional in the context? If we are reading or even listening 'literally,' the poem twice in this one passage says *gar secg* 'spear man' not 'sea,' even though the word *sæ* 'sea' does exist in Old English.

'Ocean' of course does not. Other kennings and metaphors clearly are working in important ways in the immediate poetic context. Then too we are dealing with a poet who demonstrates over and over again an ability to let traditional language link, interlace, or weave together subtle, evocative patterns of sound and meaning. By the time the word *garsecg* hits our ears the second time in this passage, we have been taken through a series of violent conflicts, from Hrothgar's talk of a blood-feud long ago involving the hero's father, to Grendel's ravages, to Unferth's 'battle-rune,' to the two vivid descriptions of hostile nature and stormy seas in winter, and finally to the sea-monsters seeking their demonic joys at a banquet on the sea-bottom. The answer that emerges in my mind, then, to the question of what to make of the recurrence of the kenning *garsecg* in the rival accounts of the swimming match is this: the whole passage, the lead-in as well as the verbal contest of the flyting itself, tells of conflict and strife in several modulations, in highly figurative language that invites the metaphorical meaning of *garsecg*. The corporeal image 'spear-man' does fit, usefully, in a passage and in a poem in which the natural is made unnatural, and the unnatural (the fictional) is made natural. There is an important point here for criticism. From a perspective many centuries after this poem's genesis and fabulation of the world, and conditioned by our own cultural contexts, which are heavily laden with low mimetic and ironic biases, we should not be in a hurry to rule out possible old metaphorical meanings, even in a hoary kenning like *garsecg*. This is a poem that is filled with respect for old things and in which, in fact, just such animist, anthropocentric meanings, often etymologically suggested, are demonstrably at work much of the time.

The third large group of kennings in *Beowulf* has to do with the bodies of human beings and of monsters, in the case of the latter often as parodies of the human form. Each of these kennings has its own particular physical force as an image, but again the mode of imagining embodied in them clearly makes empirical observation secondary to metaphorical thought. One of the most graphic, almost lurid figurations of human bodies occurs in the Finnsburg story told in Heorot on the night after Beowulf's defeat of Grendel. In the account of the funeral pyre on which Hildeburh's son and brother are consumed, two vivid kennings are used in association with the dead warriors' bodies: *banfæt* 'bone-cup, bone-vessel, body' (1116) and *bengeat* 'wound-gates, wound-openings, gashes' (1121). In the first of these the metaphorical conception is that of human bodies as containers, cups or vessels, held together by bones. The cups or containers hold lives inside them, as welcome drinks, but when the lives, the times for drinking, the banquets of life, come to an end, the cups/bodies are burned on the pyre. In the vivid phrase *bengeatu burston* 'wound-gates burst open,' as 'heads melted' (*hafelan multon*) and 'blood sprang out' (*blod ætspranc*) from 'hate-bites of the body' (*laðbite lices*), we have another architectural metaphor, like *banhus*, for the human body. The kenning *bengeat* may be the poet's own coinage, since this is the one recorded extant use of it.

Somewhat later in the narrative, in the important epic passage in which the hero arms himself for the climactic battle in the mere (1441 ff.), we find another kenning for the human body. Beowulf's war-shirt, helmet, and sword are being singled out one by one and characterized in terms of the specific protective function each is meant to serve. In this context the *herebyrne* 'war-shirt' is described as knowing how to protect the *bancofa*, a kenning meaning 'bone-cove, bone-cave, bone-chamber' or, more remotely, 'body,' so that the *hildegrap* 'battle-grasp' of an angry enemy cannot harm the life inside. Some of the same sense of the physical body as a crucial protective covering for the precious content inside it can be seen in the kenning *banloca* 'bone-locker.' This figure occurs twice: once of Hondscio's body, as Grendel bites into it (742); once of Grendel's own body, when a huge wound opens up in his shoulder, his sinews spring apart, and his bone-locks break (816b–18a). Not surprisingly, given that in *Beowulf* we are not dealing with precise descriptive language focused mimetically on the physical world, the kenning is anatomically imprecise. *Ban* could be the literal referent, in which case it refers to the bones that are the locks protecting the life inside from anything that would break in and do harm. If on the other hand *loca* is the referent and it is the bones that are being locked in or enclosed, then it is the muscles or flesh that are being alluded to. The last kenning in this group is *banhringas* 'bone-rings,' usually understood in our more scientific age as 'neck-bones' or even 'vertebrae.' The bones in question belong to Grendel's mother and are mentioned as the hero seizes the great sword miraculously provided and strikes angrily at the monster, so that the weapon 'grasps' her hard and breaks through the 'bone-rings' of her neck (1563–7a).

A small number of kennings are used effectively not to describe or represent but figuratively to characterize emotions and thoughts. We have seen how in the emotionally alive, interrelated world of the poem, feelings, thoughts, and attitudes are imagined to be present in non-human physical things (spears keep watch, a ship is eager to travel, a sword hates and sweats) in a thoroughgoing anthropocentrism. When the diction turns to internal mental processes, again the language is intensely physical. There is a stylizing of empirical observation that effects a kind of sublimation of feeling or thought into graphic physical images which are simultaneously connected with bodily processes or particular objects and quite distinct from them. The verbal language focuses not on actuality but on some emotional truth between the mind and the world, which is invoked by the obliquity of the kenning. One example of this is Unferth's unbinding of a battle-rune, already mentioned. The poet is characterizing

Hrothgar's thule (499 ff.) as a man caught deep in self-love or pride to the point of not wanting any other man in the middle dwelling to achieve more glory than he has and, consequently, as being envious of the fine effect the newly arrived Beowulf is making in Heorot. When the poet wishes to show Unferth in the process of sowing discord by discrediting the hero, he uses the 'battle-rune' kenning. A rune is at once a physical linear marking and something secret, its meaning known only to the initiated. In this case the secret that is being unbound may be a deliberate lie; Unferth's rune is certainly a radically different interpretation of an event from the one provided by the hero himself, and Beowulf's version is supported and vindicated later by his even greater triumphs in Denmark. Even before that happens we have been told clearly when Beowulf was first brought into the narrative that he is the greatest in strength of any man in the middle dwelling. When Unferth says then that Breca 'overcame' (*oferflat*) Beowulf because 'he had greater strength' (*hæfde maran mægen*, 517–18), we know it is not true. One purpose of Unferth's rune is clear. Once it is unbound it is meant to lead to a fight, and it does, in the form of a vigorous, mutually insulting verbal exchange. To say that Unferth 'unbound a battle-rune' is poetry, of course, Old English poetry. To say that he started a fight is modern prose.

The narrator uses a similar kenning, *inwitnet* 'malice-net, net of malice' (2167), when he tells of Beowulf's gifts of horses and treasure to Hygelac on his return to Geatland. The purpose in the particular narrative context is didactic and it is almost as if the narrator is obliquely reminding the audience or readers of the contentious fratricide Unferth: 'So a kinsman ought to do, not weave a malice-net for another with secret craft, prepare death for hand-comrades' (*Swa sceal mæg don, / nealles inwitnet oðrum bregdon / dyrnum cræfte, deað renian / hondgesteallan*, 2166b–9a). Of an opposite emotional content, the kenning applied by the poet to a woman who counteracts the force of the *beadurun* and the *inwitnet* in the poem's heroic society is a *freoðowebbe* 'peace-weaver, lady.' This actual term for peace-weaving, as distinct from the concept (embodied also in Wealhtheow, Freawaru, and Hygd), is used only once in *Beowulf* (1942). In *Beowulf* the female figure explicitly designated by the term is the uniquely beautiful but vengeful and ferocious Modthryth, who certainly does not initially weave peace. Prior to her conversion through marriage she 'practises a dreadful brutality' (*wæg ... firen ondrysne*, 1931–2) and has anyone other than her own lord who stares at her (possession through lustful staring?) put to death by the sword.

The kenning *breosthord* 'breast-hoard, breast, mind, heart' (found also in *Daniel*, *Andreas*, and *Guthlac A*) occurs twice, first in connection with the disastrously bad king Heremod (1719) and secondly with the dying Beowulf

(2792). In each case the figure depicts powerful, irresistible feeling that builds under pressure to a violent explosion. Heremod is *bolgenmod* 'bulged [or 'swollen'] in his mind, enraged' and kills his table-companions and shoulder-comrades as the feelings hoarded in his breast burst out with murderous force. In the case of Beowulf, Wiglaf has just hurried back to him from inside the dragon's lair. Beowulf's strength is gone, although he is still bleeding, and the young thane sprinkles his king with water. After the narrator tells of Wiglaf doing this he uses a strange two-metaphor expression to introduce the old king's last words: *oð þæt wordes ord / breosthord þurhbræc* 'until a word's point broke through his breast-hoard' (2791b–2a). The suggestion, circuitously but effectively made, is that the words about to be spoken are a pointed weapon about to break through or pierce, either out of or in to, the feelings and thoughts hoarded inside Beowulf's breast. The spatial direction of the metaphor is not clear, but the emotional significance is. When uttered, these last-ever thoughts and words of the hero express three things about which he feels intensely: his gratitude to the King of Glory that he has won the treasure for his people; his naming of Wiglaf as his successor as protector of the Geats; and his commissioning of a memorial mound for himself high on Hronesness.

The few additional kennings applied to monsters are various and distinct each from the others, so that in no real sense do they form a group. Grendel's 'nail' or 'claw' is called a *handsporu* 'hand-spur' (986). Grendel's mother is twice called a *brimwylf* 'she-wolf of the sea' (1506, 1599), with the connotations of a beast of prey and carrion who lives in or beneath the sea, gives birth to a cannibalistic monster, and herself comes out on at least one occasion to devour a human being. As a carrion creature she arrives on the scene of the great battle fought the night before in Heorot between Beowulf and Grendel, after the fighting has stopped, but the body she eats is not that of a dead warrior who has fallen in battle. *Æschere* 'Ash-War' or 'Spear-War' is a still-living man. When Beowulf, the Danes, and the Geats arrive at the mere, they find it teeming with serpents, sea-dragons, and other wild beasts, one of which, described as a *wundorlic wægbora* 'wondrous wave-bearer' (1440), is shot by Beowulf. The etymology of *bora* is uncertain, but understood as 'bearer' it makes kenning-like sense, as if someone has once observed a sea-creature moving through water and pushing up a wave, thus suggesting that the wave is being borne by the creature. The kennings *hringboga* 'ring-bow, coiled creature' (2561) and *uhtfloga* 'dawn or night (just before dawn) flyer' (2760), applied to the dragon, accord with the other diction indicating the creature's serpentine shape and movements and its habit of travelling in darkness.

A kenning can be used in a poetically effective way or badly, within the range of its semantic potential and depending on the skill and talent of the one who deploys it. Whether traditional or newly coined, the kennings are metaphors of a special kind. Because they turn even further away from direct descriptiveness than a *kent heiti* does, they create a tension, sometimes a large one, between their two parts as compounds or between themselves as compounds and what they are alluding to. This tension or incongruity seems to have little to do with the age of the compound. It is simply there as long as the word is used, for anyone alive to its meaning. The kenning *banhus* 'bone-house,' for example, although we have it only in *Beowulf* (2508, 3147), *Andreas* (1240, 1405), *Exodus* (524), and *Guthlac B* (1367), may or may not have been old long before the time of these poems' composition. At a particular point, when someone originally uttered it, the compound caught on because it is vivid and strong, and capable of staying that way no matter how often it is encountered. Its metaphorical illogicality is just as right poetically the fifteenth time it is heard as the first. A human body is not a house, says our logical mind. But as soon as we say this, the kenning urges us to consider or puzzle over why, after all, a human body in some special, important way is a house, and why moreover it is a 'bone-house.' The aptness of the metaphor is easily grasped. If we dissect it – and possibly we should not – the skeletal bones are the structural elements (joists, uprights, beams, rafters, so to speak) of a house. They structure the house and hold it together. They enclose and protect the life inside. Like a timbered dwelling, the human body is easily destroyed and lasts only for the days 'loaned' to it. The inhabitant, the life or soul or the individual human being, can leave the house/body at any time, and there will come a day when he/she will not return.

Banhus occurs twice in *Beowulf*, first when the hero still at the height of his powers crushes with his own body the 'bone-house' of an enemy of the Geats, the second when this same mighty body of Beowulf is being consumed by 'the greatest of funeral-fires' (*bælfyra mæst*, 3143b). Appropriately enough, the first of these comes just before Beowulf attacks the earth-dragon. It is the hero himself who uses the kenning, referring to *Dæghrefn* 'Day-Raven,' the champion and standard-bearer of the Hugas for whom Beowulf was the 'hand-slayer' (*to handbonan*) as part of his obligation to Hygelac in the war against the Frisians: 'a sword-edge was not his slayer; rather my battle-grip broke open his heart-wellings, his *bone-house*' (*ne wæs ecg bona, / ac him hildegrap   heortan wylmas, / banhus gebræc*, 2506b–7). A little later (3137–55), after the fatal battle with the dragon in which Beowulf dies, his people build two structures, one meant to be temporary (the pyre), the other more permanent (the memorial barrow). The first of these is *unwaclicne* 'not weak-like' or 'mean,' that is, it is 'splendid,' and in fulfilment of Beowulf's request earlier it is 'hung with helmets, battle-shields, and bright byrnies' (*helmum behongen, hildebordum, / beorhtum byrnum*). It is in the midst of these trappings of the heroic world that the lamenting *hæleð* lay the body of their lord – the physical house in which he lived his life – and then set the cremation wood on fire. As the roaring flames and black smoke mingle with the weeping of the Geats, the fire breaks down the bone-house, 'hot at its heart' (*he ða banhus gebrocen hæfde / hat on hreðre*). It would be difficult to imagine a more apt use of the kenning.

We have seen how the essence of the kenning is the way it withdraws from direct description in favour of periphrastic or oblique uses of words to suggest metaphorical identities. It is usually possible to see how a particular figure in some way is based on an observation, somewhere, sometime, of something in the actual world, but it is also clear that this observation has simply provided perceptual raw material with which to fashion a metaphor or puzzling verbal pattern. Details from the actual world of people, places, and things have been selected, removed from their empirical contexts, refashioned in words that avoid direct statement or naturalistic description, and projected imaginatively. Each such coinage becomes part of the world of words that makes up the poetic diction of *Beowulf*. One important result of this process is that the human world projected and created with words in the poem is a fictionalized or purely verbal one which exists, literally, only in poetry. That in no way trivializes or diminishes the poem. I shall try to show in what follows that it is what gives it its unique power.

3

Þryðword Sprecen: The Language of Myth and Metaphor

In one important way the experiencing of the poetic language of *Beowulf* is not unlike what happens when we open our minds to the verbal imaginings in a play by Shakespeare. Both the poem and the play involve a highly metaphorical art heavily dependent on patterns of sound and imagery to establish rich and often strange perceptions, intuitions, and identities. The word-play is meant to take us well beyond the language of rationalist logic or simple description. In both *Beowulf* and Shakespeare the fictional beings that we encounter, human and non-human, often are surrounded by multiple verbal associations. As happens when we first look at the images and patterns on an Anglo-Saxon *hyrsted sweord* 'figured sword' (or on an ornate brooch or on the illustrated page of a manuscript), some of the identities and interconnections between and among these beings will elude us initially. Some will do so permanently, partly because we do not know the poetic language subtly and well enough, and partly because we permit obstacles in our own too-prosaic minds to preclude our accepting the metaphorical invitations made by the language. But repeated hearings and readings do reveal additional meanings, which are available in the words themselves, if we keep an open attitude and do not assume we already have achieved full understanding. So far as *Beowulf* is concerned, it is through the figurative language, especially as it concentrates in the kenning and in the wealth of associated metaphors, that we either experience the text as an Old English poem or as a translation of something that reads so oddly in translation we might well wonder why so many people in the last two centuries have thought it important at all.

But there is more to this matter of the language of *Beowulf* than simply a rich store of kennings and other figures being used with skill and subtlety to convey the kinds of meanings and effects that I have been probing. I have indicated already how little emphasis there is in the poem on the separation of subject and object, how the emphasis instead is on the feeling that the various beings are linked by a common power or energy with each other and with the imagined environment in which they are placed. In specific passages, ships, swords, stormy seas, and the rising sun are closely identified with the human and the non-human beings associated with them. In our materialist, object-obsessed culture with its trust in empirical evidence, these things or images in the poem easily are seen as objective, as paralleling or providing evidence for our 'historical' inquiries. There is probably nothing wrong with such studies, provided that we also learn how to take into account what is going on metaphorically, on what we might think of as a more primitive and basic level where even things like charms, spells, and curses operate as the words come together in the poem. A weapon or ship or boar-helmet is not just an object, or even an object at all; it is a living being, part of a humanly important event. The event and its situation are primary, primitive, metaphorical, a product of the poet's awareness and of the inherited power of the traditional heroic diction. Because *Beowulf* is the product of a pre-technological culture, it is free not to devalue the skilfully fashioned, handmade swords, helmets, byrnies, shields, wine-cups, halls, harps, tapestries, banners, and ships that are its technical achievements. The devaluing of technological mechanisms comes much later historically, with the exponential growth of a technological culture. In the poem both the natural environment and the shaped human environment – including poems, songs, and stories – are indivisibly linked together in a pervasively anthropocentric way. These two environments are treated as one and are directly interconnected with heaven and hell. As we have already seen, those two imagined spatial polarities are not remote or distant places far out in the cosmos or far down in the remote depths of the earth. They closely surround and interpenetrate the middle dwelling, the human world, and they make their influence known by direct intervention in the lives of men and women. A host of epithets for God relate both to the imagined unity of the heavenly dryht and to the Deity's influence and control throughout the cosmos. In the case of hell, the demonic powers take decisively corporeal forms in the monsters that prey on the human world.

We noted, in connection with Hrothgar's sermon, that even in that 'conceptual' part of the poem the language remains concrete and metaphorical and does not retreat into allegorical abstractions. In *Beowulf*, as in Homer's epics and in much of the Bible, such conceptions as soul, mind, time, space, courage, emotion, and thought are intensely physical. The human soul is something that can be destroyed by a physical enemy like Grendel, the *gastbona* 'soul-slayer.' The mind or heart of a man is a *breosthord*, a metaphorical place in which thoughts and feelings, like treasure objects and poetic words, are stored. Time for a human being is *lændagas* 'loaned days,' a number of days loaned out as a temporary gift to an individual but subject to recall when the fated death-day comes. The space in which Beowulf's enormous strength becomes known is 'between the seas over the broad world' (*be sæm tweonum / ofer eormengrund*, 859) or 'under heaven's going forth' or 'circuit' or 'course' (*under swegles begong*, 860). Courage is swimming, wrestling, and sword-fighting against monsters. It is also speaking powerfully to revivify frightened or downhearted people. Concrete metaphors for thoughts and emotions tend to images of burning and swelling. Curiosity is a physical and mental force pressing or tormenting someone or bursting forth from him (*fyrwyt* or *fyrwet*, 232, 1985, 2784). Strong affection is a secret longing burning against the blood (*dyrne langað / beorn wið blode*, 1879–80). Fear or terror is something that 'stands up,' as it does in the Danes when they hear God's adversary Grendel, mortally wounded, expressing his pain (783b–8a). Rage (*abelgan, gebelgan, belgan, gebolgen, bolgen-mod*) is a condition in which the *mod* 'mood,' 'mind,' or 'spirit' actually 'bulges' or 'swells.' This last emotional condition appears frequently at key points, always I think in its root metaphorical sense with the meaning of swelling, which Klaeber in his Glossary entry for *belgan* says the word originally had.[1]

It is instructive briefly to follow the bulgings, as a particularly good example of the way the corporeal imagination that fashioned the poem anchors feelings and ideas in physical images connected with bodily or material processes. The bulging metaphor is used of monsters, Heremod, the hero, and the Deity. When Grendel's hand touches the door of Heorot as he tears open 'the mouth of the building' (*recedes muþan*), he is described as *bealohydig* 'bale-' or 'evil-minded' and as *gebolgen* 'bulging' or 'swollen' (721b–4a). When the Danes and Geats arrive unexpectedly at the mere, whose waters are welling with Æschere's blood, they disturb 'many of worm-kind [or 'of the race of serpents'], strange sea-dragons' (*wyrmcynnes fela / sellice sædracan*), also the 'water-monsters' (*nicras*) and the 'worms' or 'serpents and wild beasts' (*wyrmas ond wildeor*) that are moving about in the water or lying on the headlands. As these strange, hostile beings rush away from the human presences, they are characterized as *bitere ond gebolgne* 'bitter and bulging' (1425–31a). In the underwater fight with Grendel's mother, just after Hrunting has failed and Beowulf has decided to trust in his mighty hand-grip, the hero is described as 'hard in battle' (*beadwe heard*) and 'bulging' (*gebolgen*) as he hurls 'the life-enemy' (*feorhgeniðlan*) to the floor (1539–40). Heremod's swollen heart (*bolgenmod*) causes him to kill his table companions and turn away from the joys of men (1713–15). The dragon is three times characterized as bulging with rage: twice when he first discovers the theft of the cup, because he, 'the people's foe' (*þeodsceaða*, 2278, 2688), who 'for three hundred winters has held in the earth a certain one of its treasure-houses' (*þreo hund wintra / heold on hrusan hordærna sum*), has been made by one man to bulge in rage (2220, 2279–81a); again, as he waits *earfoðlice* 'with difficulty' for evening to come, so that he can vent his pent-up fury and pay with fire for the loss of the precious drinking vessel (2302b–6a). Against this monster of vengeance, as with Grendel's mother, Beowulf expresses his own rage; *stearcheort* and *gebolgen* he storms his challenge into the dragon's barrow (2550–3). Earlier, when he has learned of the horror unleashed in his kingdom by the dragon (2324 ff.) and has realized that his own dryht-hall and gift-throne have melted in welling flames, he is plunged into uncharacteristic gloom and feels 'rue' or 'grief' in his heart (*hreow on hreðre*). We are told that he thinks that 'over against the old right he has bitterly enraged the Wielder, the eternal Dryhten' (*ofer ealde riht ecean Dryhtne / bitre gebulge*).

This is a poem in which fire does not simply burn things. Fire is 'battle-wellings of hostile flames' (*heaðowylmas ... laðan liges*) closely identified with human hatreds (as in the anticipated end of Heorot, 81b–5). It is the 'greediest of spirits' [or 'of guests'] (*gæsta gifrost*) that completely swallows up (*ealle forswealg*) human bodies, as on the pyre at Finnsburg (1122b–3a). It is an enraged dragon that spews flames which destroy the 'best of dwellings' (*bolda selest*, 2326) of the Geatish society and whose 'gleaming fire' (*bryneleoma*) stands up 'to the horror of men' (*eldum on andan*), as this 'foe of the people' (*þeodsceaða*, 2278, 2688) demonstrates his wish not to leave alive there any living thing (*no ðær aht cwices*, 2312–15). Sounds, like sights, are exaggerated. A captive in hell (*helle hæften*) defeated in a gigantic struggle in the middle dwelling does not just make a noise; he sings a 'horror-lay' (*gryreleoð*), 'a song without victory' (*sigeleasne sang*), and howls over his wound, to the terrible fear of the humans who are listening (782b–8a). During the battle in the mere we are told (1521 ff.) that the 'ring-sword' (*hringmæl*) Hrunting 'Thrusting' 'yelled out a greedy war-lay on the head' of Grendel's mother (*on hafelan hringmæl agol / grædig guðleoð*), even though this fierce sword-warrior 'was not willing to bite, to harm her life' (*bitan nolde, / aldre sceþðan*); also that Hrunting's failure in this battle is his first one and that by it his *dom* 'reputation' has 'fallen' or 'failed' (*his dom alæg*).

At times *Beowulf* is 'animal language,' to use Rousseau's term for primal language, as in the *Essai sur l'origine des langues* (1740s or 1750s?). Such language owes its origin not to reasoning but to feeling, and often it is conceptually unclear and descriptively inexact (we ask, 'What is the antecedent?'). It is performative language, meant to speak to the heart as it tells of bodily contact and physical action, and expresses powerful feelings: of joy, exuberance, and great happiness, and of pain, misery, horror, and a profound sense of loss. *Beowulf* is not a poem that substitutes ideas for feelings by addressing itself to an intellectualizing consciousness or to an analytical, precise intelligence. This means that as we moderns read, translate, edit, annotate, word-process, and print our thinking about the text, we have to be careful not to silence the voices of the poem, not to repress its peculiar powers while piling up our rational scholarship. If we are possessed of an ironic or detached intelligence, it can require considerable mental and imaginative effort to translate our minds into this highly metaphorical, concrete, non-abstract language in which emotions and thoughts, like the beings who have and express them, are writ large, and are meant to be taken seriously, however easily they can be rendered ridiculous by a postmodern ironic consciousness. If we are to begin really to understand *Beowulf* as it once was and as it once had meaning, we have to move into a non-Cartesian frame of mind. Our dominant technology of language, including most of our descriptive and analytical scholarly language, abstracts us from words as material powers or forces, as verbal elements that create and re-create realities. The actual words of the poem are the reality, and the ground of communication is the total human experience made possible because of the interaction of two Gestalts: the tradition speaking through the poet's words and the traditions in the audience, then and now, that make response possible.

The lifeworld projected in *Beowulf* is one of emotional and physical extremes, in which even the rhetorical device of litotes or ironic understatement regularly acts, implicitly, as hyperbole. When for example Hrothgar has just told how a stag put to flight by hounds and driven to the edge of the horrific mere will die rather than lower its head into the waters, he says, *nis þæt heoru stow* 'that place is not pleasant' [or 'safe' or 'good']' (1372b). A moment later he says openly what he really means, by calling the mere 'a terrible place' (*frecne stowe*, 1378). Something similar happens with the occurrences of the word *unbliðe*. When Hrothgar's 'feasting' (*wiste*) and 'joy' (*dream*) in the new Heorot have been turned to 'weeping' (*wop*) and 'a great morning cry' (*micel morgensweg*) by Grendel's feasting on thirty of the Scylding thanes, the narrator describes the miserable old king with an understatement which builds its strength on contrasts: Hrothgar is sitting *unbliðe* 'not happy' (126–31). Similarly, when the last survivor (*an æfter eallum*) has finished his powerful lament over the vanishing of his dryht, he is described (2267–70a) as *unbliðe* 'not happy,' as he moves about 'day and night until death's welling' (*dæges ond nihtes, oð ðæt deaðes wylm*) touches 'at his heart' (*æt heortan*). Yet again, when the messenger near the end of the poem has finished his *laðra spella* 'hateful messages' to the Geats, a troop of them, their eyes 'welling with tears' (*wollenteare*), go *unbliðe* 'not happy' under Eagles' Ness to see their dead king and the dragon (3028–32).

The Language of Myth and Metaphor 89

In this book so far I have repeatedly used the terms 'metaphor' and 'metaphorical' to describe the ways words function in the poem. I recognize that there may have been no conscious intellectual conception of metaphor in the minds of any of those involved with the poem in Anglo-Saxon times, including perhaps even the poet himself. On the other hand, there may have been. We cannot know. In any case we must have such a conception, because in the critical discourses of our time metaphor is no longer one figure among others. It is the figure of figures. It has become a figure for figurality itself, for the imaginative or poetic uses of language as distinguished from descriptive or representational ones. Metaphorical language is a mode of using words based on identification *as* and identification *with*, between two or more things. It is a way of perceiving and describing similarities and identities which do not have full, direct connections with anything in the actual world. Metaphor is the statement 'The middle dwelling is the guest-hall of Eden,' which carries with it for us modern readers the realization that the middle dwelling is not in the least Eden. For us the metaphor is not logical in what it asserts. This means that metaphorical language is counter-logical, creating identities and opening currents between the mental processes of the poets and things external to those processes. As William Wordsworth realized, coming much later culturally, the poetic thoughts that emerge in a poet's mind are a product partly of creation and partly of what has been perceived (*Tintern Abbey*, 102b–11). In the case of an anonymous and traditional Anglo-Saxon poet, the creation may be that of a predecessor and the perception of the external world may be far in the past, but the two elements, perception and creation, are still there in the poetic expression. It is this kind of language that dominates in *Beowulf*. Since I do not think that this is sufficiently recognized either in scholarship about the poem or in interpretations of it, I wish now, in the remainder of this chapter, to broaden the discussion, to step back intellectually from the corporeal imaginings of the poem itself and try to locate them within a broader theoretical construct.

I turn again to Frye's *theoria*.[2] In describing earlier the mode of imagining that prevails in *Beowulf* – romance combining frequently with myth, with some partial sorties into limited kinds of mimesis – Frye's adaptation and use of a concept from Aristotle's *Art of Poetry* was useful. When Frye (1957) borrowed and critically revisited Aristotle's idea for characterizing different kinds of literature on the basis of whether the protagonist in the fiction is *spoudaios* or *phaulos* (relatively weighty or light, having more or less power of action), he combined the newly interpreted Aristotelian concept with another idea, drawn from the Italian philosopher and jurist Giambattista Vico (1668–1744). In his *Nuova Scienza* (1725, revised 1730 and 1744), Vico postulated a philosophy of history that defines it in terms of cycles, each with three ages: a mythical age or age of the gods, in which the dominant social form is theocracy; a heroic age, or an age of aristocracy; and an age of the people. At the end of this series, according to Vico, there is a *ricorso* or return, and the three-part sequence starts over again. Frye's modification of this pattern in 1957 led to his theory of five historical modes of Western literature and to the suggestion that in the midst of the dominance of the mode of irony in the twentieth century it is possible to discern the beginnings of a *ricorso*. Later in Frye's career in his two-volume study of the Bible, called respectively *The Great Code: The Bible and Literature* (1982) and *Words with Power, Being a Second Study of the Bible and Literature* (1990), he again used the Viconian three ages as a starting-point, but this time for a theory of what he called *langage*. He did this because he had found it necessary to deal with a particular question, one that is immediately relevant to studies of Old English poetry, although that part of our literary culture was not in any immediate sense Frye's concern.

The question Frye was addressing is whether it is possible to have a history of *langage*, 'a sequence of modes of more or less translatable structures in words, cutting across the variety of *langues* employed, affected and conditioned but not wholly determined by them' (1982, 5). His task, since his subject was the Bible and literature, was to account somehow for the large historical fact that the Bible has communicated itself and had most of its influence on literature and civilization in the form of translations. This suggested to him that there must be some sense common to the original languages and the receiving languages that can be translated, some basis of mutual intelligibility. It was that that took him again to Vico and, I think, at least in a second-hand way (this does not emerge into the foreground in either of the Bible books), to Rousseau's *Essai sur l'origine des langues*. Both Rousseau and Vico thought that language originates in metaphor and that figurative language precedes literal language (Rousseau, 95, 97; Vico, books 3 and 4, especially 340–2). In Vico's view, each age produces its own kind of *langage*, so that in each complete historical cycle there emerges a series of three types of verbal expression: the poetic, from the mythical age; the heroic or noble, from the aristocratic age; and the vulgar, from the age of the people. Frye found these terms 'extremely suggestive' and used them as the basis for his theory of modes of language, although, as he himself acknowledged, Vico got left far behind in the process.

I set out in what follows a summary of Frye's account of these three *langages*, as a way of assisting recognition of the particular mode of language that is central in *Beowulf*. I note in passing that in *The Great Code* (1982, 3–30) there are three phases of language and in *Words with Power* (1990, 3–29) there are five modes, the latter being consistent with the former but providing a more detailed set of distinctions. There is nothing crude or simplistic in the schematic theory that Frye developed out of Vico's three ages. The ideas of language and literature set out in the two Bible books were distilled by a brilliant thinker from an enormously broad and deep cultural experience over a half-century of sustained intellectual work. Clearly the theory of the three phases of language is meant to be applied flexibly and non-categorically. Both Vico and Frye recognized, and so do I, that all three phases exist in all human societies. It is a matter of which one is culturally ascendant in any particular period of history. The specific question being addressed with the help of the theory in this chapter is parallel to the question set out and discussed in chapter 1. There we asked, 'Where in literary history among the broad modes of fictional imagining does *Beowulf* sit?' The question now is 'In which of the main modes of verbal language available historically in our culture is *Beowulf* composed?'

First phase, poetic language – Frye also calls it hieroglyphic and metaphorical – had cultural ascendancy in the ancient Mediterranean and Near Eastern world and is found in most Greek literature before Plato (427?-347? BCE), especially in the Homeric epics. It is also found in the Near Eastern pre-biblical cultures and in much of the Old Testament. Its main defining characteristic is that in it 'there is relatively little emphasis on a clear separation of subject and object: the emphasis falls rather on the feeling that subject and object are linked by a common power or energy' (1982, 6). Many so-called primitive societies have words to express this common energy of human personality and natural environment. The example Frye gives is the Melanesian *mana*. In Old English literature, including *Beowulf*, the operative term is *mægen* 'might, strength, force, power, vigour, ability,' and a host of compounds including it, as for example *mægencræft* 'mighty power.' *Mægen* normally is thought of in Old English poetry as the might of God himself or as a force he has granted to other beings, such as angels and exceptional individuals, or to whole peoples chosen for special divine favour. This *mægen* enables the recipient to exert extraordinary influence in and on the physical world.[3] The corollary to this power is that there may be magical powers in the uses of words, as in spells and charms. Because of the special energy or force present in the human beings, their words are instrumentally interconnected with many other things. 'Words in such a context are words of power or dynamic forces' (6). It is not the case that the *mægen* of such words is 'nonphysical' (Greenfield and Calder 1986, 255). First phase *langage* is a language of immanence with no true abstractions and with a heavy reliance on myth and metaphor.

Second phase or heroic language – Frye variously calls it metonymic, hieratic, or dialectical – is more individualized, less formulaic than poetic or metaphorical language. In it words are 'primarily the outward expression of inner thoughts or ideas' (7). Subject and object are more consistently separated, and, as the intellectual operations of the mind become distinguishable from the emotional operations, abstraction becomes possible. Here Frye contrasts the Homeric heroes, in whose bosoms there revolves 'an inseparable mixture of thought and feeling,' with Socrates, in whom thought is to be in command of feeling. In this second phase, language moves away from the metaphorical 'with its sense of identity of life or power or energy between man and nature' to a relationship that is metonymic and in which words are 'put for' thoughts. They are the 'outward expressions of an inner reality' (8). But, and this is important, this reality is not only 'inside.' Thoughts 'indicate the existence of a transcendent order' with which human beings can communicate. Thus metonymic language tends to become analogical language, 'a verbal imitation of a reality beyond itself that can be conveyed most directly by words.' This is the *langage* of Plato and of medieval Christian theology. It is a language not of immanence but of transcendence, pointing analogically or allegorically to a reality beyond itself.

Third phase 'vulgar' language (13) – Frye calls it demotic or descriptive – is present in all historical periods but begins to emerge (13) in a major way in the sixteenth century (Francis Bacon, 1561–1626), 'and attains cultural ascendancy in the eighteenth' century (John Locke, 1632–1704). In this descriptive language there is 'a clear separation of subject and object, in which the subject exposes itself, in sense experience, to the impact of an objective world.' The objective world is the order of nature, and thinking follows the suggestions of empirical experience. Words are meant to be 'primarily descriptive of an objective natural order' and a verbal structure is 'true' or convincing to the degree that it faithfully describes or mirrors the objective world. As in first phase or metaphorical language, so here in descriptive language there is a direct relation between the order of nature and the order of words, but there has been a radical change – in fact, a huge cultural shift: the observing subject and the observed object are now sharply distinguished from each other. The corollary of this break or separation is a strong reaction against the transcendental metaphysics that underlies metonymic uses of language. At the same time the mythical sense of immanence characteristic of poetic or metaphorical language, which dominated the earliest age of Western culture, becomes culturally even more disadvantaged in the modern world.

Third phase language is perceptual, based on an assumption of its correspondence with an objective, empirical world of nature. This is the world of early modern science and of increasingly mimetic literature and visual art. To use Frye's phrase, its 'great bastion' (14) was the assumed objectivity of the material world. But then Einstein brought the realization that matter was an illusion of energy. The earlier scientific sense of a clear separation of subject and object started to disintegrate, and it was no longer possible completely to separate the observer from what was being observed. In all the natural and social sciences, as in the literary and visual arts of the modern world, the realization took hold that the observer had also to become an observed object. Otherwise not only would each act of perception and description be irretrievably subjective but the perceiver and describer would be unaware that it was. It would be a naïve physicist or painter or poet today who did not know that his or her involvement in the particular experiment, painting, or poem represents some degree of interference with and reshaping of the material world. Whether the main intention is objectively to observe and accurately to describe or deliberately to reshape something, it is known that there will be a reshaping. Subject and object historically have come together again and are known to be interdependent. It is this kind of cultural change that suggests to Frye the idea that we may have completed a gigantic cycle of language from Homer's time, where the word evokes the thing, to our own day, where the thing evokes the word, and are now about to go around the cycle again, as we seem to be confronted once again with an energy common to subject and object which can be expressed verbally only through some form of metaphor (15). Whatever the descriptive validity of this major intuition, and whether or not we are 'entering a new phase altogether in our understanding of language,' it is certainly true that much of contemporary thought is preoccupied with language and linguistic models. It is my view that studies of Old English literature, including *Beowulf* – these texts from a thousand or more years ago – can both help in this larger exploration and themselves be illuminated by it.

Although no one knows where, when, by whom, or for whom *Beowulf* was composed, it certainly came into being in its present form sometime in the four centuries leading up to 1000–1025, the time of the extant manuscript. It took shape, that is, well into the historical period which Frye thought of as 'medieval,' long after Plato had helped metonymic, hieratic, analogical language (Vico's heroic or noble language of the age of aristocracy) to gain cultural ascendancy over the earlier dominant language of the mythical age of the gods, called poetic by Vico and, variously by Frye, hieroglyphic, mythical, and metaphorical. Knowing this large cultural fact, but not consciously articulating any such modes-of-*langage* formulation as the Vico–Frye one, numerous scholars have assumed that the extant poetic records from the Anglo-Saxon period, many of them obviously theocentric, are medieval allegorical texts and that they point primarily to a transcendent reality beyond themselves. This has often been taken simply as a given, especially in recent decades by the so-called exegetical critics, because it is known that the metaphysics of the early Christian centuries and of the medieval era was based on the assumption that reality ultimately lay beyond what we post-Kantians think of as the phenomenal world.

The corollary assumption was that human beings, even with the help of divine revelation, were not capable of experiencing or knowing metaphysical or supernatural reality fully while still in the *middangeard*. But the mythopeic poems in the canon (*Genesis A, Genesis B, Exodus, Christ I, II,* and *III*, the first seventy-seven lines of *The Dream of the Rood, The Descent into Hell, Christ and Satan, Judgment Day I* and *II*), the charms, many of the riddles, parts of *The Phoenix* and, in a major way, *Beowulf* all are part of what Vico might have called a *ricorso*, a reemergence of the poetic *langage* of myth and metaphor which is dominant also in Homer and Hesiod, in much of the Bible, and in Norse myth (at least in the oldest layers of the Eddas). Several of the other less purely mythical Old English poems also are extensively involved in first phase language, even when in the poems themselves – for example, in *The Wanderer* and *The Seafarer* – the language of transcendence is explicitly being shown ultimately to be more valid than the language of immanence. The Anglo-Saxon poetic corpus includes large measures of the first two phases of language, in numerous permutations and combinations.

Chapter 1 of this book is an exploration of the idea that *Beowulf* is romance with a marked tendency to move into the mythical mode but that it also includes some elements of mimesis. Romance is the dominant fictional mode of a great deal of medieval literature. This might lead to an expectation that, so far as the language of *Beowulf* is concerned, it will be, in Frye's terms, metonymic. If we were naïvely to follow from the theory of the historical modes of fiction set out in *Anatomy of Criticism* (1957) to the more recent theory of the phases or modes of language in the first chapters of the Bible books, we might easily fall into the same trap that various exegetical critics have. By that I mean the working assumption that the language of *Beowulf* is medieval and hieratic, functioning mainly by analogy with a metaphysical reality beyond itself and the world it expresses. In fact the bulk of *Beowulf* criticism in modern times, whether of an exegetical cast or not, has proceeded on the assumption that the language of the poem is predominantly in what Frye calls the heroic-hieratic or second phase, although there have also been plenty of misguided attempts (in my view) to read it as if it were in third phase language, or at least to translate it into one or another of the 'descriptive' vocabularies available to modern scholars.

The first misconception is perhaps not surprising, since the 'social content' of the poem is an aristocratic one centred on kings, queens, lords, and warrior-thanes, and, whatever was the case in Anglo-Saxon history, Vico's 'age of the people' clearly is not being expressed in any way in this *æpeling*-centred work. It is a commonplace of Old English scholarship and criticism that *Beowulf* and most of the other extant Old English poems are composed in a heroic diction remote from the ordinary language of ordinary people. That this language is not demotic is obvious to anyone who thinks about it. What is not so clear is that we understand the extent to which the poetic language of *Beowulf* is *more than heroic* and is not the hieratic language expressing analogical thought and metaphysical assumptions that came to dominate medieval literature and culture. It is the main argument of this chapter and an important theme of this book that *Beowulf* is in an important sense 'pre-medieval,' engaged directly in a *langage* of myth and metaphor, and, as such, is due for a radical critical reappraisal in the light of the illuminating Vico-Frye theory. Such a reappraisal is part of a larger intellectual enterprise that has been in process in recent years but which so far has not had much impact on the studies of the earliest English poetry; nor has the larger effort sought or received much help from such early texts. Jean-François Lyotard, in *La condition postmoderne* (1979), has identified two powerful but divergent philosophical and critical tendencies at work in modern culture, both involving a severe interrogation of rationalism and Cartesian thought and driven by the realization that the language of descriptive analysis and abstract reasoning leads to a distancing self-reflexivity, to an anxious alienation of humanity from the natural and the material world. One modern response to this realization has been a sense of powerlessness, melancholy, and regret for a lost presence. The other, with which I would align this book, focuses on the empowered word, on the increased valorizing of metaphorical thought, and on a criticism interested in a poetics of process. If we do exist in a post-metaphysical age in which the very idea of truth may have been destroyed, as many of our contemporaries think it has been, it is vital that we value the primordial, metaphor-making mode of thinking that is present in literary language. In a period of human history increasingly preoccupied with difference and *différance*, particularities and distinctions, deconstruction and destruction, it is important to value the human capacity to construct identities, to forge unities, and to make syntheses, without reducing variety and undervaluing discreteness.

We have seen that in first phase language 'there is little emphasis on a clear separation of subject and object: the emphasis falls rather on the feeling that subject and object are linked by a common power or energy' (Frye 1982, 6). There is a common energy of human personality and natural environment, and words can be used to express this, even to bring the power or energy itself into being. In *Beowulf* we first experience this imaginative energy in the account of the emergence from the flood of 'Shield, Son of Sheaf' (*Scyld Scefing*) and his return into the sea, then again in the close association of *Heorot* 'Stag, Hart' and the Creation of the *middangeard* and, in rapid succession, in the numerous epithets and phrases for Grendel and his mother which identify them with the repugnant, threatening, terrifying aspects of the physical environment: darkness, mystery, other monsters, stormy waters, wind, ice, fire, rocks, twisted

96   Modes of Imagining and the Workings of Words

vegetation. In contrast to the monsters, Beowulf is closely associated with light, the rising sun, sheer physical power and exuberance balanced with mental and moral powers, and with the *Liffrea* 'Prince of Life.' An identity is established for the hero as master of the stormy seas, as a being capable of destroying sea-monsters and those other misshapen creatures of darkness and destruction that threaten the continuance of life as it is meant by heaven to be.

In the poem there are numerous clear examples of how the articulating of words brings mythical power or energy into action. From the first dramatic energizing word *Hwæt*, the poet's remembering and telling, using the resources of the word-hoard, brings into being the *þrym* 'might, force, greatness, glory' and the *ellen* 'brave deeds, valour' of the Spear-Danes. In a real sense the poem itself is part of this heroic power, in the form of an extended pattern of sound and speech. This is true right to the end of the text, even though by then the emphasis has shifted to the theme of the cessation of Beowulf's heroic energy, and also of the energies of the two peoples with whom he has lived his life. His people the Geats and the poem itself are still continuing to praise him and his great deeds. At the beginning, when God sends Scyld a son (12; 25) as 'comfort' or 'help' or 'consolation for the folk' (*folce to frofre*) and in his role as divine 'Wielder of Glory' (*wuldres Wealdend*) grants the Scylding Beowulf favour in the world, this action by heaven generates a momentum that leads to articulation of the son as *breme* 'renowned' and causes his *blæd* 'prosperity' or 'abundance' to spring up far and wide. It is this process of dispensing words by the narrator that creates in the poem the glory of the Scylding dynasty. Scyld's splendid funeral itself is the direct result of the dead king's word-power earlier (*swa he self bæd, / þenden wordum weold*). Hrothgar is characterized as having wide power with his word (*se þe his wordes geweald   wide hæfde*) when he commands the building of the greatest mead-hall ever heard of by the sons of men, and then dispenses gifts in accord with God's gifts to him (67b ff.). In this passage the metaphorical association and identification of the original Creation with this new work of building and ornamentation can take place because of the buildup of verbal power already in process. As Hrothgar carries out his gift-giving *beot* 'boast, promise,' it is evident that his words do have power and that they release not only his own energies but those of the many people 'throughout this middle dwelling' (*geond þisne middangeard*) who come at his bidding to decorate the great hall. The scop's song of Creation, in turn, further expresses the power by which the myth of origins is reenacted, as a way of identifying Heorot and of showing that the Scylding throne and guest-hall are founded on the power of *se Ælmihtiga*. Words – the poet narrator's, those of the folk who spread the glorious fame of the Scylding kings, Scyld's words, Hrothgar's words, and those in the song of the scop (pointing to the original Word or creating Logos in Genesis) – all, in the mythical exordium to the main narrative – 'are words of power or dynamic forces' (Frye 1982, 6).

The *Beowulf* poet does not compose as a writer of representational or naturalistic fiction does. Rather he works within a creative process in which, instead of describing the sixth-century world of the Danes and the Geats, he calls an imagined form of it into being. He makes or invents it for human listening from the raw data of inherited stories, traditional poetic language, and his own sensory perceptions. As with the original idea of Heorot for Hrothgar, so with the conceiving of the poem, it comes into the poet's mind to tell a tale about brave men long ago, a tale that will embody the life and work of the greatest of all men between the seas. In the kind of radical metaphor that he uses to do this, the semantic impertinence of identifying Heorot with the Creation, or the mere with the Flood and hell, gives dialectical energy, epistemological power, and emotional intensity. As the poet's mind experiences its own inventive capacities, as the word-hoard once again is unlocked and some of its contents come together in the curious ways of this poem, connections and identities emerge that have little to do with either accurate centrifugal observation of the external world of early Denmark and southern Sweden or with logical rational thought about moral and doctrinal codes. These associations and identities are, rather, the realities of poetic thought. They are the world that is the poem. In experiencing them we simultaneously have a sense of being part of a larger design and of containing it, of coming closer to knowing radical metaphor, including something of its ungroundedness and instability. *Beowulf* does not give us the homiletic security (*fæstnung*) of the end of *The Wanderer*. Even as from time to time it points to that same enduring reality, it mainly chooses to stay attached to the glories and ruins of the world of the *dryht*. It values more the possibility of *dream* in the *middangeard* than the certainty of the *ece* 'eternal' order whose reality and overall control it acknowledges.

Beowulf is a process of words in action. In it, persistently, there is a collective yet personal voice, and a consciousness which makes us as listeners or readers continuously aware of the process and the successive acts of remembering, telling, feeling, metaphorical compounding, thinking, and commenting. This narrative presence not only leads us into the multifaceted story of the poem but also into the process of telling a story, by means of highly figurative, intensified uses of words. *Beowulf* emphasizes the process of narration and word-shaping more than the finished product, with the result that associational, formulaic, cumulative meanings emerge in profusion. This is a work of performative verbal art more interested in sharing experience than in producing an aesthetic thing as something separate from the poet and from the ones who are meant to receive it.

The sense of how human beings express or exercise power through their words is continued as Beowulf's exploits unfold. This can be seen especially in his use of the *beot* type of speech.[4] His 'boasts' are not prideful culpable acts of boasting but a harnessing or mobilizing of his God-given strength for the coming battles. As can be seen when he arrives in Heorot, his words of resolve work powerfully even before he does anything with the monsters. His speeches to Hrothgar and the court and his verbal victory in the flyting with Unferth have reintegrating, vivifying power in a hall community previously in catastrophic physical, spiritual, and moral disarray because of Grendel's twelve years of nightly feasting. In Beowulf's account of the contest with Breca we see the earliest example of the protagonist, in what would now probably be called his adolescence, 'psyching himself up,' along with his friend, for a Herculean exploit: 'We two, being boys, agreed and vowed – we were both in our youth – that we two out on the spear-man would risk our lives, and we carried that out accordingly' (*Wit þæt gecwædon cnihtwesende / ond gebeotedon – wæron begen þa git / on geogoðfeore – þæt wit on garsecg ut / aldrum neðdon, ond þæt geæfndon swa* (535–8). Much further on in the story (2510 ff.), what the narrator calls Beowulf's last *beot* words are spoken just before the hero addresses his comrades for the final time (*beotwordum spræc / niehstan siðe*). As 'old guardian of the people' (*frod folces weard*) he prepares to seek out the feud and 'perform a glorious deed' (*mærðu fremman*) against 'the evildoer' or 'wicked ravager' (*manscaða*), the dragon. It is significant that this last mobilizing of heroic energy, like the one in Heorot many years ago, looks back to an earlier *sið* 'exploit.' The heroic momentum builds and is cumulative, from the youthful North Sea adventure, to the Danish exploits, through many other battles, and now to the last great conflict, against the enemy of Geatland and of life itself. The verbally induced momentum has to be verbally maintained to the end. Recognizing this, Beowulf says, 'In my youth I fought in many wars' (*Ic geneðde fela / guða on geogoðe*) and then goes on to show – twice using the word *gylp* and describing himself as *from* 'bold,' 'strong,' 'eager' – that he knows that he cannot go weaponless to this battle as he did against Grendel. Nevertheless, and whatever *wyrd* and *Metod* decide, he 'will not flee a footstep' (*Nelle ic ... oferfleon fotes trem*). He, 'a man of the Weather-Geats' (*Weder-Geata leod*), takes his stand before the dragon's barrow and, swelling with rage, lets 'a word go forth from his breast' (*Let ða of breostum ... word ut faran*, 2550–51). When his 'battle-clear voice' (*stefn ... heaðotorht*) roars in under the grey stone, the 'hoard-guardian' (*hordweard*) knows 'the voice of a man' (*mannes reorde*, 2555). The final climactic battle of the poem is already started.[5]

In first phase language it is not only the physical or material world that is controlled by words of power. The operations of the human mind as well follow the dictates of words, since it is the words, whether formulaic or newly coined, that become the foci of mental activity and then lead to physical action. Words serve as creating, shaping, or destroying forces. In this poem they are the prerogative of human beings. The monsters are mute and God does not speak. The conception of the word-hoard is of a verbal treasure-chest that can be locked and its contents hoarded away, or it can be unlocked and the jewelled, carefully fashioned verbal treasures shared with others, for good or ill effect, for calls to necessary action or for impotent lamenting, for stirring up emotions and bestirring bodies, for peace-weaving or for unbinding a battle-rune. Once released, the contents of the hoard are intensely social. They can create or they can destroy. In the first age – metaphorical language of any time or place is part of the first age – the culturally ascendant language of myth and metaphor is communal, traditional, and formulaic, and it is essential to the coherence and survival of the society that uses it. In important ways the society is created by the language, by the metaphors and myths.

When Frye points out that the central expression of metaphor is the 'god,' as in sun-god, war-god, sea-god, and so on, and that this is an identification of a form of personality with an aspect of nature, it might seem that *Beowulf*, a product at least in part of a monotheistic mythology, would not share the same kind of mythical and metaphorical possibilities. But this is not, I think, what we find in the poem. It is true that the protagonist is not a god, however extraordinary he is as a man, but he is closely associated with the Deity who has all real power in the poem. Beowulf's huge strength and his triumphs over sea-monsters, stormy seas, bitter cold, darkness, God's foes in the mere, the human enemies of the Geats, and the fire-dragon all are gifts loaned to him for his allotted *lændagas* 'fleeting' or 'loaned days.' His source and sustenance are the Creator. There are three closely interrelated orders of reality in the poem, each presented in a traditional imagery and vocabulary: the order of Creation (the order of the physical world), the order of kinship (family and tribal relations), and the order of the dryht (socio-political relations). When Beowulf speaks or acts, he does so as the poem's prime exemplar and champion, in the middle dwelling, of each of these interconnected orders: in the Creation he is the one gifted with the greatest strength of any man between the seas; in his kinship identities, he is Ecgtheow's son, Hrethel's grandson, Hrothgar's adopted son, Heardred's uncle, and Wiglaf's uncle; socially and politically, he is, successively, Hygelac's thane, regent to Heardred, and king or *dryhten* of the Geats.

In general, Old English poetry is monotheistic. Aside from references to false pagan gods, there is no effective plurality of gods, as there is in ancient Near Eastern, Greek, Roman, and Norse mythologies, but there is something of the same literary effect in the plurality of the one God's names, characteristics, and activities. Somewhat as with the numerous, often contradictory conceptions of 'God' in the Bible – ranging there from a capricious, irrational, and often brutal tribal deity to a figure of perfect universal love made flesh to dwell among humankind – so in the mythopeic Old English poems, there are many and various characteristics attributed to the Deity. The glaring contradictions in the character or characters of the biblical Deity are not present in Old English poems. As far as *Beowulf* is concerned, we can probably best appreciate the range of connotations in the conception of God if we understand the names of the Deity not as static nouns or simple assertions of existence, to be passed over quickly or ignored, but as verbs or adjective-verbs (participles), or as nouns indicating characteristic actions – as a process accomplishing part of itself in the events and situations of this poem, as a Creator or Prince of Life actively engaged in the lifeworld of *Beowulf*.

There is a wide range of names (nineteen) and meanings:

Ælmihtig	*Alwalda*	*Anwalda*
Demend	*Dryhten*	*Ealdmetod*
Fæder	*Frea*	*God*
heofona *Helm*	wuldres *Hyrde*	*Kyning-wuldor*
Liffrea	*Metod*	rodora *Rædend*
Scyppend	sigora *Soðcyning*	*Waldend (Wealdend)*
Wuldur-cyning		

In all there are eighty-six occurrences of these names, one on average for every thirty-seven lines of the poem. But that is a misleading way of putting the matter, since not infrequently several of the names are clustered together, for cumulative impact at important narrative and thematic points. Seventy of the eighty-six occurrences come in the first 2199 lines of the poem (part I) and sixteen in the last 988 (part II). This means that the average frequency in part I is approximately twice that in part II, one for every thirty-one lines compared to one for every sixty-one. This is not surprising. It reflects the fact that part I is (on the whole) a successfully completed heroic romance centred on a God-empowered protagonist and that part II moves the romance through more tragic phases in which the days loaned to the hero are shown coming to an end. In part II, so far as the *middangeard* and Geatland are concerned, the divine favour that gives life and strength is in a process of being withdrawn. But the Deity is still thought of as very much in control of all things, a fact referred to directly by the narrator (2291–3a, 2329–31a, 2855–9, 3051–7) and recognized by both Beowulf (2468–71, 2524b–7a, 2741–3a, 2794–8) and Wiglaf (2650b, 2855–9, 2874b–6, 3105b–9).

The nineteen actual names and epithets for the Deity vary greatly in their frequency. They embrace a considerable semantic and poetic range. Four are used much more than the others: *God* 'God' (thirty-two times, nineteen by the narrator either directly or describing what someone else says [13, 72, 113, 181, 227, 625, 701, 711, 786, 811, 1056, 1271, 1397, 1553, 1626, 1682, 2182, 2858, 3054], six by Hrothgar [381, 478, 930, 1716, 1725, 1751], four by Beowulf [570, 685, 1658, 2469], one by Hygelac [1997], and two by Wiglaf [2650, 2874]); *Dryhten* 'the Dryht Lord, Retainers' Chief, Lord, Lord God' (fourteen times, seven by the narrator directly or describing what someone else is thinking [108, 181, 187, 696, 1554, 1692, 2330], four by Hrothgar [940, 1398, 1779, 1841], and three by Beowulf [441, 686, 2796]); *Metod* 'the Measurer, One who metes or measures out a *wyrd* or fate, Ordainer of Fate, God, Governor' (eleven times, seven by the narrator [110, 169, 180, 670, 706, 1057, 1611], one by Hrothgar [1778], and three by Beowulf [967, 979, 2527]); *Waldend (Wealdend)* 'the Wielder, Ruler, Lord' (eleven times, six by the narrator [17, 183, 1693, 2292, 2329, 2857], one by Hrothgar [1752], two by Beowulf [1661, 2741], and two by Wiglaf [2875, 3109]).

The other fifteen terms, proceeding alphabetically, have the following frequencies and users: *Ælmihtiga* 'the Almighty' (once, by the *scop* through the narrator in the song of Creation [92]); *Alwalda* 'the All-Wielder, Ruler of All' (four, once by the coast-guard [316], twice by Hrothgar [928, 955], and once by the narrator [1314]); *Anwalda* 'the One Wielder, the One Ruler' (once, by the narrator [1272]); *Kyning-wuldor* 'the King of Glory' or 'the Glory of Kings' (once, by the narrator; without editorial capitalization the reference here would be to Hrothgar not God [665]); *Demend* 'the Judging One, Judge' (once, by the narrator [181]); *Ealdmetod* 'the Measurer of Old, God of Old' (once, by Hrothgar [945]); *Fæder* 'Father' (once, by the coast-guard [316]); *Frea* 'the Lord, Prince, King' (twice, respectively, by the narrator [27] and by Beowulf [2794]); *heofena Helm* 'the Helm of the Heavens, the Protector of the Heavens' (once, by the narrator [182]); *wuldres Hyrde* 'the Keeper of Glory, Guardian of Glory' (once, by Hrothgar [931]); *Liffrea* 'the Lord of life' (once, by the narrator [16]); *rodera Rædend* 'the Ruler of the Heavens, the Heavenly Counsellor' (once, by the narrator [1555]); *Scyppend* 'the Shaper, Creator' (once, by the narrator [106]); *sigora Soðcyning* 'the True King of Victories' (once, by the narrator [3055]); *Wuldur-cyning* 'Glory King' (once, by Beowulf in his dying speech [2795]).

Such a list of first phase language names for the Deity in *Beowulf* is useful but serves only as a pointer towards real critical examination of how central the mythology is in the poem's stories and metaphors. It is helpful to consider in abstraction how often these various words and phrases are used and by whom, but it is still essential to follow them doing their actual work in the verbal fabric of the poem, as I have been doing and will continue to do. In general, what these eighty-six namings of the Deity indicate is a complex, dynamic process fundamental to the structure and meaning of *Beowulf*, a process of creating, giving gifts, empowering, sustaining, rescuing, protecting, directing, counselling, measuring, deciding, judging, punishing, and revealing truth and glory. The religious versus secular dichotomy does not work with this poem, pervaded as *Beowulf* is by a religious and mythological sense of an interanimated world created and controlled by God. Whatever we readers as existential beings living in a modern or postmodern culture may think of the metanarrative or mythology that these terms point to, it is clear that as critics and readers we need an imaginatively resurrected conception of God if we are to make sense of the interrelations and interpenetrations expressed in the poem through the creative and re-creative uses of these metaphors.

As second phase metonymic language historically gains the ascendancy, language becomes more individualized. Words become 'primarily the outward expression of inner thoughts or ideas,' with subject and object 'becoming more consistently separated' (Frye 1982, 7). The sense of words 'reflecting' something beyond themselves becomes linguistically dominant, and we have the conception of words as a *speculum* 'mirror' held up to nature. This is not what we find in *Beowulf*, where often it is impossible to separate the intellectual operations of the mind from those of the emotions. This impossibility becomes obvious whenever we try to translate any of the following wide range of words and phrases for emotional and mental processes, and quickly discover that we have no sure basis for tipping our translation either way, because the probable meaning includes both mind and feeling, and in some cases 'soul' or 'spirit' as well: *bealohydig* 'bale-minded, intending evil'; *bealonið* 'baleful hostility'; *bolgenmod* 'with bulging mind or heart, enraged'; *modes brecða* 'heart's or mind's breaking, grief'; *breost innan weoll þeostrum geþoncum* 'his breast welled within with dark thoughts'; *breostgehygd* 'breast or heart-thought, thought of the heart'; *wordes ord breosthord þurhbræc* 'a word's point' or 'front' or 'beginning broke through a breast-hoard'; *fæstrædne geþoht* 'a firmly counselled thought'; *ferhð* 'mind, spirit, heart'; *fyrwet* 'intense curiosity'; *galgmod* 'gallows-minded, gallows-hearted, gloomy-hearted'; *garcene* 'spear-keen, brave'; *glædmod* 'glad' or 'kind' or 'gracious of mind' or 'of heart'; *gromheort* 'grim-hearted, hostile-hearted'; *gromhydig* 'grim-minded, angry-minded, intending hostility'; *heteþanc* 'hate-thought, thought of hate'; *hige* or *hyge* 'mind, heart, soul'; *hygemeðe* 'heart [or 'mind' or 'soul']-weariness'; *higeþihtig* 'mind [or 'heart' or 'soul'] strong, strong-hearted, strong-minded, strong of soul? determined' (all of these); *higeþrymm* 'might, force, greatness of mind ['heart', 'soul']'; *hygegeomor, modgeomor, geomormod* all meaning 'mind or heart or soul-sad'; *hreohmod* 'rough, fierce, savage, troubled of heart ['mind,' 'soul']'; *inwitnet* 'malice-net'; *inwitþanc* 'malice-thought, hostile purpose'; *mod* 'mind, heart, spirit' and its numerous compounds, as, for example, *modgehygd, modgeþonc, modlufu, modsefa*, none of which can be narrowly delimited; *sefa* 'mind, heart, spirit' is perhaps not quite so indeterminate, but there is no way to translate or understand it as having exclusively to do with the intellect *or* the feelings.

One passage from the poem, not untypical in this matter, can illustrate well the intricate fusion of thoughts and feelings that may be present in the breasts or hearts of human beings at times of extreme tension:

> *Þone cwið æt beore   se ðe beah gesyhð,*
> *eald æscwiga,   se ðe eall geman,*
> *garcwealm gumena   – him bið grim sefa –,*
> *onginneð geomormod   geongum cempan*
> *þurh hreðra gehygd   higes cunnian,*
> *wigbealu weccean,   ond ðæt word acwyð* ... (2041–6)

The following E. Talbot Donaldson translation of these lines into modern English, however readable and clear, is largely a failure in its renderings of words for mental and emotional processes, not because of any incompetence in the translator but because modern descriptive language forces distinctions and separations of these processes that are not part of the first phase language of the poem.

> Then at the beer he who sees the treasure, an
> old ash-warrior who remembers it all, the spear-
> death of warriors – grim is his heart – begins, sad
> of mind, to tempt a young fighter in the thoughts
> of his spirit, to awaken war-evil, and speaks this
> word ... (2041–6)

'Heart,' 'mind,' 'thoughts of his spirit' – they are reasonable attempts, but they particularize and separate what is ontologically integrated in the Old English. In second phase or metonymic *langage* there developed a sense in which thought and abstraction, independent of feelings, became possible. But Hrothgar, Wealhtheow, the coast-guard, Wulfgar, Beowulf, Unferth, Hygelac, Wiglaf, and the Geatish messenger are all like the human figures in Judges, 1 and 2 Samuel, Homer's epics, and *The Epic of Gilgamesh*. What burns or turns or wells in their hearts/minds/spirits/souls and gets expressed in their words is usually an inseparable mixture of thought and feeling.

Conceptual allegoresis of *Beowulf* develops when the poem is translated into second phase language, when its concrete metaphors are turned into conceptual abstractions, in a process of 'medievalizing' what in this particular sense is a 'pre-medieval' or 'non-medieval' work of imagining. Such commentary is a kind of deconstruction of the text, an attempt to assimilate it to other linguistic procedures and ideological concerns, a displacing of the primary images and metaphors by ideas assumed to have greater authority. Allegory, as Frye points out, 'is a special form of analogy, a technique of paralleling metaphorical with conceptual language in which the latter has the primary authority' (1982, 10). In *Beowulf*, although there are numerous thematic and didactic elements, the primary emphasis is the other way around. The poem is first and last a product of a corporeal imagination, not of a conceptualizing rationalizing intellect. If it were formal allegory, the host of discrepancies in its metaphorical structure would have been made to conform to a conceptual pattern. If it were 'historical allegory,' there would have been conformity to a pattern of events in history.

Second phase language involves the assumption that there is a world of thought 'separate from and in some respects superior to the physical world of nature' (Frye 1982, 8). In Plato's dialogues it is the search for this separate world that underlies the teaching method of Socrates, who, 'unlike his predecessors in Greek philosophy, professed not to know anything but only to be looking for something' (8). The famous 'irony' of Socrates involves his renouncing the idea that he has personal possession of wisdom. Instead of having it, Socrates purports to be a detached observer of it, as it emerges through discussion and argument. As the Platonic dialogue or symposium unfolds, usually with Socrates guiding the talk, it proceeds to 'a world of ideas, where it can be followed only by the intellectual soul within the body of the seeker' (8). But the language Plato uses to describe this process involves a major break with typically literary forms of expression, a replacement and downgrading of what we have been calling first phase language, which is founded on myth and metaphor, in favour of dialectic.

Socratic irony is absent from *Beowulf*. The narrator and his audience are assumed to have possession of the necessary truth and wisdom. The narrator (like Hrothgar, Beowulf, and Wealhtheow) can and does make judgments about what makes a good life or what, in each circumstance, is a proper or wise kind of behaviour. The human figures in the poem are not seeking wisdom or knowledge or understanding. They all articulate parts of the traditional lore which they already know themselves to possess. Their duty is not to engage in intellectual or spiritual questing but to act according to what they already know. In contrast to the situations in *The Republic* or *The Symposium*, in *Beowulf* when human beings are gathered together – as in the speech-centred scenes in Heorot, beside the mere, in Hygelac's hall, by the dragon's lair, and back in the Geatish stronghold – the large questions of human existence are not open for discussion, nor are they seriously in doubt. There may be particular uncertainties about what *Metod* and fate will unfold in the near or mid-term future, but that does not generate questions and dialectical argument about what is the good, the true, and the beautiful, or about how best human beings can live justly and well together. These things are known. They are integral parts of a lifeworld in which identities and codes of behaviour are familiar and the realities of heaven and hell are experienced directly in the *middangeard*. The problem is how to ensure that what is right and true is not defeated by monsters or by human evil in any of its numerous individual forms.

There is of course acceptance that either of two possible fates awaits each human being from middle earth, after life's battles and banquets are finished, and that both of these are eternal, but heaven and hell are not remote, transcendent concepts. Grendel comes from 'a flood under the earth' (*flod under foldan*, 1361) which is not far from Hrothgar's hall. When he first encounters Beowulf he quickly realizes (750 ff.) that he is in a harder hand-grip than he has ever met before 'on middle earth, in earth's regions' (*middangeardes, / eorþan sceata*). His immediate desire is to flee through the darkness back to hell as fast as he can (*Hyge wæs him hinfus* 'His mind was for him hence-eager'), 'to seek out the company of devils' (*secan deofla gedræg*). That is where he goes, mortally wounded, a little later. Similarly, although heaven is known to be eternal, to be a reality beyond the *middangeard* as well as influential in it, and to be a destination for human souls after the destruction of the *banhus*, it is not imagined or imaged forth in the poem as it is in numerous other Old English texts. The only accounts of blessedness and joy in *Beowulf* are in connection with the great gold-halls fashioned by human beings, most especially Heorot in either its pristine or its restored form. When the frame of reference is to the individual rather than the group, as when Hrothgar predicts everlasting *dom* for Beowulf and that the *Alwalda* 'Wielder of all' will grant the hero every good thing 'as he just now has done' (*sum he nu gyt dyde*, 956), it is clear that these blessings are to be experienced in the here and now of Beowulf's existence as it unfolds on earth, as well as in the hereafter. The eternal reward (*awa to aldre*) begins right now with gift-giving and admiration in Heorot.

If *Beowulf* were primarily a verbal imitation of a transcendent reality beyond itself, it would lend itself more readily than it does to the kind of commentary on it practised in recent decades by those scholars sometimes called 'patristic exegetes.' Frye points out that what makes possible the substitution of analogical or allegorical thought for metaphorical expression is the development of continuous prose, 'the main instrument of thought in the metonymic period' (1982, 10). This was the stock in trade of the Church Fathers and the early exegetes, who took the myths and metaphors of the Bible, of Jewish and Christian apocryphal and hexaemeral writings, and of ancient Greek and Roman culture, and 'rationalized' them into creeds, doctrines, moral instructions, and theological systems. The dominant literary genre used by these men was prose commentary. Their mode of thinking and linguistic expression is also the chosen vehicle of those modern interpreters who seek to understand Old English poetry, including *Beowulf*, by resorting primarily to exegetical commentaries rather than to the poetic language of *Beowulf* itself and also to the functioning poetic diction of other Old English poems. It is the contention of this book (and was also of *The Guest-Hall of Eden*) that there is evident in these texts a much greater diversity of poetic expression and meaning, within the constraints of the traditional word-hoard, than any doctrinal or conceptual analysis can account for, and that it is this poetic fact that continues to have cultural value long after the conceptual systems of patristic and early medieval thought have receded into intellectual history.

Nonetheless there are allegorical elements in *Beowulf* which can be recognized without causing the myths and the particular metaphorical images of this Germanic, Anglo-Saxon, Christian poem to disappear or get sidelined in favour of conceptual formulations. There is in *Beowulf* no closed circularity of logical or doctrinal consistency and coherence. Instead we find a host of logically loose connectives (*Þa ... þa, Ða wæs, Eft wæs, Swa, swa ... swa*), unexplained juxtapositions, and a primary narrative that knows itself free to associate or metaphorically identify human figures and events in the main story with others that are part of the larger verbal culture. Because *Beowulf* is metaphorical, it does not proceed in a resolutely linear way held together by cogent 'therefores.' What we find instead is an extraordinary fusion of sudden, unannounced transitions and an intricate interweaving of daring identifications out of what otherwise would have been insignificant fragments of ancient Germanic life. The primary critical task is not to find reason and concepts veiled in the metaphors but to recognize that it is these very metaphors that best express the realities which the poem embodies. All metaphor is revolt against totalitarian claims. It is a kind of thinking that destabilizes doctrines and ideologies. Metaphor clashes violently in a poem and works against thematic simplifications. It helps the poem to speak several languages and tell several stories at once, and even makes that inevitable. The reason conceptual allegoresis of *Beowulf* is, finally, so disappointing is that it tries to ensure a tautological nicety of rational thought in the poem which falls far short of the imaginative or metaphorical thinking going on in it. We need to accept that the literal surface of the language of *Beowulf* is not somehow incidental to something deeper or higher and to realize that it is by working with this very surface that we gain real insight into the language, thought, and humanity of the poem. There is polysemy in abundance in *Beowulf*, but it is not primarily the polysemy that is constructed by translating its words into metonymic or analogical forms of verbal expression.

It may be, as often surmised, that the architectural ruins that poets of the Anglo-Saxon period absorb into their poems are the symbolic ruins of Roman power. It may also be, as Frye suggests (1982, 12), that the rise of European culture on the ruins of Roman power during the early Christian centuries saw something of a Viconian *ricorso* in literature. Certainly the vernacular languages, including Old English, were bringing in the new poetic features of alliteration and heavy accentual rhythm, so that when Latin was used for poetry it was obliged to use vernacular-dominated patterns quite unlike those of classical Latin. *Beowulf* and the substantial number of other mythopoeic Old English poems, also the Old Saxon *Genesis* and *Heliand* and the oldest layers of the Eddas, all have myth and metaphor as their primary language and may well be part of such a *ricorso*, an early European return to first phase *langage* of the kind used by Homer and Hesiod and by many of the original writers and later redactors of the books of the Bible. Still, the culturally dominant *langage* in Anglo-Saxon times and for a long time after was metonymic and dialectical. It is this mode of thought and verbal expression, with its transcendental perspective and its belief that ultimate reality is beyond the tip of the church spire or on the other side of the *littera* on the manuscript page, that dominates in theology, philosophy, biblical commentaries, and homilies.

The metonymic phase of language commands the cultural centre at least until the sixteenth century. By then the inherently tautological character of medieval thought increasingly was being seen as problematic. If it is revelation that divulges truth about reality and if human reason and language can proceed only syllogistically to make deductions dependent on an original revelation, then there can be nothing genuinely new. The metonymic verbal resources of analogy and syllogism, moreover, contain no way of distinguishing between what actually exists and what does not exist. For centuries it seemed acceptable to believe that the study of God included the study of the created world, as the second Scripture, and to rely on an allegorical language of transcendence as the main verbal tool for such study. But the unicorn in the garden with the lady, like the great Fastitocalon in the Old English *Physiologus* and the fire-dragon in *Beowulf*, logically and verbally has as much or as little reality as has a Norman horse in the Bayeux Tapestry. The fact that historically there were horses in William's expedition and that there never was a unicorn is irrelevant to this kind of closed-system thinking. God may be reality and language may have to be metonymic, always an abstraction from the reality it would speak about, but how do we know the existential difference between the fabulous unicorn and the actual horse? As Frye points out, 'the question of actual existence does not enter the ordering of words as such' (1982, 12).

To get to that question, as Francis Bacon realized, and as John Locke showed, you had to have some criterion of reality external to words. You had to start treating things in nature as real objects, not simply as coded images of divine truth. With the establishment of empirical thought, the mythical sense of the inseparability of subject and object, expressed in the first phase language of immanence, is thought to have been shattered. So, too, the separation of subject and object that was beginning to emerge in the second phase is now in the third phase assumed to be complete. Philosophy now starts with a clear separation of subject and object, and nothing exists in the human intellect that has not previously existed in the senses. The observing subject exposes itself through its senses to the impact of an objective physical world. Thinking follows the suggestions of sense experience. Accordingly, verbal language comes to be thought of as primarily descriptive of an objective natural order. No longer is the order of words (like the languages of music and the visual arts) a huge *speculum* meant to show forth reflections of the mind of God. Rather, the criterion of truth is thought to be related to the external physical source that words are supposed to describe, as accurately as they can. If the verbal construct corresponds to the physical or objective facts, if it provides a convincing description of them, it is a 'true' statement.

In this third phase 'descriptive' language, metaphysics sits very uncomfortably, if at all. The allegorical language of medieval culture with its conception of a transcendent 'God' increasingly is relegated to the fringes of the dominant culture. Still, at least as late as Immanuel Kant (1724–1804), who dealt drastically with what he saw as the extreme eighteenth-century confidence in reason, the earlier metonymic universe continues to function, albeit in a foreshortened way. Although Kant ruthlessly rebutted traditional arguments for the existence of God and was particularly hard on the Deists, he also continued to think of God as the ultimate being, in a noumenal world beyond the phenomenal (spatial and temporal) world of experience. Because, beyond reason, human beings in Kant's philosophy have a feeling of moral obligation and are confronted by the 'categorical imperative,' they can be pleasing to God. But the dominant post-Kantian culture tended increasingly to the view either that 'God' was dead or, at most, that he was not relevant in serious inquiry into the nature of the actual world.

It was Vico who countered the emerging rationalist dogmas of the Enlightenment with the idea that the deepest layers of human creativity, of culture, and so of human history lie not in reason or in the human will but in the imagination, particularly in the human ability to think in images as well as in concepts, to fashion myths and metaphors and put them to work as a basis for action in, against, and with the rest of nature. When this creative work is engaged in, nature is humanized and made into a dwelling or home, sufficient to the fulfilment of distinctively human (as compared to animal) desires and needs. For Kant and the Enlightenment, metaphor and myth were the source of error. For Vico, and it is this that gives him his influence on James Joyce and other moderns, they were the basis of a uniquely human kind of intellection which is projective as well as reflective or mimetic. This mode of thinking is capable not only of registering and combining perceptions and experiences but also of shaping them, in the ways that poets (like the *Beowulf* artist) shape language and, by shaping it, reanimate, revivify, and make it new. The art of the shaper reveals previously unnoticed potentialities for expression in the words, and so permits the world to emerge in a new and unexpected light.

There is one sharply limited sense in which the descriptive, third phase of language is a return to the first phase. As in *Beowulf* and *The Dream of the Rood*, also in *The Iliad*, *The Odyssey*, and much of the Bible, there is assumed to be a direct relation between the order of nature and the order of words. But the relation between the two in the third age is not an integral one between words and the world of immanence within which they function, free from the subject-object split. The nature described in third phase language is not one in which an initially mighty Hrothgar through words of power can command a Heorot into being, or a God-man dying in battle on a cross can cause the weeping of all Creation. The earlier integrated, interpenetrating cosmos, with its identity of subject and object, is not part of the descriptive phase of language, however many times that kind of cosmos can still be invoked in the metaphorical expressions of poets and other creative minds. So far as the imaginative literature of the eighteenth and nineteenth centuries is concerned, simile is much more characteristic than metaphor, and the similitudes described usually have their primary reference point in the actual world, as they do, for example, in Wordsworth's conception of the poetic process as half-perceiving and half-creating.

It is not only in this kind of historically later 'low mimetic' literature itself that we see the assumption that phenomenological reference points are the really important ones. The scientific, inductive mode of thinking comes to dominate in scholarship as well as in philosophy and the physical sciences. This is true of the scholarship directed to the texts of earlier periods, most of which were written within the context of first or second phase cultural assumptions.

The problem, a large one, is that much of the scientific, historical scholarship focused on pre-medieval and medieval literary texts (including the first two centuries of *Beowulf* studies) was not yet sufficiently aware of its own 'descriptive phase' assumptions. Not only was it taken for granted, for example, that *Beowulf* should be studied as a means to learning about part of early 'European' or 'German' or 'Danish' or 'British' history but also that the poem in some important way is a verbal representation or description of an objective world that actually existed in the sixth, seventh, or eighth century. Even the manifestly mythological elements of the poem, what we might now call the most obviously metaphorical or figurative language, were thought by some to have a necessary, direct correlation with natural phenomena of the actual world outside the text. As Karl Müllenhof (1889) would have had it, Beowulf in some phenomenal sense *is* a rescuing god who struggles with the elements and the forces of nature, Grendel *is* the stormy North Sea in the spring threatening human dwellings, his mother *is* the depths of the North Sea, the dragon *is* autumn and the coming of wild weather, and Beowulf's death *is* the coming of winter. Other scholars, interested in history and intent on finding phenomenological reference points, but not, like Müllenhof, in grounding mythology empirically and chronologically, tried to read *Beowulf* as a political or historical allegory, as a representation of actual people, places, and events, or at the very least as a work whose most important elements were so-called real world ones. John Earle, for example, thought in 1892 that the poem was written in the last quarter of the eighth century to help Offa's son Ecgferth. Much later, in 1943, George Bond treated the text as a description of actual people, situations, and political events in the reigns of the Mercian kings Beornwolf (823–6) and Wiglaf (828–38). More recently, but with a good deal more awareness that *Beowulf* is primarily a fictional work of the imagination, such scholars as Patrick Wormald, Roberta Frank, and John Niles seek clarification of the poem's meanings by linking it with particular historical situations or events (Wormald 1978; Frank 1982; Niles 1993).[6]

The purposes of this kind of scientific or historical scholarship are good and necessary, provided that they do not obscure or dismiss the purposes of a poet thinking in poetic language, whether the poet is contemporary with the scholar-critic or from a thousand years earlier. One cannot read far in the Anglo-Saxon poetic records without confronting the large fact that this is not a literature of verisimilitudes, natural or historical. In *Christ II* (ASPR 3, 22–3:712–43), in a passage I have referred to already, we find a particularly vivid use of first phase language. The figure of the cosmic Christ as *cyning engla, / meotud meahtum swið* 'the King of angels, the Measurer strong in power' comes wreathed in glory, bounding over the mountains and leaping over the high hills, to free the world and all earth-dwellers by performing six further 'leaps': incarnation, nativity, crucifixion, deposition and burial, harrowing of hell, ascension. The sense of power and energy that is being verbally released in such a passage (the metaphor comes partly from the Song of Solomon, 2:8, through a sermon by Gregory the Great, *PL*, 76.1218–19) depends radically on a conception of reality in which there is no split between subject and object. The leaping Christ (like numerous other mythical and metaphorical conceptions in Old English poetry, including in *Beowulf*) is in no way a product of careful observation and detailed description of the objective world of nature, society, and history. Nor is the figure of the leaping God-man even the result of thinking theologically about nature as the revealed, second book of God, and interpreting each image metonymically as an allegorical sign pointing to a transcendental reality. The leaping Christ and his other Old English poetic companions are a product of a metaphorical sense of the identity of life or power or energy or reality itself between human beings, the cosmos, and God.

What I am concerned with here is not the question of whether in writing about Old English poetry it is possible to follow an interest in the history of ideas and doctrines or in the history of people, places, and events in Anglo-Saxon times, but with the question of what resources of language and poetic thought the Anglo-Saxon poets were using. What kind of criticism will help us understand this old poetry without translating (or distorting) it into either second phase allegorical language or into third phase descriptive language? It is my contention that in much of Old English poetry first phase language is used with an immediacy and vitality that the later poetry in the English language never consistently captures. There is enormous imaginative confidence in the way Old English poetry presents its visions of reality. The modern or postmodern consciousness, aware of multiple ironies in the later products of our multicultural world, meets in this poetry no aporetic anxieties about whether Christ really was God or whether the Creation-Doomsday story told to Cædmon was true or not, or about whether Beowulf could actually have the strength of thirty men in his hand-grasp, or whether the door of Heorot could or would fling itself open at the mere touch of Grendel's hand.

That there are enormous limitations in such first phase language is, to us, obvious enough. Even if we do make ourselves receptive to the exuberance and confidence of the myths and metaphors expressed in the poems which have survived, we do so with an awareness that this kind of language is restricted by its identity with nature in the ancient sense. *Beowulf* does not even begin to escape the assumption that the earth-dragon is as real as anything else in the poem, nor is there any evidence to suggest that the poet or his audience would question the possibility of a hall falling into the possession of a Grendel from hell. It is not difficult for us, accustomed to scientific and historical explanations of natural and man-made disasters, to interpret the monsters in the poem as projections of natural or human destructiveness, and to interpret the metaphors for the Deity also as human projections, but in doing so we distance ourselves from the cultural assumptions of first phase language. The exegetes would release us from the tyranny of nature implicit in such language by translating the poem into metonymic or allegorical formulations, but that is not only an unhistorical distortion of what *Beowulf* is and does, but an unsatisfactory way for us to try to experience this early English poem as it actually functions verbally, and then critically to describe it. If first phase imagining does not distinguish between subject and object (between human consciousness and things external to it), second phase language is little better, because, as I said above, it has no way of distinguishing between what exists and what does not exist. Its epistemological starting-point in revelation and its deductive mode of reasoning preclude such empirical analysis.

It is clear from the main body of modern criticism about Old English literature that there is still a great deal of conscious or unconscious reliance on the assumption that *Beowulf* and most other Old English poems are imagined and expressed in descriptive language and that we can learn a good deal about the materiality of Anglo-Saxon life and customs from them. Because of the cultural dominance of descriptive language in the last two centuries, most literate people are aware of the endless variety of what literature can express about the objective empirical world (including internal psychic realities objectified). Our scholarship, say in a field like Anglo-Saxon studies, is endlessly inventive in the number of general and miscellaneous subjects and topics it can identify for description, cataloguing, concording, inputting, and analysing – all such materials being in some way or other a part of Anglo-Saxon culture and so capable of being objectified, described, and recorded. The whole vast data bank becomes something that we are professionally responsible for knowing about. So far as *Beowulf* among the poems of the extant Anglo-Saxon poetic records is concerned, our scholarship is particularly inventive in the number of things it can think to say about just this one favoured poetic text.

Yet as we work through the annual bibliographies and make our decisions about what we must read and what we should read, whether we ever do or not, a curious malaise can take over. What is it, we may ask, that is being revealed to us in this endless, productive round? Which of these studies and acts of description and analysis take us back inside the myths and metaphors of the strong, sinewy poem itself, and which leave it an objective textual thing to observe, poke at, analyse, measure – and diminish? When a colleague experienced in Old English says to me, '*Beowulf* is so boring,' I think, it is not *Beowulf* that is boring, it is some of the mental operations prescribed by our kind of scientific culture for observing and describing such texts that are boring. Or, even though they may be endlessly fascinating for certain kinds of scholarly minds, they tell us almost nothing about what *Beowulf* is and does when experienced from within its own words and poetic language. As long as we continue to think in demotic, third phase language while describing *Beowulf*, we remain outside it, treating it as an objective thing and preventing its metaphors from working in our heads. There have been a lot of pseudo-historical fantasies in *Beowulf* scholarship. The poet/narrator says simply, 'We have heard,' and then tells his story. It's a story: what do we make of it? As scholars we ask how much of it is true, meaning by that based on actual people and events, but since it's also a poem held together by myth and metaphor a better question is 'What does the poet make of it?' – whatever 'it' was, or was not. What is really happening as the myths and metaphors come together in this particular shaping of words into this particular story?

Stories with strong mythical or romance plots often are presented as something the teller has been told or heard, with the suggestion that we have to listen and respond actively to something that otherwise might be lost or forgotten. If the unique *Beowulf* text from a millennium or more ago has any real capacity to justify the endless attention it gets, it has to be because it takes us into modes of thinking and possibilities of experience not normally encountered in our faculty offices, classrooms, and private studies. Either there are real treasures hidden in the word-hoard as it is used in *Beowulf*, and they are still available to us, or we have no good reason for encouraging students and others to go on trying to penetrate the poem's linguistic lair. If the poem is to continue to live as more than a ruin of the past, we have to bring out its metaphors and myths. We have to identify with them and let them work in our heads. Until we do, the realities of the poem are hidden, secret, and unknown. When we engage in this direct, inner search, we are doing the opposite to looking for the poem's meanings in the facts and events of history outside the text. We are relearning the fact that metaphor destabilizes facts, and creates its own identities and meanings. The real meaning is metaphorical. The mere, Heorot, the Scyldings, the hero, and the dragon, and much else in the poem, are *radically* metaphorical. This apparently is the only way in which the language of the word-hoard could convey the sense of the presence of the numinous in the middle dwelling.

4

Ealdgesegena Worn Gemunde: Memory and Identity

More than any other of the extant long narrative poems in Old English, *Beowulf* is an intensive, respectful remembering and re-creating of the world of the Germanic *dryht*, from imaginative perspectives shaped in significant ways by biblical myth. In this poem the aristocratic world of the *dryht* in middle earth is the main object of attention. It is imagined with a plenitude and detail accorded it in no other extant text. Its social and political forms, its rituals, its concept of property, its sense of ancestral and kinship values, and its definitions of ethical human behaviour all are presented with high seriousness, and with admiration. These cultural realities, situated and deeply rooted in what the Anglo-Saxons thought of as the middle dwelling, are never devalued or held in contempt in favour of other-worldly loyalties, as they regularly are in the hagiographic narrative poems and in some of the shorter poems in the surviving corpus. For whatever communal or private reasons, *Beowulf* clearly is the product of a desire to remember and honour the codes and rituals of the gold-hall world, even while scrutinizing them *sub specie aeternitatis*. The poem is a sustained act of remembering and thinking about past glories and tragedies, with a view to understanding how best human beings might live together. It is apparently addressed to the human faculties of memory and intelligence, and also to the capacity to look ahead and foresee the implications of particular kinds of individual and group behaviour. *Beowulf* is a text about both wisdom and prudence: it looks to the traditional past for guidance and inspiration in order to live well in the present and the future. But it is not sanguine about the possibility of any *dream* 'joy' enduring in middle earth.

The two preceding chapters have been attempts to show how *Beowulf* is a curiously inwrought verbal composition in which figurative or metaphorical language functions powerfully to suggest or establish poetic identities for a diversity of things, places, beings, and events. The overall result of this metaphorical thinking is a poem that is imaginatively alive in all its parts, each of these contributing to a flexible interwoven unity of images that contains within it many daring poetic correspondences. In this present chapter, I concentrate on what the poem expresses and shows about the processes of memory and association in establishing such identities, as a crucial part of its narrative art.

The three most memorable spatial images in *Beowulf* are the great gold-hall Heorot, the turbid monster-infested mere, and the space around the dragon's barrow. It is in these metaphorical places that the figure of the hero, in youth and age, performs his major acts of rescue on behalf of two beleaguered peoples. Around these imagined *loci* the poet has shaped a strong primary narrative whose outline is stark and simple. It is a story not easily forgotten once heard or read. It is articulated in the forceful, sinewy language of the traditional word-hoard in ways that make abundantly clear that whoever fashioned the poem was a master of a traditional art and was using it to tell an absorbing tale, and so to stir the imaginations of listeners or readers by involving them directly in an intricate, connotative experience of words, as these words interact with each other in evocative, shaping ways. But the connotative art of *Beowulf* goes beyond the imaginative interweaving of verbal formulas and phrases from the word-hoard. Even as one word finds another, and then others, to provide variations and incremental meanings, so the main story finds other stories. Memories and half-memories of past events in Scylding and Geatish experience, legends of ancient Germania, biblical stories, and prophecies or foretellings of events yet to unfold all come into focus in greater or lesser detail. Each of these stories, some merely alluded to or obliquely indicated, adds narrative depth and resonance to the main narrative. *Beowulf* is one story, and it is many stories.

In another sense as well, the foreground narrative about the hero and his three great battles does not stand as complete in itself. Although the poem is demonstrably a complex integrated whole (even with the fairly minor inconsistencies long since noted by scholars), it is also an open-ended tale of two kingdoms, both of which are expected to experience future disaster. These unhappy coming events are not yet clearly known in the narrative foreground of the poem, although they are to some extent foreseeable and foreseen. In the total fiction, Heorot and the Scyldings fade from view gradually, first when Beowulf back in Geatland tells Hygelac about his recent experiences among the Danes and, in the telling, predicts their probable bleak future. Then again, later, at the end of Beowulf's life, the battles with the Grendel kin are importantly but vestigially recalled, as part of the protagonist's recessional memories (2345–54a; 2397–2400, perhaps; 2426–7; 2510–21). Similarly with the Geats, when they are last described they are anticipating a disastrous future as soon as their enemies come to know that their protector-lord is dead (2884–91; 2910b–13a; 2922–

3007a; 3014–27). Neither the Scylding nor the Geatish story is fully told, then, within the poem itself, though theoretically both stories could have been, since they are imagined as having long antedated the poet's own time.

Nor, for that matter, is the story of Beowulf himself completely told within the poem. At the end of the narrative about him, the great memorial barrow sits there on *Hronesnæs* 'Whale's Ness' addressing itself to the memories, intelligences, and physical and moral capacities of future *sæliðend* 'seafarers' 'when from far off they drive their tall ships over the darkness of the floods' (*ða ðe brentingas / ofer floda genipu   feorran drifað*, 2807b–8). The barrow invites all such who will come after to remember this greatest of men and then, presumably, to think ahead in order to live well in a dangerous world. *Beowulf* is a work of verbal art devoted not only to recalling the storied past – ancient, several generations back, and more recent – but also to expressing deep forebodings and anxieties about the future, and to giving guidance to an Anglo-Saxon audience or readership about how to face that precarious prospect. It is a poem whose imagining remains incomplete, both for those early people and for us. As in a kenning or a riddle, the audience and we are told all we need to be, but we are not told everything. Rather we are invited by the poem's narrative incompleteness and by its inclusive communal rhetoric to engage in a mental response of actively assisting the story to go on being further developed. *Beowulf* is a work that resists closure and opens out into further 'seafaring' space, through its being centred on the decentring device of metaphor. It comes to us as a scribally written manuscript, an absence, as Derrida might say, invoking a mythical presence of a live hero and his world 'behind' the manuscript; the background presence gradually shifts to a foreground, the re-creation of that living reality in our minds as readers. Once that act of historical imagination has taken place, we are in a state of mental readiness in which the metaphors and myths of the poem's language events can move into the foreground of our minds.

If we are to understand how *Beowulf* depends for a large measure of its impact on its capacity to appeal to the faculty of memory, and then through that mental process to generate thought and right action for the future, it is necessary to consider how it has been organized with these purposes in mind. It seems clear that for Old English poets generally and for the *Beowulf* poet in particular, the word-hoard served as what Frances Yates (1966),[1] if she had focused on this part of English literature, might have called a memory bank, and that much of the extant Old English poetic corpus was composed as an *ars memorativa*, both in the specific verbal resources it uses and in its narrative and thematic subject matter. When a verbal formula or poem was composed, it was stored in the treasure-house of memory – both in actual human memories of people living at the time and, when the culture moved into literacy, in manuscript forms. So fashioned and preserved it became part of Anglo-Saxon England's imaginative, spiritual, and moral resources, to be taken out and used to inspire, instruct, and bind together the particular society that possessed it. During the history of *Beowulf* scholarship and criticism there have understandably been many and varied explorations of the question of what kind of social and cultural uses could have been made of the poem in its own time and place, whatever that time and place may have been. The most valuable of such efforts in recent years, each attempting to relate *Beowulf* to a particular historical situation or events, are Wormald (1978), Frank (1982), Earl (1983, 1987, 1991, 1994), Howe (1989, especially 143–80), Niles (1993), and Hill (1995).[2]

As in the traditional memory theatres described by Yates, so in *Beowulf*, the poet's use of selected spaces and the association with them of many lively images is crucial to the memorability of the poem. Within *Beowulf*, as we have seen, the spatial areas of both the humanly fashioned environment and the surrounding physical world are not naturalistically or representationally described. Rather they are symbolic metaphorical settings in which things are said and events take place. The hall interiors (both on the surface of middle earth and underwater or underground), the seascapes, the mead-fields outside Heorot, the nesses or promontories, the seacoasts, the unknown paths to the mere and to the dragon's lair, the twisted, frost-enshrouded woods surrounding the terrible waters over which the heavens weep – all these spatial areas are the imagined *loci* in which the poet puts images of particular things, people, and monsters, and in which particular actions and counter-actions take place. These imagined *loci* are identified and characterized in a variety of memorable ways and they are the settings in which the characters do three things: they tell their respective versions of events or situations, they interact with each other, and sometimes they perform actions that advance the plot. It is the verbal ordering and filling of these imagined spaces that constitutes the curiously inwrought tale that is the poem's main narrative, and its engagement in a world of myth.

If it is true, as I am convinced it is, that this poem imaginatively is not 'medieval,' that it is a product of first phase metaphorical language not of metonymy and analogical thought founded on similes or implied similes, then it is not 'Augustinian' in the way that some modern 'exegetical' commentaries would have it: a work whose main significance is a Christian conceptual and doctrinal one. But *Beowulf* is Augustinian in a more general and important way. For Augustine, memory was one of the great powers of the human soul and was crucial for any didactic art designed to discourage wrong behaviour and encourage virtue. In his *Confessions* (10, 8–21:208–21) there is a brilliant extended account of the faculty of memory. Augustine there speaks of the fields and spacious palaces of his memory into which innumerable treasures of images are brought, from things of all sorts perceived by the senses. His main point is that we human beings cannot remember or understand subtle or spiritual things without the help of these lively images, which appeal initially to our senses and through them to our imaginations. Yates's study adds to this influential Augustinian tenet about the necessity of lively images the equally important realization that remembering depends heavily on how the images are associated and ordered in relation to each other. Whether the *Beowulf* poet had ever heard of Augustine's ideas on memory, or had any conscious concept of a memory bank as this tradition had come down from classical times, it is clear that he did have a functioning concept of the word-hoard and that in the poem there are numerous junctures at which a particular event, place, thing, or character provides a mnemonic starting-point. At such points a speaker in the text assists others within the poem, as well as the audience (and readers), to remember something else that either parallels or contrasts with the immediate foreground subject, and so helps identify that subject and vest it with wider meaning. This process of association, this combining of background and foreground, has the function of making memorable whatever is being told about in the main story, by linking it with something already known, by locating it, that is, in a traditional space in the collective memory.

The linking of Beowulf's killing of Grendel with Sigmund's slaying of a fire-dragon is one example of how prestige and authority can be given to a recent event by 'placing' it in a particular category of things important to be remembered, in this case stories about heroes killing monsters. Through the association with something already well known and probably unforgettable, Beowulf's victory over Grendel is firmly fixed in the collective mind in the society's mythology, where it will continue to resonate both as part of the still-unfolding story of Beowulf's own life and, perhaps, although we have no direct evidence of this from the Anglo-Saxon period, in the wider memories of its culture. Such memories, the poem reminds us in many ways, are all part of one large, complex, interweaving story in which, in one of the grappling hero Beowulf's several metaphorical identities, he too is *Sige-Mund* 'Victory Hand'. Persons or objects in this metaphorically conceived story achieve existence by being processable through a traditional model or generic character. As hero, Beowulf is not analogous to or like Sigmund: he is Sigmund, because he shares Sigmund's being.

Both Beowulf and Sigmund become famous for their brave deeds. That is what heroes do. The poet's linking of them has both a general and several particular meanings. In a wide cultural sense it implies that no one who ever lives bravely and generously in the *middangeard*, as Beowulf is doing throughout the poem, is free from the procession of humankind's heroes. There is also, as the narrator indicates, a demonic procession, through whom the audience can see their own corruption in a series of inversions, as in the case of Heremod, described in this same part of the poem, and in the monsters. Heremod, according to Anglo-Saxon and Norse genealogies, was the father or predecessor of Scyld, belonging to a line of kings earlier than the Scylding dynasty (Murray 1981; Frank 1981, 162–3). After his fall the Danes for a long time endured the misery of being *aldorlease* 'lordless' (15) and needing a protector in the true procession of heroes.

In a more particular frame of reference, the scop's characterizing summary of Sigmund's life, with its experiences of 'many strange' or 'unknown things' (*uncupes fela*, 876), its far journeys, and its involvement in the endless feuding of the Germanic world, could almost equally well apply to Beowulf's own life experiences. Sigmund is especially renowned, moreover, for slaying a fire-dragon and retrieving a treasure-hoard, as Beowulf will be, though Sigmund, unlike Beowulf, survives to enjoy his treasure. We are told as well that Beowulf's illustrious predecessor has already laid low with his sword many of the race of giants (883–4a), as Beowulf in his story still unfolding also has done. Finally we are also reminded that Sigmund has received 'after his death-day not a little fame' (*æfter deaðdæge dom unlytel*, 885). Beowulf will too. Depending on what we make of the final judgment of the poem on heroic values, it may be that Beowulf receives a fame meant to be understood as more splendid than that of Sigmund. His hearth-comrades mourning his death remember his great deeds, his acts of courage, and his desire for recognition, but they also memorialize their tribe's great one from among 'the world's kings' (*wyruldcyninga*) for the humane qualities of mildness, gentleness, and kindness (3169 ff.).

In actual human existence, one of the better tricks that human memory plays is to associate with each other people, places, things, and events that never touch outside of dreams, imagining, and story-telling. When this happens in poetry it may still be a trick, but if so it is either planned or permitted by the poet, and it is basic to the art involved. The language of poetry is associative, proceeding centripetally to juxtapose and link, often metaphorically, what previously has been unrelated or has not been related before in just this way. The crowd of people inside the *Beowulf* poet's memory hoard who emerge into the poem includes numerous dryht lords and warrior thanes, kings and queens, princes and princesses, and monsters. During the almost two hundred years of *Beowulf* scholarship which we students of the poem build on, many of the cultural associations surrounding these figures have been identified, and it is a reasonable surmise that some at least of these associations would have been known by early audiences or readers. Twenty-five of the human figures in the poem appear in other texts, beginning with Hygelac (*Chochilaichus*), who actually lived and was recorded in the sixth century in the *History of the Franks* by Gregory of Tours (Garmonsway 1980, 112–13). The Danes of the poem who appear in other records are Heremod, Scyld Scefing, Sceaf, Beowulf the son of Scyld, Healfdene, Hrothgar, Halga, Hrothulf, Heoroward, Healfdene's daughter, and Hrethric. The Swedes with outside appearances are Ongentheow, Ohthere, Onela, Eanmund, and Eadgils. The Anglian king Offa, the Heathobards Froda and Ingeld, the Frisian Finn, the Volsungs Sigmund and Fitela, and the Goths Eormenric and Hama also appear elsewhere. In addition, there are analogues for Beowulf's fights with humanoid monsters and with the dragon, but there is no Beowulf outside our text. There are references to the Brosing necklace, and there are parallels for the funeral customs in the poem.

These analogues appear in a wide assortment of texts – of many types and dates and in several languages – which have survived from the several hundred years following Gregory's chronicle.[3] These texts, along with the Old English poetic corpus, especially the poems of the Junius manuscript, can be read intertextually to illuminate the study of *Beowulf*. But even giving full recognition to this diverse centrifugal verbal context, it still appears on the basis of the external evidence available that a substantial number of the associations between events, people, places, and things in the poem are made only within the poem itself, as for example in the case just discussed of Sigmund and Beowulf or in the implied comparison between the queens Wealhtheow and Hildeburh. Whether or not the correlations and identifications encountered in the text are newly made in this poem, they are important to the way it holds together, both structurally and thematically. The great figures from the past are meant to form indelible impressions, as Scyld does, and Sigmund does, and as Ecgtheow and Hrethel do, and as Heremod, in a negative way, also does. They are extraordinary romance figures in the imagination which shaped the poem and, as such, are meant to inhabit listeners' and readers' minds.

It is not only the significance of the characters, human and non-human, and their actions that is partly revealed through these associations. Places (Heorot, the mere, the dragon's lair) also are surrounded by an accumulation of metaphorical meanings to the point of achieving mythical identities connecting them with paradise, hell, and Doomsday. Things or objects – weapons, bodily ornaments, pieces of armour, other treasures – also come into focus encircled by cultural memories and associations so that they carry stories with them and take on new narrative identities as they move through time and space, from one owner to another. Perhaps 'owner' is the wrong word for those who receive and hold, for a time, the treasured objects that loom large in the poem both in the gift-giving rituals and in their opposite, that antisocial hoarding and stinginess which the poem anathematizes. The human figures themselves regularly are identified in terms of their kinship and dryht relationships and interactions, that is in their semi-public and public roles rather than as sharply individualized or private psychological entities. Similarly, the physical objects bestowed on some of them as gifts, like their lives themselves, have more the character of a loan than of a private possession to be held for some individualistic purpose.

We have noted already some of the ways in which an object like a sword – Hrunting, for example, made by the archetypal Germanic smith Weland, or the *eotenisc* 'giantish' sword found in the mere, with its Genesis story of the conflict between God and the giants – serves as a rich focus of meaning even while playing a role in the unfolding narrative. Another of the vivid story-telling objects in the poem is the necklace bestowed on Beowulf by Wealhtheow at the banquet celebrating the victory over Grendel (1195b–1214a). In the ongoing foreground narrative this extraordinary object is associated by the narrator with the Brosing necklace from the world of Germanic myth and legend. The necklace given Beowulf is one of several handsome gifts from the courteous, cup-bearing queen of the Scyldings. But the narrator singles it out as something especially wonderful. As a physical object it is introduced as *healsbeaga mæst* 'the largest' or 'finest' or 'most glorious of neck-rings' which he the narrator, has heard spoken of on earth. Then, piling up meanings, he says that he has 'heard of no better hoard-treasure of heroes under the heavens' (*Nænigne ... under swegle   selran hyrde / hordmaðum hæleþa*, 1197–8a). Next he links it with the Brosing necklace, a story-encrusted heirloom with a rich past identity, which brings some of the associations of that other fabulous object into the story of the hero in his relations with both the Danes and the Geats. Both necklaces are story-laden objects. Both have positive and negative connotations and their stories interpenetrate each other.

The narrator's method of introducing the Brosing necklace is allusive and oblique. Because of this we cannot be sure of the extent of the narrative echoing and foreshadowing involved with it. This much we are told directly: someone called Hama 'carried away the Brosing necklace to the bright city' (*Hama ætwæg / to þære byrhtan byrig   Brosinga mene*);[4] in doing so, Hama was fleeing 'Eormenric's cunning hatred' (*searoniðas ... Eormenrices*); Hama 'chose eternal help' or 'benefit' (*ecne ræd*).' We are also told (1202 ff.) that Hygelac was wearing the necklace from Wealhtheow on his final, disastrous expedition against the Frisians and that when his *feorh* 'life, body' came into 'the embrace of the Franks' (*in Francna fæþm*) the ring was part of the plunder they took 'after the war-shearing' (*æfter guðsceare*), when they left the Geats to hold 'the dwelling-place of corpses' (*hreawic*). In this passage we have another of the poem's curious reorderings of time. Even as Wealhtheow is presenting the neck-ring to Beowulf, we are being told part of the sequence of events that it will pass through much later in the main narrative. When the Scylding queen says, then, 'Enjoy this ring, dear Beowulf, young man, with happiness' (*Bruc ðisses beages, Beowulf leofa, / hyse, mid hæle,* 1216–17a), her words sound almost ominous, following as they do hard on the account of the bloody fate of Hygelac. It is almost a thousand lines later (2172 ff.) that we learn that Beowulf, whom we are seeing here receiving the necklace from the queen of the Danes, gives it to the queen of the Geats. We are not told how or why it afterwards comes into Hygelac's possession, but, since Hygd is his wife and queen, it hardly seems necessary to speculate about possible forgetfulness on the part of the poet (Klaeber, 179, n. 1202).

The allusion to the Brosing necklace is almost opaque. If it is to be understood in any other than a minimal way, it requires a verbal context of other stories and legends beyond this poem to fill in its substance and meaning. Because the mention of the necklace does in fact point to this wider context, it indicates something important about the narrative art of the poem, a feature analogous on a macro level to the way in which the figurative language itself works on a micro level. Like the language, the stories expressed are artful, oblique allusions to some wider area of significance, but often with no real definition or description of any specific meaning in that area. Much of the time in this text we are involved in a narrative art of suggestion and indirection rather than one of full and complete story-telling. Traditional narrative materials and newer elements are combined in allusive, circuitous ways that make real demands on listeners and readers. Generally, in human experience, poems come out of other poems and stories out of other stories. *Beowulf*, in fact, is at once a unique poem and a product of the formulas, themes, and tales already contained in the word-hoard. It is apparently a rich innovative gathering and combining of traditional materials from several times and places. It unavoidably depends then for some of its impact and meaning on how many of its stories the audience or readers know, and so are in a position to remember in a sufficiently active, participative way that the stories can do their allusive, suggestive work in this poem. If there ever were in existence exclusively oral accounts known to some of the original audience(s), they are irretrievably lost. We who come a thousand or so years later have either to immerse ourselves in the other relevant texts of early medieval Germania or depend on the documentary findings of scholars, in order to enter even partly into the collective acts of remembering which ideally are involved in reading and understanding *Beowulf* as an expression of its own cultural world.

In the case of the Brosing necklace and the human figures associated with it, what do we as hypothetical members of an original audience of *Beowulf* need to know? If we look at the first ring of intertextual readings, other Old English poems, it is *Deor* and *Widsith* that are most immediately relevant, since it is they that allude, as enigmatically as *Beowulf* itself does, to the figure of Eormenric. In *Deor* he is characterized as a 'grim' or 'fierce king' (*grim cyning*, ASPR 3, 179:23) of 'wolfish thought' (*wylfenne geþoht*, 22) who held sway in the kingdom of the Goths, and whose warriors sat in misery and dread, wishing his rule would end. In *Widsith*, Eormenric is similarly characterized, at one point, as 'the savage treacherous one' or 'the savage one who breaks' or 'is false to his pledge' (*wraþes wærlogan*, ASPR 3, 149:9), but at two others (88–92; 109–11) he is acknowledged as a figure of generosity. It is the first of these characteristics with its malignant connotations of power and wealth ruthlessly used that seems to be working in *Beowulf*, where the narrator tells us that Hama was fleeing Eormenric's 'treacherous' or 'cunning quarrels' (*searoniðas*, 1200) when he fled to a bright city carrying the necklace. So far as Hama is concerned, *Deor* does not mention him, but *Widsith* does (124b–30), referring to him as one of two *wræccan* 'exiles' (the other is Wudga) who 'with twisted gold' (*wundnan golde*) wield power over men and women in the land of the Goths over which Eormenric rules. This vignette in one of Widsith's lists adds only a little information to the equally sparse allusion to Hama in *Beowulf*. None of this advances understanding very far. It seems clear that the original audience or readers of all three Old English poems were expected to know something beyond what these texts themselves mention. As Muir (1994, 2, 566–7) says of the poets of *Deor* and *Widsith*, 'both treat of Germanic history and lore in an elliptical manner which assumes a wide knowledge of traditional material on the part of the audience.'

It is this something additional that has been assembled over the decades in modern times by a series of scholars who began with the Old English poems and moved outward in a centrifugal way, through the numerous texts that seemed most relevant for explicating the allusions in the Old English poems. Their searches have revealed a rich intertextuality for Eormenric, Hama, and the Brosing necklace, some of which is summarized in Klaeber's and Wrenn's editions of *Beowulf*, in Chambers's *Introduction*, and in editions of *Widsith* and *Deor*.[5] The essential texts are translated and brought together in chapter 8 of Garmonsway (1980). The writings included there span the centuries from the fourth to the fourteenth. Obviously, even on the basis of dating alone, most of these could not have been known directly as texts by the poet or his audience. But since each of them briefly or more fully provides part of a body of traditional interconnecting lore – composed of history, legend, and myth – about Eormenric, Hama, and the Brosing necklace, and because even the texts that post-date *Beowulf* convey traditional older material, each text in its own way can cast some light on the force of the association of the necklace given to Beowulf with the famous *Brosinga mene*. My purpose here is not to recapitulate these old writings – that is easily done by readers for themselves – but to recognize the fact of this object's narrative resonance from romance and myth. The cultural memory or intertextuality tells a good deal about the Brosing necklace, including its once having been the prized possession of the goddess Freyja. Now, somehow, at least part of that resonance has come into the primary narrative of our poem, as Wealhtheow's gift moves from her hands to go round the neck of the man who is greatest in might between the seas, from where it will go next to Hygd and then to Hygelac and then, in an apparently open-ended and ongoing story, into the possession of the Franks, where new stories will accrue to it. Metaphorically Wealhtheow's necklace has been associated with Freyja's, so that in an important way the mythical ring also enters *Beowulf* to serve as a reminder of the stories attached to it and to play a role in the primary narrative, before it passes out of the poem again to continue its narrative travels. It is in pondering such echoing and foreshadowing that we get glimpses of why some scholars have seen *Beowulf* as a text central to all early Germanic literature.

Not all harking back in *Beowulf* involves memories of glorious objects, deeds, or human characters. On the contrary, what more often is recalled is a story that is a mix of triumph and disaster. During the same celebration in which Wealhtheow presents her gifts to Beowulf, there is the highly allusive lay about Finnsburg, a story of bloody confrontation between Danes and Frisians (1063–1159a). This memorable interlude, in vivid images used by Hrothgar's scop, serves several mnemonic purposes: it recalls an earlier Danish victory over one of their enemies; it serves as a recollection of the ways in which the loyalties of lord and thane can be fractured by events; it reminds those celebrating happily in Heorot how treachery and broken vows can play havoc within families and between tribes; it points up the severely limited capacities of a 'peace-weaver' queen when masculine bloodlust takes over. The tale of Finnsburg helps subvert the apparent well-being of Heorot after the death of Grendel. The poet places the Finnsburg passage just after Hrothgar has paid *wergyld* for Beowulf's thane who was devoured by Grendel. We have been told by the narrator (1053b ff.) that *witig God* and the hero's *mod* have prevented further fatal bloodshed; also, the narrator, keeping his larger controlling myth in mind, provides an interesting generalizing or universalizing interpretation of what he sees as the meaning of the Beowulf-Grendel encounter. He says that in their battle 'the Measurer' (*Metod*) was wielding power over 'all ... the race of men, as he now still does' (*eallum ... / gumena cynnes, swa he nu git deð*). This sounds reassuring, but it is followed immediately by a monitory counsel of prudence which looks to the future: *Forþan bið andgit   æghwær selest, / ferhðes fore-*

þanc 'Yet discernment is best everywhere, forethought of mind.' Why is it best to look ahead, even when things are going well? Because 'he who for long here makes use of the world must experience many things, desirable and loathsome, in these days of conflict!' (*Fela sceal gebidan / leofes ond laþes   se þe longe her / on ðyssum windagum   worolde bruceð!*). The singing and music (*sang ond sweg*) in Heorot are desirable and good and the victory over Grendel is wonderful, but the song now to be sung about Finnsburg tells of the *laþes* or repugnant part of existence. By doing so it alters, intensifies, and darkens the meaning of Heorot itself, even while the recent heroic triumph is still fresh in the memory.

The remembering of the events at Finn's fortress resonates mainly as an account of disaster and builds to its climax through three stages: the initial battle, ending in a precarious truce, which the *scop* ironically calls *fæste frioðuwære* 'a firm peace agreement' and by which the now-lordless Danes are committed to following Finn, the slayer of their own ring-giver Hnæf (1071–1106); the cremation of the war dead (1107–24); the passing of a tense winter, followed by the outbreak of a fierce battle in which the Danes kill Finn, defeat the Frisians, and return to Denmark, taking with them Hildeburh and rich treasure booty (1125–59a). In each stage the remembering is centred on the unhappy queen Hildeburh. As she gives the command for her dead son's body to be placed on the pyre, not in life but in death a shoulder-comrade to his uncle (*eame in eaxle*, 1117a), the theme of internecine hatreds comes to a precise personal focus. Hnaef has been the lord of the Danes and so at this nadir in the relations between the two peoples he is the enemy of both Hildeburh's Frisian husband Finn and her dead Frisian/ Danish son. The song of lamentation she utters while 'the greatest of death-fires' or 'murderous fires' or, less metaphorically, 'funeral fires' (*wælfyra mæst*, 1119) winds up to the skies is part of an inexorable, still-unfolding pattern in whose tortuous weavings she is shortly to lose her husband as well.

The cremation scene is made memorable through stark corporeal images in two cumulative series, one before the fire is lit, metaphorically linking armour, beasts, and warriors, the second as the flames, 'greediest of spirits' (*gæsta gifrost*), roar and swallow up the bleeding corpses: (1) *swatfah syrce* 'battle-shirts shining with blood-sweat,' *swyn ealgylden* 'swine all golden,' *eofer iren-heard* 'an iron-hard boar,' *æþeling manig / wundum awyrded* 'many a noble one, fate-finished by wounds'; (2) *hafelan multon* 'heads melted,' *bengeatu burston* 'wound-gates burst open,' *blod ætspranc* 'blood sprang out.' The image of melting heads links and identifies warriors' heads with the melting metal of their helmets. The kenning 'wound-gates' identifies the men's corpses as human dwelling-enclosures with several or many gates (wounds) out of which living beings (blood) now burst forth, because 'war has seized' these men (*guð fornam*) from both the Danish and Frisian peoples. The poet ends this second stage of the Finnsburg tale with a succinct but resonant half-line, *wæs hira blæd scacen*. No single exclusive translation of *blæd* or of *scacen* will capture all the connotations here. We can understand *blæd* as 'power,' 'strength,' 'energy,' 'exuberance,' or 'glory,' and it is probably all these. *Scacen* from *scacan* 'to shake' (as in Icelandic) would give us the meaning 'shaken,' and that just might not be too radical a translation here, but perhaps the meanings 'hurried away' or simply 'gone' or 'departed' (cf. Old Saxon) will do.

The bloody tale on the human level is thrown into stark relief by the imagery of nature's daily and seasonal rhythms continuing uninterrupted while men kill, brood, and kill again, and a woman laments. The coming of morning reveals to Hildeburh the slaughter of her kinsmen: 'Not without cause did Hoc's daughter mourn the measure of fate when morning came, when under the heavens she could see the evil killing of kinsmen where earlier she held greatest joy in the world' (*Nalles holinga   Hoces dohtor / meotodsceaft bemearn,   sypðan morgen com, / ða heo under swegle   geseon meahte / morþorbealo maga,   þær heo ær mæste heold / worolde wynne*, 1076–80a). The coming of winter in Friesland sends the Danish and Jutish survivors of the first battle inside their dwellings. With the arrival of stormy weather, the Danish Hengest, confined to a hall in enemy territory, broods unhappily about slaughter and remembers his home, but he cannot 'drive the ringed prow over the sea' (*on mere drifan / hringedstefnan*). His conflicting emotions and thoughts about his kinship and dryht ties and his physical confinement all are identified metaphorically with the welling movements of the storm-tossed sea as it fights against the wind, and with the waves locked by winter in ice-bonds. With the coming of a new year to human dwellings the order of the created world proceeds as it always does, says the scop, with wondrously bright weather observing its schedule: *Ða wæs winter scacen, / fæger foldan bearm* 'Then winter was gone, earth's bosom fair.' Ideally the coming of spring should be a time for human joy, but it simply frees for action the desire to take vengeance and kill: the exiled Hengest sets aside his wish to return home and turns instead to 'terrible sword-evil' (*sweordbealo sliðen*). The result is a violation of all three orders of reality in the poem – Creation, kinship, and dryht – as a benevolent nature, a bereaved mother and sister, and a binding peace agreement all are plunged into disaster. A hall is reddened with the blood of the slain, Hildeburh's husband Finn is killed, and the Danes, having rejected the priority of a peace agreement over the duty of vengeance, plunder Finnsburg and return home, taking with them whatever skilfully fashioned jewels and brooches they can find in Finn's home. At this point the listener or reader, who has been told several times about the rich ornamentation of the great hall of the Danes, linking it with the order of Creation itself, will perhaps think again of that other gold-shining building and so be led to consider the dark side of Heorot's splendour as well.

The pattern of blood-feuding and war does not end when the *drihtlice wif* 'driht woman' Hildeburh and her fellow Danes return to Denmark. The Finnsburg interlude is closely related poetically to the situation in Heorot. No one in the audience in Hrothgar's hall who remembers these past events and is conscious of the current situation in Denmark, even with Grendel dead, could believe that all is really well. It is now a long time since these Scyldings have lived innocently and in blessedness. The Finnsburg lay is meant to be heard by the Danes, the visiting Geats, and the audience of the poem as ironic and unsettling. As the scop finishes singing, *gamen* 'mirth' again mounts up in Hrothgar's hall, cupbearers pour wine from wondrous vessels, and the regal Wealhtheow comes forth 'under a golden ring' (*under gyldnum beage*, 1163). But typically the narrator leaves only one moment of graceful, ritualized happiness before alluding to two other tales of treachery and bloodshed, one that remains to be told more fully sometime in the Danish future, the other already familiar in their past. The *sib* 'peace' that exists at present between the uncle-nephew pair of Hrothgar and Hrothulf well may end in disaster, as the one between Hildeburh's son and his uncle has. Unferth, however respected now in Heorot for his *ferhþe* 'spirit' and *mod micel* 'great bravery,' is a known fratricide and a likely source of future trouble (1165b–8a).

The whole narrative sequence in Heorot, including the singing of the Finnsburg lay, is an excellent illustration of how remembering in *Beowulf* often leads to a sense of foreboding, to a remembering of the future as well as the past, and sometimes to urgings that precautions be taken to avoid disaster. Queen Wealhtheow now begins her peace-weaving efforts, reminding Hrothgar of his duties, then Hrothulf and Beowulf of theirs, and finally the whole dryht community in Heorot of theirs: 'Here each earl is true to another' (*Her is æghywlc eorl oþrum getrywe*), she says, 'mild of spirit, loyal to his lord; thanes are united, a people all willing, dryht-men having drunk deep do as I bid' (*modes milde, mandrihtne hold, / þegnas syndon geþwære, þeod ealgearo, / druncne dryhtguman doð swa ic bidde*, 1228–31). It is clear that the exemplary queen of the Danes, who is always associated in the poem with Heorot and its ideals, speaks and acts on behalf not so much of what *is* as of what *should be*. But the powerful images of the unhappy Hildeburh and the bodies being consumed on the pyre in Finnsburg are still fresh in our minds and presumably in those of the people in the hall among whom Wealhtheow is moving. The adverbial *þa gyt* 'then still' destabilizes the *sib* 'kinship, friendship, peace' with Hrothulf, Unferth is sitting in a place of honour at the feet of

Hrothgar, and another mother, in her hall beneath the 'terrible waters' (*wæteregesan*, 1260), is remembering her misery and taking thought on behalf of her son, who also is now mutilated and lying dead.

In *Beowulf* there are numerous points at which we hear or encounter the words *gemunan* 'to bear in mind, remember, think of,' *myndgian* 'to recollect, remind,' and *gemyndgian* 'to call to mind.' What follows these verbs regularly tells of the obligations and relationships by which the participants in the action know themselves and others, and the demands being made on them by the codes within which they exist and to which in word and deed they give expression. Hrothgar turns over custody of his guest-hall to Beowulf and tells him to remember his fame and show great courage (659). A little later, as the wrestling match in Heorot begins, Beowulf remembers his 'evening speech' (*æfenspræce*) and then stands upright to come to grips with Grendel (758–60a). Similarly in a later recollection of this same event (1266b ff.), we are told that when Grendel finds 'a watchful man waiting for war' (*wæccendne wer wiges bidan*) with him in Heorot, and proceeds to take hold of the hero, Beowulf remembers 'the great strength, the generous' or 'ample gift' (*mægnes strenge, gimfæste gife*) God has given him and relies on the *Anwalda* 'Only Ruler' for help. After the victory over Grendel, Wealhtheow asks Hrothgar to be mindful of gifts and gracious to the Geats (1173) and in the same speech tells her husband that Hrothulf will hold their sons in honour following Hrothgar's death, '*if* he remembers all ... the favours' (*gif he þæt eal gemon, / ... arna*) she and Hrothgar have done 'for his pleasure and honour when he was a child' (*to willan ond to worðmyndum / umborwesendum ær*, 1184–7). She herself will remember to reward Beowulf if he will be of kind counsel to her boys (1219b–20). Life in the orders of the dryht and of kinship, and in the order of the created world itself in this epic of the creature, is a complex interwoven fabric of pressing memories and obligations.

Late in the poem, the old warrior-king Beowulf recalls many things, including how at the beginning of his reign he accepted the obligation to exact payment for the death of the Geatish king Heardred. Heardred had been killed by the Swedish king Onela who had seized the throne of Sweden after his brother Ohthere's death and had driven Ohthere's sons Eadgils and Eanmund out of the country. Eadgils was to have become king of Sweden but, forced with his brother to take refuge in Geatland, he was befriended by Heardred. Because of this liaison between the Geatish court and the exiled Swedish princes, Onela attacked Geatland and both the Swedish Eanmund and the Geatish Heardred were killed. Beowulf was then permitted by the Swedish king Onela to succeed to the Geatish throne. But his sense of duty to his dead king led him to befriend Eadgils, in Eadgils's successful bid to take the throne of Sweden and to kill his usurper uncle. This is how Beowulf as a new king, mindful of duty according to the codes of dryht and kinship, was obliged to act. The other major kind of obligation that King Beowulf has always to remember, even now at the end of his life, is to pursue fame to the very end, not primarily for the purpose of personal glory but to defend his people. It is this desire to gain fame through performing his duty as protector-lord that underlies the main story of part II, and it is this, we are especially told, that he is mindful of when in the second of the three clashes with the dragon he strikes unsuccessfully with his battle-sword Naegling: 'Then again the war-king was mindful of fame, with his war-sword struck with great strength ...' (*þa gen guðcyning / mærða gemunde,   mægenstrengo sloh / hildebille*, 2677b–9a). It is important to note, even at this late point, that the courage and strength of the hero-king are still intact. It is the weapon he uses, not he himself, that is metaphorically characterized as a weakened old warrior now failing in battle: *gomol ond grægmæl* 'old and grey-marked,' Naegling breaks because the hand that wields it is 'too strong' for it (*wæs sio hond to strong*). The cause of Beowulf's defeat is not that he does not remember and adhere fully to his obligations as hero and king but that he is, after all, a mortal creature and so at last must face the dragon, the old 'foe of the people' (*þeodsceaða*) who also is 'mindful of feuds' (*fæhða gemyndig*) and now rushes at Beowulf to seize his neck with his 'fierce bones' (*biteran banum*, 2692) – that is, with his teeth.[6]

Within the order of the dryht, the other half of the core relationship between lord and thane is the duties required of the thane. It is the remembrances of these obligations, joined to those of a kinsman, that find their point of cynosure in the young warrior Wiglaf late in the poem. Identified as *leoflic lindwiga* 'a precious' or 'admirable' or 'rare linden-' or 'shield-warrior,' he first appears at the fateful moment when the rest of Beowulf's dryht creep away into the woods to protect their lives (2596 ff.). When Wiglaf sees his lord suffering the heat of the fire-dragon under his helmet, he remembers the honours and rich dwelling-place given him by Beowulf. The antithesis between this one thane from Beowulf's troop and the other thanes is complete. The fictional modes of romance and myth deal in blacks and whites and do not introduce finely discriminating analyses of behaviour: here at the moment of crisis the thane is either loyal or treacherous. There is no middle ground. The code simultaneously being violated and upheld is so important that the poet stops the action of the fight and has Wiglaf make a lengthy speech about his and his comrades' obligation before he plunges into the battle. Wiglaf appeals to his companions' memories of the time he and they drank mead together and promised their lord in the beer-hall that they would repay him for the rings and war-arms he had given them, if ever such a need should arise (2633–7). But the other thanes do not accept the challenge. After Beowulf's death they are fiercely denounced by both the narrator and Wiglaf (2845b ff.) as 'battle-sluggish ones, cowards' (*hildlatan*) 'false to their oaths' (*treowlogan*). The young Waegmunding bitterly predicts for these men and their kinsmen a general contempt and the loss of all possessions and privileges as they are driven into disgrace and exile.

Not to remember, not to think about and act on one's obligations within the orders of the Creation, the dryht, and kinship, is to default in relation to one's functions in life, to forget what one has been loaned days for. This is why frequently in the world of the poem someone will speak or sing while others listen, and the purpose will be, literally, to remind those present of their identities and their duties within a network of kinship, dryht, and creaturely relationships that extend through space, time, and eternity. Always in the background of what the particular speaker or singer is expressing there is the overall tragic outline of the fundamental story within which they live. It goes like this: 'In the olden days brave men received gifts from heaven and from their lord. When the time came for service they did battle gloriously, but then the monsters came, evil thoughts sprang up, and the splendid troop was torn apart. Warriors lay on their deathbeds, the ravens croaked, and the sounds of the harp and of laughter were heard no more in the windswept halls.' What is remembered and sung about is a vision of *dream* 'joy' and of the way things are meant to be, but will not be if those in the middle dwelling default on their obligations. The song is meant to break the listener's heart. But since *Beowulf* is a heroic poem not just an elegiac meditation, it is meant to galvanize into action or right thought the ones who hear the words; it is meant to confirm their identities as members of a community and transform them into human beings confident and ready to serve that community. When the Danes or Geats in the poem listen to such utterances – the reminders come to them from the singers in Denmark, from Hrothgar and Wealhtheow, from the hero, and from Wiglaf – when they hear, they are meant to be transformed. As they listen, something inside them as Danes or Geats is reidentified and their actions or attitudes are meant to change. When the change is well done, as on the whole finally it is in the foreground narrative of part I of the poem (though not in part II), the life of the society changes for the better. Why should this be?

One reason the *Beowulf* poet makes extensive use of the story-telling value of memory is that it gives two views in one: depth in time and contrast. A dryht besieged remembers an earlier, happier time. A joyful troop remembers when things were not so good and knows such a time may come again. But this is not all. Memory, as the poet knows well, is the means by which a human society survives. Acts of remembrance and imaginative re-creation – remembering is imaginative re-creation – are essential if human beings are to be bound

Memory and Identity 131

together. Such acts, moreover, are often cathartic and spell relief after great tension has passed, as in each of the banqueting scenes in Heorot and, in a different cadence, in the memorial dirges and circling of the riders in the funeral rituals following the death of Beowulf. Because memory is what it is, both a retrospective and a prospective faculty, the first thing the scops, the *hæleþ*, and the narrator remember is that time passes. In thinking back *in geardagum*, they know that they and their people have so far survived the passage of time, however many of their fellows have died, and, since they have survived what they remember, they may also have a future. Memory, especially the acts of communal remembering, the singing of songs and the telling of stories about old things, can also then be a form of hope. Even though the songs heard long ago in a particular hall may have ended, and the hall itself may have fallen into ruins, someone is still calling into mind that earlier place and its people. If the song of those who have disappeared is still being heard, there is the possibility that those now living will not be annihilated by oblivion.

Part of elegiac art is that if a particular memory is a sad or unhappy one recalling something far back in time, it tends to mingle with good memories so that its sharpness and pain are softened and absorbed into a pattern of resignation and acceptance, even hope. This tendency is perhaps most notable in the account at the beginning of the poem of the death and sea-burial of Scyld Scefing, an event presented movingly and with emotion but also as something now remote in time and thoroughly absorbed into folk memories about the glories and triumphs of the early kings of the Scyldings. It is possible years later to lament again such a loss, as in this passage, but when that is done it gives rise to a diffused, melancholy sense of the passing of time itself, to a pattern of meaning in which glorious deeds and death, joys and sorrows, have peacefully joined each other in the collective memory. This elegiac combining of pleasure and pain is even more succinctly expressed in Beowulf's account to Hygelac of the songs sung in Heorot on the day after Grendel's death (2101 ff.). Initially, on this occasion of triumph, there is much gift-giving, feasting, and mirth, and the first songs in the celebration are happy ones. But then 'the old one of the Scyldings' (*gomela Scildinga*), Hrothgar, 'informed about many things' (*felafricgende*), tells of times far off. Then again someone, perhaps Hrothgar himself, touches 'the harp's joy, the glad wood' (*hearpan wynne, / gomenwudu*) and tells tales 'true and sad' (*soð ond sarlic*), 'strange stories according to right custom' (*syllic spell ... æfter rihte*). 'The great-hearted king ... bound with age, the old warrior' (*rumheort cyning ... eldo gebunden, / gomel guðwiga*), begins to speak of his far-off youth and his earlier battle-strength, as 'old and wise in years,' he remembers many things and his heart wells within him (*hreðer inne weoll, / þonne he wintrum frod   worn gemunde*). Interestingly, it is through the voice of Beowulf that we are shown this glimpse of a special moment in the existence of the Danes: the hero ends his recollection with the evocative words *Swa we þær inne   andlangne dæg / niode naman,   oð ðæt niht becwom / oðer to yldum* 'So there inside we took pleasure the livelong day, until another night came to men.' The night which comes is the night in which Grendel's mother strikes. Here the elegiac sense of melancholy, of sorrow in the midst of joy, and of joy within the shadow of great danger, seems almost to have as much to do with the passage of the years and days themselves, of youth giving way to age, of daylight giving way to darkness, and of the morning that will surely come, as with the actual events remembered. Here too in the remembering we see a foreshadowing by the young warrior-prince of his own character as the wise, thoughtful king who emerges to dominate part II of the poem.

When the faculty of memory is filled with some recent pain or loss, because of murder or defeat or treachery – as with Hrothgar's tormented recollections during the Grendel ravages, or those of the Scylding warriors trapped for a winter in Finnsburg, or those of Wiglaf after the display of cowardice by his fellow thanes – the painfulness is just as sharp and clear as with a memory of something positive and good. The sense of injury has not been blunted by time and the desire for some compensatory counter-action or vengeance is acutely felt. Such emotions lead directly into one of the main obligations placed on members of both the order of the dryht and the order of kinship. The intense recalling of recent wrongs sometimes points specifically into the heart of the custom called *wergyld* 'man-price,' in which each human being is believed to have a specific value that must be repaid if he is killed: repaid in blood or in goods equal to his worth. In the world of *Beowulf* the law of *wergyld* is no abstract theory but the flashpoint of endless bloodshed and disaster. The truce between the Danes and the Frisians in the Finnsburg lay is based on an agreement (1095 ff.) that, if the murderous hate between the two peoples is called to mind (*myndgiend wære*) in a rash speech by any of the Frisians (1104–5), the sword will settle the conflict. Inevitably the fateful reminder does come, and an aggrieved Danish son whose father has been killed but not avenged lays his dead father's sword in Hengest's lap. According to one of the codes by which Hengest lives, it is intolerable that he and his fellows in their 'lordless' (*ðeodenlease*) state should be following 'their ring-giver's killer' (*hira beaggyfan banan*). He now must act. But, as in other such instances, adherence to that code in conflict with the higher code of the peace oath exerts a perverse, antisocial force that destroys human beings and their societies.

Another act of destructive remembering is woven into Beowulf's report to Hygelac about the situation in Denmark, in his prediction of the coming conflict between the Heathobards and the Danes. He speaks (2041 ff.) of 'an old ash-warrior' (*eald æscwiga*), an elderly Heathobard who will 'call to mind at every opportunity' (*myndgað mæla gehwylce*, 2057) all the grievances and hatreds between the two peoples, and with grim heart will tempt a young fighter to start up again the feud demanded by the law of blood vengeance. Apparently, although once more we are dealing with allusion not assertion, it is this particular act of remembering and telling that will lead to the disastrous events that complete the story of Heorot in a final destruction by fire. In the passage here, describing this future episode, we see a curious juxtaposition of temporal perspectives in the narrative art of the poem. From Beowulf and Hygelac's point of view, the passage is a prophecy, a foretelling of something that is still to happen at some future time, but the passage also paradoxically tells, even as Beowulf talks, of acts of remembering by a malevolent participant in the future events. The art of memory is being stretched to include the recalling of events that have not yet taken place. From the perspective of the narrator – perhaps also from that of an early audience familiar with the story of Heorot – and from the poet's and our own perspectives based on knowledge of the structure of the whole poem, Beowulf's prophecy is an allusive rounding out of the main narrative of part I.

In human existence, loss of memory at its most devastating is not to know who you are. When the messenger late in the poem (3010b–17) foresees disaster and annihilation for the Geats as a people, he gives the order that the rings from the dragon's hoard, 'grimly purchased' (*grimme geceapod*) with Beowulf's life, are to be devoured in the flames of the funeral pyre, so that 'no earl will wear an ornament in remembrance' (*nalles eorl wegan / mæððum to gemyndum*) and 'no bright maiden will have a ring adornment on her neck' (*ne mægð scyne / habban on healse   hringweorðunge*). This is because the man who was their ring-giver gave them not only rings but identity and that identity has now been destroyed. They and others now will not know who they are and they will not belong anywhere. As we have seen, the human figures in *Beowulf* regularly are shown identifying themselves, or being characterized by the narrator or someone else, in terms of their kinship or dryht relationships and in terms of their identity as members of a world created and ruled over by a heavenly Dryhten. If in such a world, defined in intensely ancestral (familial), political (social), and mythical (theological) ways, these human figures know themselves and are known by other people by such identities, both they and those to whom they speak and with whose fates they become involved will have a sense of their likely behaviour, and probably also of their human worth. All the figures in the many stories in the poem are in a real sense fictions in the tales of others and, sometimes, in their own self-narrations as well. It is their fictive, that is their imagined reality, that is their reality.

Beowulf knows and regularly identifies himself as the recipient of God's favour. In the exuberance of his sea-voyage to the land of the Scyldings he embodies still untold potential stories that are to be used by the narrator to tell the wyrds of the Danes and, later, the Geats. In his first speech (258–85) he introduces himself and his men to the Danish coast-guard. He and his troop are 'Hygelac's hearth-companions (*Higelaces heorðgeneatas*) and he is Ecgtheow's son. He notes that 'every wise man, far and wide over the earth, remembers' his father Ecgtheow (*hine gearwe geman / witena welhwylc wide geond eorþan*). In such designations lies a range of powerful narrative expectations and obligations. In a real sense Ecgtheow already has become a story known to many, including the Danes to whom the son is now presenting himself. The son is continuing the father's story as it now picks up in another sequence, once again involving the Scyldings. Simultaneously, Beowulf lives and tells part of Hygelac's story, and others' stories as well. Towards the conclusion of the Geats' stay in Heorot, both Hrothgar and Wealhtheow sketch out possible future interchanges between Danes and Geats, stories and plots yet to be unlocked. Stories never live alone. Like the leaves and branches and the living creatures in the scop's song of Creation when Heorot was new, and like the serpentine figures in Anglo-Saxon manuscript drawings, stories have to be tracked forward, backward, and sideways. This elaborating of the narrative art of the poem provides constraints that allow the poet to be maximally creative, even as the adherence to traditional accentual and alliterative constraints frees him to construct curious and daring metaphorical variations.

When the human figures in the world of the poem remember who they are and to whom they owe gratitude and loyalty, they also recall the places and events by which the significance and even the reality of their own existence has come together, through involvement with those other people. When Beowulf towards the end of his life remembers his father placing him at the age of seven in Hrethel's court, the memory evokes in him a feeling of gratitude about how well the treasure-lord of the Geats remembered the obligations of kinship (*sibbe gemunde*, 2431) and so treated him like a son. This in turn recalls other events in the Geatish royal house, especially those involving the lives of Hrethel's three sons, Hæthcyn, Herebeald, and Hygelac, and so we are told fragments of their stories. In the circling rings of narrative characteristic of the poem, for Beowulf to be a child again in memory means that he calls up his father Ecgtheow, his maternal grandfather and former king, Hrethel, and the three young princes who were his uncles. Similarly, to be a young man again is to recall the time when Hygelac was his lord, and also the people, monsters, and events long ago in Denmark (2510 ff.).

Memory and identity to a large degree are other people. As Beowulf revolves his many memories, he thinks more of those others than of himself. People are the landscape of memory. It was they he was observing long ago, not himself. It is the relations with them and with the many others encountered over the years, always in the overall context of acting in a middle world created and ruled over by God, that structure and give meaning to his life. He remembers and forever moves as a dryht-man and kinsman, and as someone cognizant of the laws of the *Anwalda*. This is the rhythm of his life. Finally for him, as shown in the last words he ever speaks, remembrance is more than honouring and speaking respectfully of the dead. Remembrance is joining them, being one with them: *ic him æfter sceal* 'I must follow after them' (2816). Also, as the passing of his arms to Wiglaf, the memorial barrow, and the poem itself all indicate, being remembered means becoming one with those who will live after. To be remembered is one form of survival. As Beowulf's death approaches, there are many dead in his past, friends and enemies, each of them involving one or more stories. Each of their stories is part of the story of his life. The account of his life, moreoever, its major events writ large in the primary narrative of the poem, is presented as the story of humankind in middle earth. As God's champion, Beowulf acts in obedience to heaven's will and is shown doing so throughout his *lændagas* 'loaned days' on behalf of the human race in their struggle with stormy, treacherous waters, encroaching darkness, destroying fire, and the monsters both inside and outside their societies.

If we read or listen to *Beowulf* sequentially, it becomes a myth, first by tautology, in the sense in which all myths are *mythoi* 'narratives' or 'plots,' and secondly in a more specific sense, of being a very open, comprehensive narrative that contains within itself, sometimes only allusively, a large number of supporting myths and stories. These include especially significant material about Creation, Paradise, Satan, Cain and Abel, the biblical giants and the Deluge, the descent into hell, and mentions of the Judgment, as well as a great deal of what we think of as semi-historical material to do with the Danes, the Geats, the Swedes, and other peoples who once lived in what is now northwestern Europe. Finally also there is Germanic legendary and mythical material about Sigmund, Fitela, and Weland. Throughout this wide-ranging collection of stories and parts or mere hints of stories, the main narrative about the hero Beowulf proceeds, to some extent as a linear plot. He goes to Denmark, performs certain acts, and returns home. Then, many years later, having been made king, he fights a battle with a dragon in which both of them are killed. But the linear plot or *mythos* becomes an increasingly resonant myth to which meanings accrue as it goes, because of two things: the richly metaphorical language used and the wealth of stories that feed into and interpenetrate it.

It is clear that, whatever else, *Beowulf* is not a tightly closed work of art, especially in its narrative aspects. The story of Beowulf is not sealed off in a world of its own. It is not caught in a self-contained poem or novel to be studied and admired as something so structurally and artistically complete in itself that it defies correlation with other works and with human life itself. The story of Beowulf's engagement with the Danes and the Geats constantly reaches out and takes into itself materials not strictly necessary for the development of its own main plot, to such an extent that we realize that however central and important the primary narrative is, it is only the beginning of the matter. It is not plot, in fact, in the later historical sense – of a lengthy, carefully deployed providing of information in a suspenseful and finally complete and consistent way – that is the main concern or achievement of the poem. *Beowulf* tells a story, certainly, but in a remarkably open, inclusive, and spacious way. In connection with the two necklaces, Wealhtheow's and Freyja's, I used Julia Kristeva's critical term 'intertextuality' to describe the poem's centrifugal tendencies. The term belongs to the late twentieth century, perhaps, but the phenomenon indicated by it was integral to the manuscript culture out of which *Beowulf* has come to us.[7] As Walter Ong and others have shown, that manuscript culture accepted as a given that texts come out of other texts and are not simply created out of lived experience. Still shaped in part by the traditions of the old oral world, the manuscript culture deliberately fashioned texts out of other texts, stories out of other stories, and poems out of other poems. It regularly borrowed, so to speak, what had in any case only been loaned to the previous users; it adapted as seemed appropriate, and it shared the common resources, including everything from the biblical mythology and traditional stories to the particular verbal formula or kenning. The second word of our poem, *we*, is a companionable word, and so is the poem that follows.

The main theme of this chapter is the role of memory and association in the poem's narrative art. The subtheme is the parallel between the pervasively metaphorical use of language in *Beowulf*, partly documented and explored in the two preceding chapters, and the way each discrete unit in the main narrative finds or associates itself with another story or myth that helps identify it and give it resonance. What this means is that in the poem's larger narrative art there is a phenomenon parallel to the more minute elements of compounds, variation, and cumulative style, by which one word or phrase finds another in the intricately interconnected verbal art characteristic of the poem. We saw earlier that this art depends heavily on a language of immanence, and this in turn led to the concept of first phase or metaphorical language, as distinguished from both metonymic and descriptive language. I should now like to suggest briefly (for elaboration in part two of this book) how the acts of remembering and associating in the poem, both on the level of particular imaginative figures of speech and of larger narrative units, help locate the poem securely in a recognizable mythological framework.

Trying to think within the categories of metaphor, myth, and mythology – all of these being 'primitive' categories from some of our contemporary perspectives – can be difficult, because they involve illogicalities and a good deal of disregard for empirical facts and for what we think of as history, in favour of some imagined reality or truth. But suppose we say, as I think Tolkien half a century ago suggested we should, that the hero and the monster metaphors in *Beowulf* are the poetic and therefore the primary meaning of the work. They are the mythical core out of which the poem grew and they do not depend for their imaginative power either on the moralizing comments of the narrator or on the predicative language of scholars about what actually happened in the historical world that surrounded the poem. If *Beowulf* has a doctrinal cortex or a historical myth, it is doctrine and history that bypass conventional theological and historical criteria. The exegetes who comment on and interpret the poem by rationalizing its myths and metaphors into metonymic language, and think that by so doing they are explaining it, simply fail to accept it for what it is. To say, as some have, in our ideological period of criticism, that Beowulf's fight with the dragon and his retrieval of the treasure are the consequences of pride and avarice in the hero is an imposition on the poem, not a reading of it. But sooner or later, if readers of the poem stay true, in this respect, to Tolkien's penetrating insights, the intellectual mortality of such efforts fades away and the dragon and his treasure are still there in all their metaphorical and mythical force, and the hero is still there in all his exuberant magnamimity.

The poem is a product of first phase language, a structure of poetic meaning that sustains a number of moral and theological ideas and absorbs into itself certain aspects of people, places, and things from Germanic life. But it universalizes and is not subject to criteria of accurate description of externals, either of doctrines or of the physical and actual historical world. Although myth and metaphor may introduce ambiguities undesirable in descriptive writing which aims at analytical precision, the case is different in poetry, where the ambiguities are functional. This means that the reader or listener has to surrender precision for flexibility of imagining, as in a *kent heiti* or a kenning, and so be imaginatively ready, when he or she finds sea-monsters proposing banquets on sea-bottoms, to recognize in the dryht-halls and treasures found down in the depths under the headlands that these images are participants in the dryht of hell. He or she may also realize that, in a poem in which things are identified both *as* what they are and *with* what they are not, in some curious but important way Unferth may well *be* Grendel, and so may Hrothulf, because Grendel is a destroyer of the fraternal society of Heorot and so are they, and he belongs to the race of Cain, and so do they.

PART TWO

STRUCTURE AND MEANING

5

Fyr on Flode:
War against the Creation

Early in part II of *Beowulf*, the narrator tells of the destruction of 'the best of buildings' (*bolda selest*, 2326a), the royal hall and gift-throne of Geatland, by a fire-dragon who is enraged that his long-hoarded treasure has been disturbed while he sleeps. An unnamed fugitive characterized as 'a sin-troubled man' (*secg synbysig*, 2226a) has taken a shining treasure-cup and then, seeing the sleeping dragon, has fled in terror and gone to his lord, with whom he has successfully made a 'peace-treaty' (*frioðowære*, 2281). The furious dragon goes berserk and sets out to wreak total vengeance on the land of the Geats. As he spews forth flames that burn the bright dwellings, a blaze of fire stands up 'to the horror of men' (*eldum on andan*, 2314a), and we are told that 'the loathsome air-flier did not want to leave there any living thing' (*no ðær aht cwices / lað lyftfloga læfan wolde*, 2314b–15).

Whatever are the meanings of the puzzling, brief account of the theft of the cup, the cataclysmic nature and scope of the dragon's response seem out of all proportion to the apparently inadvertent desperate action of the son of warriors who happens upon the treasure while fleeing *heteswengeas* 'hate-blows' (2221–5). Something more than a plausible cause-effect sequence is at work. The 'serpent's warfare' is 'seen far and wide, his pressing hostile vengeance, from near and far' (*Wæs þæs wyrmes wig wide gesyne, / nearofages nið nean ond feorran*), as the 'war-enemy,' 'destroyer' (*guðsceaða*) shows his hatred and his determination to humiliate the Geatish people (2316 ff.). By means of these extraordinary and mysterious events the poem moves inexorably into its final phase, a depiction of bloodshed and human misery that reaches extensively into the past and the future even while the foreground story about the man Beowulf is taken to its conclusion.

The major event at the beginning of part I is the building of the great hall Heorot by the renowned Hrothgar, lord of the Scyldings, who has emerged as

142 Structure and Meaning

the fifth king in the splendid dynasty begun by Scyld Scefing. Hrothgar has subdued all his enemies and brought peace and prosperity to his people. It has come into his mind 'to bid men to make a hall-building' (*Him on mod bearn, / þæt healreced hatan wolde ... men gewyrcan*). This will be 'a mighty mead-house ... great[er] than any of the children of men have ever heard tell' (*medoærn micel ... þonne yldo bearn æfre gefrunon*). In it he will 'distribute all things to young and old even as God gave to him, except for public land and the lives of men' (*ond þær on innan eal gedælan / geongum ond ealdum, swylc God him sealde, / buton folcscare ond feorum gumena*, 67b ff.). The thought of this mighty enterprise having entered the king's mind, the work is commanded 'of many nations throughout this middle dwelling, to adorn a place for the people' (*manigre mægþe geond þisne middangeard, / folcstede frætwan*, 75–6a). The task is quickly carried out and soon 'the greatest of hall-buildings' (*healærna mæst*) is 'all ready' (*ealgearo*). 'He who with his word' (*se þe his wordes*) has 'power far and wide' (*geweald wide*) shapes or creates (*scop*) a name for it, *Heorot* 'Hart, Stag,' and then proceeds to carry out his promise to give gifts by distributing rings and treasure at a banquet.

There is no question here, as there is with the fire-dragon, of the possessor of a hoard avariciously clinging to a treasure or being enraged by the loss of one item from it. Again it is clear that the poem is telling of something more than simply the building of a dryht-hall. To build the hall is not enough. The Scyldings have to absorb and be absorbed by the original Creation. The narrator juxtaposes closely with his account of the creation, naming, and first enjoyment of Heorot the memory of the Creation of the world itself (89b ff.), in the form of harp music and 'a clear song of a scop' (*swutol sang scopes*) who knows 'from long ago how to tell of the origin of men' (*frumsceaft fira feorran reccan*) and now recounts how 'the Almighty fashioned the earth, a radiantly bright plain surrounded by water' (*se Ælmihtiga eorðan worhte, / wlitebeorhtne wang, swa wæter bebugeð*), and then 'exulting in victory set in place the sun and the moon as lights for land-dwellers' (*gesette sigehreþig sunnan ond monan / leoman to leohte landbuendum*). Like Heorot, adorned or ornamented with the help of many people throughout the middle dwelling, so the 'regions of the earth' (*foldan sceatas*, 96) in the first Creation are adorned, by the Creator, 'with leaves and branches' (*leomum ond leafum*). Later we are told that Heorot sits in the midst of 'mead-fields,' 'mead-plains' (*meodowongas*, 1643). The scop's song ends with words whose mythical resonance and meaning extend throughout the verbal fabric of the whole poem: *lif eac gesceop / cynna gehwylcum þara ðe cwice hwyrfaþ* 'life also he created for every kind of being that lives and moves.' Immediately after these words about the origins of all life come others that metaphorically identify the inhabitants of Heorot with the life of the primal Creation itself: 'So those dryht-men lived in joy, blessedly' or 'happily' (*Swa ða drihtguman dreamum lifdon, / eadiglice*). This is a signature passage for the poem, involving three creators or shapers and three kinds of creation: the Almighty fashioning the order of the world and all living things; Hrothgar by his word-power bringing into existence and naming the greatest of hall-dwellings; the scop, whose clear song is the associative linking of the other two shapings.

With the destruction at the beginning of part II of Beowulf's gift-hall by 'the people's foe' (*se ðeodsceaða*, 2278, also at 2688) 'made eager [or 'ready'] by fire' (*fyre gefysed*, 2309), a rich metaphorical complex of meanings moves into the dominant narrative position, and remains there until the end of the story. As the *mythos* of widespread destruction unfolds, there is a massing of images and themes of blood-feuding, social disintegration, and death. It is as if all the hatreds and hostilities of many years of existence have suddenly coalesced into one monstrous, objective form, the fiery, vengeful dragon, and his long pent-up rage has been unleashed in a wild orgy of destruction. The images that dominate the last third of *Beowulf* are the polar opposite of the paradisal metaphors and themes associated with the building of Heorot and the joy-filled existence all too briefly experienced there. For part II, the Lay of the Last Survivor is the signature passage. It tells not of life and a newly created dryht-hall but of a vanished dryht and ruined hall. Here we have a powerful expression of the radical sense of alienation and separation that is the core of Old English elegy: the thane is part of the light-filled centre of a functioning hall, favoured by and loyal to his lord, or he is an exile from such a centre. In this apostrophe to the earth by the one living 'keeper of rings' (*hringa hyrde*, 2245) there is no mention of God, the harp is silent, and we are told that 'Baleful killing has sent away many life-kinds!' (*Bealocwealm hafaþ / fela feorhcynna forð onsended!* 'War-death' (*guðdeað*), 'terrible life-evil' (*feorhbealo frecne*), has taken away all human lives except that of one survivor (*an æfter eallum*), whose heart also soon is touched by *deaðes wylm* 'death's welling' (2268–70a). However diametrically opposed the two complexes of meaning are in the two songs – one to do with creation and life, the other with the undoing of creation, destruction, and death – they are never separate for long in the narrative art and meaning of this poem. Even as the first gift-giving begins in Heorot, in close association with the Creator's purposes for his Creation, there is reference to the 'battle surges' (*heaðowylma*) and 'hostile fire' (*laðan liges*) that wait for the great hall, and to 'the sword-hate between son-in-law and father-in-law' (*se ecghete aþumsweoran*) that will 'be born' (*wæcnan*) and bring about 'deadly slaughter' (*wælniðe*, 82b ff.). Further to intensify these polarities, which emerge early in the narrative to define existence in the new middle dwelling, the ominous prediction about the ultimate fate of Heorot is immediately juxtaposed, without explanation, with its mythical source, the *ellengæst* who waits and suffers in dark places. This 'fiend in hell ... called Grendel' *(feond on helle ... Grendel haten,* 101–2b) is unprovoked by any human action other than the happiness of the Danes; in his misery he cannot bear the sound of the music and joy coming from the hall. So he begins to do evil and as he does so the pattern of life-destroying influence, which is still continuing much later in the poem in the form of the 'people's foe' *(ðeodsceaða),* begins its ineluctable sabotaging of the world of the idealized, paradisal dryht.

The Need for an Explicit 'Ars Poetica'

The preceding chapters of this book have been attempts to describe *Beowulf* in three aspects: the dominant modes of its imagining; the ways in which its kennings and other metaphorical language function; and the allusive, associative, and mnemonic nature of its story-telling. At numerous points it has been clear that this is a poem whose imaginative and fictional boundaries are wide, whose language is richly connotative, and whose multiple narrative strands take the listener or reader through a complex interweaving of legend, folk-tale, and myth. This present chapter and the final three, by focusing in a concentrated way on certain major metaphorical complexes, builds on those preceding chapters and is an attempt to illustrate how the poem tells or otherwise indicates much of what it means. The questions for consideration now are these: How does *Beowulf* invite its listeners or readers to understand and respond to it? What major meanings are to be heard and seen in and through the imagery of the poem, as a result of its characteristic modes of imagining, its metaphorical language, and its interweaving allusive narrative art? For those who think about such things, and there are a sizeable band of us who do, this kind of critical task of interpretation bristles with literary theoretical implications. We are now in a period of Old English studies in which there is little excuse for anything less than a fully articulated *ars poetica* from each of us who would interpret the old texts. This is why, in what follows, I try to keep clear a number of the more important of the theoretical implications, beginning with a few general principles.

It is well known that when the writings of Jerome, Ambrose, Augustine, Isidore, Gregory, and others of the Church Fathers made their way into Anglo-Saxon England, they brought with them the traditions of scriptural exegesis.[1] Bede, for example, was profoundly influenced by the exegetical lore that permeated Latin Christianity in his time and was a practitioner of it. The extent, however, to which exegetical theory and practice influenced vernacular English poetry, in its composition or in its being understood by Anglo-Saxon listeners or readers, has for some decades now been one of the most hotly discussed questions in Old English scholarship. The fact that a large portion of the approximately thirty thousand lines of extant poetry is intimately and pervasively connected with Scripture suggests, on the whole, that how Anglo-Saxons were understanding the Bible had a good deal to do with the kind of poetry they composed, and with what it probably meant to them and to their audiences and readers. There were of course numerous ways other than exegetical commentaries by which Anglo-Saxons became familiar with the Bible and the many early accretions to it: the liturgy, sermons, service books, illuminated manuscripts, saints' lives, apocryphal writings, church architecture and decoration, stone sculptures, wood carvings, metalwork, jewelry, tapestries and embroidery, and a wide range of other sacred objects. The text of *Beowulf* contains a significant amount of explicit biblical and hexaemeral material, in prominent places in the narrative. It also shares with other more manifestly Christian and biblically inspired Old English poems a host of 'baptized' Germanic images and themes.[2] What is interesting about this, and important not to forget, is that the poem stays deeply immersed in the imagery, trappings, and values of the old dryht world; these old elements are not culturally 'displaced' or submerged in favour of an exclusively Christian ideological framework. Unlike the other extant long poems in Old English, all of which use the traditional heroic diction and varying amounts of Germanic cultural content to serve Christian stories and themes, *Beowulf* is not the product of an other-worldly Christianity teaching contempt for the world of the dryht. Interpretation of the poem must confront these facts, and many commentators have done so, with varying degrees of success. There is still, however, a good deal of theoretical confusion and some unnecessary acrimony about what constitutes valid commentary on this in some ways enigmatic poem.

The critical confusion does not arise from any shortage in the number of theoretical formulations about literature, poetics, and language available in our time. On the contrary there are numerous critical approaches or schools, each offering its own particular preoccupations and insights. Interpreters of Old English poems have not only patristic exegetical theory and commentaries to draw on, but the following critical formulations as well: the work done on orality in relation to literacy; various kinds of formalist and structuralist criticism; myth or archetypal criticism; semiotics; the now fairly old but not exhausted 'New' criticism; historical criticism, in its old and new varieties, including intellectual history or the history of ideas; psychoanalysis; phenomenology; hermeneutics; reception theory; poststructuralism; and the various kinds of political criticism such as Marxism and feminism. There are no doubt others, and there are many subdivisions and combinations within and across this list. Confronted with this abundance of theory and practice and the claims made by the various schools or persuasions, the student of *Beowulf*, like the student of any other text or body of literature, can do one of three things. He or she can take an exclusive view in favour of one or two of the critical claims and assume that the others are wrong, a waste of time, or simply irrelevant to his or her interest. Alternatively he or she can take a relativistic stance, recognizing some validity in most or all of the approaches but no special authority in any of them. But the exclusivist approach shuts off too many avenues to knowledge and the relativist one risks being overwhelmed by the variety of competing claims. There is, however, a third possible attitude and approach, one that we can see foreshadowed in the patristic and medieval theory of the four levels of meaning. Recognizing, as did the early exegetes, what has been called a principle of polysemous meaning, that is, that a literary text contains a variety of kinds of meanings, we can look for a critical *theoria* comprehensive enough to account for this variety of theories. To be really useful, the *theoria* will have to be based firmly on the diverse facts of literary experience and will need to recognize interconnections between the different kinds of meaning as they do their work in the text in question.

In the ferment of theoretical and practical criticism in the second half of the twentieth century, there is one critic who has explicitly articulated a wide-ranging post-Hegelian *theoria* of polysemous meaning which, used astutely and flexibly, can serve in ways analogous to the earlier medieval formulation, with its four levels: literal or historical, allegorical or typical, tropological or moral, and anagogical or mystical. In essay 2 of *Anatomy of Criticism: Four Essays* (1957), also in the conclusion of *The Great Code: The Bible and Literature* (1982), and finally in the first half of *Words with Power, Being a Second Study of the Bible and Literature* (1990), Northrop Frye attempted to show how emphasis on the commonalities and interrelations between various critical schools and perspectives can lead to a major clarification of the intellectual discipline of criticism itself, and so to a greatly improved ability to gain real knowledge and understanding of what literary texts are and do in a culture. The overall long-term consequences of that daring effort remain to be seen. The ideas about verbal language in Frye's last two major books (1982, 1990) are now making their way globally both in English and, in the case of *The Great Code*, in an increasing number of translations (Lee/Denham 1994, xxvii–xxxii). In the meantime there is something in this wide-ranging, inclusive *theoria* that can be very useful in showing how a correlation of patristic exegetical perspectives with twentieth-century critical ones can assist understanding of Old English poetry generally, and *Beowulf* in particular.

Like other great poems and literary works, *Beowulf* invites and repays many rereadings, providing new meanings and discoveries each time. Some of the new findings are what was overlooked or simply not absorbed on previous occasions, but others come from new contexts in the reader's own experience. The implication is that when the act of reading starts, some kind of dialectical process begins to unfold, so that any given understanding of what is read is one of a series of phases of comprehension. In a general way that is what the ancient exegetical theory of four levels recognized and tried to articulate: first it directed attention to the historical or literalist references, and to the multiplicity of tropes and figures that could function on the literal level of a text; then, having recognized these two distinct kinds of literal meanings, it moved on to other, what our *ealdfæderas* 'ancestors' thought of as 'spiritual' levels of apprehension. Similarly in our time, the growing acceptability of a principle of polysemous meaning is an important realization in our emerging world culture. It may now be desirable and possible to bring some order and clarity into the numerous ways we approach the challenge of trying to understand literary texts, and other verbal formulations as well. One of the main differences between the old conception of four levels and a modern/postmodern conception is dictated by the fact that the old three-tiered cosmos is gone, except for imaginative purposes. So also, for most of us, is the attendant theology. This means that we should not think of each phase of meaning in a text as arranged in an ascending hierarchy or even in a progressive sequence. Each phase is better understood as a different aspect of the same thing. Our contemporary theoretical understanding also indicates that, strictly speaking, there is no such thing as 'literal' ('literalist') meaning except in historical and descriptive writing. *Beowulf* is not either of these. From most modern or postmodern perspectives, the three 'spiritual' levels of the ancient-medieval theory of polysemy look just as literalist and historically dated as the first or literal level does. In a confessional context, old or modern, of Christian belief, the four irreducible 'facts,' causally related in the four-level scheme, are these: what you read; what you believe; what you do (because you read and believe); and what result follows for your soul, eternally (because you have read, believed, and acted according to the rule of *caritas*, or not). The problem for most modern interpreters is not that three of the old levels are too symbolic or allegorical but that they are too literal(ist), not symbolic enough, for those of us who inhabit a post-Hegelian world and cannot be placed back in a believing early medieval community.

It is clear from the mass of criticism and interpretation which *Beowulf* has generated over the decades that it is a work that invites polysemous reading, and richly rewards it. The problem for *Beowulf* criticism now, it seems, is to begin to try to establish some coherence in and among these efforts without in any way seeking to impede them, so that we have a sense of how each partial act of understanding is part of a larger body of knowledge, of and about the poem.[3] This is why the following pages refer to and use some of the main features of the old exegetical theory, in close correlation with certain major insights and realizations of late twentieth-century theory. But, even as I recognize the usefulness of such theoretical considerations, the primary interest in this book is still with the poem itself. I make a serious attempt to let this unique text dictate which part of polysemous theory, old or new, to call on at each stage of interpretation. To go the other way, to let the many theoretical ramifications of both the ancient-medieval and the modern-postmodern ideas of interpretation dictate the course of the discussion, would lead to a project of unmanageable dimensions, and almost certainly would lose *Beowulf* in the process, to say nothing of the critic writing the book. What follows in this chapter and the next – also to a significant degree in chapters 7 and 8 – is an outline of a polysemous reading of *Beowulf* designed to show both old and new meanings. I have drawn, briefly or at more length, on quite a number of critical approaches, without permitting any one of them by itself to assume undue authority. By letting the poem not the theory carry the burden of the discourse, and by building on the previous chapters, I present an understanding of *Beowulf* that is meant to be both richly evocative in its appreciation of details and broadly illuminating in a large literary and cultural context.

Responsible interpretation has first to address the far from easy question, What would *Beowulf* have meant in its own time, as in its curiously circuitous and allusive way it led its listeners or readers through its two-part story about its protagonist and his actions in the lands of the Scyldings and the Geats? What would have been the meaning, for them, of the great hall Heorot? What would they as Anglo-Saxons have been led to think about as they pondered the significance of the fire-dragon and his acts of destruction, including the slaying of the hero at the same time as he, the monster, is slain by the hero and Wiglaf? These are primary questions. But there is also a corollary interest in this inquiry, based on the realization that great works of the imagination like *Beowulf* take on additional or different meanings as they move through history and come into contact with succeeding generations of readers. In the case of this particular poem, which apparently sat largely unregarded in a fairly nondescript manuscript for several centuries, that kind of accrual of meanings was delayed for a very long time. Even so, much has been done with and to it, in the last two centuries, and a comprehensive critical account has to recognize the existence of this history of accumulated meanings.

A comparison of the old exegetical theory with certain modern and postmodern critical approaches reveals three things: first, there are similarities, at times surprisingly fundamental, between the two sets of theories and practices; secondly, modern and postmodern criticism appears in certain essentials to have grown out of medieval exegesis and to have taken the cultural place formerly held by it; thirdly, it is intellectually desirable, perhaps even necessary, to achieve a critical balance between two kinds of consciousness, the one a product of the painstaking work of reconstructing parts of the past through careful re-creation of perspectives and meanings from former centuries, the other the possession of the critic both cognizant of the thought forms and sensibilities of his or her own time and interested in describing in our contemporary world the significance of Old English poems like *Beowulf*. The hypothesis that permits these two kinds of consciousness to work together is an assumption that literature is a coherent and intelligible body of knowledge not capable of ever being fully understood by means of the perspectives of any one historical period or of any one critical school. Part of this assumption is that literature possesses within itself enough knowable structures and recurrent elements that we are not prevented, as radical historicist arguments would suggest we are, from a substantial measure of genuine understanding of texts from earlier historical periods.

I take as an established fact that the text of *Beowulf* does contain various kinds of meaning. As I said above, what indicates that this is so is the variety of critical and scholarly approaches that have been brought to it, each of them distinguished from the others by the particular kind of verbal elements in the poem that it chooses to focus on. But, whatever the critical interest, it is probably a safe assumption that any serious interpretation of the poem must somehow deal with the following questions: What is Heorot and who are the Scyldings? What is the mere and who are the Grendel race? Who are the Geats in the poem and what is their kingdom? What are the dragon and the treasure? A polysemous exploration of possible answers to these 'What' and 'Who' questions, interested equally in both early medieval and in our current interpretive needs, can take us some considerable way towards understanding this unique poem. That, then, is the main task of this chapter and of what follows in the remainder of the book. The last three chapters continue and extend the polysemous inquiry begun here by examining how part II of the poem, focused on the dragon and Beowulf, completes and finally defines the overall structure and heroic theme of the poem. This last critical task brings us back to the question, Who is Beowulf? That query may not be as simple in the answering as sometimes is assumed, but clearly it is central to any interpretive reading. Chapter 1 has already given a broad preliminary answer to the question of what or who Beowulf is. The matter of his imaginative identities has also been addressed more incidentally in chapters 2, 3, and 4, but the main response will come in the last three chapters.

Literal Meanings

What is Heorot and who are the Scyldings? On the most obvious literal level of meaning, Heorot is one of two principal settings for the major events in part 1; the other is the mere. The Scyldings are the *þeod* 'people' who make up the majority of the human figures in this part; they are, so to speak, the main social and political content of the fiction. We have already seen, in the discussion of modes, kennings, metaphorical language, and narrative remembering, how *Beowulf* points to and draws on a historical and physical world outside itself but at the same time moves away from that world into the centripetal, self-referential world of the poem's own internal patterning and fiction-making; also something of how it inhabits or functions within the context of the word-hoard and Old English poetry more generally. We have recognized as well, at least in broad contours, that *Beowulf* is part of the wider world of words, of imaginative literature as a whole. Definition of such critical contexts for understanding the poem is a modern or postmodern intellectual activity, at least in the way we formulate the definitions of the different contexts of meaning, but I know of no reason to assume that the poet and at least some of his listeners or readers would not have been cognizant of the same essential contextual facts, even though they would have conceived of them and described them differently. It is probably safe to assume the presence in their minds of two kinds of awareness: like us, they would have been more or less conscious of an art of story-telling and entertainment at work in the poem, as they listened to an oral performance or as they read through a manuscript version; at the same time, Heorot and the Scyldings of the poem would for them in some sense have been historical, a place and a people that at some probably indefinite time in the past actually had existed and, in the form of their historical successors the Danes, still did exist. Similarly, numerous modern scholars, with varying degrees of confidence, have granted this imagined place and people inside the poem a connection with prehistoric or early historical Denmark and its inhabitants. Numerous frustrated attempts have also been made to link the poem's composition with its own immediately contemporary context in Anglo-Saxon England, whatever that may have been.

Unfortunately, in my view, much of the effort to reconstruct or fashion historical context and meaning for *Beowulf* has assumed or hoped for a degree of representational descriptiveness in the poem that simply is not there. If I am right, it would seem to be critically healthy, and historically accurate, to recall that in patristic and exegetical practice the literal or descriptive focusing on words as signs pointing to places, people, things, and events outside a text in the actual world is only part of what medieval exegetical interpretation included on the first level as literal meaning. Literalness or the sign value of words was only part of the *sensus litteralis*: the literal or first level of composition and interpretation included as well figures of speech and embraced a wide range of tropes (metaphors, similes, allusions, allegories, parables), sometimes to such an extent that the figural qualities of the text precluded the taking of a simple, straightforward literal meaning at all from what was written or uttered. So far as extant Old English poetry is concerned, it is probably the case that, although this kind of imaginative and verbal turning away from direct description is pervasive, it is never pushed to the degree familiar to us in the 'abstract' modern literary art of the twentieth century, in such works, for example, as *Finnegans Wake*, with its exuberant, sustained exploration of the possibilities of verbal language. Even so, no one, I think, familiar with Old English poetic language would now claim for the linguistically formulaic works found in the Anglo-Saxon poetic records a high degree of mimetic realism or naturalistic descriptiveness: not, that is, if these Old English works are compared with the poems and fictions of the dominant modes of imagining in the last two or three centuries of our literary history. All Old English poems including *Beowulf* immediately announce their 'poeticness' or separateness from the world outside them, not only by their diction but also by the alliterative accentual metre in which they are shaped and by a wide range of other poetic devices, including the frequent use of assonance, verbal echoing, and paranomasia (also favoured by Joyce). The scope within such devices for playing with similarities of sound and different connotations of meaning, and for drawing the listener or reader away from any simple-minded literalistic response, is considerable. One thinks here of some of the more obscure Old English lyrics, including many of the riddles, and also of the kennings observed in chapter 2, in all of which the verbal expression is highly contrived and the focus of meaning is inward, away from direct, literal description or statement.

Considered literally or 'literarily,' in this second, centripetal sense, Heorot and the Scyldings emerge as a rich figurative pattern of images whose main poetic features are easily recognized and whose metaphorical connections within the poem are numerous and far-reaching. It is important to bring this literal (literary) motif into critical focus before consideration of any 'higher' or more 'spiritual' meanings, either those indicated in the text itself by the poet or narrator or those likely to have been discerned by hierarchically minded early medieval imaginations responding to the poem; also before consideration of any 'wider' or 'deeper' phases of meaning that might be recognized by a modern or postmodern critic, of whatever persuasion. It is important also to recognize that meanings which would have been apprehended or understood by Anglo-Saxons as historically literal are now, for us, literary and largely metaphorical, because what the two ages accept as history is by no means the same thing.

The Danes in *Beowulf* are the *Scyldingas,* 'the sons [or 'the men'] of Shield.' The succinct telling of Shield's mysterious origin, conquests, dynastic achievement, and funeral is a parabola-like introduction to two major structural patterns in the poem: the rise, fall, and restoration of the Scyldings, the main concern of part I; and the overall story of the unpromising beginning, rise to triumph and glory, and eventual death of the hero, revealed in a sometimes non-linear way in both Parts I and II. Joy and sorrow, the ebb and flow of human life in the Northern lands, the ongoing war between God and his adversaries – in *Beowulf* these large narrative and symbolic rhythms are inextricably interwoven with the lives and deaths of great kings and protector-lords, like Shield first and, later, like Beowulf. The rhythms are present in all parts of the poem. Appropriately, the imagery of victory in war appears at the very beginning of the text, in association with the eponymous ancestor of the Scyldings, and is quickly taken to its first narrative climax in the account of the building of Heorot. This act of construction is presented as the crowning act of Hrothgar's reign after he has been given *heresped* 'success in war' and is ready to reward his people with generous gifts.

As a verbal image of a physical entity, the great hall is never naturalistically or representationally described (the same is true of the mere and the dragon's lair). Even putting together all the language applied to Hrothgar's dwelling we do not end up with anything like a complete overall empirical sense of this 'best of houses' (*husa selest*), nor would we expect to, given *Beowulf*'s place early in the history of English poetry and its reliance on 'first phase' or metaphorical language for most of its meaning. Nonetheless many of Heorot's 'physical' attributes are mentioned, even as the hall's more obviously figurative or metaphorical identities unmistakably are being established. This dual verbal task is carried out in several ways: by a wide range of characterizing compounds and phrases which, as in kennings and other figures, combine some degree of empirical observation with fictional imagining; by what happens to the hall in relation to other images in the narrative; by the fact that the towering structure of Heorot is the main point of cynosure for the life of the Danes; and by what the narrator says directly in the form of value-laden comment about the meanings of the hall and the Scyldings.

Interestingly, Heorot is mentioned first as an imaginative idea, as a vision that *comes into* Hrothgar's mind (*Him on mod bearn,* 67b) and then gets 'worked' (*gewyrcean*) into the form of a *healreced* 'hall-palace,' a *medoærn micel* 'mighty mead-hall' greater than any ever heard tell of by the children of men. The clear statement of the building's purpose indicates the source of the visionary idea leading to its creation: 'and there within [Hrothgar] would distribute all things to young and old, even as God gave to him, except for public land and the lives of men' (71–3). Mindful of what God gives him, of divine plenitude directed towards him as king, and also of the fact that he himself is not the disposer of human lives or public land, the lord of the Scyldings commands many 'tribes' or 'races' (*mægþe*) 'throughout this middle dwelling to adorn a place for the people,' a *folcstede*. In a kind of coded language, the telling of the origin of the extraordinary edifice moves quickly through a particular creative process: from an initial visionary concept which enters Hrothgar's mind to verbalization of the concept as a royal command, then to actualization of the building, and finally to the naming of the new structure.

Like much else in this long interconnected work, the connotations of Heorot as a poetic motif emerge gradually. Because the hall is both an integral part of an unfolding narrative and in itself a rich cumulative pattern of symbolic meaning, it is intermingled with two other major motifs in part 1: that of the mere and the Grendel kin, and that of the hero. In itself Heorot has two distinct aspects: on the one hand, it is a poetic expression of an idealized state of human existence; on the other, it shows human life taken over by demonic powers. Although these two existential conditions are radically different, and clearly presented as such, they are shown, in the account of what happens to the great hall, as coexisting in fierce antithetical tension with each other. Because Heorot is built by and for the Scyldings of the poem and is dwelt in by them, the dual aspect of its meaning is inseparable from their own bifurcated existence. It is Beowulf's function to rescue these Danes, once they have been taken from a state of primal blessedness into one of demonic possession and grim despair. To do this he must eliminate the forces from hell which are preying on them and by so doing cleanse both the hall and the mere. He does this. Even so, it is his own expectation (shared by the narrator and, it seems, by Wealhtheow) that the fatal contradictions within the Danish society itself eventually will destroy Heorot. In one sense the monsters are irrelevant. Some of the real destroyers are right inside the hall.

If we literally and literarily follow the imagery of Heorot as a 'physical' entity, this is what emerges. The building towers up high and horn-gabled (*Sele hlifade/ heah ond horngeap*, 81b–2a) and has a 'steep' or heavily pitched roof (*on steapne hrof*, 926b). It sits on a high place (*on heahstede*, 285) in the midst of a plain or fields (225, 1413, 1643, 2003), and its impressive elevation is referred to several times: *hean huses* 'the high house' (116); *to þæm heahsele* 'against the high hall' (647a); *in sele þæm hean* 'in the high hall' (713b); *reced hliuade / geap ond goldfah* 'the hall towered up, vaulted [or 'spacious'] and shining with gold' (1799b–1800a). Quite unnaturalistically its light shines 'over many lands' (*ofer landa fela*, 311b). There are outer buildings around the central structure, including sleeping-quarters for those who do not spend the night in the main building (138–9; 920b–4; 1310–11a). Heorot is approached by a 'road' or 'street' 'shining with bright stones' (*Stræt wæs stanfah*, 320a) which leads from the seashore where Beowulf and his troop arrive; this road also apparently connects with 'distant roads' (*widwegas*, 840a) along which 'leaders of the people from far and near' (*folctogan feorran ond nean*, 839) come to examine the marvel of Grendel's hand, arm, and shoulder. As the narrator tells of the exuberant horse-racing that follows after this gathering of admirers, he refers to 'a sand-coloured street' (*fealwe stræte*, 916a) somewhere near the hall. A day and a half or so later in the story, as the triumphant Geats return from the mere following Beowulf's victory there (1632 ff.), they are described as marching forth 'on the foot-tracks' (*feþelastum*) and measuring 'the earth-way, the well-known road' (*foldweg ... cuþe stræte*).

Literally a timbered structure (*sæl timbred*, 307b) with horned gables (*horngeap*, 82; *hornreced*, 704) and 'adorned with bones' or 'antlers' (*banfag*, 780), Heorot is repeatedly characterized in images of radiance and splendour. It is a 'gold-hall' (*goldsele*, 715, 1253, 1639, 2083) not only because it is the royal house of a munificent treasure-giver in which golden objects are dispensed but because it itself is 'splendid and shining with gold' (*geatolic ond goldfah*, 308, 1800), 'a hall gleaming with treasure in the black nights' (*sincfage sel sweartum nihtum*, 167), 'the bright dwelling of brave men' (*hof modigra / torht*, 312b–13a). On the evening of Beowulf's battle with Grendel, as the monster approaches Heorot, he passes 'under the clouds, beneath the sky' (*under wolcnum*), until he can very clearly make out 'the wine-building, the gold-hall of men, gleaming with plated gold' (*winreced, / goldsele gumena ... fættum fahne*, 714b–16a). Heorot's radiance is internal as well as external: 'The tapestries along the walls / Shone with gold, many a wondrous sight / For each man who gazes on such things' (*Goldfag scionon / Web æfter wagum, wundorsiona fela / secga gehwylcum þara þe on swylc starað*, 994b–6). Even the mead-benches are adorned with gold (*golde geregnad*, 777) and the floor is *fagne* 'decorated, shining' (725).

There is no sustained or detailed description of the interior of the hall (or, as already noted, of its exterior), but certain physical features beyond those already mentioned are referred to: the gift-throne (apparently elevated above the rest of the floor, 1815), the hearth (404), the eating and drinking places, the areas cleared for sleeping, and the door or 'mouth' (*muþa*, 724) of the building. This last is important; the door is 'held fast by forged bands' (*fyrbendum fæst*) but is flung or torn open with a touch from the hands of Grendel (721b ff.), the cannibalistic 'mouth-destroyer, devourer' (*muðbonan*, 2079) whose hand, arm, and shoulder later are displayed above the door, under the vaulted roof (833b–6). That the hall is imagined to be large inside can be deduced from the presence in it of a considerable but unspecified number of Scyldings, who are joined by fifteen Geats and, during one of the gift-giving rituals, by 'eight horses with gold-plated bridles' (*eahta mearas / fætedhleore*, 1035b–6a). There is one final but not unimportant physical feature, the iron bands and hinges designed to hold the hall fast within. Quite possibly these are 'literal' in a general historical sense, in that they may reflect actual architectural practice, but they also appear to be metaphorical and symbolic, analogous to a similar motif in the Old English poem *The Order of the World*, in which the order of Creation is described as held fast and prevented from decline or destruction by mighty locks placed round it by God (*ASPR* 3.166: 86–9). Heorot is at once similar to that other Creation and different from it; as a 'fair earth-dwelling' (*fæger foldbold*, 773) Hrothgar's hall is strongly bound together and favoured by heaven, but it is also shown to be destructible. During the conflict with Grendel, for example, the narrator says that only the roof survives intact. But importantly Heorot is capable of being restored and is restored, by the hands of many willing men and women who after Grendel's defeat make the building ready again to serve, for a time, as a *gestsele* 'guest-hall' (991 ff.).

If one reads the imagery of Heorot in this way as a literary motif, a considerable number of characterizing terms accumulate. One group, including compounds and phrases utilizing the base words *bold, ham, hof, hus,* and *wic,* designates the hall as a home or dwelling. Another group indicates the type of building itself, the large hall structure just discussed: *flett, heal, reced, healreced,* and *sele.* Many of the compounds indicate or allude to functions for which the structure is built and used. It is a *dryhtsele* 'dryht-hall' (485, 767) in which the lord of the Danes and his retainers enjoy comradeship together. It is a place for gift-giving and is variously called a *gifheal* 'gift-hall' (838), a *beahsele* 'ring-hall' (1177), a *hringsele* 'ring-hall' (2010), and a *goldsele* 'gold-hall' (715, 1253, 1639, 2083). Beyond these two major functions of serving as a place of fellowship and gift-giving for Hrothgar's 'hearth-troop,' Heorot is also a place for showing hospitality to guests (hence *gestsele*, 994), and for convivial eating and drinking by whoever is present (hence *beorsele* 'beer-hall' or 'banquet-hall,' 482, 492, 1094; *winsele* 'wine-hall,' 695, 771; *winreced* 'wine-hall' or 'wine-building,' 714, 993; *medoærn* 'mead-house,' 69; *medoheal* 'mead-hall,' 484, 638; and *winærn* 'wine-house' or 'wine-hall,' 654). Finally, and disastrously, because hell and the spirit of Cain cannot tolerate such a favoured, harmonious place, Heorot becomes a 'war-hall' (*guðsele*, 443) in which an uninvited guest, a savage, gluttonous monster, feasts on human flesh and the Scyldings experience an evil 'dispensing of ale' (*ealuscerwen*, 769).

We have said that the poetic identity of the Danes is closely linked to that of their hall. Who, then, in the centripetal or inward verbal patterning of the text are the Scyldings? One of the first things that may strike the modern or postmodern reader, coming to this 'epic' about *þrym* 'glory' and *ellen* 'brave deeds,' is the sharp contrast between the rulers on the one hand and their subjects on the other. Aside from the royal figures in the Denmark of the poem, beginning with Scyld and including Queen Wealhtheow, the rest of the Scyldings are a curiously passive and mainly anonymous group of human beings. When, in their lordless state at the beginning of their existence as a people, heaven acts to send them a king, they are grateful. Similarly 'at the appointed time' (*to gescæphwile*, 26), when their first great king goes into the keeping of the heavenly Prince, they mourn and carry out the appropriate funeral rites. So also when Hrothgar commands them to build a hall, they do so, and appropriately are filled with joy as they banquet and receive gifts in it. When a guest from hell comes to visit, they are completely paralysed and victimized. Twelve years later when a deliverer appears, they are momentarily heartened and make room for the foreign visitors. After the first evening of banqueting they clear the hall so that the Geats may deal with the monster. And so on. The Scyldings consistently are characterized as the largely passive recipients of actions by others: God, their rulers, the monsters, and the hero. The only times they themselves 'act' they do so in direct response to what some higher or lower power does to them. Literally they have no initiative or apparent will of their own. This is all very curious because in the rhetoric of the poem – including things said by Beowulf, the narrator, the Geats, and the Danes themselves – they are idealized and romanticized to a considerable degree. They are described as brave warriors living in joy, 'blessedly' (*eadiglice*), until the 'fiend in hell' (*feond on helle*) begins his crimes (99–101). Years later, after each decisive action by Beowulf in their kingdom, there is a resurgence of their primal joy. But how can human beings who are identified mainly as submissive recipients of grace or of demonic attack, whichever comes at any point, be ideal? This is a question that cannot be answered convincingly, I suggest, on the level of plausible cause and effect, of literalistic meaning. The Scyldings are symbolic and their primary significance emerges metaphorically.

It is illuminating, to a point, to read and identify patterns of words and physical images for the Danes and Heorot, interpreting them both literalistically as signs having some connection, however oblique, with an actual historical world and, literarily, as motifs in a unique verbal structure. Such critical analysis is elementary and necessary as the first step in recognizing the particular environment of images that in its totality constitutes the unique structure that is the poem. But identification and analysis of the main physical images in this centripetal-centrifugal manner lead logically to more intensive probing into how these verbal elements accumulate, vary, and move within the fabric of the poem and, as they do so, how they take on significance in relation to each other, as well as to other similar or antithetical motifs. Much good critical work has been done in recent decades with this level or phase of meaning in *Beowulf*.[4] Given the length of this text, its interconnectedness, the figurative richness of its language, and its unique structure, this kind of close reading of the internal or centripetal part of the *sensus litteralis* holds almost unlimited scope for discoveries of new things to delight and please connoisseurs of the art of *Beowulf*.

Typical and Typological Meanings

But even as *Beowulf* entertains and pleases, and also, in one special sense, instructs, by pointing outward to what modernity is pleased to call the 'real' historical world of the Northern Germanic peoples, the poem also makes clear that it is intended to inspire and instruct on other levels as well. It is perhaps not surprising that some modern and postmodern critics resist this fact. The dominant scholarly culture in which we live and work is not on the whole patient or understanding when confronted with those elements of Anglo-Saxon (or later medieval) culture that emphasize, or simply assume, religious or metaphysical realities. Many would prefer to stay with the *sensus litteralis*, with what the Fathers and the artists and exegetes who followed them thought of as the purely human language and meaning of a text. In the case of *Beowulf*, after all, for the reasons just mentioned, reading on this level can be very rewarding. Among Old English longer poems it stands out as *sui generis*, as a moral and religious poem that does not ask its listeners or readers to despise the world, to escape from the middle dwelling and the individual *banhus* as soon as heaven permits. Rather, *Beowulf* shows and invites a deep loyalty and attachment to ideals, things, people, and experiences in middle earth. Even so, other perspectives and levels of meaning also are at work, and the poet reminds us of them over and over again; it is this set of directions within the poem itself that now needs to be identified, and analysed in the light both of exegetical theory and of certain twentieth-century critical concepts.

To conduct such an analysis it is necessary to confront directly a central fact about *Beowulf*, one that has been hovering over the whole discussion in this book so far: for an early medieval Anglo-Saxon and a modern scholar-critic, reality and history are by no means the same. As Dorothy Whitelock pointed out years ago, for members of an Anglo-Saxon audience of *Beowulf* the deliverance of Heorot from a monster's ravages would be an event on the same level of reality as the attack by Ingeld and the Heathobards: 'The average man would believe in the monsters, in the creatures of evil lurking in the waste lands round him' (1951, 71–2). For us, in contrast, the hall and the monsters, and even the Scyldings themselves, are symbolic and mythological, however true and important we may think the human and social meanings they point to. For the Anglo-Saxon, and for the verbal language he or she used (or was used by) to express 'reality,' there was no split between the phenomenal and the noumenal worlds, no post-Cartesian scientific sense of empirical facts as things divorced from their moral and spiritual dimensions. This has many implications for those trying to understand the poem, especially in relation to the question of whether or not the literal imagery – of Heorot, the Scyldings and the Geats, the mere, the monsters, the dragon's lair, the treasure, and the hero – invites a degree of allegorical understanding.

I have been suggesting that the reading of *Beowulf* as signs and the reading of it as centripetal motifs should be seen as distinct but complementary critical activities, without both of which an imbalance occurs in the act of interpretation. Failure in this area of criticism leads either to a too-complete ironic withdrawal from the world outside the text or to a slighting of the integrity of the work itself, all delight and no instruction, or vice versa. But we need not stop with this unresolved dichotomy any more than medieval exegetical theory stopped with the literal and historical level of interpretation. In fact, as soon as the critic's attention moves beyond saying what the poem refers to in the external world, and beyond examination of how its verbal elements work internally, he or she is led irresistibly, by directives within the poem itself, into further matters of polysemous interpretation. If the response to the text is intellectually conscious, it is impossible not to wonder what all the literal and literary imagery is meant to signify. What is the poem or the poet trying to tell listeners or readers? Part of the attempt to answer such questions involves a critical process closely analogous to the medieval search in texts for the second level of meaning, the one called allegorical or typical and having to do with moral teaching or doctrinal and devotional matters. Here again Frye is helpful. Thinking as a modern but well aware of the medieval theory, he called this next phase of interpretation 'formal criticism.' It begins in much the same way as textural or rhetorical analysis, by studying the imagery of the poem with a view to bringing out its distinctive structure or pattern, but it goes beyond this perspective to another kind of activity. Formal criticism as such is commentary, the process of translating into explicit or discursive language what is implicit or only partially explicit in the work itself. The critic or exegete as commentator tries to find out what the poet meant to say and then tells his or her own reader what the poet had in mind. He or she tries to explain, for example, what is meant when Heorot and the Scyldings are linked with the first Creation, or when the Grendel race are identified with the race of Cain; or, more difficult, what is meant by the close association of the dragon and Beowulf with the ancient accursed treasure.

There is a possible major pitfall in this kind of exegesis and criticism, one that has dogged the controversies in *Beowulf* studies for some decades now. If we unthinkingly adopt the view that the poet's main intention was to convey a meaning or teach a lesson to his audience, we risk forgetting the hypothetical nature of all imaginative expression. We may also neglect the corollary point, that the words in every poem or literary work are part of a unique literary motif or structure. One of the main achievements of criticism in the mid and late twentieth century, of special importance when reading a marvel-filled work like *Beowulf*, has been to demonstrate how correspondence between words in a text and what those words describe outside the text is of primary concern only in discursive writing. Nor is that all. As moderns and postmoderns, we have emphatically demonstrated to ourselves that, even in verbal expression that is primarily discursive or descriptive, the correspondence is more precarious than was once recognized in the heyday of mimeticism. It is now a critical axiom that a poet's intention, even that of a didactic medieval poet, is to a considerable degree always centripetally directed and each image or idea in the poem is there primarily as part of the poem. It is this fictional or literary or imaginative fact about *Beowulf* that provides one of the main themes of this book: whether the concern at a particular point is with the overall mode of imagining, the metaphorical way the language works, or the circuitous and allusive manner in which the story gets told, it is the essentially poetic and imaginative nature of the structure of words entitled *Beowulf* that is being kept in the foreground. It is this imagined fictionality, moreover, that will continue to dominate, as the outline of a polysemous interpretation emerges further in this chapter and in what follows.

Partly because of our assumptions and predispositions as moderns or postmoderns, controversy surrounds the question of the degree to which exegetical theory about the second, third, and fourth levels of the *sentence* (allegorical, tropological, and anagogical) is relevant to Old English poetry, including *Beowulf*. But there are also inherent characteristics of the poem itself that make undesirable any critical or interpretive flat-footedness in the way the exegetical scheme is used. Although a large number of passages in *Beowulf* direct attention to one or more of the second, third, and fourth levels of meaning – and I shall discuss enough of these to establish the point – there still remains a good deal of obliqueness and mystery in the presentation of the poem's metaphors. (There is no implication in the present interpretation that anyone responsible for the composition of *Beowulf* was a sophisticated exegete of biblical texts, thoroughly versed in patristic commentaries. All that is argued for, and demonstrated, is the major presence in the poem of biblical elements, deployed in shaping, informing ways which show an awareness of the moral and spiritual perspectives traditionally delineated in the four-level concept: the kind of awareness that any intelligent Anglo-Saxon Christian imbued with the dominant theocentric world view and a traditional sense of the meanings of the biblical story and stories would have.) *Beowulf* invites a measure of *allegoresis* or allegorical interpretation, but it is not formal allegory. It conveys spiritual and moral teachings, certainly, but it does not subordinate the pronounced physicality of its metaphorical images to abstract concepts or doctrines. It is a work obviously intended in its own time to invite and encourage meditative, thoughtful responses to its tale of joy and horror. But it is also clear that, like other great works of the imagination conceived in highly figurative language, *Beowulf* could not have yielded up all its meanings to anyone in its own time, including the poet himself, regardless of the imaginative responsiveness or the religious piety and exegetical insights brought to bear on it. Nor, it should be readily acknowledged, does it permit definitive interpretation now, for all the learning and critical ingenuity that may be brought to it.

Henri de Lubac indicated in the following way the exegetical difference between reading for literal or historical meaning and reading for allegorical meaning: 'De l'histoire à l'allégorie, on passait comme de la lettre à l'esprit, du fait sensible à la réalité profonde, ou du miracle au mystère' (*Exégèse Médiévale*, part I, II, II, 549). The movement to this second 'mode d'explication' is dictated by four great teachers, Jerome, Augustine, Ambrose, and Gregory, and also by a long list of others, including Isidore, Bede, and Hrabanus Maurus. These seven exegetes all wrote before or during the period of Old English literature, Hrabanus coming last, 784–856. According to the tradition developed and furthered by them, the essence of allegorical meaning is the spiritual mystery that rests in the events and words (*facti* and *dicti*) of a text and so directs the Christian to see in them a revelation of divine truth. The search for the allegorical meaning is not at all a matter of detached speculation about some non-temporal truth; rather, the one who searches for it, according to the dominant exegetical tradition of the Latin West, will find the concrete mystery of the revealed Christ himself. Beneath the surfaces (*superficies*) of the historical or literal text the awakened understanding sees another dimension, that of spiritual reality.

Real allegory is typology, leading the mind and soul in a process of upward metamorphosis from types to the antitype, to the reality in relation to which everything else is a type. The allegorical level is supposed to answer the question *quid credas* 'what do you believe?' It is precisely at this nexus that many moderns and postmoderns become uneasy. Some take comfort from the fact that, although there are biblical elements in *Beowulf*, the most obvious ones are from the Old Testament and there apparently is no overt reference in the poem to Christ. Common sense tells us that this apparent absence (it may evoke a presence) can only have been deliberate on the part of the poet, who would certainly have known that for Anglo-Saxon Christians the normal way of understanding the Old Testament was to interpret it in relation to the New Testament. The words and events of the Old Testament, as the Old English poems *Genesis*, *Exodus*, and *Daniel* make abundantly clear, were read as prefigurations of the New Testament revelation. The Old Testament types are part of a view of history which sees the temporal and spatial ordering of human experience as understandable only in the context of eternity. As such they are part of myth. Typology is the reversal of most modern historiography, the latter being conducted according to a principle of causality in an attempt to provide explanations for events in terms of previous chronological causes and effects in the actual world of time and space. The typological pointers to biblical matters that are provided by the *Beowulf* poet help keep the poem from dissolving into a mass of decentring allusions. Still, some will argue, such typological or allegorical knowledge on our part may not be useful with *Beowulf*. Would it not be better to continue to scrutinize *this poem* for social or historical realism or for correspondences to the archaeological finds about Anglo-Saxon England that have been piling up in our time, or even simply to the poetic and imaginative intricacies that the text provides so generously? Even if, the argument continues, *Beowulf* may long ago have lent itself to allegorizing responses from certain Anglo-Saxons attuned to logocentric and metaphysical ways of perceiving and thinking, why should our interpretation pay heed to such things?[5] In what follows I hope to show that our critical and cultural biases are unnecessarily delimiting and that the 'metaphysical' gap between the poem and ourselves may not be as unbridgeable as we think.

There is a gap of another kind between the literal and the literary aspects of meaning within the *sensus litteralis*, and it is this that the second level of exegesis existed to close. It did so by thinking beyond words as signs or motifs, by moving on to consideration of them as allegories of spiritual mysteries or moral truths. In the same way, the exegetical consciousness also considered the events of history and the order of the physical world themselves as revelations of the workings of heaven and hell. It is this kind of reading, interpreting, and commenting on texts, events, and the things of the world that in Frye's theory of polysemous meaning is called formal criticism. On the one hand, form implies what we have been considering as the literal/literary unity of the structure and, on the other, such complementary terms as content and matter, what the structure shares with external nature. In this second, formal phase of criticism, analogous to the medieval second level, the imitation of nature is not the kind of handling of the world and ideas outside the poem that is comprehended in the literalistic half of the first level of exegetical reading. In formal imitation the work of art is a secondary imitation of human action or thought. This does not mean that it is two degrees removed from 'reality' but that, according to a long and durable tradition, it is one step closer to universal truth and the reality that ultimately matters. This level emphasizes the exemplary nature of what is being described and sets forth what tradition says are typical action and typical thought. This emphasis or assumption is what makes interchangeable the terms 'allegorical' and 'typical' to designate the second level of meaning. From the allegorical perspective, the work of art stands as exemplary between actual history or philosophies or theologies, on the one hand, and the reader or interpreter, on the other. Once again, though, it is important to realize that the word 'allegorical,' in this interpretive sense, does not imply that a particular text like *Beowulf* is structurally a sustained, formal allegory with its imagery subordinated to a parallel and more important structure of concepts or doctrines.

It is evident that a great many of the literary texts of the medieval and Renaissance periods are more involved in this formal phase of meaning than in the more externalized or descriptive following of an empirically known nature found in the European literatures that come later historically. The *Beowulf* poet often directs interpretation of the actions set forth in his poem by having the narrator or another character stress their typicality: Grendel is 'of the race of Cain' (*in Caines cynne*, 107a); 'Wyrd often saves an undoomed man, if his courage is good' (*Wyrd oft nereð / unfægne eorl, þonne his ellen deah*, 572b–3). He stresses their exemplary function: Beowulf is 'the gentlest and worthiest of men, kindest to his people and most eager for fame' (*manna mildust ond monðwærust, / leodum liþost on lofgeornost*, 3181–2). When the poet does these things he is working in a very broad humanist tradition in which serious or major poetry was expected to illustrate the typicality of human experience and the universal forms of behaviour. That this tradition still helps assure a readership not only for *Beowulf* but also for many other texts from the ancient, medieval, and Renaissance periods is perhaps a tribute to the human accuracy or truth expressed in it. That it also has a fundamental and direct historical connection with the way believers throughout the history of Christianity have looked to the persons, events, and teachings recorded in the Old Testament (and other texts) as allegories pointing to the ideal human form, Christ, is clear.

As biblical mythology worked its way through the centuries of European literature, it encountered many different social and cultural contents which, on the face of them, would seem to have nothing to do with the Christian Bible, Old

Testament or New. But over and over again these cultural contents were swallowed and interpreted in the light of the powerful mythology which we see starting its large cultural task in the English language during the Anglo-Saxon period. In *The Dream of the Rood,* for example, the Christ who goes to battle on the Cross is unmistakably presented as the ideal embodiment of the thane-lord loyalties of the Christian *dryht* society which is the product of the fusion of Germanic tradition and biblical myth. Some hundreds of years later, in *Piers Plowman,* the Jesus who jousts in Piers's arms at Jerusalem is presented as the ideal embodiment of Christian feudal values. The question for us is where, if at all, in its exemplary and moral dimensions, *Beowulf* belongs in this kind of ongoing reimagining of biblical story and myth. Who, according to the typifying expressions within the poem itself, are the Scyldings and what, beyond the historical and literal/literary level, is their hall Heorot? What, moreover, does the poem say or suggest about the meanings of the Scyldings and Heorot on the third and fourth levels, those parts of the *sentence* traditionally called tropological and anagogic?

In the patristic and medieval exegetical scheme, movement beyond the letter or the image was thought of as progression to an order of truth in which the human being learns what it is that he or she is to believe. Often but not always a writer will make clear what moral or spiritual lesson is intended by overtly linking images within the text with biblical and other traditional Christian matters. *Beowulf* does this. It is an Anglo-Saxon poem based on inherited folkloric tales associated with places and events in the Germanic past. That earlier world and its tales have been reshaped by a biblically educated imagination able to see and interpret correspondences between the Germanic stories and some of the most profoundly influential biblical and hexaemeral narratives. This reimagining is carried out to the extent that the overall outline of biblical myth from Creation to Doomsday and a significant number of discrete myths within the large containing narrative are functioning in the poem in shaping and informing ways, without at all overwhelming the Germanic tale. When the first presentation of Heorot is linked with Genesis, it is as if the poet is laying a mental map of the first Creation over a map of the land of the Scyldings. By placing the unique story of Beowulf within the coherence of the larger biblical story, by inviting us to see the tale of the Scyldings and the Geats not only in the middle distance of the Germanic past but also in the farther distance of biblical myth, the poet provides glimpses of the power and the workings of a far greater design than any earthly hall or worldly code can achieve. The periodic scanning in the text of that larger poetic and mythic horizon is an invitation to us to engage in featural analysis in which close reading goes hand in hand with attention to the larger rhythmic structures of the metanarrative. Much of the vitality of the poem inheres in its corporeal details, but its profundity and vision depend as well on its large contours.

Metaphorically Heorot is an *imago mundi* and the Danes are humankind or, as the poem has it, 'mankind' (*moncynn*, 110, 164, 196, 1276, 1955, 2181). Although there is a significant degree of historical particularity about this place and people, their typicality or universality is made clear in several ways. As mentioned more than once already in this book, the creation of Heorot is linked in exemplary fashion with the origin of the earth itself, a 'radiantly bright plain' (*wlitebeorhtne wang,* 93) illuminated by the sun and the moon and adorned by the Almighty with all living things. Its inhabitants, the Scyldings, at the moment in which they take possession of their great hall, similarly are linked with 'the origin of mankind' (*frumsceaft fira*, 91). In each of the three occurrences, early in the text, of the theme of ornamentation, there is a sense of the broad world coming to a central focus in the story of the Scyldings: in the case of Scyld's sea burial, the ornaments and treasures laid in the bosom of the ship are brought from 'far ways' (*of feorwegum*, 37); in the case of Heorot, it is said by the narrator that the work of ornamenting this 'people's place' (*folstede*, 76) is required by Hrothgar of 'many peoples throughout this middle dwelling' (*manigre mægþe   geond þisne middangeard*, 75); and when the world itself was formed, says the singer in Heorot, the Almighty 'ornamented the earth's regions with branches and leaves' (*gefrætwade   foldan sceata / leomum ond leafum*, 96–7a). The treasure-laden burial ship of a good king, the mightiest of mead-halls heard of by the children of men, and the pristine Creation itself, all, because of their inherent excellence deriving from the Creator, establish Heorot and the Scyldings as powerful metaphors for ideal or typical human life as heaven created it, and as the *Alwalda* 'All Ruler' intends it to be. This is why in Heorot in its early hours, we are told, 'those dryht-men lived in joy, blessedly' (*ða drihtguman   dreamum lifdon / eadiglice*, 99–100a).

Despite the catastrophic fate that soon engulfs Hrothgar's kingdom, most of the characterizing epithets applied to the Danes are laudatory or sympathetic. Socially and politically it is the Danes who are the point of cynosure throughout part I. They are the collective human reference point round which all ethical and spiritual values come to a focus. In the very first line they are called the *Gar-Dene* 'Spear-Danes,' a martial epithet paralleled in its general meaning by the numerous uses of *Scyldingas* 'Sons of Shield.' Hrothgar twice describes his people as the *Ar-Scyldingas* 'Honour-Scyldings' or 'Grace-' or 'Favour-Scyldings': first, when he tells Beowulf how the hero's father embroiled in a blood feud fled the land of the Weders and sought the favour of the Danes (464); and secondly, when he contrasts Beowulf with the murderous, stingy Heremod, whose reign over the *Ar-Scyldingas* was a disaster (1710). In this latter passage Hrothgar calls the Danes 'the sons of Ecg-wela,' *Ecgwela* apparently being an early Danish king whose name 'Sword-Wealth' literally and metaphorically combines connotations of both war and treasure. In the Finnsburg episode, continuing the martial theme, the narrator calls Hnaef, the king of the Danes who has been slain in battle and whose body is being placed on the pyre, 'the best battle-warrior of the Army-Scyldings' (*Here-Scyldinga / betst beadorinca*, 1108b–12a). It was noted earlier how, in Beowulf's decisive put-down of Unferth as an ineffective coward in the war with Grendel, the hero calls the Danes 'the Victory-Scyldings' (*Sige-Scyldinga*, 597); he uses the same epithet for them when he is describing to Hygelac (2004) his 'mighty meeting' (*micel gemeting*, 2001) with Grendel. Hrothgar's venerability is characterized twice by the narrator in terms of the old king's relation to Ing, the legendary king of the Danes: while presenting Beowulf with gifts after the slaying of Grendel, Hrothgar is referred to as 'the protector of Ing's friends' (*eodor Ingwina*, 1044); later Beowulf, not knowing of Grendel's mother's attack during the night and her slaying of Aeschere, is shown going cheerfully in the morning to inquire whether 'the prince of the Friends of Ing' (*frean Ingwina*, 1319) has had a pleasant night according to his desires.

Additional terms identifying, characterizing, and idealizing the Danes accumulate throughout part 1, underlining the typicality and universality of what they symbolize. For both Beowulf (427) and the narrator (609), Hrothgar is 'the lord of the Bright' or 'Glorious Danes' (*brego Beorht-Dena*). Hrothgar's people are the 'Ring Danes' (*Hring-Dene*), a term used directly by the narrator (116, 1279) and by Hrothgar (1769); 'Ring Danes' is at once a literally descriptive term, pointing to the rings and mail-coats or corslets that appear frequently in part 1, and an important symbol of several things. A ring is both inclusive and exclusive, encircling even while it delimits and excludes. It becomes a many-faceted spatial metaphor for the Danes, who are represented at the beginning of the poem as singled out for special favour and, for more than alliterative reasons, are designated eight times by one of the four compass points (383, 392, 463, 616, 783, 828, 1578, 1996). As the East Danes, the West Danes, the North Danes, and the South Danes they inhabit a kingdom which in the poem's metaphors and in its universalizing or all-encompassing typicality symbolizes the ideal *middangeard*. They live in a hall in the midst of a *wong* 'plain' (225, 1413, 2003), a *meodowong* 'mead-plain' (1643) metaphorically linked with the *wlitebeorhtne wang* 'radiantly bright plain' (43) of the primal Creation. In the midst of this *imago mundi*, in this enclosing and protecting ring-hall of the people favoured by God and their king, is situated the gift-throne from which the lord of the rings circulates treasures among the *dryht* men. Near the throne and throughout the hall, from time to time, Wealhtheow, Freawaru, and hall stewards pass wine-goblets or pour clear mead from beautiful ale-cups. The Ring Danes and their middle dwelling symbolically embrace the full circle of God's originally bright Creation. It is into this light-filled centre that the foe of mankind and adversary of God comes out of the darkness, intending to destroy human harmony and joy. Against him, twelve years later, from across the sea and assisted in his voyage by God, comes a deliverer who is the mightiest of the human race, as this race lives in this poem in the imagined spaces enclosed by the seas.

During his first meeting with the hero, Hrothgar recalls how, long before Grendel's attacks when he himself was young and enjoying his early kingship, Beowulf's father *Ecgþeow* 'Sword Servant' came to the *Suðena folc ... Ar-Scyldinga* 'Southern people ... Grace Scyldings' to escape the consequences of having killed a man of the Wylfings, thereby starting 'the greatest of feuds' (*fæhðe mæste*, 459 ff.). Hrothgar settled the matter by paying the *wergyld* 'man-price,' in the form of *ealde madmas* 'ancient treasures' which he sent 'over the water's ridge' (*ofer wæteres hrycg*, 471b–2a) to the Wylfings. In return Ecgtheow swore oaths to Hrothgar and by so doing assumed an obligation that Beowulf now, years later, appears to be resuming as he volunteers to help the Danes. The first thing Hrothgar says to the young man – who is standing before him on the hearth 'hard under his helmet' (*heard under helme*) with his byrny shining (404–5) – shows the king's realization that that event long ago is now coming full circle: 'Because of deeds done, my friend Beowulf, and because of kindness [or grace], you have sought us out' (*For gewyrhtum þu, wine min Beowulf, / ond for arstafum usic sohtest*, 457–8). The deeds done and the kindness or grace referred to here can mean any and all of the following: the generosity shown earlier by Hrothgar to Ecgtheow and the Geats; the grace or kindness of Beowulf that is being demonstrated by his coming at this time to Denmark; and the grace of God which, years earlier, prompted Hrothgar to settle a feud and, similarly now, has sent Ecgtheow's son to stop the bloodshed of another feud. The phrase *for arstafum* has precisely this last meaning in the statement made slightly earlier by Hrothgar when he is told by the herald Wulfgar about Beowulf's arrival: *Hine halig God / for arstafum us onsende* 'Holy God in his grace is sending him to us' (381b–2). Because this is a poem in which human expressions of magnanimity and heroism regularly are presented as imitative of and made possible by the grace of the heavenly Dryhten, the formulaic phrase *for arstafum* in this passage functions both literally and typically to suggest all three meanings. Hrothgar's earlier kindnesses to Ecgtheow and the Geats were the gracious, peace-making acts of a king who himself is favoured by heaven. Similarly, Beowulf has been accorded by the Almighty powers far beyond those of normal men and is generously offering to put these to work helping the Danes against the powers of darkness.

War against the Creation   167

The passage under discussion culminates in a description by Hrothgar of Heorot drenched in blood (*drihtsele dreorfah*, 485) after a night of Grendel's ravages. The old king uses a cluster of formulas which by virtue of their scriptural and scripture-inspired associations convey allegorical meaning about the situation of the Danes, both at the beginning of Hrothgar's reign when Ecgtheow sought him out, and again now years later. Perhaps the best way into these typifying and typological associations is through the one other occurrence in Old English poetry of the phrase *ealde madmas*, which is used here by Hrothgar of the *wergyld* he paid for Ecgtheow. The formula is found in *Exodus* (*ASPR* 1; 107:586) and refers to 'Joseph's treasure' (*Iosepes gestreon*, 588), that fabulous traditional (but not explicitly biblical) wealth that washes up on the seashore after the great miracle of deliverance and judgment enacted in the Red Sea waters. Like Grendel, the enemy of the Israelite *dryht* in *Exodus* is identified as *godes andsaca* 'God's adversary' (503). The Egyptians led by Pharaoh have at this point been put to death in the depths of raging flood-waters by 'an ancient sword' (*alde mece*, 495) through the power of 'the Guardian of the mere-flood' (*mereflodes weard*, 504). Under Moses as their mighty leader in war, the Israelite *dryht*, like the Scyldings prior to Grendel's incursions, are meant to enjoy the *brade rice* ('broad kingdom,' 557b) of the Promised Land with its *burh* and *beagas* ('fortress and rings,' 557a). Both peoples, the Israelites and the Scyldings, because of the leadership of mighty war-lords assisted by heaven, are permitted in triumph to occupy *beorselas beorna* 'the banquet-halls of men' (*Exodus*, 563-4a; *Beowulf*, 482) and to use 'ancient treasures' for peace-making purposes.

The kingdom of the *Ar-Scyldinga* newly ruled over by Hrothgar to which Ecgtheow flees is called, by Hrothgar, *gimme rice* 'gem kingdom' or *gimmerice* 'gem-rich' (the manuscript says *gim merice*), or perhaps *ginne rice* 'broad kingdom' (several editors' emendation). In the next phrase, Denmark is called the *hordburh hæleþa* 'treasure city of heroes' (466b-7a). Whether the first of these two formulas is read as a compound noun 'gem kingdom' (*gimme rice*) or 'broad kingdom' (*ginne rice*) in apposition with *hordburh* or as an adjective 'gem-rich' modifying it, the reading makes good sense, in the *Beowulf* context. In the former reading ('gem kingdom'), the words would be a characterization of the land of the Scyldings paralleling the reference in *Exodus* to the broad kingdom and gold-halls of Israel's Promised Land. If however the text is read as saying *ginne rice* 'broad kingdom' there is an illuminating parallel in the Old English *Genesis* (*ASPR* 1, 9:230), where the wide or spacious kingdom referred to is the broad land through which the second stream of paradise flows; this follows in the *Genesis* text immediately after a description of the first paradisal stream, characterized as watering a place where the best gold and gems are found. Typologically the Promised Land has been traditionally understood in one of its main meanings as a restoration of paradise, so that the alternative analogues in the two Cædmonian poems for Hrothgar's kingdom have similar allegorical significance.

Interesting as well, in the light of the prominence in *Beowulf* of the newly built Heorot's association with the first Creation, is the fact that the passage in *Genesis* includes a description of the newly established paradise (*Neorxnawong*, 208 and 217) as it stands 'good and ready for guests, filled with gifts' (*god and gastlic, gifena gefylled*, 209). Even if the manuscript *gastlic* is read as 'spiritual' instead of being taken as a variant of *gæstlic* 'ready for guests,' as it is by some editors, the immediately following reference to paradise as a place filled with gifts for the use and enjoyment of God's thane Adam and his wife Eve retains the basic metaphor of the guest-hall of Eden.[6] For that matter, there is good reason to assume that the *Genesis* poet was engaging in paronomasia, one of the polysemous devices available to him for letting two perfectly intelligible and compatible meanings work together simultaneously. Paradise as first created is both physical and spiritual, and there is no split in *Genesis* between the phenomenal world and the noumenal one, any more than there is in *Beowulf*. It is in this idealized mythical place, this *temenos* 'sacred precinct,' that Adam and Eve are blessed by the 'happy-hearted King' (*bliðheort cyning*, 192) and are given for their enjoyment all that the Dryhten has brought into being, 'every created thing in the world' (*eall worulde gesceaft*, 199). Like the 'radiantly bright plain' of the new Creation in *Beowulf* (*wlitebeorhtne wang*, 93), the human pair are described by the adjective *wlitebeorht* (188), and as being 'in their youth' (*on geogoðe*, 187). The speech of Hrothgar to Beowulf looks back to an earlier and better time when he himself also was 'in his youth' (*on geogoðe*, 466) and his splendid kingdom had not yet fallen under the influence of hell. In that long-gone period early in 'the one hundred half-years' (*hund missera*, 1769) of his reign, the man Ecgtheow who started a feud and so came into Hrothgar's kingdom was willing to swear oaths and be bound by the law of *wergyld*, unlike Grendel now. It was a time, like that of the primal paradise, when, as can be seen in the account of the founding of Heorot, the folk-share or common land and the bodies of human beings were inviolate, not to be treated as dispensable possessions to be disposed of at will (*Beowulf*, 71–3). It is, I suggest, such verbal echoes and elegiac memories as these, of a lost paradise and early promise thwarted long since in Hrothgar's guest-hall, that permeate the language and hover over the scene in which Hrothgar receives the hero.

Since Heorot and the Scyldings in their ideal aspect are identified typically by means of paradigmatic models found in the biblical accounts of the origin of the world and the human race, it is not surprising to find the story of Cain emerging early in the narrative. Because the poem is largely concerned with Germanic stories about how savage blood-lust and war regularly undermine human efforts to create and sustain social harmony, it is not strange at all that the enemies of such divinely assisted human work should be identified by an Anglo-Saxon poet with the archetypal figure of Cain. Interestingly it is not literally Satan as such, even in disguise (as in *Genesis B*), who introduces hell's influence into Hrothgar's world. But in another way Grendel's attacks on Heorot do parallel the fall of man in the Cædmonian poems. As in *Genesis A* (442–851) and *Genesis B* (852–964), so in part 1 of *Beowulf*, the 'fall' of the human race into the clutches of hell takes place because of an assault by hell, not because of any discernible human failure.[7] The poet does not try to give a human explanation, that is a human-behaviour explanation, for the fall of Heorot. Hell goes to work on Heorot and that is that. Like Adam and Eve in the poems of the Junius manuscript, the Scyldings are happily enjoying the gifts of the *middangeard* when suddenly and without provocation an uninvited visitor from hell arrives to destroy their joy. In *Beowulf* and in both parts of the Old English *Genesis*, the emphasis is on the way that the war already started between the Creator and his adversaries is now being continued, with the Scyldings and Adam and Eve caught in the middle. In this traditional mythology the real demonic is pre-human. It is true that in both the Cædmonian *Genesis* and *Beowulf* the human victims do 'fall,' in the sense that they do not (cannot?) successfully resist the attack from hell. But they are victims of crime, not instigators of it. In neither text is there a sense of the human beings having independent wills or any real freedom of choice in the matter. The mythical presence of the heavenly and demonic influences impinging on and determining human existence is too complete. In *Genesis,* to be sure, it is said that the two trees in paradise represent God's gift of human freedom to choose good or evil (460 ff.), but the emphasis throughout is on the skill of the demonic tempter and on the good intentions of Adam and Eve.

Something similar is true of *Beowulf.* Not only does the narrator present the Scyldings as having done nothing to deserve Grendel's hatred but, even when some of them in desperation fall into devil worship, they are said not to know any better. This, it should be noted, is in spite of the fact that *Beowulf* is a poem replete with sententious and moralizing comments and judgments on people and events, by both the narrator and other characters inside the narrative. The 'fallen' Danes are not judged negatively, except in the case of Unferth, who is arraigned for cowardice by Beowulf; perhaps also, by anticipation, as the narrative proceeds and the ambiguities of Heorot intensify, Hrothulf also is implicated. It is never said or apparently even implied that the Danes really could have helped themselves in the war with Grendel. For those of us accustomed to the play of free will in Shakespearean tragedy, and to John Milton's emphasis on the adequacy of human reason and foreknowledge for resisting hell's assault in *Paradise Lost* ('sufficient to have stood but free to fall'), this may seem curious. In one sense the conception in the Old English poems of how human beings are conditioned and determined by forces beyond their understanding or control is like the treatment of human figures in modern ironic texts, as for example in a Samuel Beckett play or a Franz Kafka novel; or as in the conception of human beings in some modern science in which they have no real identity and are simply local modifications of the energy field. In *Beowulf* when human figures are characterized as weak or strong or as good or bad it as if their strength or weakness and their good or evil disposition are assigned to them by external forces: a savage spirit wells up in someone and drives him to murder; a soul-slayer attacks and induces despair and devil worship; God gives prodigious strength to one man so that he is able to perform gigantic acts of rescue. Even more arbitrarily, in the case of the Geatish prince Herebeald remembered by Beowulf, an arrow accidentally kills someone and the one who has shot the arrow, the elder brother of the dead man, is viewed by the father of the two brothers as a loathsome, guilty, but unpunishable fratricide.

For us, the sense of a set-up, of numerous set-ups, at once arbitrary and objective, pervades the poem. It is also built into the biblical and hexaemeral myths that help structure and inform the *Beowulf* vision of existence in middle earth. Most unnervingly perhaps for those who would still see the biblical metanarrative as doctrinally authoritative, its use in practice, as in this and other Old English poems, leaves a strong sense that free choice is highly theoretical. Theoretically Guthlac or Juliana or the Scyldings and Geats can say yes to the Creator, thus affirming their gratitude and obedience to the *Liffrea*. When instead in the normal course of existence most human beings, other than saints and heroes, say no and prove disloyal, they are Grendel, or they are the Danes in their devil worship, or they are the cowardly thanes about to be driven into exile late in the poem. Such beings in principle are cut off from knowledge of the real good by which alone they might have directed their lives rightly. It will be necessary to return at greater length to this point in the last chapter of this book. What is important here is to recognize how the mythical mode of imagining and certain structural metaphors characteristic of the Cædmonian poems have close parallels in *Beowulf*. Whether or not direct 'influence' is assumed, recognition of these similarities is important if the patterns of imagery in *Beowulf* are to become clear and if the typifying part of their polysemous functioning is to be understood.

When the rebel archangel Lucifer in *Genesis B* says *Ic mæg wesan god swa he* 'I can be God as well as he can, (283b), theoretically he is right. In a world of pure hypothesis and imagining, Lucifer or any other of the archangels could as well be God. But that is not what the myth or the orthodox doctrines that emanate from it say, and so Lucifer is presented as an exemplar of *ofermod* 'overreaching pride'; consequently there is dissension and war in the dryht of heaven which must be punished. In *Genesis A*, the *Waldend* 'Wielder' (67) is 'furious' (*yrre*, 34) and 'wrathful' (*wrað*, 35) because of the way the original perfect harmony of the dryht of heaven has been violated. He engages in the mythically first wrestling match in the extant Anglo-Saxon poetic versions of the biblical metanarrative (65b ff.). Like Beowulf dealing with the monster Grendel – who also bears 'God's wrath' (*godes yrre bær*, 7ll) – the Deity is described as seizing his foes with hostile hands, crushing them in his bosom, and then driving them forth from their glorious possessions 'on a long journey' (*on langne sið*, 68b). As in *Beowulf*, predictably there is a place that has been prepared for those who 'contend against God' (*wiþ gode winnan*, 77). In the Cædmonian poems, especially *Christ and Satan*, this demonic place is characterized at length in imagery depicting a perversion of the dryht of heaven, which is described at the opening of *Genesis A* and many other places in the extant Old English poems. Where heaven is symbolized by joy in the high halls, hell like Grendel's mere is 'a place of exile' (*wræcstowe*, *Genesis A*, 90) and misery 'down under the headlands in the lower abyss' (*niðer under nessas   in ðone neowlan grund*, *Christ and Satan*, ASPR 1, 136:31).

The antithesis between the two dryhts is absolute in the Cædmonian poems; in the somewhat displaced version of it in *Beowulf*, important identifying connotations of the dryht of hell surround Grendel's hall down under the headlands. Most especially, the mere, like the dryht of hell inhabited by the former archangels who once were princes and thanes in heaven, is a place of joylessness and unending misery. The dryht of heaven is symbolized metaphorically as a harmonious divine body. God as mighty King of Glory is 'the head of all the high Creation, the Almighty Prince' (*heafod ealra heahgesceafta, / frea ælmihtig*, *Genesis A*, 4–5a). He is eternal, having no beginning and no end, and he enfolds in his bosom (*sweglbosmas heold*, 9) the thrones of heaven and the kingdoms of the sky. This unitary harmony in the highest level of being is intended by God to be indivisible and the heavenly troops in the beginning are 'limbs about the dear One' (*leomu ymb leofne*, *Christ and Satan*, 154a). But after the war in heaven, in which the body of heaven metaphorically is dismembered, hell is created and the corporate source of all true being can no longer be reached by Satan's hands or seen by his eyes, nor can the sound of its brightest trumpet be heard by his ears (*Christ and Satan*, 168–71). Satan's acute sense of himself and the other wretched monsters around him as stained and wounded parts (129–30, 155–6a) of a mutilated body, now cut off from their source, is supported by other images of monstrosity, the dragons at hell's door and the venomous adders and serpents that twist about there, to strive with the bodies of human beings who come to the dryht of hell (132–5). We remember here the welter of writhing monsters and serpents that greet the Geats and the Danes when they arrive at Grendel's mere, some of which tear at Beowulf during his descent into the turbid waters (1425 ff.).

The imaginative parallels between this hexaemeral mythology (recast in Old English poetic language in the Cædmonian poems) and the imagery of *Beowulf* are close and detailed. They suggest that the *Beowulf* poet, telling his Germanic tale in a poetic language already heavily invested with associations derived from Christian mythology, saw as useful to his purposes considerably more of that mythology than just the Creation myth and the story of Cain and Abel, those two parts of the biblical narrative acknowledged by most modern critics as present and functioning in the poem. By verbally recalling or echoing the war in heaven, which preceded both the Creation of hell and the Creation of the *middangeard*, the poet alludes to a wide imaginative context for his presentation of Heorot and the mere, and for the beings, human and other, who move about in and around these typical, exemplary locales in the imagined space of the poem.

Early in Christian tradition, in exegetical commentaries and in the development of the liturgies that gave communal, ritual form to the spiritual and moral truths contained in scripture (the Christian mythology), the fall of Adam and Eve, the crime of Cain, and the rebellion of the race of giants were all, as wilful acts of disloyalty and disobedience, seen as connected with Lucifer's rebellion. This is why, in the Cædmonian poems, among the rich profusion of words and formulas indicating various attributes of the Deity, his identity and function as 'Lord of victories' (*sigora Waldend*, *Genesis A*, 126) has to go on being repeated, as it is in the Bible itself, in the successive episodes of the story of humankind. In *Beowulf* as well, in the scop's song of Creation, the Almighty is characterized as 'exulting in victory' (*sigehreþig*, 94) as he puts the sun and the moon in their places. But because the Deity is anthropomorphized and caught in a story, that is, in a narrative form that cannot exist without tension and conflict, even his victories are never final, as long as the tale that is human history continues. Triumphant, the Lord of victories is said in the hexaemeral myth to win the war in heaven, but, because he also creates hell and middle earth, he sets the scene for further conflict and battles, and the war goes on, until the final Doom. It is not only Beowulf's battles and conquests that have no lasting or absolute effectiveness within time. The mythographers' and the poets' sense of the contradictions of actual human existence determines that the telling of stories must continue.

As in Jewish and Christian tradition so in *Beowulf*, the story of Cain and Abel is closely linked with that of the primeval giants and Noah's Deluge. Although the most explicit focus for these stories in the poem is on the Grendel race and the mere, the theme of the social destructiveness of fratridical strife and enmity among human beings pervades much of the text. From the time of the narrator's first association of 'the terrible waters' (*wæteregesan*) and 'cold streams' (*cealde streamas*) of the mere with the *westen* 'wasteland' of Cain's exile (1260 ff.), the symbolic identification of the two places and their inhabitants – Cain, the 'many spirits fated of old' (*fela / geosceaftgasta*, 1265b–6a), and the Grendel race – is meant to lead the listeners' and readers' minds to realization of the close connection between demonic and human killing. The knowledge of good and evil that comes to Heorot as a result of the fall into Grendel's clutches is a projection of the struggle of brothers and kinsmen: Cain against Abel, the Grendel race against the Scyldings, the monsters against God, the Scyldings against each other. The God-empowered hero appears in the form of a champion of the good fraternal society. Beowulf, adopted by Hrothgar, is the true brother of the Danes and of Hrethric and Hrothmund. Grendel, Unferth, and Hrothulf are the antithesis. When Beowulf is older he acts as the true father of Heardred, whose own father has failed in his duty to his family and his people, and has got himself killed, for no good reason. Especially from the time of Hrothgar's reading of the runes on the sword-hilt, from that day onward in *Beowulf*, the mystery which the king reads about the origin of ancient strife is also the thing that is to be feared: the same war that led to obliteration of the first Creation goes on even after Grendel and his mother are dead. Its continuousness depends on the history of changing forms. Each fratricide and traitor, each evil ruler or disloyal thane, each monster has his or her own identity, and each one can be destroyed by God or by one of his warrior-champions. But everybody knows that the race of monsters and monster-humans will take on new forms to attack and bedevil the Creation. The myth of the archetypal fratricide plays a major role in conveying an allegorical sense of the universality and typicality of many of the particular events of killing that are described or alluded to in the stories of the Scyldings and the Geats.

In the poet's artful ordering of his materials, the introduction of Grendel, rather like the presence of serpentine forms in illustrated Anglo-Saxon manuscripts, encircles the song of Creation. The monster is mentioned first just before the song is sung, after the anticipative allusion to Heorot's final destruction by hostile fire. Then comes the narrator's brief description of the Danes as dryht-men living in joy and blessedness (*Swa ða drihtguman   dreamum lifdon, / eadiglice*, 99–100a). This is followed by the second mention of Grendel. So far as the monster's moral and spiritual meanings are concerned, the terms by which he is immediately characterized could not be more clear and unequivocal (100b ff.). Literally and typically he is 'a fiend in hell' (*feond on helle*) who begins 'to do evil' (*fyrene fremman*). He is 'the fierce spirit called Grendel' (*se grimma gæst   Grendel haten*), 'a famous walker in the border lands' (*mære mearcstapa*) who, like the biblical Cain wandering apart from the favoured part of Creation, rules 'the moors, the fen and fastness' (*moras ... fen ond fæsten*). It is important to realize what is going on here metaphorically. It has just been said that Grendel lives in hell and that he also lives on earth, albeit out on the fringes beyond human habitations. Completely antithetical to the blessed dryht-men living in joy in their newly created hall, Grendel is described as a *wonsæli wer* 'an unblessed [or unhappy] man' who 'for a time' (*hwile*) has inhabited 'a dwelling of the monster race' (*fifelcynnes eard*). Earlier he has been 'proscribed' (*forscrifen*) by the 'Creator' (*Scyppend*) 'in Cain's race' (*in Caines cynne*). The Almighty who created the world is directly involved in Heorot, and hell is close by waiting to enter the hall. Grendel *is* a devil (*feond*) and a man (*wer*). This is illogical, but it is what the poem says, and shows. Because he is both devil and man, he is not fully either one: as a devil he fails, because he is also mortal; as a man, he fails because he embodies everything that brings about the destruction of human beings, bodies and souls, including his own. The man-devil equation is necessary so that we can be shown both that Grendel as an individual is destructible and that as a member of a particular lineage he is indestructible, so long as time and history continue.

The narrator proceeds immediately to illustrate and explain how Grendel comes to have his dual identity. Because Cain slew Abel 'the eternal Dryhten' (*ece Drihten*) avenged the killing, so that the first fratricide had no joy from the feud he started. Instead, because of his crime, God drove him out (we remember God driving Lucifer out of heaven) 'away from mankind' (*mancynne fram*). 'From there' (*Þanon*), that is from Cain as an exile from the human race, 'all' *untydras* 'came awake' or 'sprang up' (*onwocon*). The verb *tydran* means 'to bring forth, to propagate; to be fruitful,' but the negative prefix gives the related noun *tydras* 'progeny, offspring, growth' the sense of something evil and unnatural, of beings who are monstrous or, in the root Latin sense, abominable, away from man, inhuman.[8] It is from Cain, no longer part of the Creation favoured by God, that there came 'all unnatural broods, monsters and elves and orkneys [water-monsters], also giants' (*untydras   ealle ... / eotenas ond ylfe   ond orcneas, / swylce gigantas*). There is nothing empirically precise or descriptive about this cluster of monstrous disnatured beings, but their kinship identity with Grendel is explicit and their main typological significance is clear enough. These are the adversaries 'who fought against God for a long time' (*þa wið Gode wunnon / lange þrage*, 113b–14a), thus continuing Cain's crime of doing evil against the Creation. Even as the archetypal brother-slayer acted to violate the primal human family and spill blood on the earth, so Grendel cannot bear the sound of happiness coming from those human beings favoured by God, the Scylding successors to Abel. Just before the narrator describes Grendel's first visit to Heorot he concludes the account of Cain's progeny with these words: 'He paid them their reward for that' (*he him ðæs lean forgeald*). Given the identity just established for Grendel, the remainder of part 1 of the poem can be seen as the telling of how Grendel and his mother as particular enemies of God and Creation, in a long line of such enemies, commit their crimes and receive their appropriate retribution.

The summary account of Grendel's twelve years of visits to Heorot in lines 115 to 188 is polysemously concentrated. The first visit takes only eleven lines in the telling, but the passage is informative. After night has come Grendel sets out for 'the high house' (*hean huses*) where the Ring-Danes have settled in after the beer-drinking. When he gets inside he finds an *æþelinga gedriht / swefan æfter symble* ('a dryht of noble ones sleeping after the banquet'). 'They did not know sorrow,' says the narrator, allegorizing, 'the dark fate of men' (*sorge ne cuðon, / wonsceaft wera*). Grendel is characterized as 'grim and greedy ... fierce and furious' (*grim ond grædig ... reoc ond reþe*). The epithet *Wiht unhælo* applied to him is suggestive; taken literally it means a creature or being that is not well, not hale, someone sick or unsound. C.L. Wrenn, not unreasonably, given the context of this passage in the poem, in which primal or paradisal blessedness is being attacked, suggested reading *unhælo* as a noun meaning 'damnation' (as compared to *hæl* 'salvation'), thus giving for Grendel the sense of 'creature of damnation' (Wrenn 1973, 281). It is war – physical, moral, and spiritual (these distinctions are not drawn in the poem) – that Grendel brings to Heorot, and this central theme is continued in the account of the seizing of thirty thanes. Grendel begins demonically, with cannibalistic feasting, and never develops from this. In the metaphorical phrase *huðe hremig* 'exulting in plunder' the bodies of the Scyldings that provide Grendel with his nightly feast are the spoil in the first battle in the twelve-year war now starting.

The brevity and starkness of the account of Grendel's first attack and the scope of his ravages, thirty human lives, create a startling effect. In accord with the sharp polarization between the world of the innocent Heorot and the demonic force now directed against it, the imagery in the passage is sharply antithetical. The Danes peacefully sleeping and unaware of 'the dark fate of men' (*wonsceaft wera*) are in stark contrast to the ravening marauder who comes through the darkness to murder those who sleep. Grendel's 'fill of slaughter' (*wælfylle*) contrasts with the Scyldings' banqueting (*symble*). Their *wop* 'weeping' the following morning alliterates with their innocent *wiste* 'feasting' the previous evening, but it represents a total reversal in their fate (128–9a). Where only a short time ago Hrothgar's people have been joy-filled inhabitants of Heorot they now have become terrified fugitives from their own hall and must find places to sleep in the outlying buildings. Grendel is parodically described as a hall-thane, as filled not with loyalty but with hatred (*healðegnes hete*, 142); he is fast in 'feuds and crimes' (*fæhðe ond fyrene*); he literally and figuratively takes possession of the great building which until now has been held by 'the friendly lord of the Scyldings' (*wine Scyldinga*, 148). Since Grendel symbolizes and actualizes everything that is hostile to Heorot and its purposes, his possession renders useless this 'best of houses' (*husa selest*). He now rules and has power (the verb is *rixode*, 144) as he sets himself 'against what is right' (*ond wið rihte wan*). This sudden turnaround in the Danes' situation quickly becomes a long-term pattern and, as it does so, in sharp contrast to the song of Creation earlier, 'mournful lays' (*gyddum geomore*, 151) are sung, ensuring that the tragedy of Heorot becomes 'known, not secret' (*undyrne cuð*, 150) to the sons of men. The truth of Heorot's fate is now known. The question that poses itself, then, naturally and according to the old fourfold scheme, is, What is the appropriate human response to Grendel?

6

Swa Sceal Man Don:
Germanic Tales and Christian Myths

Grendel's unwillingness 'to settle with money' (*fea þingian*, 156) or to pay any compensation has a clear meaning on the literal-historical level of the narrative, where it serves to advance the plot by initiating against the Scyldings a hostile action that somehow must be dealt with if they are to recapture any of their former well-being. On the level of allegory, of typicality, Grendel is the enemy of the Creator and also 'the enemy of mankind' (*feond mancynnes*, 164b, 1276). As a 'creature not healthy,' 'a creature of damnation' (*Wiht unhælo*, 120b), he is a being not functioning as he was created to. In this sense he is unnatural, the joyless foe of life itself. The adjective *feorhseoc* 'life-sick' (820), applied to him when he is mortally wounded, succinctly identifies his essence. As a cannibalistic devourer of human beings, he is the embodiment of blood-lust directed against life itself. In his contempt for the laws of *wergyld*, he symbolizes a wild, antisocial lawlessness that left unchecked will take possession of human life and destroy it. He is those savage, chaotic forces that prey on ordered societies and undermine humankind's attempts at civilization. There is something surrealistic and hallucinatory in the way Grendel literally eats the bodies and drinks the blood of the *hæleþ*, in futile attempts to get their *dream* from which he is forever barred. When 'in the black nights' (*sweartum nihtum*, 166b ff.), rather like a dragon taking possession of a hoard, he seizes as his dwelling-place 'the hall shining with treasure' (*sincfage sel*, 167), he still cannot 'approach the giftthrone, the precious object in the presence of God' (*no he þone gifstol gretan moste, / maþðum for Metode*). He can have no joy of it (*ne his myne wisse*). Like Lucifer and Cain before him, Grendel is barred from the throne of grace and forever joyless. He is allowed for a time to separate a human society from its Creator, but his victories are time-bound and he himself is eternally damned, never to be reunited with the Lord of the heavenly gift-throne.

Tropological and Anagogic Meanings

Tropologically the member of the audience or the reader, observing the nature and consequences of this 'dark death-shadow' (*deorc deaþscua*, 160) who creeps about among 'those familiar with hell's secrets' (*helrunan*, 163), is meant to recognize within himself or herself, or among his or her fellows, those same savage impulses and perverse desires that threaten to destroy all hope of joy and happiness among human beings. See, the listener is meant to understand, what happens when hatred, envy, wrath, anti-social self-absorption, and the spirit of damnation take over. Avoid these vices. The positive exemplars for emulation, by which the *quid credamus* is to become the *quid agamus* of tropology, are the hero, the good king, the good queen, and the faithful thane.

At this stage in the *Beowulf* narrative (164 ff.), however, the Danes and Hrothgar apparently are powerless and some of Hrothgar's subjects do the worst possible thing. After 'many a mighty one' has sat in secret council (*Monig oft gesæt / rice to rune*) deliberating what would be best 'against the sudden terrors' (*wið færgryrum*), some of them pray for help to the *gastbona* 'slayer of souls' and offer sacrifices at heathen shrines. Interestingly, as noted earlier, the narrator does not really censure this action, which is based on a counsel of despair. He suggests (178b ff.) that the hard-pressed Danes do what they do simply because they know no better: 'Such was their custom, the hope of the heathen; they remembered hell in their hearts' (*Swylc wæs þeaw hyra, / hæþenra hyht; helle gemundon / on modsefan*). It was their custom because 'They did not know the Measurer, the Judge of deeds, nor did they know the Dryhten God, nor indeed did they know how to praise the Helm [or 'Protector'] of the heavens, the Wielder of glory' (*Metod hie ne cuþon, / dæda Demend, ne wiston hie Drihten God, / ne hie huru heofena Helm herian ne cuþon, / wuldres Waldend*).

It is important, on all levels of interpretation, to try to understand what is going on at this point in this telling of a Germanic tale in the light of Christian story. Years ago, Klaeber said (135), commenting on this passage, that Hrothgar is consistently represented as a good Christian. But such a statement is too bald, too unsubtle for dealing with the indirect, riddling ways in which this poem does much of its work. It is true that Hrothgar is idealized and praised almost beyond the point of believability, even in a fiction composed in the modes of romance and myth, and even in a poem that is open and direct in presenting many of its meanings. But it is necessary to remember that *Beowulf* works obliquely as well, often juxtaposing and suggesting rather than spelling out all the identities and connotations involved actively in its verbal functioning. *Beowulf* depends much more on symbolic metaphor than on clear conceptual statement. It appears to have been composed on the assumption that those who hear and receive the poem will recognize and respond to its allusive language. Because of this assumption there is often indirection, a kenning-like or riddling obliquity, and the words are able to convey much of their polysemous content without being overly explicit. Allegoresis is probably unavoidable when commenting on such passages as the one about the devil worship, but if such commentary becomes too mentally prosaic it risks losing important parts of the poem's ability to resonate. Rather than calling the theopathy-prone Hrothgar a good Christian, it is better simply to remember, when told of the Danes' honouring of the *gastbona*, what has already been established about these people, by means of certain poetic facts: the song of Creation, sung when the guest-hall Heorot was new, and the resultant paradisal associations of the hall; the other indications of the 'unfallen' or 'blessed' (*eadig*) state of 'joy' (*dream*) in which the Scylding 'dryht of kinsmen' (*magodryht*) exist prior to Grendel's attacks; the metaphorical identity suggested between Cain and Abel, on the one hand, and Grendel and his victims, on the other. These connotations make it difficult – I would say impossible – to think of the Danes simply as devil-worshipping pagans or as good Christians.

The alternative is to understand the passage as saying that, as a result of hell's attack on the Danes, that is, because of Grendel, it is their custom, during the twelve years of their misery, to offer sacrifices at heathen shrines. By doing this, they do not know – that is, they forget – the God whose influence and generosity earlier informed their existence and made it possible, in that earlier condition, for them not to know 'sorrow, the dark fate of men' (*sorge ... wonsceaft wera*, 119b–20a). Because 'the greatest of night-evils' (*nihtbealwa mæst*, 193) has taken possession of their hall and, it appears, of their souls as well, it is the night of death and damnation that now threatens to engulf them. They have been pushed to the physical and spiritual limits and are ready for the heroic deliverer to reintroduce them to the reality they have forgotten. Such a reading makes coherent sense of the internal fiction of the poem. The problem of a historical pre-Christian Denmark arises only when we go to a history and chronology outside the fictional text, when we press for a centrifugal historical meaning rather than staying with the poem's own centripetal and metaphorical frame of reference, and with the meanings that take their rise there. Paganism or heathendom in *Beowulf* begins and ends in the influence of the mere, which is quelled, and (in part II) in the heathen hoard, which is reburied in the earth.

The narrator does spell out clearly for his audience what the choice between damnation and salvation entails. As individual listeners and as members of a community, they have been prepared for this homiletic point by seeing the ravages of the race of Cain and the influence of hell on the Scylding society. The tropological lesson (183b ff.) now driven home by the narrator arises from the literal (literary) and allegorical account of the war waged against Heorot by the one familiar with hell's secrets: 'It is woe for him who must through fierce distress thrust his soul into the fire's embrace, expect no comfort, change in any way' (*Wa bið þæm ðe sceal / þurh sliðne nið   sawle bescufan / in fyres fæþm,   frofre ne wenan, / wihte gewendan*). The metaphor of a man thrusting or shoving his soul into the bosom or embrace of hell's fire accentuates the idea of choice available to the listener or reader who has knowledge of the Christian redemptive scheme; it is there, I think, that the *sentence* is pointed, not at the Danes within the poem. Similarly, says the narrator, explicitly continuing his tropological or moral teaching, 'It is well for him who can after his death-day approach the Dryhten and seek peace in the bosom [or 'embrace'] of the Father!' (*Wel bið þæm þe mot / æfter deaðdæge   Drihten secean / on to Fæder fæþmum   freoðo wilnian!*). There is as well as tropology a strong anagogical pull in the passage, as the narrator invites his audience to meditate on last things, specifically on the radical dividing of the damned from the blessed that will take place in the Judgment. The presence here of explicit anagogy is interesting because it occurs in a context in which the literal narrative in itself makes excellent story-telling sense. It is on that first level that Hrothgar is shown as powerless (*ne mihte snotor hæleð / wean onwendan* 'the wise man could not turn aside his trouble,' 190b–1a), his earlier glories in war and the building of the great hall now temporarily eclipsed by the devil-man who has come out of the dark places to possess Heorot by night. And yet on this literal base the other levels of meaning rest easily. The passage illustrates two important facts about *Beowulf:* its meanings are multi-levelled but the different levels or phases of significance are not in separate compartments. Rather, in the hands of a master artist, they interpenetrate each other, with little or no sense of strain or incongruity.

As Hrothgar tells Beowulf about the humiliations he has endured, while fate through Grendel's terror has utterly swept away (*forsweop*) his Danish warriors and diminished his hall-troop (473–88), he states his belief that this disaster could be stopped if God so wished: 'God can easily restrain the foolhardy ravager from his deeds!' (*God eaþe mæg / þone dolsceaðan   dæda getwæfan!*). The king goes on to recall how, after drinking beer, his men have vowed to wait with terrible swords for Grendel's attacks, but, in the event, have been powerless and have instead seen the bench-boards of their hall drenched with blood and their numbers lessened. In this speech the 'helm' or 'protector of the Scyldings' (*helm Scyldinga,* 456) is recognizing a brutal fact, one that looms large both literally and allegorically in the meaning of the poem. He and his troop are completely powerless to protect themselves. Their desire to act is real enough, but their powers of action have been circumvented. They and their hall are possessed. Hrothgar does recognize that this wretched fate could change, if God so wished, but he himself cannot do anything to make this happen, other than to welcome Beowulf. Still, this willingness to look to the champion sent by God and to rely on the man from Geatland is crucial, both to the development of the narrative fiction and to its moral significance. It demonstrates Hrothgar's realization of his and his people's absolute need for heroic action. It is the spiritual precondition of humility that is necessary before deliverance from hell's powers can take place. In brief, Hrothgar is the perfect embodiment or exemplar of the lesson of *humilitas* that he seeks to teach Beowulf later in the sermon against pride. Although it may be difficult for most of us moderns and postmoderns to see such acquiescence to the forces of heaven and hell as fitting or right, it does seem to be how this poem is conceived.

Simultaneous Polysemy

The account of Grendel's approach to Heorot on the night he encounters Beowulf and of the fight between them (702b–836), like much else in the poem, is a simultaneous functioning, in both literal and literary (imaginative) ways, of images of the corporeal world and of moral and spiritual meanings attached to those images by virtue of the language the narrator uses. In this functioning the phenomenal and the noumenal are one. There is no split between mind and body, no sustained separation of the physical and the metaphysical. Heaven, hell, and middle earth metaphorically come together. Grendel is 'the one who goes in shadows' (*sceadugenga*) in 'the dark night' (*on wanre niht*) and he is 'the demon foe' (*scynscaþa*) who wants to drag men down into those shadows, but, as is well known, he cannot do any of this unless God permits him to. He is the one who comes walking 'under the misty slopes' (*under misthleoþum*) having in mind 'to ensnare someone of mankind in the high hall' (*manna cynnes / sumne besyrwan   in sele þam hean*). He bears 'God's wrath' (*Godes yrre*). The curse or proscription that was placed on him earlier, like the one on Cain, was not so much an act of divine vengeance as a protecting of the Creation, by casting out the evil that threatens it. Grendel is joyless (*dreamum bedæled*) and has 'a mind bent on evil' (*bealohydig*) as, 'bulging with rage' (*bolgenmod*), he touches with his hands the door of Heorot, causing it to give way, and then tears open 'the mouth of the hall' (*recedes muþan*). As the monster enters, 'an un-fair [or 'horrible'] light very like a flame' (*ligge gelicost leoht unfæger*) stands out 'from his eyes' (*of eagum*), and he sees the Geatish fighters and kinsmen sleeping peacefully together. The narrator has already told us, at the beginning of this important polysemous episode, that 'the marksmen who were to protect the horned building, all except one, were asleep' (*Sceotend swæfon, / þa þæt hornreced healdan scoldon, / ealle buton anum*, 703b–5a).

Not only is there no modern split in such a passage between mind and body, or between the physical and the metaphysical, there is not even a sustained and characteristically 'medieval' emphasis on the spatial separateness of 'this world' from heaven and hell. In *Beowulf*, the close interrelatedness of what in more characteristically medieval formulations would be projected as a diagrammatic hierarchy of the levels of being is perhaps most evident in the handling of physical bodies. Even though the poem does speak of bodies as bone-houses (2508, 3147) and does include the conception of them as places within which souls dwell, and from which in due course these souls go to their heavenly reward or to the company of devils, the primary emphasis is on the concrete bodies of the monsters and the human beings as the living, and dying, forms of moral and spiritual realities. There is a profusion in *Beowulf* of images of heads, hands, claws, arms, shoulders, chests, feet, bones, sinews, and blood. These body parts are not empirically described in detail so that we can 'see' them in any minute naturalistic way, but neither are they mainly abstract or lacking in physicality. They are enlarged in their presentation, and boldly stylized. Often they are contorted or strained or mutilated, according to where they occur in the narrative, but they are always solidly placed and corporeally present in the *middangeard* of the poem.

Heorot is literally a place for feasting, and that is what Grendel has been doing there each night for twelve years. The hall also allegorically is the guest-hall of the world in which humankind dwells and is visited relentlessly by the enemy both of God and the human race, who comes from hell to destroy the bonds that link human beings with their Creator, to attack again and again the primal *dream* from which Cain and the race of monsters are forever barred. The battle between hell and heaven for humankind could hardly be more completely grounded physically than it is in the account of Grendel's last visit to Heorot. It seems from what the narrator says that on this occasion 'the horrid monster' (*atol aglæca*, 732) is even more berserk than usual and is driven to outdo his previous crimes. As Grendel steps quickly on to the shining floor of the hall and looks at the sleeping Geats, his spirit laughs out loud (*þa his mod ahlog*, 730) and he has in mind that, before day comes, he will separate 'the life from the body of every one of them' (*anra gehwylces / life wið lice*, 732b–3a). It is interesting to notice here how Grendel, like the other beings in the poem (human, partly human, and not human), is not in control of himself. He does not act as a result of some inner motivation that he has considered and decided on. The way the narrator presents him is theatrical and choreographed and suggests that he is compulsive and unfree, that he is 'on automatic': 'an un-fair [or 'horrible'] light very like a flame" (*ligge gelicost leoht unfæger*) stands out from his eyes; his spirit (*mod*) not he himself laughs out loud; it is in his mind to kill everyone in the hall; and now 'the hope of filling himself on a feast comes to him [or befalls him]' (*þa him alumpen wæs / wistfylle wen*, 733b–4a). Grendel is surcharged with demonic energy and externally driven, and he is ultimately powerless. He is a creature of mystery and darkness, estranged from human and divine companionship, and will be exposed and recognized as such when his claw hangs in the morning light above the doorway of Heorot. It is his *wyrd* that after this night he will not be permitted 'to partake of more of mankind': *Ne wæs þæt wyrd þa gen, / þæt he ma moste   manna cynnes / ðicgan ofer þa niht* (734b–6a). But he is allowed, partly for story-telling effect, to indulge in what he hopes is to be a sweet foretaste of a fuller gluttonous banquet still to come. The eating and drinking of one of Beowulf's sleeping warriors is gruesomely described (739 ff.) in a detailed account of bloody cannibalism, with the monster seizing the sleeping thane, slitting him open, biting into his bone-locks, drinking blood from his veins, and swallowing him chunk after chunk until the hapless, innocent victim is 'all eaten up, even his feet and hands' (*eal gefeormod, / fet ond folma*). This brief account of the brutal despatching of the young Hondscio without opposition from Beowulf has about it an archetypal resonance: in a kingdom being wasted by a monster a youthful figure is sacrificed to appease the attacker. In addition, the episode provides Beowulf with a direct personal reason for taking vengeance on Grendel, to supplement his altruism towards Denmark and his desire to honour his father's obligation to Hrothgar. Hondscio's death also invalidates any sense in the audience that Grendel's destruction by Beowulf is not legally required or that Grendel's mother is in any moral or legal sense justified in her vengeance.

Having disposed of Beowulf's thane, Grendel reaches with his own hand for Beowulf. When Beowulf fiercely seizes it the monster knows instantly that he has not previously 'in the middle dwelling, in earth's regions, met in another man a greater hand-grip' (*þæt he ne mette   middangeardes, / eorþan sceata   on elran men / mundgripe maran*, 751–3a). At the moment of this very palpable, crucial encounter between the monster and the hero, the language is at once physically specific and allegorically general, keeping the large, exemplary environment of formal meaning present even as the immediate physical action unfolds. The assailant who reaches for Beowulf is called 'the keeper of crimes' (*fyrena hyrde*, 750), and the narrator reminds the audience that this attack is one of numerous assaults on humankind by 'the evil enemy' (*se hearmscaþa*, 766). The hand-grip that now seizes Grendel tells him at once that he is encountering something radically different from his previous victims: 'his experience there was not like any he had met before in the days of his life' (*ne wæs his drohtoð þær / swylce he on ealderdagum ær gemette*, 756b–7). He, the one who has for many years brought terror, is now terrified and panic-stricken. His hand is caught, but 'his mind for him is,' literally, 'hence-eager' (*Hyge wæs him hinfus*, 755a), instructing him 'to flee into the darkness and seek the company of devils' (*on heolster fleon, / secan deofla gedræg*, 755b–6a). His hand 'in the grip of the fierce one' (*on grames grapum*, 765a) tells him he cannot get away. There is economy and simplicity in the words used: 'Then the good one, kinsman of Hygelac, remembered his evening speech. He stood upright and grasped him fast; fingers burst' (*Gemunde þa se goda, mæg Higelaces, / æfenspræce, uplang astod / ond him fæste wiðfeng; fingras burston*, 758–60). Given the powerful linguistic buildup that has been provided by this point in the poem, for both the monster and the hero, and the metaphorical establishment of the profound split between what Heorot was and what it has become, the next six words are a quiet marvel of compressed meaning: *eoten wæs utweard, eorl furþur stop* 'the giant was outward, the man stepped forward,' 761). The giant and the man. This is the agonistic moment, the first of three major ones in the poem, when heroic and divine energy mobilized in human form decisively meets demonic hatred, and, in this instance, makes it strain to escape.

The narrator, good story-teller that he is, helps his audience to respond appropriately by allowing himself to gloat a little: 'That was a sorry journey that the evil enemy had taken to Heorot!' (*Þæt wæs geocor sið, / þæt se hearmscaþa to Heorute ateah*). Having said that, he then describes the tumultuous rage of the two assailants as it breaks out in a wild wrestling match that terrifies the Danes, almost destroys their wine-hall, and determines which of the two powers will possess 'the fair earth-dwelling' (*fæger foldbold*, 773). In the midst of the uproar, a song is sung. This time the music that is heard comes from the far pole of the fiction from the one that provided the song of Creation for those inside the hall when Heorot was new. From the ramparts outside, not from a safe, happy seat inside, the frightened listeners hear 'God's adversary wailing, singing a dreadful lay, a song of no victory' (*gryreleoþ galan Godes andsacan, / sigeleasne sang*) as 'hell's captive howls over his wound' (*sar wanigean / helle hæfton*, 785–8a). For a time that has seemed endless to Hrothgar, Grendel has been permitted to do his deeds of hatred, but now he has been stopped, and is being held fast by the one who of men is 'strongest in might in the day of this life' (*mægene strengest / on þæm dæge þysses lifes*, 788b–90).

The poet unerringly chooses words that evoke the physicality of the material world even as they serve to identify the things, beings, situations, and actions in that world by means of symbolic metaphors which imaginatively place the whole verbal fabric securely in the marvel-filled world of heroic romance and biblical myth. The words the narrator uses to describe the durability of the hall as Beowulf and Grendel do battle in it – *þa wæs wundor micel* 'Then it was a great marvel' (771a) – are similar to those applied by Hrothgar (925 ff.) to the entire episode about the cleansing and saving of Heorot by the one who has come from far away (825–7a) and has driven the mortally wounded Grendel back into his fen retreat. There, says the narrator, hell receives his heathen soul (851–2). Standing on the steps of the hall, Hrothgar looks up 'at the high roof shining with gold and at Grendel's hand' (*steapne hrof / golde fahne ond Grendles hond*, 926b–7). He utters a brief prayer of thanksgiving to the Ruler of all, and then says, 'Always God, Keeper of glory, can work wonder after wonder' (*a mæg God wyrcan / wunder æfter wundre, wuldres Hyrde*). What could be ordinary, a hand or a roof or a wrestling match, is suffused and surrounded by the extraordinary. Metaphorically and allegorically the struggle has been about whether humankind, assisted by heroic effort and the Creator, or hell, embodied in a gigantic man-devil descended from Cain, will possess the middle dwelling. The question has been, Who will be permitted to feast in Heorot? All the Danes believe that this has now been answered in a way that satisfies their desires: *Denum eallum wearð / æfter þam wælræse willa gelumpen* 'For all the Danes after that rush of killing desires were fulfilled' (823b–4).

It is one of the larger narrative ironies of *Beowulf* that no sooner do the Scyldings think that they and Heorot have been freed from Grendel than another tormentor emerges, in the form of Grendel's mother, introduced by the word *wrecend* 'avenger' (1256). Her literal meanings are immediately established in the narrator's description of her (1255b ff.) and then in Hrothgar's account of what the people of his country have reported to him about the 'two mighty border-prowlers' (*twegen micle mearcstapan*), 'spirits from elsewhere' (*ellorgæstas*), who hold the moorlands out from Heorot (1345 ff.). Literally this second major threat to the Danes is the mother of the slain Grendel, and she now, according to the laws of blood vengeance, will exact the price of her son by slaying Æschere, one of the most illustrious of the Scylding counsellors. Like Grendel, the female monster is a parody figure, a grotesque perversion of what, within the value system embedded in the poem, womanhood, wifehood, motherhood, and peace-weaving queenship should be.

She is *ides aglæcwif* 'a lady monster-woman' (1259a), and, as far as those who have seen her can make out, is 'in the form of a woman' (*idese onlicnes*, 1350–1a). Grendel, 'in the form of a man' (*on were wæstmum*, 1352), though earlier called a giant or *eoten* (761), was her only offspring (1547a), and it seems clear from the extreme physical difficulty of Beowulf's struggle with her that she too is oversize, a giantess. Though a mother she has no known husband.

Since she gave birth to a son there must have been a partner, but who that might have been trails off in the surmises of those who have brought accounts of her back to Heorot: 'They know no father, whether for him any in earlier times was begotten from secret spirits' (*no hie fæder cunnon, / hwæþer him ænig wæs ær acenned / dyrnra gasta*, 1355b–7a). Grendel – a 'momma's boy' turned sociopath – and his terrible mother are a conspicuously incomplete family. In some way each seems to be the body of the other's death. The mother, driven only by a desire for blood vengeance, is also the main narrative instrument for continuing the feud between hell and Heorot after Beowulf's initial cleansing of the hall. She is as well the third disturbed mother given prominence in the middle third of the poem. Her concern for her son – not to be sentimentalized by any Romantic or modern sensibility prone to the idealization of monsters – is a parodic version of Wealhtheow's anxieties for her sons, and of Hildeburh's grief over the death of her son. As mistress of an underwater *reced* 'building' or *niðsele* 'hostile hall' from which she makes her murderous attack on Heorot, she is a grotesque mockery of peace-weaving. Her domain is not in the midst of a mead-plain, as Heorot is, but down beneath the headlands and turbid waters, in depths unknown to any of humankind before Beowulf penetrates them (1366b–7). The demonic light of her hall is antithetical to the radiance of the gold-hall, its treasure is hoarded not circulating (1557, 1613), its would-be banqueting (on the body of the hero) is cannibalistic, it is a place in which *dream* is totally absent, and its guardians are in stark contrast to the alert guardsman who early in the poem watches from a ness or promontory over the Danish shore. The guardians of the mere are a writhing mass of 'the race of serpents' (*wyrmcynnes*), 'strange sea-dragons' (*sellice sædraca*), 'nickers' (*nicras*), and 'wild beasts' (*wildeor*) which move about in the blood-stained waters or lie on the nesses. Some of them, says the narrator, are those which make their way in the mornings across the sea. The iconography of this tangled fusion of demonic beasts of the waste land and the chaotic sea almost certainly has one of its origins in the Bible, in the great land-monster or dragon Behemoth and in the treacherous destroying whale or sea-monster named Leviathan (called Fastitocalon in the Old English *Physiologus* poem). Both these archetypal creatures have long-established metaphorical associations with hell. The domain over which Grendel's mother presides and in which she tries almost successfully to destroy the hero, in Hrothgar's words, 'is not a pleasant place' (*nis þæt heoru stow*, 1372b).

Allegorically or typically, the narrator establishes the main meaning of Grendel's mother when he first mentions her. As with Grendel earlier and as with Heorot and the Danes, this level of significance is indicated explicitly by means of biblical myth, specifically by the second of two direct tellings in the poem of the story of Cain's crime and its aftermath (99 ff.; cf. 1255b ff.). Grendel's mother is a being who remembers her miseries and is forced, because of her ancestor Cain's murder of his brother, to live in 'terrible waters' (*wæteregesan*) and 'cold streams' (*cealde streamas*). She has her lineage and draws her code of kinship from the one of Adam's two first sons (Seth came later) whose act of fratricide introduced bloodshed and crime into the Creation and so led to his being forever outlawed. Cain was forced 'to flee the joy of mankind' (*mandream fleon*, 1264) and to inhabit a wasteland (*westen*), metaphorically and allegorically the same waste place in which the mere is located and from which attacks are launched on the patriarchal and fraternal world that Heorot is meant to be.

In chapter 3 critical attention was directed to the runic inscription on the hilt of the huge sword from the depths of the flood as it was being read by the king of the Scyldings, after Beowulf had cleansed both Heorot and the mere. It is now time to return to that metaphor and to inquire further into its meaning. What were Hrothgar and the Danes meant to understand by the runic telling of the story of the biblical Deluge, placed before them at the moment of the second of the hero's two major victories over the race of Cain? What truth were they meant to perceive in the runic account of the 'origin of ancient strife' (*or ... fyrngewinnes*, 1688b–9a) which led to the punishment of 'the race of giants' (*giganta cyn*, 1690)? What tropological lesson were they meant to take from these ancient but recently relived tales? What, for that matter, were the original audience or readers to understand from this dramatically direct linkage of the story of the Scyldings with happenings back when the world was young?

The careful and intricate patterning of the poem provides answers to these polysemous questions. The identification of the story of the Danes with events early in Genesis and in hexaemeral accretions to the biblical tales, in the exemplary way just indicated, has been fully prepared for well in advance of the appearance of the runic sword-hilt. Certain key images and symbolic metaphors appear first in the exordium of the poem, where the narrator establishes the genesis of the Scylding people in the figure of the mysterious Scyld Scefing. Scyld is said to have emerged from the waves 'in the beginning' (*æt frumsceafte*, 45) and to have founded a dynasty which quickly is shown coming to its most glorious expression in the great hall whose light shines over many lands, but whose joy immediately is made precarious by 'the dark death shadow' (*deorc deaðscua*) who emerges from beneath the flood-waters. This is the hall whose name means 'hart' or 'stag,' whose roof remains intact during the climactic battle with Grendel, and whose antlers reach towards heaven, as do those of the stag described by Hrothgar. There is an important three-part metaphorical identity established between Heorot, the king of Heorot who never surrenders to the

Grendel race, and the stag pursued by hounds. This last of the three victims, like the other two, does not surrender to hell; he chooses to die rather than lower his head and descend into the hell of those same flood-waters out of which the monsters come to bring death and damnation (1368–72). Neither 'Hart House,' communal humankind, nor the 'hart,' the individual human soul or heart seeking deliverance from enemies and longing to drink at springs of living water (Psalm 41), can deal unassisted with the 'soul-slayer' (*gastbona*) or dares risk descending into the serpent-filled hell-waters. A miracle of deliverance has to take place, both in the human dwelling and in the depths of the mere.

In the *Anglo-Saxon Chronicle* listing of the mythical ancestors of the West Saxon king Æthelwulf, in the entry for the year 855, Scyld's father Sheaf is placed in a genealogy stretching back through Woden to 'Adam the first man, and our father who is Christ'; in this series Sheaf is the son of Noah and was born in Noah's ark (Whitelock ed. 1955, 175). As Whitelock's notes indicate, Æthelweard's version of this annal has the name of Scyld in the same form as in *Beowulf* and then, as in *Beowulf*, omits all the names until Sceaf (*Scef*). Æthelweard also adds the story of the mysterious arrival of Scef (not Scyld) in a ship on the island of Skane as a child, and his acceptance as a king. In *Beowulf* (4 ff.), the mysterious Scyld emerges from the flood as a helpless (*feasceaft*) foundling who lives to find 'comfort' or 'consolation' (*frofre*) and becomes a powerful and good king receiving tribute 'across the whale-road' (*ofer hronrade*). God, says the narrator, has seen the wretchedness of the lordless Danes, and, in addition to sending them the boy Shield who becomes a great king and protector, also later sends a son to Shield 'as a comfort for the people' (*folce to frofre*). The prominent association of the theme of consolation with the origins of the Scylding dynasty parallels an integral part of traditional Flood typology in a way that may assist understanding of the exemplary significance of Scyld. If the first king of the Scyldings who comes out of the flood was thought by the poet and his audience to be the son of someone born in Noah's ark, it makes excellent metaphorical sense to have such a connotation leading into the story of Hrothgar's new creation. The Hebrew meaning of the name of the last of the antediluvian patriarchs, *Noah*, is not certain, but in Genesis 5:29 it is explained by a pun on the word *naham* 'to comfort,' giving the meaning 'consolation.' Hrothgar's timbered hall, ark-like, is associated with the first Creation of the earth itself, surrounded by waters (92–3), and with all living things, with 'every kind of being that lives and moves' (*cynna gehwylcum þara ðe cwice hwyrfaþ*, 98): with, that is, those same life-forms from the first Creation that Noah was commanded to rescue and protect in the ark, for release later. Again like Noah, who was the one just man chosen by God to make possible a new creation, the Scyldings are singled out for God's special favour. These images and allusions suggest a richly evocative pattern of meaning that goes as follows. Out of the line of humankind stemming from Adam came Noah, whose son Sheaf was born in the ark. Then comes Sheaf's son Shield, who provides a new beginning for the Danes, after (we learn later) 'the long evil to the people' (*leodbealo longsum*, 1722) caused by the bloody savagery of *Heremod* 'War-Mind,' who is included in the annal for 855. Whether or not the specific tradition recorded in the *Chronicle* entry for 855 is known to the poet and his audience, it seems probable that they are aware of something typologically similar to it. It is clear, at least, that the Creation myth and the myth of the Flood do surround and inform the story of the Scyldings in important ways and that these myths play a major role in establishing the typicality or exemplary meaning of the story of Heorot and the Danes.

Although there are close imaginative and thematic parallels between the account of the origins of the Scyldings and the Genesis stories of the Creation and the Flood, the differences, of course, are of equal importance, if we are to understand what the poem is doing and how it invites recognition of its polysemous meanings. Allegorically or *sub specie aeternitatis*, Heorot is the guest-hall of Eden about to have its blessedness marred by the blood-feuding that was initiated by Cain and eventually quelled in the Deluge. But literally the hall is a construction by human hands in middle earth, imagined as existing somewhere in time after the Deluge which was sent as punishment for the early representatives of the race of Cain. The great hall comes into being at a moment of equipoise in Hrothgar's reign when apparently there is peace. On this 'historical' or literal level, the narrator's allusion to the fate waiting for the initially splendid building is to the fire and slaughter that will come later as a result of Ingeld's treachery. But in a poem in which heaven and hell interpenetrate middle earth as thoroughly as they do in this one, and in which biblical patterns are being interwoven with a Germanic tale, the mention of the surging hostile fire which ultimately will destroy Hrothgar's creation can hardly fail to carry connotations of the final destruction by fire which awaits all things in the *middangeard*.

In both biblical and Northern myth, the end of the Creation is Doomsday. Everything in the imaginative economy of *Beowulf* sooner or later comes full circle. The poem is a curiously inwrought verbal fabric in which, among other motifs, a pattern of rings and circlets comes together to symbolize a basic structural and thematic circularity in the shape and meanings of the poem itself.[1] In Heorot's beginning is its end, the narrator tells us right at the beginning, because the ancient strife quelled temporarily in Noah's time is always potentially present and will burst out disastrously after Hrothgar's 'one hundred half-years' (*hund missera*, 1498, 1769) of successful kingship have come full circle. Even as the primal Creation was led inexorably towards the Judgment of the

Flood-waters, so Noah's and Hrothgar's new creations are assailed by postdiluvian evil and must be rescued, again and again. Even when they are, as Beowulf after his return to Geatland shows that he realizes, Heorot will still move unavoidably, and despite the best peace-weaving efforts, towards a final destruction. The biblical myths that the poem is using do also of course provide a frame of reference outside this closed circle of fate, in the order of eternity, but so far as human existence in time is concerned – and this is the main burden of the poem – the fate of all created things is circular or cyclical. In Heorot as in Adam all men die, because hell will not let them be, will not let them remain in the primal *dream* for which they are created. With the help of 'the Wielder' (*Wealdend*), both Noah and Beowulf do bring cleansed, restored creations out of the F(f)lood-waters, but the destruction by F(f)ire is still to come.

Through examination earlier – of the markedly fictional mode of the poem's imagining, of the highly metaphorical way its language works, and of the associative and mnemonic processes by which its narratives come together – I demonstrated that this is a verbal composition which permits no easy paralleling of itself with things and events in the actual external world. There is no literalistic or historical meaning that actually is *Beowulf*. At the same time I recognized that the poetic language being used does have important *potential* (as well as residual) connections with that world. It can readily be seen that *Beowulf* points selectively or alludes, on the one hand, to an actual Germanic world and that it also goes in another direction; it turns away from what we moderns and postmoderns think of as history and the world of actual places, people, and things into a world of metaphors, stories, and biblical myths which are thought to contain or point to crucially important truths. When the narrator directs attention beyond the types and exempla reenacted in the images, situations, and events of the poem into questions of tropological meaning, into consideration of what, for example, a new enactment of Cain's crime has to do with the lives of the poem's audience, it is some part of those potential outward-reaching connections that begins to come into focus. We can sense this even though we know little about the audience. *Beowulf* in its conception and its telling is not bound by history, but it is obvious that it is meant to have an impact in the actual world in which what we think of as history is unfolding.

In medieval exegesis the allegorical, tropological, and anagogic meanings were thought of as three successive aspects of the spiritual meaning. What is composed or written as literal record (the first level) and read as prophetic allegory or typology (the second level) has to be explained *moraliter*, that is, tropologically, in terms of human conduct. Tropology must come third in the sequence because literal meaning, on which doctrine is based, and allegory, in its concern with truth, are the necessary predecessors of virtue. According to

Jerome, Bede, and others, the 'fruits' of morality can come only after the 'flowers' of allegory. It is, so to speak, by contemplating in the Bible and other writings, in history, and in the order of Creation what God did and does that humankind comes to know what it ought to do. Tropology comes after the objective aspect of what allegory shows and is the interiorization of the truth in the individual and in the community. It is the phase or level of understanding in which listeners or readers recognize that they are being addressed and that an active response is being elicited from them. Allegory tells what is to be believed as truth, the *quid credas.* Tropology is concerned with the *quid agas,* what is to be done, through charitable action, once the truth is told and recognized. Anagogy, literally 'a leading up,' takes the mind and soul of the individual from the visible to the invisible, from the earthly to the heavenly. Anagogic understanding enables the human being to see in the actual events of this world the realities of the order of eternity.

So far as Grendel is concerned, the brute literal fact of his life, the eating of human bodies and the drinking of human blood, is ended when Beowulf mortally wounds him. He, 'a creature stained with crime' (says his conqueror, thinking anagogically), 'must wait for the great Doom, for how the bright Measurer will sentence him' (*ðær abidan sceal / maga mane fah   miclan domes, / hu him scir Metod   scrifan wille,* 977b–9). In a poem as ideologically uncomplicated and mythically strong as this one is, the nature of Grendel's reward at Doomsday is not in doubt, even though, in comparison, the fate of the Danes and their dwelling will prove to be more insecure than at this moment they think it is. As the narrator describes the many men and women restoring the guest-hall (991ff.), he again focuses on the roof, which alone has survived intact when the stained and guilty monster fled. This double image of the enduring roof and the fatally wounded enemy fleeing the ruined hall prompts a *sentence* that functions on all four traditional levels:

>   *No þæt yðe byð*
> *to befleonne   – fremme se þe wille – ,*
> *ac gesecan sceal   sawlberendra*
> *nyde genydde,   niþða bearna,*
> *grundbuendra   gearwe stowe,*
> *þær his lichoma   legerbedde fæst*
> *swefeþ æfter symle.*

>   It is not easy
> To flee from death   – try it, he who will – ,
> Driven by necessity   he must seek out the place

> Made ready   for soul-bearers,
> Children of men,   earth-dwellers,
> A place where his body   fast on its bed of death [perhaps 'grave']
> Will sleep after the banquet. (1002b–8a)

The literal image of Grendel fleeing and despairing as his life comes to an end becomes an explicit metaphor for the life and death of all men, an allegorical exemplum reminding each individual soul-bearer listening to or reading the story to take the tropological lesson and prepare for the inevitability of death, for that anagogic time after the body lies fast on its deathbed. The *sentence*, which begins in a daring juxtaposing of the dying of the man-monster with that of all men – those in Heorot and those in the audience – comes to its completion in the double metaphor of human life as banqueting and death as the sleep that surely follows.

The interpreter of the passage does not have to be critically sophisticated or a trained theologian to see what the poem is saying here: human beings caught in the antithetical tensions of existence in the middle dwelling either do or do not behave as they should at the banquet provided in the guest-hall of the world. Either they live with, and for, the created order and human life or they become destroyers of them. What will come after their particular banquets are ended will be determined by the use they have made of the gifts distributed to them. We notice at this stage in the story that just after the mention of the great Doom that awaits this latest member of the race of Cain, and even while the Danes are looking at Grendel's hand and claw, the fratricide Unferth, who has verbally impugned the abilities of the hero, is singled out by the narrator and described as having been silenced (980ff.). As the day proceeds, the euphoria builds, culminating in a great banquet and munificent gift-giving by the king. But as the evening wears on the harsh tale of the Danes' experiences at Finnsburg is told. Then Wealhtheow – queen and would-be peace-weaver, concerned wife, mother, and generous aunt, gracious hostess passing a communal cup – expresses enough anxieties to remind everyone of the threats that still exist for life in the world of the hall.

Tropological and Archetypal Meanings

In the polysemous schema used by Frye, archetypal criticism parallels or replaces tropology in the older formulation. It studies each poem as part of poetry, and poetry as part of the total human imitation of nature that used to be known as civilization, before we moderns and postmoderns came to see how precarious that term is in the light of the enormous atrocities perpetrated by our

Germanic Tales and Christian Myths   193

race in the twentieth century. But obviously civilization, or whatever we call it, is not merely an imitation of nature. Rather, says Frye (1957, 105), it is 'the process of making a total human form out of nature, and it is impelled by the force' that Frye, following William Blake, calls 'desire.' This humanizing work recalls, in a fundamental way, the role of tropology in medieval exegesis. In the tropological perspective, we remember, it is by contemplating what God does as Creator, Redeemer, and Judge that the human individual learns what he or she as a member of a community is to do, what rituals to engage in, and what models to follow in building, through acts of charity, the edifice of faith. Whether in their public ritual acts of the giving and receiving of gifts or in private dreams and longings, the protagonists of Old English Christian poetry are shown as drawn towards the *dream* of the gold-hall and towards spiritual warfare in the dryht of the Creator. It is this powerful desire that appears to have been the driving force for much of the creative, culture-building work that defined Anglo-Saxon England.

Desire in the Blake-Frye sense is the social aspect of emotion. Tropology is the understanding of faith that leads to works. What action, then, does desire or the tropological understanding of biblical story lead to in Old English poetry? It leads to veneration of the Cross, warfare against demons and monsters, trying to govern in accord with heaven's imperatives, acts of rescue for those enslaved by hell, longing for the heavenly dryht, adoption of the ascetic life, pilgrimage by seafaring, the building of churches in formerly heathen lands, artistic creation, prayer and fasting, or the willingness to die the life of a martyr. Desire, we observe, is not satisfied by objects but is the energy that leads the society to develop its own form, the Anglo-Saxon gold-hall world which exists only precariously in middle earth but securely in eternity. The conclusion seems to follow that tropological exegesis, with its understanding of the social implications of spiritual doctrine and moral teaching, is the historical precursor of archetypal criticism, with its interest in literature and the other arts as ethical instruments, as tools in the work of building or shaping a culture. The centrality of the Bible in medieval culture has been largely superseded in modern and postmodern culture by the human arts and sciences and by the productions that arise from human creativity rather than, as once was thought, from divine creation. Tropological meaning and interpretation have been succeeded by archetypal criticism interested in the broad literary and cultural significance of texts.

Beowulf is a narrative poem of heroic action, but it is far from being simply a straightforward tale of adventure. Along with the main story and the numerous supporting sub-stories, there is religious, philosophical, moral, and political teaching. One has the sense on finishing reading this work that whoever the poet was, this for him was a definitive composition. Whatever else he might have done, this poem shows a fullness of conception, a maturity of thought, and a verbal and imaginative ability to reshape old stories using the rich treasures of the ancestral word-hoard in poetically powerful ways that have no equal in the extant Old English poetic records. These observations hold true whether we assume oral or written composition and even if we take into account that in each oral presentation of a poem (as in each scribal copying of it) changes are introduced, deliberately or otherwise.

That *Beowulf* is meant to teach as well as entertain is clear. In its didactic aspects the voice of the narrator is central. How closely this voice is identifiable with or as that of the anonymous poet (or poets) there is no way of knowing. Largely because of the narrator's presence, many of us think that we encounter in the text an active personality that both enters and eludes us as we read. Since both the narrative materials and the poetic language are deeply traditional, the voice we hear doing the remembering, telling, expressing feelings, commenting, praising, and judging is a persistently collective one. Yet, to a limited degree, it is also personal. After the first and only use of the plural first-person pronoun *we* in line 1, the singular forms *ic* and *mine* occur from time to time: 38, 62, 74, 776, 837, 1011, 1027, 1196, 1197, 1842, 1955, 2163, 2172, 2685, 2694, 2773, 2837. But these occurrences do not define or in any way express an individualistic, objective, or alienated artist standing aside from his tale. On the contrary, the narrator identifies himself as the ears through whom what is getting told has been received and so is now being made available to listeners/readers: 'I have heard' (*hyrde ic*, *ic ... gefrægn*); 'by my hearing' or 'by what I have heard' (*mine gefræge*); or sometimes in the negative, 'I have not heard' (*ne hyrde ic*). *Gefrignan*, we remember, is 'to learn by inquiry' as well as 'to hear.' The person or narrative voice that we come to know is the one so actively and deeply engaged in the composition and performance that to a considerable degree he is, simply, the poem.

Part of what is meant in reading *Beowulf* literally, then, is reading it as a first-person narrative directly transcribing the narrator's performative imagination and mind at work. Such reading permits recognition of two distinct human or social contexts: that of the various peoples or societies told about by the narrator, and the narrator's own society, existing at some unidentified later time, perhaps several centuries later, somewhere in Anglo-Saxon England. The authenticity of the literal transcription is not like that found in the ironic writing that comes in the more modern periods of our literary culture, in which the writer either has removed himself or herself completely from the text or else is present within the text but still deliberately distancing himself or herself from the material. The opposite is true of *Beowulf*, where the narrator is present, relevant, and an active part of the intricately interconnected verbal world of the poem. Although in some undefinable way he is also the creation or voice of a poet in the historically later of the two societies, he is presented as identifying sympathetically with his hero's life and story to such an extent that we learn a good deal more about the first society than about the second. We can in fact do no more than speculate about the second, and of course we do.

But questions arise from the fact of these two social contexts. For example, when the narration ends, has the Beowulf story as much reason to go on as to stop? Because of the narrator's identification with his subject and his evident attempts to involve his audience, does the conclusion of the poem suggest indeterminacy and inconclusiveness or a real end? Does it imply both? We have heard repeatedly during the telling of the stories of the Danes and the Geats that, within time as it is experienced in the poem, the chronic reemergence of evil and the need for it to be destroyed are never finished. The apprehensions about the future expressed by human figures within the narrative in both parts I and II are extensions of the terrors of the recent past, and these in turn have been mythically identified with ancient, ongoing evil. Does this mean that the poem, like time itself, does not come to a conclusion, that the temporality of the narrator's re-created past reaches towards and envelops his own and his audience's future? And ours? Does it mean that there is an implied obligation or at least an invitation to reassimilate the story and the myth, and to have one's life changed by doing so? I think it does.

Here we approach a crucial dimension of *Beowulf* criticism. To clarify, before proceeding to a discussion of the structure and major themes of the poem, let me highlight one consequence of those large 'decisions' made by the poet which I have been describing, analysing, and discussing so far: the decisions to use the mythical and romance modes of imagining, first phase *langage*, and a richly allusive polysemous narrative art, and to assume the role of an engaged narrator.[2] The consequence of all these choices in combination is a unique poetic vision in which hearers or readers are expected to participate. But there is a problem. The vision of existence projected by the poem is in some senses monstrous and bizarre. It is meant, it seems, to be truly sobering, even at times terrifying. But however tragic the poem's conception of human life within time and history becomes, it does stop short of nihilism. It does present a basis for human beings achieving understanding and becoming wiser about how their societies hold together and how they disintegrate. It also shows how individuals and communities can live their lives well or badly, either in the service or in contravention of ideals which, although they can never be fully realized in middle earth, do inform and structure human existence in vital, meaningful ways.

Without any predetermined definition of what 'vision' might be generally in literature, we can say that in *Beowulf* the particular poetic vision that is projected involves seeing both up close and beyond, seeing the concrete physical people, things, and events of the remembered world of the gold-hall, and also seeing beyond the separate realities of these people, things, and events to their vital interconnections with each other, and so to the whole imagined cosmos of the poem. Vision in *Beowulf* involves an ability to show large coherences and interactions within and among the three orders of the Creation, the dryht, and kinship. It shows a capacity to look for and imaginatively call into being an idealized social order in which human existence could be one of joy and comradeship, but an ability also to stare unblinkingly at how vulnerable and precarious all such human constructions are, even when they are fashioned according to a divine model and are maintained or restored from time to time by infusions into human beings and situations of *mægen* 'power' from the *Alwalda*.

Beowulf is an expression of a poet's deeply felt concern for what creates and sustains a human society, in the face of what, finally, in this world, are seen as unbeatable odds. Perhaps the poem is also meant to show glimpses of a third order of experience – beyond the ordinary experiences of hall life and the miseries of an existence racked by demonic influences, feuds, and wars – glimpses, that is, of a world projected as a great gold-hall enveloped in a *dream* 'joy' that may never have existed fully in time and space but which completes existence for those who once lived in the actual world of the dryht, and dreamed there of human joy and fulfilment. Perhaps it is in these glimpses that we see the realized form of the definitive experience for the dryht culture, the one that Old English poetry urges Anglo-Saxon men and women to have, but which they never quite get. Of course if such a joy-filled world really existed, no individual could have lived in it, because the actual society he or she belonged to was part of himself or herself, and it included all the exiles, wanderers, and slaves, all those too cold and hungry and sick ever to have got near the ideal gold-hall and gift-throne. No society, even the smallest and most loyal, could live in such a world, because the innocence needed continuously to exist *eadiglice* 'in blessedness' – that is, in the world of the Creation symbolized in the primal Heorot – would have required an individual and social integration far beyond anything that the music of the harp and the song of the scop could induce. If actual Anglo-Saxon men and women could have lived in the original Heorot, the poem itself would have been unnecessary, because the distinction between poetry and life would have disappeared and life would have become the continuous incarnation of a creating Word.

The Anglo-Saxon period of history appears above all to have been an age of warfare, physical and spiritual. Its education theory, if it can be called that, was based on the fact that both primarily physical warriors and primarily spiritual ones had their major social roles defined in terms of warcraft, and of the loyalties and duties integral to such a life. So far as the spiritual warrior, the *miles Christi*, is concerned, several of the surviving poems set forth ideal types of behaviour: *The Dream of the Rood, The Fates of the Apostles, Guthlac A* and *B, Andreas, Judith, Elene,* and *Juliana,* to name the most obvious. For the primarily physical warrior the exemplars are described in poems like *The Fight at Finnsburg, The Battle of Maldon,* and *The Battle of Brunanburh. Beowulf* is about a champion who is at one and the same time both types of warrior. Because he is a fusion of both, he is unique in Old English, more unlike than like the protagonists in either of the groups of poems just mentioned. The poem about him has been seen, plausibly enough, as a cyropaedia or teaching instrument for the education of a young prince. Whether or not one of the intentions underlying its composition was that specific, it is clear that *Beowulf* is much involved in setting forth the ideal behaviour of a hero who becomes a king and whose great achievements are inextricably both physical and spiritual. In a fundamental way, the poem about him is a tale of conflict which reaches back to ancient, ongoing battles preceding it and, ominously, to battles yet to come. In both the larger three-tiered cosmos and in the middle-earthly part of it, war is chronic. Feuding goes on and on in an endless bloody pattern of offence and retaliation, of vengeance sought on land and sea, and beneath them. The dual theme, of war between hell and the human hall-world, and among individuals and peoples in the world, is so emphatic that even the peace-makers (Hrothgar, Beowulf) and the women who try to serve as peace-weavers (Wealhtheow, Freawaru, Hygd, and the reformed Modthryth) do not take the poem towards a vision of lasting peace on earth. For the historical times this may have been an impossible dream. As I said above, the odds finally, within history, according to *Beowulf*, are unbeatable. In order that disaster not be complete, it is the hero's high destiny to fight to the end, and that is what he does: *Heold on heahgesceap* (3084).

The Germanic Tale and Its Multiple Biblical Associations

Given what we know of Old English Christian poetry, the ideal for a long narrative poem would be one that, ultimately, derived its structure from the Bible, for that was the great story that provided Anglo-Saxons with encyclopaedic knowledge of the *Alwalda* 'Ruler of all' and of the many ways he intervenes, from the time of Creation to that of the Judgment, in the life of middle earth. In *Beowulf* the ordering of the narrative, including a combining of Germanic and biblical/hexaemeral elements, is no simple matter. Since it is obvious that much of the social and cultural content of the poem is Germanic, it will be helpful now to recapitulate and bring together the cumulative pattern of biblical/hexaemeral meanings which are identified or associated with the Germanic elements. Like the foreground narrative itself about the exploits of the hero, the biblical myths and meanings are not set down in a straightforward linear way. Instead they are worked into and around the story of Beowulf in his dealings with the Danes and Geats, as this narrative emerges in its own peculiar forward, backward, and sideways manner. The poet apparently saw in his tale of hero and monsters the potential for a rich interlacing of Christian significance known to him and his Christian audience but, until he did his work, no more than archetypally implicit in the inherited Germanic materials. It is possible, perhaps likely, that by the time he came to use the traditional poetic diction available to him it had become so saturated with the connotations of Anglo-Saxon Christian culture that many of these accrued meanings were working in the words willy-nilly, and were using him as much as he was using them. Whatever was the precise degree of cross-cultural consciousness in the poet's use of particular phrases, it seems clear overall from the version we have that he was probably well aware of a whole series of identities between the metanarrative and the narrative of the poem.

The principal identities shared between the Northern story and the biblical/hexaemeral one include the following: the linking of the building of Heorot with the Creation of the world and also, through verbal echoes, with the triumph of the Lord of victories in the War in Heaven; the fall of Hrothgar's world, because of the attacks on it by hell, not through any guilt of the Scyldings; the identification of the demonic enemy that precipitates this fall of Heorot with the biblical fratricide Cain and, by implication, the identification of the fraternal hall society with Abel; the linkage of the Grendel race with the antediluvian giants who fought against God; the arrival of a deliverer from across the sea, not identified *as* any biblical figure but clearly reenacting the kind of divinely enabled rescue action and restoration of the earlier Creation performed by several biblical champions in the poems of the Junius manuscript (Noah, Abraham, Moses, Daniel), as Beowulf destroys the enemy of the Danes, cleanses their polluted, blood-stained hall, and restores their kingdom to its primal intended state; extensive association of Grendel's mere not only with hell but with the waters of destruction in biblical myth and typology, including the waters of Chaos in the darkness that surrounds God's created world in Genesis, those of the biblical Deluge sent to punish the giants and the race of Cain, those of the Red Sea in which a sword of Judgment destroys the monster Egypt, and finally and unavoidably, given these other associations – for fuller scrutiny in the last chapter – an unspoken identification of Beowulf *with* (not *as*) Christ in his descent into hell, his miraculous conquest there in the harrowing, and his return to earth before he departs for the kingdom from which he originally came.

There are still further illuminating scriptural parallels. After Beowulf kills Grendel, Hrothgar speaks gratefully of the way the 'Guardian of glory' (*wuldres Hyrde*) always works 'wonder after wonder' (*wundur æfter wundre*, 928 ff.) and now through his might has caused a warrior to free the formerly bloodstained dwelling 'from demons and evil spirits' (*scuccum ond scinnum*). Just as the king of the Scyldings is about to declare his adoption of this 'best of men' (*secg betsta*), he uses language which echoes Gabriel's words to Mary in the Magnificat, as the archangel tells her that she is blessed among women, that her Son will achieve greatness, and that he will receive a throne and kingdom that will last forever (Luke 1:28 ff.). Hrothgar speaks of the favour shown by 'the God [or 'the Measurer'] of old' (*Ealdmetod*) to 'whatever woman brought forth this son among mankind' (*swa hwylc mægþa swa ðone magan cende / æfter gumcynnum*) and he predicts that Beowulf's 'glory will live for ever and ever' (*þin dom lyfað / awa to aldre*). Later, after the hero's triumph in the mere and his return to Heorot (1687 ff.), Hrothgar reads the rune-staves on the ancient sword hilt and again speaks of the propitiousness of the birth of 'the better man' (*eorl ... betera*) whose 'glory is raised up over the far ways ... over every people' (*Blæd is aræred / geond widwegas ... ðin ofer þeoda gehwylce*). He predicts that Beowulf's life will be 'a consolation, whole and long-lasting' to his people (*ðu scealt to frofre weorþan / eal langtwidig leodum þinum*). Here again the poet has Hrothgar use language that is rich in scriptural overtones. The primary echo this time is from another passage in the Gospel of Luke, one that would have been just as familiar liturgically as the words of the Annunciation already subliminally at work; this is the *Nunc Dimittis*, spoken by Simeon in Luke 2:25 ff. when the Christ child is brought to him. Like Hrothgar, who refers to himself as 'old in winters' (*wintrum frod*, 1724a) and as having waited a long time through the dark years of Heorot's tribulation, the old man Simeon is described as just and devout and as having waited a long time in the temple in Jerusalem for the consolation of Israel. When at last the deliverance does come, Simeon like Hrothgar gladly welcomes it, saying as he does so that Christ will be known before the face of all people and will be the glory of his people.

When Beowulf returns to Geatland he is recognized as having achieved greatness. In due course, because of his generosity, bravery, wisdom, and spirit of sacrifice, he does receive a throne and kingdom, thus fulfilling in a this-world sense Hrothgar's Simeon-like prophecy for him. Not only is he established as the greatest and strongest of men between the seas, but he is also a prosperous, upright man living a life of service to his fellows (we are told this gradually in part II). Throughout Beowulf's long life as an adult, in fact, but most especially at its conclusion, he is celebrated as the glory of his people. He is not, however, presented as Christ or, I think, even as a Christ figure, despite the verbal associations linking him metaphorically to the God-man of the Christian mythology. He knows himself as fallible and mortal, also that his life is being lived according to a fate controlled by the *Waldend* 'Wielder.' He knows moreover that his actions inevitably will be subjected to the Judgment (2327b–32, 2741–3a). It is this particular knowledge that prompts his darkest thoughts (*þeostrum geþoncum*, 2332), unaccustomed ones for this energetic, non-introspective *miles athleticus,* when he is confronted with the menace of the dragon.

It is important to observe carefully the situation in which Beowulf is presented as being plunged into uncharacteristic gloom. A sudden, wild, monstrous destructiveness has begun to engulf his kingdom. The dragon's rage, briefly kept in check after the theft of the 'precious drinking vessel' (*drincfæt dyre*, 2306), has been unleashed as soon as evening came. To the horror of the inhabitants (2314), the 'old' (*frod*) 'enemy of the people' (*ðeodsceaða*), who for three hundred winters has held in the earth an immense treasure (2277–80a), has now come spewing flames and has burned the bright dwellings of Geatland. The narrator tells us that this 'loathsome one who flies in the air' (*lað lyftfloga*) 'did not want to leave there anything alive' (*no ðær aht cwices ... læfan wolde*, 2314b–15). The 'serpent's war' (*wyrmes wig*) and 'hard-pressing hostility' (*nearofages nið*) are seen far and wide. After 'the war-enemy' (*guðsceaða*) has shown his hatred and has humiliated the Geatish people, he hurries back before dawn to his 'secret dryht-hall' (*dryhtsele dyrnne*), leaving the land-dwellers surrounded by raging fires. Each living thing is threatened, and it is as if the Creation is about to be set on fire, if Beowulf does not stop the destroyer. Geatland, which includes this serpent of death, has started to burn from within, even as Beowulf's own body burns later when the venom of the *wyrm* starts to work within it. We are told by the narrator that the dragon 'trusted in his barrow, his war and his wall' (*beorges getruwode, / wiges ond wealles*), but also that in this trusting he is deluded, that his 'thought' or 'hope' (*wen*) will betray him. We have already been told by the narrator (2275b–7) that the dragon has no benefit from the hoard in the earth which he jealously guards. The narrator later repeats this same view, along with the judgment that the dragon has 'wrongly' (*unrihte*) hidden the treasure objects in the first place (3058–60a).

The horror is quickly reported to Beowulf, including the fact that his own home, 'the best of dwellings' (*bolda selest*), and 'the gift-throne of the Geats' (*gifstol Geata*) have been destroyed in the welling flames. Like the Old Testament Job, when the 'fire of God' (Job 1:16) suddenly and unaccountably falls on his possessions, Beowulf, also as a righteous man of property and of great social responsibility – and until now much favoured by God – is devastated: 'That for that good man was a grief in his heart, the greatest of mind-sorrows' (*Þæt ðam godan wæs / hreow on hreðre, hygesorga mæst*, 2327b–8). As in the case of Job, and also of Hrothgar years ago when his *bolda selest* came under siege, Beowulf as the central victim of the almost apocalyptic catastrophe now unfolding is presented by the narrator as a good man (*þam godan*), not as someone guilty or deserving of such torment.[3] Like Job, however, he initially thinks that he has somehow 'against old law' (*ofer ealde riht*) 'bitterly enraged the Wielder, the eternal Dryhten' (*þæt he Wealdende ... ecean Dryhtne / bitre gebulge*). There is a further parallel with Job, in both Beowulf's righteousness and his humble response to the disaster that has struck: Beowulf has not been told what we have been, that the Wielder has permitted this disaster to start unfolding, though he does recognize, typically and rightly, that God is involved in what is happening. Job never learns that God has given the old foe Satan permission to bring destruction down on him. In *Beowulf* earlier, when the young man who disturbed the hoard 'by secret craft' (*dyrnan cræfte*, 2290) stepped near the head of the dragon and survived, the narrator explained it this way: 'So an unfated one can easily survive woe and misery, he who holds the favour of the Wielder!' (*Swa mæg unfæge   eaðe gedigan / wean ond wræcsið   se ðe Waldendes / hyldo gehealdeþ!* 2291–3a). It seems that once again in the poem we are being told that all events are in the hands of the Deity, and that the event which leads directly to the wildly destructive actions of the fire-dragon is sanctioned by God. The man who takes the cup from the hoard wrongly possessed by the dragon must be a *þegn* 'thane' not a *þeow* 'slave' (Klaeber's reading of the damaged manuscript; see Klaeber 1950, 85, note on 2223), because this man later (2281b ff.) bears the cup to his liege-lord Beowulf (*mandryhtne*). He asks for and receives 'a compact of peace' (*frioðowære*) with 'his lord' (*hlaford sinne*). For a slave no such relationship would be possible.

Unlike Job, Beowulf does not engage in days-long debate about the problems of theodicy. Job's question – 'Is not destruction to the wicked? and a strange punishment to the workers of iniquity?' (31:3) – is essentially the same as Beowulf's thought as he wonders about having offended against the old law. But neither protagonist identifies any evil that he has committed. On the contrary, both affirm their innocence. Job does so verbally at great length, to the final annoyance of both his comrades and the Almighty. Beowulf is different. He is much less self-assertive than Job. The main subject of his retrospective thoughts on his whole life is his people and their history. But like Job he does affirm the rightness of his own life, in two ways. Remembering how he once crushed the hated Grendel kin, he again acts decisively to destroy the enemy, as he always has when confronted with monstrous evil. Secondly, he says, just before he dies, happy, that he is content to have his moral record go before the Wielder (2732b–43a): 'I have ruled the people for fifty winters' (*Ic ðas leode heold / fiftig wintra*). During that time 'there was no king of the surrounding folk who dared attack me with warriors, oppress me with terror' (*næs se folc-cyning, / ymbesittendra   ænig ðara, / þe mec guðwinum   gretan dorste, / egesan ðeon*). In his dwelling he 'experienced the creations of time' (*Ic ... bad mælgesceafta*), 'ruled well, did not seek out treacherous quarrels' (*heold ... tela, / ne sohte searoniðas*), and 'did not swear oaths wrongfully' (*ne ... swor fela / aða on unriht*).

Many cultures have the myth of the extraordinary human being battling a dragon. This is a story that can be told in any number of ways. The Old Testament figure of Job, who is not a hero but a successful seeker after understanding and wisdom, is someone who because of his experiences comes to know himself as 'a brother to dragons' (*frater ... draconum*, 30:29); also as a man whose 'harp is turned to mourning' (*versa est in luctum cithara mea*, 30:31). Like Beowulf he has to confront the great monsters of land and sea, Behemoth and Leviathan, in order to be vindicated before the Lord (40–1). Late in Job's experiences, God in a stupendous speech tells him the mysteries of Creation and shows him an overwhelming vision of the two monsters. Beowulf from his youth onwards has periodically entered into and moved about in the depths of the sea, and, unlike Job, has seen and entered into the hall of the death-shadow (cf. Job 38:16–19). In his journey to the mere he has gone through the unknown to the boundary of the wilderness (1410) and now, to confront his dragon, must once again go to a desolate, waste ground 'wherein there is no man' (Job 38:26): *no ðær ænig mon / on þære westenne* 'there in that wasteland there was no man' (2297b–8a). Beowulf is not like 'the swift horse' (*se swifta mearh*) mentioned in the Lay of the Last Survivor (2264b–5a) which no longer 'paws in the courtyard' (*ne ... burhstede beateð*), but he is like the strong horse in Job 39:19 which paws, rejoices in its strength, is eager for the coming battle, and mocks at fear. Beowulf 'is afraid of nothing' (*contemnit pavorem*) and does not turn back from the sword (cf. Job 39:22 and *Beowulf* 2347b–54a and 2518b–24a), even though, like the fighter who attacks Leviathan in the Book of Job, he also has a sword which finally 'cannot hold' (*cum apprendenderit eum gladius, subsistere non poterit*, Job 41:26; *Beowulf* 2680b–7).

Unlike his Old Testament precursor, Beowulf is never reduced to abjection. God does not have to tell him to gird up his loins like a man (*Accinge sicut vir lumbos tuos*, Job 40:2), to remember battle, and to confront the monster. He *is* what God tells Job to be (Job 40:2ff.); he is majestic and excellent as he stands *heard under helme* trusting in the strength of a man. It is clear that the narrator both approves and expects us to: 'such is not the undertaking of a coward!' (*ne bið swylc earges sið!* 2538–41). This is no sermon denouncing Beowulf as one of the proud who must be brought low by Leviathan. The dragon pouring out streams of deadly fire evokes from Beowulf the rage and wrath that God demands of Job (*disperge superbos in furore tuo*, 40:6). The voice uttering the words of hatred that storm out of the mouth of the *stearcheort* lord of the Weather-Geats is 'battle-clear' (*heaðotorht*, 2553), and the hoard-guardian recognizes in it 'the voice of a man' (*mannes reorde*, 2555). Or is it the voice 'of man'?

The multiple biblical associations found in and brought to the inherited Germanic tales of a gold-hall rescued from demonic powers and an earth-dragon fought to the death provide rich suggestions of wider and deeper meanings, but they never overwhelm the foreground story. The larger epic action informing the poem is the story of the Bible, the comprehensive account of the relations between heaven, hell, and middle earth that came with the missionaries into Anglo-Saxon England and there, while partly repressing Northern myths and codes, also was taken into their language and was profoundly changed by it. The imported biblical epic helped bring about a major cultural transformation which is illustrated, in part, in *Beowulf*, and in small or large compass in many of the other extant poems. The interpenetration of the Christian and Germanic verbal elements in *Beowulf* does not show either cultural stream pressed into the ideological service of an orthodox predetermined theology, either Northern pagan or Christian. This is because the poem is radically metaphorical in its language. The stories, metaphors, and myths from both cultural backgrounds work together with a dynamic, unsettling energy that destabilizes any consolidating Christian or pagan ideology. This is also why many of the attempts to explain or state the poem's themes in conceptual or ideological ways end up being major abstractions from and bifurcations of the text.

It is important to remember that the poet is a story-teller as well as a poet. The stories he tells do imply a good deal about the shapes of the societies which are his concern. One of the things we learn from what is now called cultural studies is that there do seem to be stories in human societies that control all the others, and even account for the shapes of the societies themselves. But they do this primarily as stories not as ideologies. Once arranged in powerful, imaginatively authoritative ways, they become irresistible patterns, driving forces for good or evil. This says to me that it is one of the complex tasks of criticism to distinguish between those story-telling uses of words which rationalize brutality and demonic power and those which fashion stories capable of transforming for the better the unacceptable givens of existence. Stories can become controllable, to a point, but they can also control the teller. They often fight each other, as I think they do in *Beowulf* – more about this later – for power over the listeners and readers. Some exceptionally strong stories, like the metanarrative taught by the Whitby monks to Cædmon, come to control the others, not again, I think, primarily as an ideology but as a story, comprehensive and strong enough in this case to help shape a new hybrid Germanic Christian culture in Anglo-Saxon England. The *Beowulf* poet saw in this same mythology enough verbal sword-power to vest his folk-tale of a monster-slayer with enormous cultural resonance, which continues to this day for those with ears to hear. Because he was able to give more dynamism to old formulas and themes than, say, Cynewulf was – in the Byzantine, hieratic narrative stasis of *Juliana* and *Elene* – he created a tension. He destabilized the old Germanic words and, while still using them, created new identities and meanings for them.

Beowulf is a poem and must be studied and interpreted as such. Any attempt to explain it in terms of something that is not poetry will fail. Although like most of the world's greatest poetry it means many things other than what it says explicitly, this does not imply that criticism should paraphrase it into lifeless abstractions or doctrinal formulations: no ideologically obsessed mind can take in great poetry or great art of any kind. Nor should we try to explain *Beowulf* by reference to one or more particular historical situations. It is not, in other words, to be considered a poetic version of some non-poetic referent, a theology or a moral code, or a set of specific local circumstances, however much it swallows and uses elements of both such kinds of material while developing its own powerful vision of human existence. As visionary poetry *Beowulf* both demands and resists its own interpretation. Whether we are considering its words as signs, as motifs, as exemplary types, or as tropological and anagogic suggestions for a consciousness heightened by exposure to this particular structure of sounds and images, it is necessary continuously to keep in mind that we are dealing with poetic language and that this language is doing metaphorical things which can be done only in poetry. It is these considerations among others that have guided the argument of this book so far, and it is these that have particular importance as we now turn to deeper and broader questions of meaning, in the context of a discussion of the structure of the poem.

7

Heold on Heahgesceap: The Structure of the Poem, the Heroic Theme, and the Shape of the Hero's Life

In *Beowulf* the foreground action does not begin *in medias res,* as it does in the more ample epics of Homer, Virgil, Dante, and Milton. The action begins rather at the beginning of the story of the Scyldings, with the symbolism of the archetypal child Scyld, set adrift, exposed, vulnerable, and yet through divine grace soon to be hugely powerful: weakness and power, emergent life and death, all are in play together in this brief narrative, forming an epitome of the larger poem which they introduce. The story continues through a high point in the Scyldings' existence (the building of Heorot), then through a twelve-year period of disaster, followed by three climactic days and nights in which the hero restores the well-being of the Scylding kingdom. The first of the poem's two main narrative movements ends when Beowulf and his troop return to their home in Geatland. By this stage in the narrative we have also heard two references to Heremod (901, 1709), a Danish king from before the time of the Scyldings, and so have come to realize that in a wider chronological perspective the poem has after all begun *in medias res.* With any story there is always the possible question, What took place earlier? The story-teller does not have to deal with the question at all, but the *Beowulf* poet does, in two ways: he makes a few allusions to Danish experiences before Scyld; he provides mythological precedents. Still, the foreground narrative in part 1 is the story of the Scyldings. It begins at its beginning and presents *in toto* the Scylding cycle of history redeemed. As an integral part of this cycle, the protagonist completes his odyssey, which begins and ends in his homeland.

The foreground action continues in Geatland, initially with a recapitulation by the hero to his king of the events in the land of the Scyldings. After this, the story jumps to a time many years later when Beowulf, approaching the end of a fifty-year reign as protector of the Geats, sees his kingdom devastated by a firedragon. He goes to destroy his people's enemy, even at the cost of his own life.

So far as the foreground narrative of the whole poem is concerned, it is primarily the figure of the hero that holds together the tale of two kingdoms. The action begins with a gift (Scyld Scefing) from the Prince of Life to one lordless people in middle earth and follows through the 'historical' existence of the Scyldings and their kings, including the work of the youthful hero on their behalf. The story then shows, through an intricate mixture of retrospection, narration of present events, and gloomy forebodings, what happens to the hero and his own people, the Geats, during the remainder of his life. In part I of this total narrative, divine grace triumphs, temporarily. In part II a curse operates decisively. The poem begins on a theme of heaven's generosity and ends with a vision of a world in which grace is little in evidence. Scyld Scefing is the first of a dynasty. Wiglaf is the last of the Waegmundings. *Beowulf* tells first of the triumph of life, then of the triumph of death.

The conclusion of the action of the whole poem is analogous in at least one respect to what happens in certain other classics of English literature. At the end of *Piers Plowman*, for example, even though the memory of Piers is still very much alive, it is the triumph of the dark forces of Antichrist in history that are dominant. At the end of Spenser's *Faerie Queene*, in contrast to the conclusion of *Beowulf*, the destroying monster the Blatant Beast has not been killed; but the vision of destruction and social chaos that is beginning to unfold is essentially the same as in *Beowulf*. At the end of *Paradise Lost*, as in the Old English poem, human exiles defined by disloyalty to their L(l)ord are driven from their homeland into an ominous and uncertain future, as Adam and Eve 'with wandering steps and slow' move out into the wilderness of human history. At the end of the great elegy *Lycidas*, after the poem's powerful vision of corruption and death in the order of nature, there is a parallel for Beowulf's memorial barrow placed on Whale's Ness for the guidance of seafarers: the Genius of the shore remains as guide for 'all that wander in that perilous flood.' In *Beowulf*, as in each of these other works, a code and a vision sufficient to the very real evil in the world have been established. It has been shown that history includes monstrous destruction but that it also can and must include generosity and enormous human effort if the darkness and chaos are not to be complete.

The overall foreground action of *Beowulf* provides a sharp focusing of listeners' and readers' attention which brings the scenes in Denmark and Geatland (also the ones at Finnsburg, the court of the Heathobards, and Ravenswood) into forms that have almost the force of drama – a highly formalized drama, to be sure, but one with actions, defined performers' roles, set speeches, some dramatic interchanges, and enough characterization of the settings by the narrator to make possible a *mise en scène*. These dramatic features are particularly evident in the scenes in Denmark, but the foreground action of the dragon fight,

Beowulf's death, and the funeral rituals could be realized on stage, in a highly stylized way; they would require the narrator as one of the dramatis personae.

Although generically part I is a heroic romance with its main quest successfully completed, from another perspective, suggested by frequent references to unsettling and destabilizing forces always at work in the hall-world, the story of the Scyldings can be seen as the tragedy of Hrothgar and the inevitable eventual ruin of his kingdom. From this perspective part I is the account of how a heroic-age people falls into the possession and rule of a monster of destruction whose ravages require the counter-action of vengeance which the hero provides. At the end, as at the end of Marlowe's *Tamburlaine* or Shakespeare's *Macbeth* and *Hamlet*, the irrational destroyer that has been laying waste the kingdom has himself been destroyed. The cleansed, restored society which remains has a future, at least for a time. Part II deals with a different phase of tragedy. It is more elemental, more ironic, and its closely related themes of social destruction and the death of the hero, however honourable and *dom*-worthy Beowulf's death, remain the major themes right to the end. Rather like a young Fortinbras or Edgar, Wiglaf remains to rule the kingdom, but his Geatland, unlike the Denmark of Fortinbras or Edgar's Albion in *King Lear,* is given little or no prospect of deliverance from the feuds and treacheries that have come to dominance. The dragon is dead literally, but human evil in the form of warfare continues. Those faithful to dryht loyalties are not presented as at all adequate to resist the coming disasters. Whoever in Anglo-Saxon society composed this poem knew well how to express the recurrent, cyclical craving of human beings for ordered social existence, but the poem's final vision shows this strong desire as endlessly frustrated in the nightmare of history. In its overall structure this is a poem which moves from a world of dream and nightmare to a world of heightened consciousness in which the experiences of history, of existence in time, are even more terrible than the earlier twelve-year nightmare, because the ruin and killing go on for centuries.

In comparison with part I, part II has a less concentrated unity of action. Although the figure of the aged hero-king is at centre stage throughout and dominates the consciousness of the other characters even after he is dead, this part is so involved in the broad sweep of societies – past, present, and future – warring with each other and racked by internal accidents, disloyalties, and crimes that the poem takes on something of the traditional epic's encyclopaedic range. In this sense the panoramic telling of the passing generations in the last third of the text parallels the dynastic vision which begins the poem, except that the emphasis is on bloody battles and ruined societies, not on prosperity. Where part I brings into sharp foreground realization the brilliant (and gloomy) scenes in Heorot and concentrates the action on the great hall, thus providing a warm, light-filled communal centre for the depiction of human life in middle earth, part II avoids any such unifying and stabilizing architectural and social image. Instead there are an aged warrior-king, the stone arches of a ruined *ece eorðreceda* 'everlasting earth-hall,' a hoarded, accursed treasure, one loyal young thane, and a dragon on a lonely promontory by the sea, all against a backdrop of an apprehensive, beleaguered kingdom surrounded by hostile neighbours and stormy waters.

The foreground narrative action of the whole poem is flanked by the funeral rituals of two great warrior-kings, one a Scylding and one a Geat. The chronological time embraced by the story of the kingdom of the Scyldings extends from Scyld's life and death onward, and covers the reigns of Beowulf I, Healfdene (semi-historical, CE 445–98), and Hrothgar (historical, 473–525). In addition, there are intimations of future events involving Hrothgar's children, the sons Hrethric and Hrothmund and the daughter Freawaru, the last of these married as a peace-weaver (apparently unsuccessfully) to the Heathobard Ingeld. In a rough approximation, following Klaeber, this chronology would commence sometime early in the fifth century and extend to the second quarter of the sixth century, about 100 to 125 years.

The chronological events of the part of the poem concerned with the Geats date from about 500 when Hygelac, a historical king, was twenty-five years old, through his death in 521, and then through the twelve years of his son Heardred's reign, plus the fifty years of Beowulf's kingship, bringing us to 583. The allusions in both parts I and II reach backward and forward in chronological time, with destruction foreseen for both kingdoms in the not-too-distant future, because of forces recognized as already at work by characters within the poem. The persistence of the theme of the inevitable reversal of good fortune includes numerous references and allusions to latent perils and facts of existence which show the well-being of Heorot and all those associated with it as precarious and ultimately doomed: 81b–5, 1060b–2, 1162b–5a, 1165b–8a, 1180b–7, 1228–31, 1233b–5, 1246b–50, 1255b ff., 1304b–6a, 1386–9, 1481b, 1491b, 1761b–78a, 1826–35, 1885b–7, 2005b–9a, 2024b–69a, 2115–17a. Similarly in part II, the messenger and the Geatish woman at Beowulf's pyre anticipate disastrous raids from the Swedes and Franks, once the Geats' loss of Beowulf is known (2910b–3030a, 3150–5a).

Beyond these years of chronological or 'historical' time, perhaps 150 in all – allowing for partial overlap in the stories of the Scyldings and the Geats, because the young king Hygelac is on the throne while the old Hrothgar still reigns – we have what might be called mythical or biblical time, extending from Creation when Heorot is new to Doomsday, the time to which the curse on the dragon's hoard extends its fatal influence (3069). Part I pulls mythically towards the restoration of first things, part II towards last things: origins versus eschatology. Even as human actions in the foreground narrative are presented as happening either because of heaven's favour or because heaven permits demonic influences to function, so mythical time embraces or includes the poem's chronological or historical time, and gives each narrative event its real significance. Time as *chronos*, as *lændagas* 'loaned days,' exists within the context of an order that is *ece* 'eternal.' The tale of the kingdoms of Denmark and Geatland is seen from the perspective of an imagination (in both poet and audience) aware of and using these larger mythical patterns. The foreground story does contain the elements from which a chronology can be constructed, approximately, but this most definitely is not the way the narrative itself is arranged. Nor is it the way the outline of Beowulf's whole life, from boyhood to death, emerges. Nor even, as we have seen, do the particular parts of the larger biblical epic – used to help shape and inform the other stories – follow their linear ordering in the Bible. The overall structure of the poem, with its genesis-like beginning and its doom-heavy conclusion, is firmly placed on the bedrock of the Creation to Doomsday myth.

Structurally the Bible is a *commedia* or comedy and has within it a long series of heroic deliverers raised up at appropriate times, under divine guidance, to rescue and lead the chosen people from whatever destruction threatens them, beginning with Noah and including the other Patriarchs (Abraham, Isaac, and Jacob), Joseph, Moses, Joshua, Samson, Deborah, Gideon, Samuel, Saul, David, Judith, Daniel, the Maccabees, Jesus, and the apostles. In the early centuries of the Christian era this list was augmented as various religious leaders and saints emerged and stories like the biblical ones were attached to them. Often the later iterations had clearly recognizable scriptural models, and in any case each one served to continue and extend in the life of Christendom the original biblical mythology and story-telling. At the same time, the scriptural models were adapted to the cultural imperatives of widely differing times and places, often with revolutionary intentions: hagiography is revolutionary in that it normally champions individuals not in the upper echelons of the worldly power structure. In Anglo-Saxon England this ancient shaping and re-creating tradition continued in such Old English poems as *The Fates of the Apostles, Andreas, Judith, Juliana, Elene,* and *Guthlac A* and *B*, in the numerous other saints' lives, and in the stories of many of the human figures and miracles in Bede's *History*. It also continued in a particularly powerful and memorable, though unique, way in *Beowulf*. *Beowulf* is a heroic romance, of a particular kind. Its narrative is divided between a heroic rescue theme and a theme of the disintegration of a warrior society. Whatever else the poem is structurally and thematically, it is not in any overall sense a comedy, although in the story of

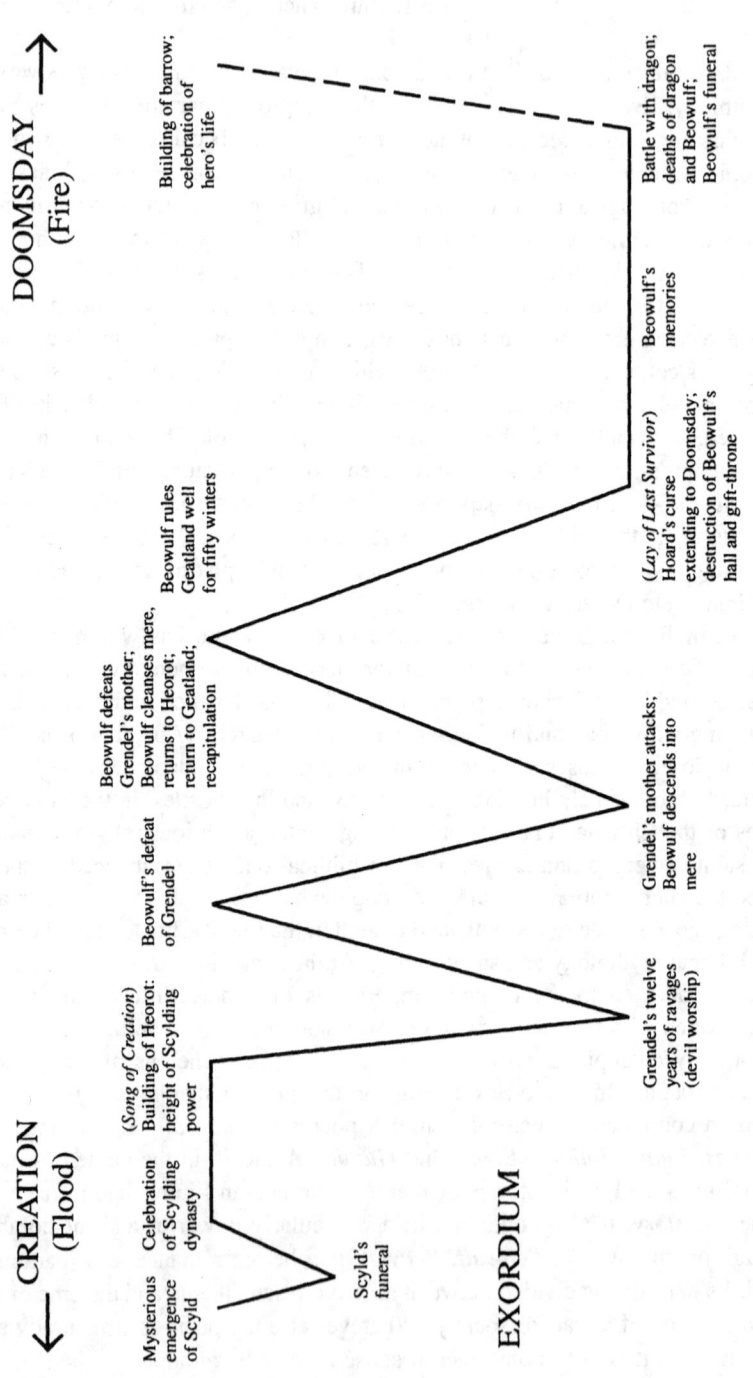

Structure, Theme, and the Hero's Life 211

BEOWULF – PART I

(Song of Creation)
Building of Heorot

Banqueting and gift-giving

Grendel's attacks

Beowulf in Geatland

Beowulf emerges from the mere and returns to Heorot

Beowulf's arrival in Denmark

Beowulf's fight with Grendel

Beowulf kills Grendel's mother and cleanses the mere

Beowulf's descent into the mere

The Danish Adventure

Heorot it does contain major elements of one, situated within the completed tragic structure of the whole poem. The poet preserves the epic feature found in *The Odyssey* and *The Aeneid* of a split in the narrative action, the second part of the composition being set in a different locale from that of the first. But contrary to the arrangement in those classical poems, it is the first part of *Beowulf*, not the second, which structurally is a successfuly completed romantic or heroic comedy.

Still, as we have seen, even in part I the commedic elements are persistently undercut by an elegiac sense of the doomed nature of all human societies and of life itself in middle earth, so that by the beginning of part II the imagery and themes of social reintegration and well-being are already fast receding into memory. Where comedy is about society as a whole and is concerned with the removal of obstacles to the fulfilment and happiness of the particular people involved, tragedy is concerned more with the individual, with the extraordinary or heroic man or woman whose larger-than-life stature and actions increasingly set him or her apart from the surrounding society, culminating in a death that leaves a huge absence in its wake as the cluster of people that remain try to pick up the pieces of their existence. By these featural definitions, *Beowulf* is a heroic romance whose first part is commedic in structure, though even there, as I have said, the theme of social fulfilment is somewhat darkened and threatened. From the beginning of part II, the poem takes what previously have been mainly latent tragic cadences and themes, places them in the poetic centre, and explores them so thoroughly that the earlier images and themes of human happiness and heroic glory recede further and further into memory, until finally they have disappeared entirely from the foreground narrative, leaving only a memorial of themselves.

Romance, like all narrative literature, is an imitation of action, even if the action could never take place in actual life. If, as I think, *Beowulf* is romance structurally as well as modally (commedic romance in part I, tragic romance in part II), we have to address the question of why this particular fictional imitation of an impossible action is granted an importance and significance accorded only to major poetry. What is special about the action in this poem or about the way it is presented? What does it really mean to act in *Beowulf*? In the case of the hero, an act is the expression of his *mægen*, a power or energy that makes him magnanimous and whose origin is in heaven. Beowulf is represented as bearing heaven's grace (*ar, este, hyldo*) and as knowing this to be the source of his strength, as well as the determiner of his fate in each adventure he undertakes. Unlike Guthlac, Juliana, and Andreas, he is not addressed directly by angels who provide comfort and advice and by devils who offer evil suggestions tending to damnation.

Because *Beowulf* breaks with the commedic triumphalism of the Old English hagiographic poems (and of its own part I), it is able to be a tragedy, and to explore at length the kinds of images and themes that are powerfully present in some of the elegies. In contrast with the stylized Byzantine abstractions of *Juliana, Elene, Guthlac A* and *B*, and *Andreas*, *Beowulf* deals much more fully with the corporealities of actual existence in the *middangeard*. The poem embodies some of the same themes about human war against the hellish enemies of Creation that the hagiographies do, but its concentration on the things of this world

Structure, Theme, and the Hero's Life 213

BEOWULF – PART II

Diagram (circular, clockwise from top):
- Beowulf rules Geatland well for fifty winters
- Beowulf and Wiglaf fight the dragon; deaths of the dragon and Beowulf
- Beowulf's memories
- Beowulf's sorrow, self-doubt, plan for vengeance
- The dragon destroys Beowulf's gift-throne and ravages Geatland (Doomsday)
- The taking of a cup from the hoard
- The dragon rules the hoard three hundred winters
- The lay of the last survivor
- Prophecy of disaster for the Geats; building of Beowulf's barrow; celebration of his life

Beowulf's Last Battle

pulls it away from theology, and leads the audience instead to a knowledge of death and human (including heroic) limitation. The resultant final vision involves a pervasive symbolism of destroying fire, ruins, earth mounds, rust, dead bodies, and ashes, those things in the actual world that the human desire for life most wants to separate itself from. The poem thus does provide insight into the separation of worlds that the homiletic themes of the hagiographic poems express more emphatically. But in these works the saints' choices are abstract and transcendentally driven. They do not define an ethical relation, other than rejection, to existence in the world. This fundamental difference between the two kinds of poems helps explain why the attempts by 'Augustinian' critics to establish sin and guilt in the primal Heorot and even in Beowulf are so unconvincing. The thematic emphasis within the poem itself ensures that such a metaphysical judgment does not apply.

Beowulf's exalted sense of duty to his fellow human beings follows from his conviction that the heavenly Dryhten is good to him. When, prior to his fight with the dragon, he is shown wondering if in some way he has offended against the old law, his short-lived attitude of uncertainty is new, but the humility in relation to God and his laws is consistent with Beowulf's characteristic view that it is heaven's favour that makes him what he is. In practice this means being someone special who is meant to make boasting speeches and pursue fame, because in so doing he is serving others and helping beleaguered human societies. When *wyrd* comes *ungemete neah* 'immeasurably near' (2420a) and his hall and gift-throne are destroyed, dark thoughts well up in his breast and he assumes that this is because the divine favour is diminishing, that in some way he has angered his heavenly Dryhten (2324–33).

Beyond his habitual awareness of God's good will towards him, Beowulf has two additional sources of knowledge: his own experiences or achievements and what he is told by others. The former are more prominent in the narrative, although what he is told is not unimportant. Early in the poem (194 ff.) he is in his homeland and hears there 'about Grendel's deeds' (*Grendles dæda*) and Hrothgar's 'need of men' (*manna þearf*). But as we learn later it is through the experiences of the contest with Breca and other acts of monster-quelling prior to the 'mighty errand' (*micel ærende,* 270b) in Denmark that he comes to know himself as a suitable champion for Heorot. Similarly, success in the many battles he underwent in his youth, including the ones against the Grendel race, gives him a self-knowledge that he refers to much later (2510 ff.) while speaking his last 'boasting words' (*beotwordum*) and deciding which weapons to take to fight the dragon. He recognizes that fate and God will decide the outcome, instructs his thanes that this is not their *sið* 'venture' but his alone, and goes forward trusting in 'the strength of one man' (*strengo getruwode / anes mannes*).

Despite Beowulf's detractors in the anti-heroic modern and postmodern age of criticism, in the poem's terms he is the ideal man who, on the basis of unparalleled physical and moral worth and achievement, becomes a king and for a long time rules as a wise, effective protector of his people.[1] He is not perfect, all-powerful, or all-knowing, as the Deity is, but among men he is without equal; he is mortal and knows himself to be so. As is normal in romance, the characters ranged round the protagonist are either good or bad, for or against the orders of dryht, kinship, and Creation within which Beowulf lives his life. The poet who shaped the tale is ethically clear-headed but he is not simple-minded, and so there are degrees both of excellence and of evil in the poem. In the case of the hero, as we have just seen, an act is the expression of an energy and magnanimity that have their origin in heaven. This is true also of Hrothgar up until the time Grendel attacks Heorot, at which point the previously heroic king loses his power of action: *unbliðe sæt* (130). No one among his people can take effective action. Even when Beowulf arrives, despite Hrothgar's welcome and ready acceptance of the *cempa* 'champion' who has unexpectedly appeared, a kind of perverse non-action tries to get in his road, as Unferth seeks to undermine the hero's credentials. Beowulf sees clearly the essential passivity represented by Unferth and the Danes, and points out to Unferth that 'Grendel never could have done so many terrible things ... in Heorot' (*Grendel swa fela   gryra gefremed, ... on Heorote*) if Unferth were as daring as he claims and if the monster expected any real 'fight from the Spear-Danes' (*secce ... ne weneþ / to Gar-Denum*, 587–601a).

Unferth, a self-regarding, narcissistic parody of the hero, has attracted a good deal of interest from moderns, even admiration, because his words are tendentious and quarrelsome, and so are somewhat dramatic in the way that those of Milton's Satan are.[2] Yet we are meant to understand, as Beowulf does, that they are words without substance, and that their source is pride and envy. This is Lucifer's starting-point when he is jealous about the high position of the Son in the heavenly dryht and decides to rebel against divine law, thus starting the war in heaven and making necessary the formation of hell. In Unferth's beginning is his end. Arrogance has to be directed against someone or something, and in Unferth's case it leads him to envy (including the invidious comparison of Beowulf and Breca, 499 ff.); it is of a piece with the earlier malice that led him to murder his brothers (587–9; 1159–68a). Unferth, who strikes some moderns and postmoderns as lively and as fulfilling a proper role as challenger of a would-be hero in a heroic society, is the kind of influence that moves towards the frustration of heroic action, towards the triumph of joyless fratricide and endless bloodshed in the world of the dryht. Part of Unferth's ultimate mythical or metaphorical significance lies not only in the pride-driven fallen angel Lucifer but also, more directly, in the archetypal fratricide Cain, and in Cain's successor Grendel. As an apparently sanctioned fratricide sitting at the feet of the king of the Scyldings, and as someone who perhaps in the end will conspire with others to destroy Heorot (1163b–8), he is no mere entertainment. Like Shakespeare's Iago, Unferth is a parasite who cannot exist except in a destructive relation to someone else: he murders his brothers, tries to defame Beowulf, and gets his importance by being seated at the king's feet. His mighty sword, even when loaned to the hero, is impotent for the task of battling against Cain's descendants. But Unferth is still in the cleansed hall after the hero has returned to Geatland. So far as Heorot is concerned, Unferth's influence outlasts that of Beowulf.

The opposition between Beowulf and Unferth can be seen as finished when Hrunting is courteously and discreetly returned to Unferth (1807-12) and the hero goes home. But perhaps the differences between these two fictional entities cannot be resolved so easily. It may be that these antitheses reproduce themselves endlessly within the poem and that they have much to do with the way the heroic romance gradually and inexorably becomes tragic. In the first place, as is abundantly clear, reversals are normal in the world of *Beowulf*. The primal *dream* of Heorot turns into a scene of devil worship. The hall is later rescued, only to await destruction by fire. The evil Grendel ends up mortally wounded, with his hand, arm, and shoulder torn off. He is succeeded by his mother; she is destroyed, but the Grendel race lives on. In his youth the hero triumphs, but with age comes a major reversal. Gold-halls shine for a time but there are earth-dragons. Creation itself lasts until the great Doom.

It may well be that the real opposition with which the poet is preoccupied is less the static opposition of good and evil, for which the poem has many terms, than the dynamic opposition between man's created nature, human society as it is intended by the *Liffrea* to be, and what a society actually is and does: the relation between human being and human doing. In the case of the exchanges between Unferth and Beowulf, this opposition can be regarded as partly a contrast between two styles of using words. When Beowulf is speaking, including when he is using *gielpworda* 'boasting words,' his language is relatively plain and direct, as transparent as it can be in expressing his thoughts and feelings, and in telling his story. Unferth, the mar-peace – this is his character whether or not that is the etymological meaning of the name, and whether that is the name, instead of the manuscript 'Hunferth' – is an ironist, filled with mistrust and suspicion fuelled by self-contempt, and he assumes or pretends to assume that the reputation Beowulf has gained is based on lies or exaggerations. He deliberately tries to create a disjunction between signifier and signified. His allegation that Beowulf was a loser in the competition with Breca and, by implication, that there is therefore no reason to think the Geat has credentials for rescuing the Danes is initially proven false. Beowulf kills Grendel and then he kills Grendel's mother. Unferth gives the hero a sword that proves worthless and he is silent when the hero returns to the hall. For the time being, despite the apparent generosity of the gift of Hrunting, Unferth has been exposed as mean-spirited and wrong in both his descriptive and his predictive utterances. He has misread Beowulf's achievements in the past and also his likely performance in the near future on behalf of Denmark. He has been silenced, for now. Since he and his sword have been exposed as unable to do deeds, he speaks no more words. His words have had no power in any case. The silenced Unferth reminds us of the wordless monsters and their deep source in the secret mere depths, connected with elemental and original evil. But in a perverse, disjunctive way, ultimately Unferth is partly right. The 'battle-rune' which in envy and jealousy he unbinds as he sits at the feet of the lord of the Scyldings (499 ff.) does its work. Beowulf cannot save the Scyldings from themselves, and there is a suggestion that Unferth will conspire with others to precipitate a feud that will destroy the gold-hall and the harmonious society which the hall is meant to embrace (1163b–8a). Blood-guilty and cowardly, Unferth is certainly not right morally, but in the long run his modes of behaviour and his cynical view have predictive accuracy.

According to the dominant themes of the poem, the typical monstrous act is meant to be seen as no more real finally than the essentially passive attitude of Unferth and the Danes. It is only the divine that really has the power to act. Power (*mægen*) in *Beowulf* means the Almighty and his champion. God is never linked with any foolish or tyrannical kingship or abuse of position. The quality of the divine act reveals itself as an act of creating life, then of constantly re-creating it by sustaining and protecting it (including providing protectors of it), and finally of taking what is good and true from the Creation back into the keeping of heaven (Scyld, Hama, Hrethel, Beowulf) while the faithless parts (like Grendel and Unferth) are consigned to hell's fire. The Grendel monsters are rebels against God. As with their predecessors Cain, the giants, and Lucifer, it is the rebels' function (in the myth and in the story) to react against the good (C)creation. In the Old English *Genesis* poem and in tradition, Lucifer sets himself up as a rival to the Lord of the heavenly dryht (as does Unferth on the human level with Beowulf) and behaves as a parody of a *dryhten* with his troop of thanes. The appearance of the devil worship in Denmark represents the entrance into Heorot of the human ability, out of desperation, to worship precisely this demonic force, to turn to the mere and hell for help in protecting and keeping a kingdom, rather than to the *Alwalda* by whose grace and favour the hall-world has been created in the beginning. Grendel is hell's or Satan's main representative in part I and illustrates well the perverted quality of parody heroism. He is a hall-thane from a dryht-hall that hides its treasure at the mere-bottom instead of circulating it usefully. He listens in rage to the sounds of human joy, to the song of Creation itself, coming from Heorot. He combines in himself the traditional envy of Satan at God's Creation of paradise for the delight of humankind and Cain's envy over the favour shown by God to Abel. As a descendant of those 'who fought against God,' this *wiht unhælo* 'unhealthy being,' 'creature of destruction,' 'spirit of damnation' is the embodiment of demonic wrath and of the spirit of vengeance as it breaks into the little world of the Ring-Danes. They as yet are 'sleeping after the banquet' (*swefan æfter symble*) and do 'not know sorrow, the dark fate of men' (*sorge ne cuðon, / wonsceaft wera*, 119–20). Grendel's exulting over his 'fill of slaughter' (*wælfylle*, 125) once he has seized thirty thanes from their resting-place and has set out to return to his dismal hall, is the spirit which, once let loose in the world, identifies human life as endless conflict. This is the vision that comes increasingly into sharp focus in the last scenes of the poem, even though by then 'the horrid one who goes alone' (*atol angengea*, 165) who was called Grendel, and his mother too, are long since dead.

Hrothgar is important for the theme of heroism. Beowulf and his men are careful to honour and praise him even when his essential powerlessness against the Grendel race is evident to all. Everything he says and does in the poem is significant. Out of warfare he brings peace. He creates a splendid hall within which to exercise great generosity. When hell intrudes into his world, there is no sign that he himself succumbs to devil worship as 'Many ... a mighty one' (*Monig ... rice*, 171b–2a) of his followers do. He is the first to recognize that Beowulf's advent into the kingdom of the Danes is because of God's grace. He facilitates the hero's work in every way and rewards it magnanimously when it is done. He demonstrates at every point all the proper kingly virtues. His only failure, and it is catastrophic, even though not his fault, is that he has no power against Grendel. Plunged into despairing grief at the slaying of Æschere, his *runwita* 'confidant,' *rædbora* 'counsellor,' and *eaxlgestealla* 'shoulder-comrade' (1325–6a), he has to be released by the hero (*Ne sorga, snotor guma* 'Sorrow not, wise man') from the tyranny of his feelings, from his elegiac remembering. Lamenting is fitting, but by itself it is futile. In this incident, which sets in contrast the misery of the powerless and the decisive action of the powerful, Beowulf demonstrates (1383 ff.) that heroism is extremely practical and socially useful. It is the antithesis to the elegiac cast of mind, which in its essential attitude of grieving is passive and often self-absorbed. 'It is better for every man that he avenge his friend than that he mourn greatly' (*Selre bið æghwæm, / þæt he his freond wrece, þone he fela murne*), says Beowulf: 'Then the old man leapt up, and to God, the mighty Lord, gave thanks for what the man had spoken' (*Ahleop ða se gomela, Gode þancode, / mihtigan Drihtne, þæs se man gespræc*). Heroism galvanizes potential strength into concrete, useful acts. It is a release of energy by those who have in mind to give real service and so attain glory before death. To sit *unbliðe* is not useful.

The poem has important things to say about kingship in relation to heroism. In part I Hrothgar is the order figure. Grendel is the rebel who attacks Heorot and usurps Hrothgar's power. Beowulf is the nemesis or avenger figure whose dual function is to kill the rebel-usurper and restore something of the previous order. In part II Beowulf is the order figure, deprived of his hall and throne at the beginning of the action. The dragon is the usurper. Beowulf and Wiglaf together are the nemesis figures. In part I, looking forward to the disorders of part II and also backwards in time to the evil days before Scyld Scefing, we have the description of Heremod, the antithesis of a good king: a murderer, a creature of irrational rages, a solitary, joyless being who is stingy and mean-spirited, and is hated and feared by his people. In the background in part II, significantly, there are several figures of kings all of whom except Beowulf fail to maintain order and one in particular, Hygelac, whose rash and foolish expedition into Friesland leads both to his own destruction and to a pattern of blood-vengeance which is expected to embroil the Geats after Beowulf's death. There is a clear suggestion, in the way the narrator keeps referring to this disastrous adventure (1210 ff., 2354b ff., 2500 ff., 2910b ff.), that Hygelac, despite his fairly favourable profile in the scene in which he welcomes Beowulf home from Denmark, does not really do a king's work. Even in that scene, where he is magnanimous with Beowulf, we learn that he selfishly would have preferred the hero to stay home and leave the South Danes themselves to settle their war with Grendel (1992b ff.). By his subsequent pride-driven attack on another people, Hygelac threatens to destroy the order in his own kingdom which, *ex officio*, he is obliged to maintain. His son Heardred is too young to reign unassisted. Apparently it is only through Beowulf's regency that disaster is averted. Significantly also in part II, which presents a vision of near-chaos in the relations between warring peoples, the counter-action by Beowulf and Wiglaf against the dragon has limited effect. The order it restores is to be short lived, more so even than the one that Beowulf reestablished years earlier in Heorot. By the end of the poem's presentation of kingship, the bleak truth revealed about it is that no matter how altruistic and prodigious the achievements of the strong ruler are he will at best pass into favourable legend and his deeds into the collective memory. He will be a vivifying memory or not, depending on the responses of those who hear the tale or see the barrow high on Whale's Ness.

Among the good kings in the poem – the *Kyning-wuldor* God, Scyld, Hrothgar, the generous treasure-giver in Hrothgar's sermon, and Beowulf – Beowulf is the one on the human level who most excels. He does not have a savage heart (*næs him hreoh sefa*, 2180b) and he is described (3181–2) by the twelve riders who circle his memorial barrow as both 'eager for praise' (*lofgeornost*) and the 'mildest and gentlest of men, kindest to his people' (*manna mildust ond monðwærust, / leodum liðost*). Faced by his greatest test in the form of the fire-dragon, he once again summons up successfully the power to fight for his people and, this time, to die for them, with no fear for himself in the conflict: *no he him þa sæcce ondred* (2347b). He means to enter into his sacrifice alone: *Nis þæt eower sið, ... nefne min anes* 'that is not your venture, ... but mine alone' (2532b–3). Because of Wiglaf's loyalty, he does receive help *in extremis*, even though he has explicitly said he does not want it (2642b–6a). As he mentally prepares for death, he takes 'joy' (*gefean*) in the fact that he has ruled his people well for fifty winters and has not compromised with the evil endemic in the world (2732b–43a).

    This persistence in right conduct to the end looks back to a prescription set out earlier in the poem. In part I, once Grendel and his mother are dead, Hrothgar makes a crucial speech to Beowulf which establishes the pattern of 'manly virtue' (*gumcyste*, 1723), of 'that better thing ... eternal rewards' (*þæt selre ... ece rædas*, 1759–60), by which Beowulf must live as he grows older if his great strength is not to lead him into pride and covetousness, and so into obliviousness of the favour that God has shown him. Hrothgar's sermon defines the moral and theological obligations by which the hero should function. The essential elements are avoiding wrath and bloodthirsty thoughts and acts; avoiding stinginess or avarice; recognizing in all humility that God in his breadth of spirit dispenses wisdom, land, and earlship, and controls all things; avoiding joylessness; not becoming over-confident in prosperity but avoiding especially the pride that destroys from within and so leads to extreme covetousness and forgetfulness of the world to come; remaining mindful of the time limit on all human glory and strength; and, finally, keeping oneself aware that reversals are inevitable and that sorrow comes after joy, because the *eald gewin* 'ancient struggle' continues always.

    Hrothgar the homilist is not speaking here (1698b ff.) in any sense as either a negative detractor of Beowulf's achievements or as a prophet foreseeing future moral failures by the hero. On the contrary, he praises Beowulf's present glory 'throughout the wide ways ... over all peoples' (*geond widwegas ... ofer þeoda gehwylce*) and sees him as holding steadily to manly virtue while demonstrating 'might with wisdom of heart' (*mægen mid modes snyttrum*). On this basis he prophesies: 'You shall become a long-lasting comfort to your people, a help to heroes' (*Đu sceall to frofre weorþan / eal langtwidig leodum þinum, / hæleðum to helpe*). This is what Beowulf does become, and continues to be until the time of his death, and even after death. In his sermon Hrothgar speaks as the voice of age and experience, complementing the hero's youth and relative innocence. There is no particular self-justification or expression of personal failure in the way the old king illustrates the theme of inevitable reversal by reference to his own early prosperity which was later destroyed by Grendel. Without self-effacement he simply expresses gratitude to God that now he can look on the monster's head and share both the restored joys of Heorot and his new adoptive-father relation with the hero.

There is a maturation in heroism in the poem that is foreshadowed in Hrothgar's mainly tropological speech to Beowulf, with its anagogic reference to last things. But even now (1785 ff.), with the great hall 'again as once it was' (*eft swa ær*), Beowulf's wisdom and largeness of spirit are evident. His innocence is relative and has to do only with the aging and kingship that still await him in the future. In the experience of the mere he has already learned a great deal. As 'night's covering helmet' (*Nihthelm*) becomes 'dark over the dryht-men' (*deorc ofer dryhtgumum*), the hall towers aloft 'spacious and shining with gold' (*geap ond goldfah*) and 'the guest' (*gæst*) Beowulf sleeps, drained of energy after his ordeal in the mere, 'until the ... swarthy raven happy of heart' (*oþ þæt hrefn blac ... bliðheort*) heralds 'heaven's joy' (*heofones wynne*). When the bright light of morning comes hastening over the shadows, the 'bold-spirited' (*collenferhð*) hero, once again comrade of the rising sun, prepares with his warriors to leave for Geatland. Before doing so he shows himself a mature, generous peacemaker. He returns Hrunting to Unferth and does not mention the sword's failure, he courteously thanks Hrothgar for his hospitality, he offers further help should Hrothgar need it, and he expresses confidence that Hygelac will support him in this. He concludes by promising that if Hrethric comes to the Geatish court he will be among friends.

Hrothgar's reply is illuminating (1840 ff.). The old king says, literally, that Beowulf's words are dictated by God: *Þe þa wordcwydas   wigtig Drihten / on sefan sende* 'The wise Lord sends into your heart these speeches.' Hrothgar has not heard 'a man speak more wisely while still so young in life' (*ne hyrde ic snotorlicor / on swa geongum feore   guman þingian*), and he draws a parallel between Beowulf's physical and mental powers: *Þu eart mægenes strang,   ond on mode frod, / wis wordcwida* 'You are strong in might, and sage in spirit, / wise in the words you speak.' He immediately goes on to predict that if Hrethel's son Hygelac dies, the Geats will decide that Beowulf is their best possible choice as king. Beowulf has proven himself a peacemaker between the Danes and the Geats, having brought to an end earlier wars that took place between the two peoples. As 'a warrior glorious with gold' (*guðrinc goldwlanc*, 1881) and 'exulting in treasure' (*since hremig*, 1882), he is now leaving Hrothgar and Denmark, but it is clear, both at this moment and in his report to Hygelac, that he is no treasure-deluded champion filled with *hybris*. Hrothgar's sermon argues for a continuation, then, beyond the victories over the two members of the Grendel race, of the *fortitudo* and *sapientia* already demonstrated. Beowulf, speaking a little later in the narrative to Hygelac about his conquest of Grendel (1999 ff.), shows his awareness that others of Grendel's kin still live on the earth, the implication being that he knows that in the *middangeard* there is no end of the need for heroism.

The pattern of 'manly virtue' (*gumcyste*, 1723) laid down by the Danish king is honoured fully in the events of Beowulf's subsequent life.³ It is already evident in the farewell commitments made in Denmark and it continues in the wise, generous use of his strength in ongoing service to his people. In Geatland it shows itself first in his duties as kinsman and loyal thane to Hygelac, who gives him rich treasures, land, and high rank and is repaid with service from the hero's 'bright sword' (*leohtan sweorde*, 2492): 'I would always go before him in the foot-troop, alone in the front' (*symle ic him on feðan   beforan wolde, / ana on orde*, 2497–8a). Later the manly virtue is demonstrated in Beowulf's regency, in an uncle-nephew relationship with Heardred that works as it should, because Beowulf, having no lust for power for himself, refuses Queen Hygd's offer of the throne and instead provides friendly counsel to the young king (2369 ff.). During his own fifty-year reign he rules wisely and well (2208b ff.), meriting the same unambiguous commendation from the narrator that Scyld Scefing received earlier in the poem, *þæt wæs god cyning* 'that was a good king' (2390b). Finally, the climax of the hero king's exemplary living out of the program of manly virtue comes when, describing himself as 'old guardian of the people' (*frod folces weard*, 2513a), he steps forward to take his stand before the fire-dragon. The phrase *heard under helme* 'hard under his helmet,' again used here (2539a), is a succinct formulaic image for mobilized heroic energy ready to serve as protector of humankind. It has been used twice before of the hero: first, when as a figure of exuberant daring, he identifies himself to Hrothgar's herald (*Beowulf is min nama*, 340 ff.); then a few minutes later as, glistening in his linked armour (*on him byrne scan*), he takes his stand on the hearth to greet Hrothgar for the first time and to offer his services against 'the Grendel thing,' ' the Grendel affair' (*Grendles þing*, 403b ff.). Sixty to seventy years later – by Klaeber's reckoning Beowulf would be about eighty-eight at the time of the dragon fight; Klaeber calls him a noagenarian – it is the same powerful heroic man, though much older, who roars his defiant challenge into the gray rock enclosure against the dragon of death.

If we step back mentally from the presentation of Beowulf's life in relation to Hrothgar's tropological thinking and instead consider this same life in archetypal terms, certain interesting structural features of the poem begin to come into focus. The most obvious large pattern is of course the part I–part II gold-hall and earth-dragon division, what I have been calling a tale of two kingdoms, held together by the hero's actions on behalf of two peoples. This is the same structure that Tolkien eloquently described as 'essentially a balance, an opposition of ends and beginnings,' 'a contrasted description of two moments in a

Structure, Theme, and the Hero's Life 223

great life, rising and setting; an elaboration of the ancient and intensely moving contrast between youth and age, first achievement and final death' (1936, 81). Almost as obvious as this bipolar structure is the tripartite pattern of the hero's battles with three major monsters, graduated in a sequence of increasing difficulty. There is nothing in the poet's use of this second pattern, even the recapitulation to Hygelac, that conflicts in any serious way with the overall duality seen by Tolkien. It is true that there is a narrative and metaphorical closeness between the battles with the two representatives of the Grendel race that does not exist between this two-phase conflict in Denmark and the later one in Geatland. The hero's last encounter with a monster is of a different order and magnitude. Even so, the mutually fatal battle between two aged guardians does parallel and complete the earlier victories in Denmark, in just the way Tolkien says.

Within the overall balance of 'two moments in a great life,' in close relation also to the division of the hero's *agon* into three major conflicts, a third important structural pattern is discernible, that of the different phases of Beowulf's own life. Once identified, this pattern helps illustrate how the heroic romance of part I gives way in part II to something darker in the poem which has been there from the beginning. Like much else in *Beowulf*, the story of the hero's life does not emerge in a linear way, but gradually and circuitously. Still, by the end of the narrative, six clearly defined but differently emphasized phases have been made known. In critical retrospect, these phases and the overall pattern they form can be seen to serve two important purposes: they metaphorically integrate the life of the hero into the fates of the Scyldings and the Geats; they reveal an archetypal level of meaning that has major structural force in the youth-age balance of the whole work, making possible the placing of an almost perfectly realized heroic quest within a larger tragic structure. The overall result of this distinctive shaping of poetic materials is a vision of being in time which becomes increasingly bleak and austere and which, although it avoids nihilism, says clearly that in the *middangeard* of human existence even totally selfless heroic effort is bounded by death and is undercut by a combination of fate and the failures of ordinary human beings. As the romance darkens and proceeds to its narrative and symbolic conclusion on *Hronesnæs*, it becomes clear that the poem is also about the limits of archetypal romance itself, in all its phases.

The rhythm and sequence of Beowulf's life are the phases of romance fiction.[4] What this implies critically can be seen if we examine the six phases in order. The first one, the archetypal myth of the birth of the hero, is the sparse account of Beowulf's beginnings, his birth, infancy, and boyhood. Here there are elements of mystery. The information given is very partial and the way in which it is divulged is delayed and fragmentary. Early in the text (371–6) it is

224   Structure and Meaning

announced that Beowulf is Ecgtheow's son and the grandson of King Hrethel of the Geats, but the name of his mother is never provided, nor do we learn anything definite about her. This is strange, given that Hrethel and all three of his sons, brothers of this same Geatish princess, do have their stories told; in the cases of the father, Hrethel, and two of the sons, Herebeald and Hæthcyn, the references to their lives also are fragmentary, but they are graphic and memorable. Hygelac's story in comparison is somewhat more extended, though by no means complete. In addition, we receive enough information about Beowulf's father to have a sense of his background presence and importance. But the mother is left a mystery, nameless and undescribed. We think we know who she was, Hrethel's daughter, but beyond that she is undefined. Is this so that Hrothgar, who has known Beowulf's father directly and helped him, can be free to speak allegorically about her (942b ff.) as if she were simply the unknown and mysterious bearer of divine grace, especially blessed among women in her giving birth to 'the best of men' (*secg betsta*)? We cannot be certain of the poet's intention in the matter, but he does have Hrothgar, just before adopting the deliverer of Heorot as his son, say these words: 'Truly, whoever was the woman who bore that son among the tribes of mankind, if she is still living can say that the ancient Creator was gracious to her in her child-bearing' (*Hwæt, þæt secgan mæg / efne swa hwylc mægþa   swa ðone magan cende / æfter gumcynnum,   gyf heo gyt lyfað, / þæt hyre Ealdmetod   este wære / bearngebyrdo*, 942b–6a). Perhaps the obscurity of the references to this mother figure really is to serve the purpose of a typological connotation, and a sense of miracle, in a kind of veiled, retrospective 'nativity ode.' But this explanation is not fully satisfying, given that the poem establishes numerous other similar metaphorical resonances around people, places, and things while identifying them on a literal level as well.

The first phase of archetypal romance is underemphasized in *Beowulf*. Still, beyond the elements of mystery surrounding Beowulf's birth we are told two things about his boyhood. The first falls into the category of the typical motif of an unpromising beginning for a heroic life, but we learn nothing of this until after Beowulf has completed his 'mighty errand' (*micel ærende*) in the land of the Scyldings. After the hero has reported back to Hygelac and been rewarded handsomely by him, thus gaining full glory and recognition in his homeland, the narrator divulges the poor reputation accorded Beowulf there early in his life. Now the audience learns (2183b ff.) that the protagonist was 'humiliated' or 'despised for a long time' (*Hean wæs lange*) and was denied 'gift-honour on the mead-bench' (*on medobence   micles wyrðne*) by the lord of the Weders because he was thought by the Geats to be 'slow' or 'sluggish' (*sleac*) and 'not bold' (*unfrom*). The second piece of information about the hero's boyhood in

Geatland comes from Beowulf himself, late in his life, in his long remembrance of things past before he goes to fight the dragon. The romance motif involved here is that of a boy being separated from his parents but shown favour by one special adult (2425 ff.). Beowulf himself does not mention what has been said earlier by the narrator about the contempt shown him by the Geats. Rather, he recalls gratefully how at the age of seven, when he was brought by his father to the Geatish court, King Hrethel gave him 'treasure and feast' (*sinc ond symbel*), 'remembered kinship' (*sibbe gemunde*), and treated him as well as he did his own sons.

The second phase of romance, the innocent youth of the hero, is easily recognizable in the next chronological part of Beowulf's life. Although this deals with events which take place before he goes to Denmark, the telling of it emerges only after he has arrived there. This is dramatically effective, since it is at this point in the narrative that the real importance of the preliminary adventures – fighting giants and sea-monsters (418 ff.) and competing in the stormy seas with Breca (506 ff.) – is about to have its main impact. This is probably also why the references to the youthful skirmishes have strong overtones of the extreme perils which normally in *Beowulf* surround human life, and so necessitate the work of heroes. It is important to note that when Beowulf decides to go to Denmark, he introduces the element of choice into the poem and embarks on a way of life, foreshadowed earlier, which continues to the very end. Like Hercules in Prodicus's fable 'Herakles at the Crossroads,' Beowulf chooses the life of toil on behalf of others.[5]

The third phase of romance, the story of the successful quest, receives full expression in the main narrative of part I. Beowulf experiences a double progress as he voyages across the sea and battles in Heorot on behalf of the Scyldings and then, in a structural *katabasis*, descends into an underworld beyond the reach of ordinary mortals. He matures in experience in ways that directly parallel the changing structure and themes of the poem. The two major exploits in Denmark, in Hrothgar's hall and in the demonic parody of it beneath the mere waters, not only extend Beowulf's consciousness but also reveal the two antithetical realities which envelop Hrothgar and his people. We are told first that the pre-Grendel Scyldings did not know the dark fate of men. Then we see how the hell-world is revealed to them and to the poem's audience. The initial intrusion into the *dream* of Heorot by the joyless *feond on helle* develops into a long occupation, during which the Danes experience the various means by which hell tries to undo creation: by destroying human lives, by violating moral law and customs, by undermining the king's authority and power, and by driving human beings into self-destructive devil worship. All these things are experienced directly in Heorot, but by showing them the poem still has not revealed the basic mythical source of these evils. It is the ordeal in the mere which lays bare the ultimate meaning of the ancient feud that has engulfed the Scyldings. At the same time in this central part of the poem there is a process of discovery and increase of knowledge in Beowulf which confirms him as a constantly perceiving, learning hero. His growth in consciousness, like that of other epic protagonists, takes him to the lowest reaches of the imagined world in the poem. Thinking archetypally, we remember that earth is middle earth in all mythologies, including the ones underlying *Beowulf* and Anglo-Saxon culture, probably because of an assumed psychological/cosmological correspondence. It is the hazardous descent into the mere and the later ascent from it that define most sharply the vertical perspective which is basic to the structure of imagery in *Beowulf*: to the metaphorical conception of the four-level cosmos, whose polarities are heaven and hell and whose middle area divides into the world of the gold-hall in the midst of a pleasant plain and the world of the ruined hall associated with nature in its repugnant aspects, including death.

The primary area of communication through literary archetypes is consciousness and recognition. But *Beowulf* is not a chant directed to some primitive unconscious. It is a waking dream addressed to conscious minds and imaginations. For Beowulf to come to know the hell-world, and so be able to report on it to Heorot, he has first to make his way (1402b ff.) along 'an unknown course' (*uncuð gelad*) into a totally malignant place which is very difficult of access. Accompanied by troops of Danes and Geats, he is guided by the tracks of Grendel's mother 'over the dark moor' (*ofer myrcan mor*), up 'steep rocky hills' (*steap stanhliðo*) and 'tight inclines' (*stige nearwe*), along 'narrow, single-file paths' (*enge anpaðas*) and over 'steep headlands' (*neowle næssas*), until the human searchers come to the mere and 'the houses of many water-monsters' (*nicorhusa fela*). This sequence stands in sharp contrast to the description earlier of the approach of Beowulf and his men to the best of houses, along the *stanfah stræt* 'street shining with stones' (320) through the mead-fields. Arrival in 'the joyless wood' (*wynleasne wudu*) beside the flood-waters, which are welling with Æschere's blood, is only the beginning of the ordeal. At this point the narrator suggests the enormity of the imminent struggle between the hero and the demonic world by having a bright war-horn repeatedly sing out a battle-lay, to the rage and dismay of the host of sea-serpents, monsters, and wild beasts which are exploring the waters or lying on the slopes of the shore. Having killed one of these strange beings, Beowulf, feeling no anxiety about his life (1442b), now fully arms himself. The narrator draws attention to Hrunting, and then to the sharp contrast between the fearless hero and Unferth, 'who did not himself dare to risk his life under the conflict of the waves' (*selfa ne dorste / under yða gewin   aldre geneþan*, 1468b–9).

Throughout the poem when Beowulf learns of disaster he does two things: he speaks words of power and then he goes to confront the monster. That is why as he now stands on the shore of the mere he describes himself as *siðes fus* 'eager' or 'ready for the venture' (1475) and goes to 'work' *dom* (*dom gewyrce*, 1491). But this time he can penetrate only with great difficulty to where no man has gone before. After the surging waters embrace him, he swims downward for 'part of a day' (*hwil dæges*, 1495) before he manages 'to perceive the ground-plain' (*þone grundwong ongytan*, 1496), the bottom of the mere.[6] At this moment there is a sharp antithesis of human and non-human. The 'sword-greedy' (*heorogifre*) being who has held 'the domain [or 'region'] of the floods' (*floda begong*) for 'a hundred half-years' (*hund missera*, the duration of Hrothgar's rule) now sees 'that someone of men from above was exploring the dwelling of alien creatures' (*þæt þær gumena sum / ælwihta eard   ufan cunnode*). The groping monster seizes the warrior in her 'horrid grip' (*atolan clommum*) but cannot hurt his 'hale [or 'healthy'] body' (*halan lice*), because its 'war-covering' (*fyrdhom*) of byrny rings keeps her 'loathsome fingers' (*laþan fingrum*) from penetrating the hero's 'locked limb-sark' (*locene leoðosyrcan*). The she-monster of the depths cannot get at the body of 'the prince of rings' (*hringa þengel*) and so, as a carrion beast (*brimwylf*) unable actually to eat the flesh she craves, she carries it away to her house. Again as in the earlier fight with Grendel – perhaps because of enchantment – Beowulf cannot use weapons: 'no matter how brave he was, he could not wield weapons' (*no he þæs modig wæs – / wæpna gewealdan*). As the perilous descent is almost complete, the narrator tells of a gang of weird, war-tusked, sea-beast thugs who have been pursuing the hero, hampering his movements and trying to break his armour. Finally the beleaguered swimmer perceives that he has arrived in some kind of *niðsele* 'hostile hall' where no water can harm him in any way. The mere is a twisted refraction of the hall-world. Like Heorot, this hell-hall beneath the chaotic, monster-infested waters has a protective roof. Like Heorot's roof, which also withstands attack (by a monster from this same flood), this one is to protect the hall from 'the flood's sudden grip' (*færgripe flodes*). Again, as part of the implicit parodic contrast with Hrothgar's radiant hall, this hostile dwelling at the mere-bottom has 'fire-light ... shining brightly with a clear flame' (*fyrleoht ... / blacne leoman   beorhte scinan*).

The words used to depict and characterize the descent narrative (1492 ff.), particularly the verbs and verb phrases, tell of two interpenetrating processes involving the hero and the monsters, one to do with enormous physical struggle and effort, the other signalling at each stage what it is that is being discovered and learned, because the different beings involved in this crucial episode are pressing the limits of their powers. This is the sequence: *Weder-Geata leod /*

efste mid elne 'the prince of the Weather-Geats hurried eagerly'; *nalas andsware / bidan wolde* 'he would not wait for any answer'; *brimwylm onfeng / hilderince* 'the surging waters embraced the battle-warrior'; *Da wæs hwil dæges, / ær ... ongytan mehte* 'Then there was part of a day before ... he could perceive'; *Sona ... onfunde ... beheold ... þæt þær gumena sum ... cunnode* 'She soon discovered ... saw ... that there someone of men ... was exploring'; *Grap ... gefeng / atolan clommum* 'She groped ... seized with horrid clasp'; *no ... gescod / halan lice* 'she did not hurt his hale ['healthy'] body'; *ðurhfon ne mihte* 'she could not penetrate through'; *Bær þa seo brimwylf ... hringa þengel* 'The sea-wolf then carried off ... the prince of rings'; *he ne mihte ... wæpna gewealdan* 'he could not ... wield weapons'; *bræc* 'broke'; *ehton* 'hurried'; *ongeat* 'perceived'; *wihte ne scepede* 'did not harm at all'; *geseah* 'saw'; *Ongeat* 'Perceived'; *mægenræs forgeaf* 'gave a mighty rush'; *sweng ne ofteah* 'did not hold back the blow'; *onfand* 'discovered.' This vocabulary for how each participant comes to know by doing continues to accumulate throughout the whole adventure of the mere.

The previously unknown world of Heorot's (and humankind's) buried life is below the monsters and waters of the mere. As with the fire-dragon fifty years later, the emergence of Grendel's mother has been abrupt and unexpected, a sudden return of those repressed forces that are meant to be banned and excluded from the hall-world. It is the monsters who destroy the great erections of kings. In perverted, death-dealing ways they incarnate the evil behaviours of real living men and women, but this unwelcome fact cannot be fully understood until the monsters are found out and defeated in their own dwellings. It is not easy for the hero to go all the way down into the mere, or once there to survive, and 'the depths-cursed mighty mere-woman' (*grundwyrgenne, / merewif mihtig*) is no helpful Sibyl offering a golden bough to lead the way. But there are three lights in turn which shine to light the hero's progress: the *fyrleoht* 'firelight' which illuminates the underwater hall when Beowulf first arrives at the bottom (1516b–17); the *beadoleoma* 'battle-flame' Hrunting (1523), revealed as useless for dealing with the evil in the mere; the light that shines just after Beowulf, rejoicing, has killed Grendel's mother with the 'giantish old-sword' (*ealdsweord eotenisc*, 1558a). This last light stands bright inside the hall, says the narrator, 'just as the candle of the sky shines brightly from heaven' (*efne swa of hefene   hadre scineð / rodores candel*, 1570–2a).

The cumulative account of coming to know through new, conscious perceptions and huge physical effort continues in the beheading of Grendel and his mother, in the reascent with Grendel's head and the hilt, and in the triumphant march back to the stag-antlered hall. This process of discovery has taken Beowulf through a series of sharply focused incidents, each bringing with it a vivid perception of something previously unknown.[7] The exploratory experience has taken him into nothingness, so far as his own strength is concerned, and has thrown him absolutely on the power of the Creator for help and rescue. He has entered, explored, and come to know the demonic world in its monstrous, anti-life aspects. He has also come to know that the power of the Creator is at work even in the depths. The ordeal of the mere has enabled him, as the most powerful human part of the lifeworld of the poem, to emerge as the 'strong-hearted protector of seafarers' (*lidmanna helm / swiðmod*) and to swim up through 'the surging waves' (*yðgebland*) and 'mighty dwellings' (*eacne eardas*) which now are 'all cleansed' (*eal gefælsod*, 1620–1a). God's enemy having been defeated, the hero returns to Heorot 'after the fall of devils' (*æfter deofla hryre*) and gives to Hrothgar the gold sword-hilt with its runic revelation (1687–98a) of 'the origin of ancient conflict' (*or ... fyrngewinnes*); also with its telling of how 'the eternal Dryhten ... the Wielder' (*ecean Dryhtne ... Waldend*) took 'retribution' (*endelean*) on 'the race of giants' (*giganta cyn*) in 'the Flood' (*flod*), 'the welling of the water' (*wæteres wylm*).

What is it, then, that Heorot and the audience are meant to learn as they contemplate 'the choicest of irons ... with its twisted hilt and serpent ornaments' (*irena cyst ... wreopenhilt ond wyrmfah*, 1697–8a) and as they are told about the experience of the mere? Through Beowulf's descent, victory over the monsters, ascent, and return to Heorot he has traced Grendel's and his mother's crimes to their source in the original crime. We have never before in the poem been told of any reason beyond Grendel's connection with Cain for the assaults on Heorot. The mystery that is now solved, through the seeing of the serpent shapes and the reading of the runes, is the identifying of the evil that has emanated from the mere-flood in Denmark with all the evil of the antediluvian world, that of the giants as well as Cain's, also apparently that of the original *wyrm* 'serpent,' and beyond these the evil of the rebel angels who became devils and began the whole ancient, ongoing conflict. Hrothgar, the warriors in Heorot, and the woman with them, all of whom gaze on the fearful spectacle of Grendel's head (1647–50), are now meant to know what it really is that twelve years ago suddenly attacked their paradisal joy, what it was that caused the devil worshippers among them to remember 'hell in their hearts' (*helle gemundon / in modsefan*, 179b–80a), and what it is that now has been conquered. The creation of Heorot was followed by Grendel's attacks on it and then by the devil worship of some of the Danes, this latter being a turning away from Creation and a forgetting of the Dryhten God so that for them he became otherness, the unknown. But now, through Beowulf's triumph and the reading of the runes, they can wake from their amnesiac nightmare and reabsorb into their midst the exuberant, fully conscious champion who has removed any reason to go on blundering through sacrifices at heathen shrines. We have earlier been told by Hrothgar (1368–72) that the harassed stag (*heort*) does not dare to lower his head and enter the mere, but Beowulf has done this vicariously for the antlered hall. Because he has, Heorot again can tower upward, a confident unbeaten symbol of human aspiration.

Even while the hero's quest on behalf of Denmark is in the process of being successfully completed, phase-four romance, with darker and more ironic cadences, already is crowding into the poem. As the story of Hrothgar's kingdom unfolds, a tragic theme is building, in the words of the narrator, of Wealhtheow, and of Beowulf: despite the hero's success on its behalf, the idealized, innocent world of the great gold-hall is nonetheless fated to be destroyed, by human treacheries. The destructive forces, according to the tragic view of existence, are an inevitable part of the world of experience set against the innocent world that heroism seeks to defend and consolidate. Because of the experience and knowledge of the hell-world which Beowulf has now gained, he is no innocent youth deluded either about his own powers or the strengths and weaknesses of Heorot. Like Theseus reemerging from the labyrinth of Minos, Aeneas from Hades, Christ from hell, and Guthlac from hell-gate, also like Dante, in a much more fully cosmologized form later in the culture, Beowulf has descended into and returned from a hostile underworld. He has recovered an unknown or repressed past and has reemerged with a submarine or labyrinthine consciousness that enables the re-creation or restoration of Heorot and the shaping of a future which takes into account the presence of evil in the world. The mere he descended into is both the demonic past, now temporarily subdued, and also the world of a foreordained future. His descent into the abyss has been voluntary and his reemergence is a miracle. By these actions the poem asserts the heroic and the divine in the face of chaos and hell and shows a partial return of the guest-hall of Eden. But by now Beowulf sees, and the Scyldings and the audience are meant to as well, that Eden no longer really exists other than as an ideal. Heorot is the world both before and after the Deluge. Part I of the poem is about the courage to bring forward into human experience the vision of Creation and then it is about the even greater courage needed to contemplate the inevitable undoing of Creation. From the time of the adventure in the mere, it is the fatal dichotomies of history and existence in time that must be confronted. It comes as no surprise that when Hrothgar preaches his sermon to Beowulf, the latter already clearly knows enough not really to need the tropological instruction directed at him. It seems likely in fact, as noted earlier, that the main intended object of the narrator's didacticism, through the mouth of Hrothgar, is not the hero himself but the audience. From Beowulf's report to Hygelac it is clear that he at least understands that the challenge now for Hrothgar's once-innocent world is to maintain itself against the assaults of experience.

By the time part II begins, fifth phase romance, which deals with contemplative reflection about actions now past, has already been thoroughly prepared for. The main 'action' in this fifth phase is not really action at all but memory and reflection within the mind and speeches of the hero, as he thinks back over the years and prepares to face death. There is of course one final agonistic physical act to be carried out, but what dominates most of the rest of the poem is an ongoing process of thinking out loud. Beowulf is now very old, heavy with the weight of adult experience, and the world about which he speaks at length is all too familiar in its essentials. There is something of the old philosopher-king in the figure of the venerable protagonist as he gazes on the stone arches of 'the works of giants,' architectural ruins of a people vanished long ago, and contemplates human existence in the context of his imminent death. Throughout part II so far, Beowulf's growing awareness of his own death has led him to delineate his whole life. Now his perspective is that of someone who has overcome time and history. By this fifth phase, the world is no longer marvellous and mysterious, surrounded by memories of the primal Creation, but the romance *mythos* is still at work, because the most powerful man in middle earth is still functioning and because a terrifying death-bringing dragon enveloped in flames has emerged to harass his kingdom. When Beowulf learns of the dragon's attack he knows immediately that further heroic action is required of him, regardless of the enormity of the challenge. Perhaps he is saying, as Socrates does in the *Gorgias* (473C), that one's judgment on how to act should not be swayed by horrors. But the horrors are there. The hero's fight with the dragon is the poem's apocalyptic showdown. The return of the repressed or banned monstrous power requires a renewal of the heroic quest. As the narrative moves into its sixth and final phase and tells of the death of Beowulf, we are shown the end of heroic action. At the beginning of part I, we remember, we were told of the genesis of the Scylding people through the compressed metaphor of the boy-man Shield, son of Sheaf, who emerged from the waters and, in a few lines of narrative telling, was sent back again into those waters. Now by the end of the poem this mysterious cyclical fusion of life and death in one archetypal human figure has been teased apart and delineated more fully, in the six phases of the hero's life. As this life come to its conclusion, funeral and memorial rituals are unfolding, and elegiac lamentation has taken the place of acts of rescue. The dryht world that the hero has fought to preserve is disintegrating.

8
Nu Is Wilgeofa ... Deaðbedde Fæst: Tragedy and the Limits of Heroism

The total pattern of Beowulf's life is lived out against a social background in which death and ruin – through war, bloodshed, treachery, accidents, weakness, and cowardice – inexorably become the dominant features. Beowulf is the greatest of men between the seas, standing against all the human and subhuman monstrosities and chaos of his time. On the whole he is a happy warrior, capable of rage when this is needed but able to rejoice in his work. He is happy in the way that only the truly magnanimous can be. Although his life is primarily one of action, it is not an unexamined life. In his speeches he converts what would otherwise be the inarticulate end or *telos* of his existence into an articulate program. In contrast to the wordless monsters, he has what is distinctively human, the power of speech, and he is able to define his life and the lives of others within a matrix of change. He is certainly not psychologically conceived, nor is he theologically rarefied in his thinking, but he is presented as a being with a sense of time, as someone for whom the organization of a lifetime is a serious problem to be dealt with, in words and deeds: his *vita activa* goes hand in hand with his *vita contemplativa*. If the two did not do so, there would be the kind of one-sidedness in the energetic exercise of his superior powers that we find in simpler, more purely folkloric protagonists. As a poetic conception, Beowulf is a good deal more than prodigious physical fitness and impressive appearance. Like Hrothgar, Wealhtheow, Hygd, and Wiglaf, he knows himself to be part of a deliberative ethical program in which each of them attempts to live well according to the values of the hall world. No one of them is completely successful, but they do the best they can in the situations in which they find themselves, and better than anyone else in the world of the poem except God. Beowulf receives the rewards of such a life, on earth and in heaven. It is Wiglaf's view that his lord 'will long remain in the keeping of the Wielder' (*he longe sceal / on ðæs Waldendes   wære geþolian*, 3108b–9). Beowulf dies confident that God need not punish him for slaying kinsmen, knowing too that he has protected his people well, and aware that a memorial barrow will keep alive in the middle dwelling the *dom* he has won. The narrator tells us that Beowulf's soul goes 'from his breast' (*of hræðre*) 'to seek out the judgment of those fast in truth' (*secean soðfæstra dom*, 2820). This is the last judgment, anagogically referred to according to the ancient eschatology at work in this part of the poem. It is the judgment in which human beings are revealed to themselves as they really are by a truly unbiased, because non-perspectival, omniscience.

We have seen that Beowulf has no strength that does not come from God and that the monsters have no final strength at all against God, even though they are permitted in time and history to conduct their ravages. Beowulf has the strength of thirty men in his hand-grip, but he is not invincible, nor is he automatically the victor in his battles. The extreme hazards – sea-beasts, darkness, cold, storms – of the prolonged adventure with Breca leave him exhausted. His wrestling with Grendel requires enormous effort and includes setbacks, before he succeeds in mortally wounding the monster. The fights with Grendel's mother and then with the dragon are increasingly more demanding. On the question of whether Beowulf is right to decide to fight the dragon single-handed, it should be remembered that in this phase of the poem we are no longer in the semi-mythical innocent world of the primal Heorot. We are in the more realistic world of experience in which the emphasis is on the closeness of death for all human beings. In Beowulf's last great battle he is still mighty but he needs help from another human being and he is killed, in the midst of victory. This last fact implies logically that God's favour loaned him in the form of *fortitudo* is now finally being withdrawn, as sooner or later it is from all creatures in the order of the world. Beowulf himself has had no illusions about this truth. As he prepares to meet his fate, he has reconfirmed what he has existed for: 'And so through life I am to do battle, while this sword endures' (*ond swa to aldre sceall / sæcce fremman, þenden þis sweord þolað*, 2498b–9). When in the event Naegling breaks, this symbolizes the imminent ending of his own enormous strength and the fulfilment of the purpose that heaven had when it initially released his powers of action, his *mægen*, into the world. Just after the narrator has described the last stage in the battle with the dragon – Wiglaf wounds and weakens the monster and then 'the protector of the Weather-Men' (*Wedra helm*) cuts 'through the serpent's middle' (*wrym on middan*) – he spells out for the audience what is already clear: this victory finishes Beowulf's 'work in the world' (*worlde geweorces*, 2711).

The admiring descriptions of the protagonist in both parts I and II show him as splendidly powerful physically. But from the anagogic perspective of God and *ece rædas* this strength is like any other magnificent physical treasure in the guest-hall of the world. It ultimately fails, and the hero's body, reduced to ashes, is consigned to the earth. Heaven's conception of real and enduring human strength is suggested in the metaphor of treasure applied to Beowulf's soul early in part II (2422), as he first becomes aware (2397 ff.) of 'the hideous guardian, the old one under the earth' (*Weard unhiore ... eald under eorðan*) holding 'golden treasures' (*goldmaðmas*). It is, after all, the hostility of this old one that is requiring of Beowulf, 'gold-friend of the Geats' (*goldwine Geata*, 2419, 2584), that he bow to the fate that is now seeking out 'his soul's hoard' (*sawle hord*) and will separate his life from his body. The metaphor of golden treasure for the life or soul of the hero-king is important to the meaning of treasure in the poem. Gold is good when intimately associated with, and used generously by, good men and women on behalf of life and other people, but ultimately the only hoard that avails is the soul of a good person. The dragon's hoard has been in the earth long before Beowulf and his people see it and it is accursed until the end of time. Although it is part of *draconitas* to hoard treasure, the dragon is still wrong to do so, and he gains nothing from it: *He gesecean sceall / hord on hrusan,   þær he hæðen gold / waraðwintrum frod;   ne byð him wihte ðy sel* 'He is to seek out a hoard in the earth where he, old in winters, will guard heathen gold; he is none the better for it' (2275b–7); *Þa wæs gesyne,   þæt se sið ne ðah / þam ðe unrihte   inne gehydde / wræte under wealle* 'Then it was seen that the act did not profit him who wrongly kept the treasure hidden under the wall' (3058–60a). Beowulf's hoard (soul, life) is 'wound' or 'wrapped' in his flesh (*flæsce bewunden*, 2424) during the days of his life, but at death it is separated from its flesh-home to go elsewhere. Even the physically and morally greatest of men finally is mortally weak. But the soul committed to lasting benefits is strong enough to triumph over the world, even while retaining a good *dom* and *lof* in the world.

The state of heroism is given only to a few in the poem (Scyld, Beowulf I, Healfdene, the younger Hrothgar, Beowulf, Sigmund, and Wiglaf), and for a limited period. When the allotted time for a particular individual is up, some other heroic champion is needed. Heroism entails major responsibility as a leader in the war against evil, as a peace-maker, and as a gift-giver. It confers authority, shared to some extent with other dryht-men. It is in accord with the way the *Scyppend* has created the world and it involves energetic, wise use of the gifts given by him. This model of heroism is the major source of human worth and dignity in the poem. Like Jahweh in the Old Testament, the Ruler of the heavens in *Beowulf* is presented as a deity who in his plenitude wills prosperity and protection for his chosen people but also permits enemies to rise up against them. Within the concepts of the patriarchal lordship of God and the mutual obligations of a fraternal dryht, the sons of men are permitted to exercise moral, which is also to say immoral, choices, to demonstrate courage and loyalty or to be disloyal cowards, to act generously with their fellows or to turn away misanthropically and hoard their life and gifts. If most men choose to act in ways that are less than ideally moral, as seems increasingly to be the case, then social catastrophe follows. The hero can effect rescues while he lives but he does not live forever.

However inadequate such a conception of how human responsibilities intermesh with the course of events determined by heaven and hell may be (it is a kind of fatalism), this does seem to be the core of the poem's view of the human capacity to act. There is little in *Beowulf* of the modern assumption that knowledgeable human beings, on their own, individually and collectively, can shape and reshape the world and human society. As long as heaven favours you, you behave bravely and generously. When the favour is replaced and malice from hell takes its place, you suffer and endure, hoping for relief and demonstrating eagerness to accept that relief when and if heaven sends it. In this world-view there is little of our post-Enlightenment assumption that human beings through their sciences and their arts can construct a better reality than circumstance, unconscious nature, the gods, and the march of history otherwise provide. There is little sense, either, that human beings, even the heroic ones like Beowulf, through their understanding and unusual efforts really can take control of event and circumstance. From one modern perspective there is in this old poem a massive human evasion of responsibility, with evil projected mainly on to the monsters and hell and good on to the hero and heaven. Most of human existence is simply a given, the result of divine and demonic forces that act on human beings and their societies. If there is temporary relief from war and bloodshed, go to your seat at the banquet and experience joy with your fellows, for the sweet joy will not last.

But the *Beowulf* poet sees more deeply into human nature and society than this sense of human limitations might seem to imply. The gaps between being and doing, between heroes and monsters, between action and words, and between the gold-hall and the earth-dragon all are powerfully set out in the poem, in the structure of a complex tragic romance held together by sustaining metaphors and an overall myth. The antithetical gaps are so well established metaphorically that when the narrator introduces his comments, maxims, or other moralizing expressions, his sententiousness risks collapsing into tautology or self-evident platitudes. The epithets of evil surrounding the monsters are all accurate enough, within the broad canons of plausibility informing the poem. But the real information the poem conveys about the evil that undermines human life and achievement points finally to the human beings themselves. The main plot or *mythos* of *Beowulf* can be seen not only as an account of the consequence of what the monsters do in the middle dwelling but also of what they do not say, because they cannot say anything. They are radically inarticulate and so it is the human characters in the poem, including the narrator, who have to come to see and then say where the real source of danger for Heorot and for Geatland is.

To a considerable degree the narrative proceeds through a series of misreadings or gaps in knowledge, by a sequence of events or situations not known or understood in advance, or at all, by the participants. Often they act in ignorance, sometimes appropriately but often inappropriately, at times disastrously. They grope towards conclusions, sometimes correct but frequently wrong, or at most only partially correct. This misreading of event and circumstance is of course part of most fictions of whatever time and place, but in *Beowulf* it is developed by the poet into a major theme, as he and his audience think back retrospectively and re-create the existence of men and women in the heroic world. The frequent emphasis on the fact that the characters within the poem do not know or understand what is happening to them is a principal cause of the profound sense of uneasiness, and at times terror, that haunts the whole structure. Most of the human figures are presented as completely vulnerable to forces beyond their control, and beyond their understanding. At certain points, moreover, when they do come to know the true state of affairs, the truth is so hideous and monstrous, so bleak in its implications, that only the bravest continue to act. Most flee from the hall to the outer buildings, or retreat into the woods when the dragon's flames begin to rage. It is not only weapons, the door of Heorot, and the dragon's treasure that have a dark enchantment placed on them.

We have already examined the theme of mystery and unknowing that surrounds the birth and death of Scyld Scefing. This aspect of the exordium sets a tone that never completely disappears from the poem. Because Hrothgar has triumphed in battle and subdued all his enemies, he and his people, not knowing about Grendel and the mere, try to build a *pax Scyldinga* reflecting the *dream* of the guest-hall of Eden. When Heorot falls victim to the monster, even the *witan* 'wise ones, councillors' do not know what to do, and so they do the worst possible thing. Grendel – doomed, damned, and fated to destroy, and to try to lead others into damnation – has come from the unknown depths to tear the Scyldings limb from limb and to paralyse their souls so that they actually worship what they detest most. Those who control access to Heorot, the coast-guard and the herald, do not know, initially, how to react to the arrival of Beowulf, but after careful inquiries they do the right thing, as does Hrothgar. Unferth either does not know the truth about the hero or deliberately lies about it, and he probably does not know (neither does Beowulf) how useless Hrunting will prove to be. So far as the home of the Grendel kin is concerned, apparently someone has seen the mere and described it to Hrothgar (1345 ff.), but we are told that no one knows the way to it, along the 'narrow lone paths, unknown road' (*enge anpaðas   uncuð gelad*, 1410). No one knows its depths. Grendel and his mother do not know what waits for them in the hall. He knows only his cannibalistic lust and she her craving for blood revenge. The hero who penetrates the unknown depths is 'one of men ... from above' (*gumena sum ... ufan*) exploring 'the dwelling of alien creatures' (*ælwihta eard*). As each of the two combatants in the mere struggles and blunders through their battle together, neither of them has any real control, and it is not until the miracle of the giantish sword takes place that heroic conquest, light, and clarity emerge. Up on the shore of the mere, meanwhile, both Danes and Geats have misread the blood-stains in the water and so have reacted inappropriately, though differently. The reading of the runes a little later is one of the few moments of genuine knowledge, but even this leads to a false sense of security, at least for Hrothgar and some of the Scyldings.

Wealhtheow is different. We see her functioning only after Heorot has fallen into the clutches of hell, so that her powers of action are always circumscribed. She is queen of the Scyldings, wife and consort of Hrothgar, mother of their two young sons Hrethric and Hrothmund, foster mother and aunt of Hrothulf, adoptive mother (perhaps unwillingly) of Beowulf, and mother of the peace-weaver bride Freawaru. In an exemplary way Wealhtheow, 'the lady of the Helmings' (*ides Helminga*, 620b), carries out her ritual functions through gracious words and actions. She is the ideal humane opposite to the 'lady monster-woman' (*ides aglæcwif*, 1259a) who inhabits the mere and emerges from it in mindless rage to wreak destruction. Above all, Wealhtheow worries and thinks while performing her duties. She is profoundly anxious about the future, and with good reason. Unlike her husband with his manic-depressive swings, she apparently sees the situation in Heorot for what it really is. She knows even before her demonic opposite emerges from the mere that the destruction of Grendel has not solved Heorot's problems. Like Homer's Penelope unweaving her shroud each evening for twenty years, to protect a family and dwelling, the peace-weaver Wealhtheow is wary of an outsider being brought into the domestic circle. In the midst of *gamen* 'mirth' and happy *bencsweg* 'bench-noise' (1159b ff.), 'the lady of the Scyldings' (*ides Scyldinga*) makes her way beneath her golden circlet to where Hrothgar and Hrothulf sit, with Unferth at the king's feet. She courteously offers a cup to her noble lord, but then she says something verging on rudeness: 'Be happy, gold-friend of men, and speak to the Geats with kind words, as one is expected to do!' (*þu on sælum wes, / goldwine gumena,   ond to Geatum spræc / mildum wordum,   swa sceal man don!* 1170b–2). Be polite, give them gifts, yes, but then she gets to her real concern:

'They have told me that you would have this warrior as a son for yourself ... Rejoice while you may in giving many rewards, and leave folk and kingdom to your kinsmen when you must pass on' (*Me man sægde,   þæt þu ðe for sunu wolde / hererinc habban ... bruc þenden þu mote / manigra medo,   ond þinum magum læf / folc ond rice,   þonne ðu forð scyle, 1175–9*). The real question is whether their nephew Hrothulf will honour his obligations to them and whether their own sons Hrethric and Hrothmund, now sitting one on each side of Beowulf, will be all right.

Unlike Penelope, Wealhtheow has her husband present. It is her sons whose well-being is far from secure. It is for them, rightful successors to the father, that she must try to bind together a strong protective fabric of security. Beowulf's adoption by Hrothgar may be acceptable, although it seems clear that Wealhtheow finds it suspect; to make it work for her sons and therefore for Heorot is her challenge. The masculine ways of ordering or trying to determine events are not hers. Hrothgar may think he has done something positive, generous, and helpful by adopting Beowulf and rewarding him richly, but, thinks Wealhtheow, this could be neglect of a more immediate charge, the future safety and success of their sons, and, we might suppose, of Freawaru, although she does not mention her daughter. It is as if Wealhtheow has intuition and knowledge about what really will happen in the future, while Hrothgar gets carried away by his feelings of the moment.

Like the other human figures in the poem, the queen of the Scyldings is who she is more by external necessity than through any individual desire. She seems to be enduring a kind of private mourning and anxiety, knowing that even Beowulf's triumphant rescue of Heorot from the monsters has not really dealt with the problems in her family and in Denmark. No matter how many times she passes the wine-cup and how many courteous words she utters, these attempts will not be enough. The narrator, without commenting directly on her actions and words, makes it clear that she is right. Her sons are vulnerable. Blood of her kinsmen will be shed. The flames will come. Wealhtheow's situation, like Hildeburh's, is intolerable, but there is nothing she can do about it except perform the rituals and urge others to do their duty, knowing or suspecting that some of them will not. What else can she do? The answer is nothing. Not in the Denmark of the poem; not in Heorot; not in the existence she has been given. Whatever may have been the case in history outside the poem, the narrator through repeated hints leaves little doubt that Hrothulf will betray his aunt and uncle and their sons (1013b–19, 1162b–5a, 1176b–87, 1228–31). The princess Freawaru, like her mother, also will be tightly circumscribed in her powers of action and will not be able to restrain the hatred of the Heathobards. The Heorot story, then, has its own conclusion and it will eventually be told.

When Hrothgar built the gold-hall he could not know the way it would end. His was the logic of innocence, not yet assailed by demonic powers from without and within, not yet battered by too much reality. What is more terrible in its implications, then, in this poem, than the crimes of the monsters is the crimes of the human beings. The monsters that emerge from time to time to threaten human societies can be destroyed by God's champion, but he cannot eradicate the weakness of human beings. It is the endless killings by human beings that are most terrible.

The presence of the two sexes in the poem makes several of the situations complex and emotionally resonant. It also repeatedly gives two perspectives, those of Hrothgar and Wealhtheow; Grendel and Grendel's mother; Hildeburh and the men in her two families; Modthryth, before and after her conversion, in her father's house and then in Offa's; the lamenting warriors at the pyre on which Beowulf's body lies and the woman who sings a sad song foretelling future terrors. Wealhtheow, Hildeburh, and Freawaru all are brides from strange lands pledged to loyalty and generous devotion in their adopted homelands. They are joined by Hygd, Modthryth, and the woman at Beowulf's pyre, so that by the time the six have all taken their places, they have evoked a composite, strong, enduring female figure striving to hold families and tribes together. They are a kind of golden ring, which shines, lights up, and embraces the darkest scenes. Somehow apart, suffering, and used for state purposes, this female figure is fated to watch the boys and men she loves as they brood over their perceived injuries, as they express their aggressions in vendetta-inspired obligations, and as they are killed. What becomes of her? She becomes the archetypal suffering female who stands and endures as a memorial to the history of masculine killings. Although men in the poem also are victimized and suffer, it is the double focus – on the male-centred world caught up in an endless series of disasters, and on the women who react to it with strong feelings and intelligence – that helps finally to destabilize the romantic delusions of that world, and by so doing helps push the poem into its darker realizations. Perhaps as well, the frequent presence of thinking, feeling women makes more notable the absence of both mother and wife for the hero, and underlines his heroic separateness, his gradual but finally complete isolation in death from everything in the middle dwelling. As part of this theme we recall that it is only the young warrior Beowulf himself who tells us anything about the princess Freawaru (in his report to Hygelac, 2020 ff.). The young man, at the height of his masculine powers and success in the land of the Scyldings, has watched her carrying the ale-cup throughout the hall, has heard her called Freawaru, has seen her offer the studded cup to warriors, has observed her youth and gold ornaments, and has learned that 'She is promised ... to the shining son of Froda' (*Sio gehaten is ... gladum suna Frodan*). As his later predictions about what will follow Freawaru's marriage indicate, he has been thinking about her.

To pursue further the idea of gaps in knowledge and their function in the tragic structure, we may ask whether Hrothgar fails to combat the monsters because he is so preoccupied thinking about them, and about welcoming and rewarding the outsider Beowulf, that he has Hrothulf by his side and Unferth in a place of honour at his feet. We may also ask whether Wealhtheow's more inward-looking feminine perspective is meant to point to the real source of danger, real in the sense that it is the determining factor after the two monsters are dead. If this is where the poem is leading us, we and the audience are also meant to see that the most dangerous unknown is not some ineffable realm beyond human knowledge – beyond the sea's horizon to which Scyld's burial ship moves, in the darkness outside the light-filled hall, beyond the unknown path to the mere, or in the stormy waters from which seafarers look to Beowulf's barrow – but the internal human facts that are overlooked or unconsciously ignored. It seems that it is not the danger that Hrothgar thinks he has come to know in Grendel that will hurt the Scyldings most but the danger he does not know that he does not know. It is the internal treacheries that will destroy Heorot and its fated *dryht*. Wealhtheow at least partly knows these errors of existence in the hall-world, and so does Beowulf as he later explains the Danish story. But it is not until we hear him as the old warrior-king speaking at length, before he and the dragon kill each other, that we have the poem's most unimpeded song of experience. The tonality for this song has been set at the beginning of part II where the Lay of the Last Survivor and the rifling of the hoard begin the imaginative deconstruction of the gift-giving and Song of Creation in Heorot.

Beyond the narrator himself, the most sophisticated and knowledgeable reader of situations, people, things, and events is Beowulf. Hrothgar is idealized though not ideal and is very much a figure in romance, which is to say there is always part of him that is naïve; he believes in the possibility of paradise restored. Wealhtheow is less naïve, but she too is a figure in romance, in a different sense; she is the conscious, noble victim of forces that she cannot control, although she can see and understand the most basic and immediate part of them. Hygelac demonstrates little in the way of wisdom or understanding. His main achievement is fundamentally to destabilize his kingdom. His wife, Hygd, like Wealhtheow, exemplifies thoughtfulness. She tries to ensure the well-being of her son and people after her husband has acted foolishly. But it is Beowulf who, more often than not, sees things clearly. He has much to learn as he goes, and in both youth and age he does learn through observation and experience, to the point of achieving genuine wisdom. By the time we hear him in part II thinking aloud at great length, it is clear that he knows far more about the meanings of events in Geatland than does any character other than the narrator. Even so, as noted earlier, his attempts to understand why God has permitted the earth-dragon to attack his hall and kingdom lead him to momentary self-doubt, which the knowledge conveyed to us by the whole poem does not verify. Although he is a central part of the tragic theme, he does not see it fully for what it is. On one level, the literal one, the final crisis is precipitated by the fugitive who takes the cup; metaphorically, the dragon's rage over the disturbance of the hoard is part of the curse placed on the hoard by those who long ago buried the golden objects; allegorically, the images of an almost apocalyptic unleashing of destruction and death, and the premonitions of final disaster for the Geats as a people, point to a Doomsday motif. Beowulf momentarily misreads these events, tropologically, as a judgment on some imagined failure in himself. But the poet, as he moves his tale of tragic heroism into its final phases, has a more comprehensive vision than that to show his audience and to have them think about.

In *Beowulf* we can finally glimpse – through the intricate interlace of welling emotions, hopes and fears, griefs and longings, conflicting interests, blood-lusts, peace-making and peace-keeping – an overall higher order of synthesis. As we proceed through to the end of the narrative, experiencing all the strong accentual rhythms and verbal subtleties of this complex composition, we do come to see an emergent order. As we go deeper and deeper the poem binds together in words the broken links between Creation and the human experiences of the hall-world, between the human work of building, creating, and ornamenting a civilized peaceful dryht and the frustration and ruin of that work. It provides a vision of a better way (*dream*) than the monstrosity and wild destructiveness of feuding. The tragedy is that the better way leads out of the lived history of men and women and into the eternity within which their actions are known. So far as the *middangeard* is concerned, the curse goes on until Doomsday. The world of time and the world of eternity are brought into alignment periodically throughout the poem, so that the vertical perspective meets the horizontal one: in the myths and metaphors of Creation, in the extended account of the undoing of Creation (of two halls and two kingdoms), in the workings of grace and heroism, and in the final Doomsday destruction heralded by the *fyr-draca* 'fire-dragon.' Through the poet's long, sustained act of narration – involving intricate verbal motifs, uses of words as signs, uses of words as exemplary images, and expressions of ethical duties – there is a continuing drive through and beyond the tropological and even the archetypal meanings to an anagogic perspective. There is at work, building gradually, a ritual meditative purpose which holds out the ultimate possibility of the separation of the world of life from the world of death. Beowulf is not deified, but he is magnificently human by his close association with the divine power and the magnanimity of the Wielder. His death in the dragon fight is not the end of his story either on earth or in heaven.

This is a poem which invites emotional, imaginative, and thoughtful involvement in it. It does not encourage detached observation of it as some strange fiction separate from listener or reader. Its invitation to involvement is what induces participation in the tragic vision, but this happens in a powerful, distinctive manner. One way in which *Beowulf* as a vision of human existence differs from some other tragedies is that it goes beyond questions of free will and necessity, and so transcends the antithesis often found in tragedy between freedom of choice and external compulsion. We have noted twice that Beowulf as protagonist considers but rejects the possibility that some failure by him may have caused the disaster unleashed by the fire-dragon. After thinking about it, he continues in his usual mode of behaviour, confident that his record will stand in the Judgment (2732b–43a). A tragic protagonist does not necessarily have to do anything wrong to make tragedy possible. There is no necessity of a tragic flaw or *hamartia*. In literary terms, the death of Christ is a tragedy. The main point of that death, powerfully expressed in Anglo-Saxon poetry in *The Dream of the Rood*, is that everyone and everything is involved in it. Even the speaking cross as the most loyal, conscious part of the Creation, like the quaking earth and the darkening sky, is obliged to take part in the killing of the *Wealdend* who has become heroic man to free humankind from their 'many sins and Adam's old works' (*ond Adomes ealdgewyrhtum, ASPR* 2, 64:99–100). This is why pity and terror are evoked and why all Creation weeps when Christ dies on the rood. The young *hæleð* who has mounted up on the high gallows 'brave in the sight of many' (*on manigra gesyhðe*, 41) is heroic, innocent, and sinless. There is terror because he takes on in his murdered self all the evil of the world. The major meaning of the tragedy lies in the impact of the death. By it the rood, the dreamer, and the listeners or readers all are drawn into (become one with) the unity of the single body of Christ which dies, descends into hell, and then is resurrected. Death without the catharsis of the resurrection would be nihilism.

In the case of Beowulf something at once similar and different takes place. The concern is with an *ænlic* 'unique' man not with a god-man, but it is also with poetry as experience, as an intense process of receiving, using, and being changed by potent, meaning-laden word-treasures, in a process of shared creation and re-creation. Both *Beowulf* and *The Dream of the Rood* emerge as metaphorical expressions of realities to be participated in, not as artifacts to be detached from. They do not invite passive staring at the blood-stained mere or the besmeared tree as if these were simply external images projected *to wæfer-*

syne 'as a spectacle' (*The Dream of the Rood*, 31) for sadistic entertainment. In *Beowulf*, in the account of human figures in relation to the mere and its monsters and to the dragon and his lair, two kinds of humanity are presented. One is primitive and passive, and cowers before the monstrous forces that assail it, both the non-human and the perverted human ones. Much of the time this humanity exists in a state of terror. The other kind of humanity is active, exuberantly energetic, and does not know fear. It stands up and speaks words of power, it swims, it wrestles, it rages, it uses its weapons, it thinks, it transforms the feelings of abhorrence into heroic songs. It does not stop until the dragon is dead. Because this kind of humanity has not surrendered to the terror, it must be remembered. It is to be identified with. It holds out the promise, ultimately, of the conquest of death, of the eternal separation of life from death.

The essence of the tragedy in *Beowulf* is an intense vision of what it is that sustains a human society and life itself and what it is that destroys them. In an important sense, the main story-line is a journey from a dream of wish-fulfilment into a nightmare, then back into the dream, and then, inexorably and completely, back again into the nightmare – the nightmare of human existence in time and history. The dream first becomes a nightmare because the Scyldings who are in the dream do not understand or know how to deal with the evil that bursts in to destroy their blessedness: 'they did not know sorrow, the dark fate of men' (*sorge ne cuðon, / wonsceaft wera*, 119b–20). They do not have the power successfully to resist. Like Job in the Old Testament, Hrothgar and Heorot have initially been in harmony with the Almighty and have had great prosperity. Then suddenly, with no provocation or guilt on their part, 'darkness and the shadow of death' strike and 'terrify' them (Job 3:5). In part II of the poem there is not the same direct presentation of an innocent gold-hall world. But we are told that when the broad kingdom of Geatland comes into Beowulf's hand he rules it well for fifty winters, until the dragon begins to rule in the dark nights (2207–11). Again as in the story of Job, it is clear that the act which provokes 'the ancient night-foe' (*eald uhtsceaða*, 2271) and 'ravager of the people' (*ðeodsceaþa*, 2278) is permitted by God. The narrator explains, in the form of a generalizing maxim, why the fugitive who has stepped close to the dragon's head is able to escape: 'So may an undoomed man who holds favour from the Wielder easily survive woes and misery!' (*Swa mæg unfæge   eaðe gedigan / wean ond wræcsið   se ðe Waldende / hyldo gehealdeþ!* 2291–3a). Beowulf's generous, compassionate response to this unhappy, needy man, who comes to him and obtains a *frioðowære* 'peace compact' (2282b), is not a guilty act. As with Heorot many years earlier, the human society attacked by the hostile monster is Job-like, in that there is nothing to indicate that it deserves such destruction. Again too, as with the Scyldings, there is no indication that any of the victimized people can withstand the wild attack – other, of course, than the hero.

We should probably ask again what reality it is in this poem that is meant to be saved and protected by the hero. More specifically, what is it in the ideality of the gold-hall world that makes possible the heroic theme, continued from the first words of the poem to the last, creating the sense of glory and great human potential whose final defeat in the process of time is profoundly moving? As *Beowulf* moves through six phases of romance narrative and gradually reveals itself structurally and thematically as a great tragic poem, what are the human realities symbolized by the hall world that make the poem resonate still, a thousand or more years after the cultural circumstances of its origin? We have discovered in the text a generous measure of the seemingly endless sources of symbolic energy that imaginative literature as a whole provides. By focusing on literature's two central processes, myth and metaphor, I have tried to show how the poem delivers this energy by helping us release its words from the inert language of the glossaries, dictionaries, concordances, and data banks. I have treated *Beowulf* as part of literature, and literature as a living system of imagining in which we find the widest possible range of human desires and frustrations. I have considered this old but still new text as a presentation of stories and myths about the poet's and his audience's mental or imaginative capacity to hear or perceive linkages between widely (and even wildly) different parts of a symbolic world. This symbolic world has become at least partly knowable through cunning, powerful uses of the verbal resources of the word-hoard. By explorations of the verbal structure from several critical perspectives, I have tried to show, in that structure, different levels or phases of meaning – words as metaphorical motifs, words as signs, words presenting exemplary types, words communicating broad communal and cultural significance, and also words that point beyond the powers of words. I have suggested that through this polysemous richness, always based on and informed by the literal/metaphorical level, there emerges an imagined vision that passes well beyond questions of moral judgment about the lives of Beowulf and the peoples around him, and comes to its final focus in his death. I should like now to say what I think the essence of that vision is.

If this poem ended with the return of Beowulf and his troop to Geatland, it would have a radically different overall meaning. It would be a fascinating but not particularly disturbing tale of a heroic quest, a *micel ærende* successfully completed on behalf of a beleaguered people. Thematically it would show a world in which the Wielder, the Almighty, lets monsters prey disastrously on unoffending human beings but also empowers one extraordinary man to rescue and restore those human beings to a generous measure of social security and well-being. In that projected world, symbolized by the poem's main *imago mundi* Heorot, the four basic needs of human beings in all times and places are recognized and permitted fulfilment: the need for physical shelter, food, and drink; the need for companionship, sexual, familial, and social; the need for material possessions; and the need not to be confined but to move freely. Human existence as *dream*, embodying the joyous, confident fulfilment of all these four needs, is powerfully projected in 'the best of houses' (*husa selest*, 146, 285, 658, 935) whose light shines over many lands (311) and inside which *wiste* 'banqueting, feasting, abundance' symbolizes the plenitude both of Hrothgar and the heavenly *Liffrea* 'Prince of life' in meeting the first human need.

In important ways Heorot is a utopia, an idealizing description of a nowhere, an allegory, so to speak, of the mind of a generous, wise man acting in accord with the will of the Almighty. In this place Heorot, which is not an actual place, the bonds of family and dryht relations – the second human need just mentioned – are shown to be potentially strong and good, capable of bringing harmony and great happiness in a hall world in which the highest value is respect for the sanctity of human lives (71–3). Possessions – the third need – come from God and are generously and freely shared. The giving and receiving of gifts and treasures is a fundamental, life-sustaining ritual. So far as the fourth requirement is concerned, the freedom to move about in safety, this is most clearly evident in the vigorous, enthusiastic building and ornamenting of Heorot by many people 'throughout this middle dwelling' (*geond þisne middangeard*, 75b), in the excited gathering of warriors and chieftains on the morning after Grendel's defeat to look at the marvel of his hand, arm, shoulder, and bloody tracks (834–41a), and again in the exuberant release of energies in the music and horse-racing on the same morning (853 ff.). In Heorot, then, set in the midst of the mead-plains, the four fundamental human needs not only are met, they are shown as fulfilled to the point of blessedness: 'So those dryht-men lived in joy, blessedly, until ...' (*Swa ða drihtguman   dreamum lifdon, / eadiglice,   oð ðæt ...*, 99–100). Sleeping after their banquet, for a time they do not know 'sorrow ... the dark fate of men' (*sorge ... wonsceaft wera*, 119b–20a).

But in part I of the poem each of the four basic human needs and desires is also shown as desecrated and threatened with destruction by the Grendel race, and in the longer term by human failures. Half the narrative burden is taken up with attacks, actual and potential, on the *dream* of Heorot. The other half concerns the actions of Beowulf, who with full assistance from the heavenly Dryhten restores the gold-hall world so that it can continue as a noble though still vulnerable place for the fulfilment of human desires. Part II of the poem is a kind of dark shadow supplement to part I, constructed out of the destabilizing subthemes that were partly pushed out of the light-filled centre in part I. It is a dystopia to follow the impossible dream set out in the utopia. The two parts together powerfully illustrate one of the central ideas of postmodern literary theory, that each work of literature both defends and attacks its own establishment. The great royal hall is destroyed at the beginning of part II and is never restored. It is as if all potential for structured human happiness is destroyed at once. We are left to consider the implications, as these are suggested by the death of Beowulf and the disintegration of his kingdom.

To understand the depth and meaning of these two visions together, we need to take polysemous thinking beyond the constraints of ideological criticism, either early medieval or modern/postmodern. As we search out the under-thought beneath the ideological surface of this great poem, it becomes clear that it is the myths of primary human concern that come to dominate over the socio-political and theological concerns also evident in the text. Centuries after the Anglo-Saxon dryht, the concept of *wergyld*, and the theology of the Fathers have all largely receded from our culture, the poem continues to speak about human dwellings and about eating and drinking, and about the possibility of being murdered while you sleep. It is concerned with families, with brothers, sons, daughters, fathers, mothers, uncles, aunts, nephews, grandfathers, and adoptive fathers, and with shoulder-comrades. It is concerned with human beings not wanting to be enslaved, with the freedom to move about: to swim, to sail across the waters, to race horses, to play. It powerfully projects the desirability of a social order in which men and women are secure and happy enough to compose or listen to stories, songs, and harp music, and to shape curiously inwrought, beautiful objects for individual adornment; or weapons to protect human bodies, or ring-necked ships meant to move eagerly with the winds. Identification of human life in terms of a dwelling-place or shelter leads to the poem's symbols of social solidarity, the communal guest-hall, banqueting, and the passing of an ale-cup; also to symbols of clothing, armour, and shared treasure. Privation of these human goods leads to the sense of desolation articulated by the Last Survivor, to the acute need of the fugitive who takes the cup from the dragon's hoard and with it regains social identity, and to the monstrous isolation of Grendel and his mother. Identification of human life in terms of play and civilized activities leads to images of athleticism and the arts.

Each symbolic image of a basic human need in the process of being fulfilled is an integral part of an idealized whole, the gold-hall world. *Beowulf* speaks of all these things in both the horizontal sequential telling of the stories of the Scyldings and the Geats and in the vertical linking of these needs, desires, and activities with the great containing myth of the Creation as the shaping, ornamenting, and sustaining by the Father-God of a middle dwelling in which to house all ongoing creative life. Ideologically, horizontally, Heorot is the dryht-hall, the socio-political centre of the Scylding version of the Germanic warrior culture as this is imagined retrospectively in a later time. Mythologically, in its fundamental iteration, Heorot is the world of the human family before the first brother-murder. In the mythological thought of the poem, the creation of the great guest-hall is the first in the progression of metaphors and myths – succeeded by Fall, Flood, re-creation, history, Doomsday – which express the poem's primary concerns. It is the combination of those myths with the stories of Denmark and Geatland that gives *Beowulf* its continuing power as words. *Beowulf* is a poem which recovers and re-creates myth.

One question posed by part I and answered there is repeated in part II, but given a harshly different answer. Over and over again in this theocentric, mythological text it is said that the *Alwalda*, under any of his names, is in control of events and situations. As we have seen, the narrator, Hrothgar, and Beowulf all express this faith. If it is true, as I have tried to show, that the primal Heorot and Beowulf at the beginning of part II have done nothing to deserve the destruction that strikes them, then the poem is a presentation of the profound problem of theodicy: why does an all-powerful God of generosity and goodness permit evil and suffering, perhaps in some sense cause them, by letting the monsters exist and by permitting human beings to identify themselves with the race of Cain? If we consider only part I, the problem of undeserved misery gets a more or less satisfactory, traditional resolution, as in the Book of Job and the New Testament: God lets the Grendel race work their evil for a time, but he intervenes by providing a redeemer figure who restores the situation from its temporary condition of demonic possession. Like Job at the end of his story, Heorot regains a prosperity comparable to its earlier one. There really is some kind of resurrection by faith in myth in part I. Heorot and the hero are the positive, creative, structural fiction which asserts something essential in the teeth of experience. They are the poem's supreme fiction: their ideality may be illusion, but it is illusion that is made reality by the poem, a reality to be participated in, even if the vanished dryht and the cremated body of the hero will in due course succeed them. As metaphors, both the gold-hall and the hero are counter-logical and counter-ironic. Even though both of them are to be destroyed, they *are* the myth which for a time in part I arrests history. They suggest that there is a structure of permanent reality beyond the hypothetical or imagined forms in which they themselves have been projected.

But in part II, thoroughly prepared for in the dark subtext of part I, there is no such deliverance or restoration of the Geats, even though the dragon is killed. From the Lay of the Last Survivor to the end of the poem we are involved in a memory world in which the vanished dryht in the Lay and the vanishing dryht in Geatland are a kind of encroaching tomb or architectural ruin filled with disintegrating objects and relationships. The metaphors of the gold-hall and the mead-fields have disappeared into images of a ruined dryht world being laid waste by human killing and a fire-dragon. The middle dwelling is now a place of rusting ale-cups and weapons. There are no bird-prowed sailing ships, racing horses, or flying hawks. As in Greek tragedy, *Beowulf* achieves its catharsis by attaining what is fundamentally a vision of God-permitted destruction according to the dictates of wyrd, of law and ineluctable process beyond the powers of human beings. It is as if the poem has reversed the traditional Christian vision in which an order of grace succeeds an earlier order of law.

Wyrd – grammatically and conceptually – is 'what is to be, what will be.' It *is* what happens in the world of experience. The *wyrd* which the narrator, Hrothgar, and Beowulf all recognize as having determining power (455, 477, 572, 734, 1056, 1205, 1233, 2420, 2526, 2574, 2814) does not mean the force of external influences, nor does it mean some moral fault. Such conceptions do not make sense in describing this tragedy. Throughout his life Beowulf's heroism has included wisdom side by side with courage. He has shown a detachment from existence even while participating exuberantly in it. The interpenetration of work and play in the poem is also the interprenetration of necessity and freedom. Because Beowulf is created and enabled to fight monsters, he willingly, freely, and happily does so. What he has to do is what he wants to do. There is no tension between internal private desires and public duty. The ego does not coexist with wisdom and goodness because wisdom understands the Creation through tradition and the law. If Beowulf survives the fight with Grendel, good, but if the monster carries his bloody corpse over the moors, Hrothgar should not grieve. He should simply send the dead warrior's mail-coat, Hrethel's legacy and Weland's work, back to Hygelac (445 ff.). Each challenge and potential disaster is something to be plunged into and then integrated into the evergrowing pattern of service and experience. In Beowulf liberty has its centre in wisdom, in that creative wisdom which shows itself as heroic action and is at once work and play, because it is in harmony with the order of Creation itself. He is part of the great principle of creative Wisdom described in Proverbs 8:30-1, as being 'at play everywhere in the world' (*ludens in orbe terrarum*) and delighting to be among the sons of men.

Too great attachment, as in Unferth and in the thanes in the dragon-fight, leads to cowardice and worse. Attachment to treasure to the point of hoarding is social death. The taking of one small cup from the hoard back into a functioning social context throws the anti-human dragon into a berserk fury. Beowulf, in addition to ensuring the death of the old night-foe, wants to see 'the ancient wealth, the golden things, the bright curious gems' (*ærwelan, / goldæht ... swe-*

gle searogimmas, 2747b–9a), and he thanks 'the Prince, the King of Glory, the eternal Dryhten' (*Frean ... Wuldurcyninge ... ecum Dryhtne*) that he has been able before his death-day to get such treasure for his people (2794 ff.). He wants the treasure to serve human life. Now that 'with his old life-law' or 'with his old allotted life-span' (*frode feorhlege*) he has bought the hoard, now that metaphorically he has made himself *wergyld* to try to save the Geats, he is completely ready to relinquish both the hoard and his personal treasures. The ultimate test of his detachment is his total readiness for death when it comes. Just before *wyrd* sweeps him away, he takes from his neck 'the golden necklace' (*hring gyldenne*) and gives it, along with his 'gold-gleaming helmet' (*goldfahne helm*) and his 'mail-coat' (*byrnan*), to the young spear-warrior Wiglaf. For Wiglaf, who misunderstands and resists the death, the losing of his lord is a torture; three times he tries to prevent the dying king from leaving middle earth, by washing Beowulf's venom-poisoned wound.

The hero has always to be engaged and detached. He has to fight the foe of life with every part of his *mægenstrengo* (2678) but at the same time be entirely willing to have his strength cancelled by death. The thanes are afraid of death. Wiglaf bitterly fights against Beowulf's death. Beowulf accepts it with equanimity. He has adjusted to the temporal narrowing of opportunity that age has brought. Unlike Job and Hamlet in their fleshly forms, he does not thrash about in frustration in the bone-house of his corporeal self. Instead he uses absolutely his still solid flesh until it is destroyed and his life leaves it. To an extent he has been imprisoned in the armour of the dryht culture, but his ability to abandon and transcend its weapons and treasures when the occasion demands is part of his freedom as hero. The cosmos remains split in *Beowulf*, but the hero can and does join the eternal part of it. The rituals at the end of the poem ask the audience to accept the hero's death. The antitype of all the treasures he has received during his *lændagas* – from his ancestors, from Hrothgar and Wealhtheow, from Hygelac, and from his time as king – is the *sawle hord* 'soul-hoard' (2422) that goes from his breast to seek the *soðfæstra dom* (2819–20). His judgment or apocalypse comes when he confronts the body of his own death in the dragon, when his life is released from its elemental *banhus* incarnation and is free to go into eternity, even as the dead dragon, a creature of earth (*eorðraca*), air (*lyftfloga*), and fire (*fyrdraca*), is pushed lower in the order of Creation, into the embrace of the flood-waters. Beowulf goes from *dom* to *dom*, from glory in middle earth to glory elsewhere.

What finally are the consequences of Beowulf's death? How do they relate to the great dream of human well-being that informs part I and cannot be forgotten in part II? What is the impact of the death on his people, on the whole poem, on us? The narrative began with the lordless Danes needing help and receiving it.

It ends with another lordless people, the Geats, filled with terror at the dark fate awaiting them. As Wiglaf keeps 'head-guard' (*heafodwearde*, 2909b) over the dead king and dragon, a messenger takes the news to the stronghold: 'Now the one who granted the desires of the Weather-Men [or '-People'], the Lord of the Geats, is fast on his deathbed' (*Nu is wilgeofa   Wedra leoda, / dryhten Geata   deaðbedde fæst*, 2900–1). The one who was the source of all their well-being, who was their *wilgeofa*, 'is resting on the place of slaughter by the deed of the serpent' (*wunað wælreste   wyrmes dædum*, 2902). The 'life-enemy' (*ealdorgewinna*) has destroyed the man who embodied the health, safety, and prosperity of the people. The world without Beowulf, predicts the messenger, will now resume its normal state of endless bloody feuding and war. The Franks, the Frisians, the Hugas, the Merovingians, and the Swedes all will ensure that *wælnið wera* 'the murdering hostility of men' (3000) will rage, bringing disaster for the Geats. Some of the rings and gold which Beowulf has 'grimly purchased ... with his own life' (*grimme geceapod ... sylfes feore*, 3012b–13) will be consumed with him on the pyre (3010b–15a). The rest will be buried in the ground at Beowulf's barrow, 'as useless to men as it was before' (*eldum swa unnyt,   swa hit æror wæs*, 3168). In a complete apocalypse, as in the Old English Doomsday poems and the Book of Revelation behind them, the whole world is raised from death and cleansed, by making Satan, the dragon, and the faithless among humankind the scapegoats. In *Beowulf*, less totally mythical, the hero has voluntarily served as scapegoat to ensure the dragon's death. The dragon also is a scapegoat, but not voluntarily. The land of the Geats remains mainly a land of decay and death. But there has been a partial splitting of worlds.

Tragedy presents a vision of glory and great human potential lost. In the moral economy of this poem, the high price paid by the *wer* Beowulf has been partly wasted. The dragon is dead, but the treasure is useless and Geatland is plunging into ruin. In the words of the messenger, the world of the once-golden dryht-hall is now desolate because 'a hero king,' 'a man both hero and king' (*biorncyning*, 2148, 2792), has laid aside 'laughter, sport, and joy' (*hleahtor ... gamen ond gleodream*, 3020b–1a). All the primary needs of the hall-world – for shelter, food, and drink, for family and comradeship, for giving and receiving gifts, and for freedom to move not as wretched exiles but safely – all these needs and desires will go unmet. Instead 'many a spear cold in the morning will be wound round by fingers, raised in hands' (*Forðon sceall gar wesan / monig morgenceald   mundum bewunden, / hafen on handa*, 3021b–3a). It will not be the sound of the harp that wakens the surviving warriors but a hideous story-telling about the poem's last anti-human banquet. The 'dark raven' (*wonna hrefn*), which now usurps the place of a human story-teller, is the antithesis of the 'happy-hearted raven that announced' (*bliðheort bodode*) the sun, 'the joy of heaven' (*heofones wynne*), on the morning of the triumphant Beowulf's departure for home (1801–6). This last dark bird in the poem, 'eager [or 'ready'] for doomed men' (*fus æfter fægum*), will tell many tales and 'will say to the eagle how he fared at the eating, when with [or 'in competition with'] the wolf he plundered the corpses' (*earne secgan,   hu him æte speow, / þenden he wið   wulf wæl reafode*, 3026–7). The tragedy of this very corporeal, metaphorically thought poem is that it has expressed huge desires and has shown great human joy, and then has cancelled the joy, leaving only the desires and a memorial barrow with twelve circling riders singing an ancient lament.

Conclusion

This exploration of the *Beowulf* that we may think we know has been a ransacking and sorting through of those elements of the Old English word-hoard that are used in the poem, in the hope of putting the metaphors back together as once they must have been. If the attempt has been even partly successful, the poem should have emerged in a new, energizing way.

But how did it all begin? asks the poet-narrator, looking back on Danish history. How will it all end, for the Sons of Shield and for the fabulous warrior who for a time brings relief from monstrous destruction? How will it end for Beowulf's own Geatish people? These questions, as the poet well knows, are eternal ones – originary and teleological. They invite the telling of stories and myths which lead us back to the time when the kingdom of the Scyldings did not exist, even to the time when the radiantly bright plain of the earth itself first was being fashioned, surrounded by water, illumined by the sun and the moon, its folding surfaces adorned by the Almighty with branches and leaves and every living thing that moves about; then forward again, all the way to the death of Beowulf, which marks the end of the age of this hero; and, above and through Beowulf's story, inexorably, to the great Doomsday when all societies will have vanished. But for us the listeners and readers the end-day is not yet: we are given an exemplary tale by which to steer our tall ships through the dark waters of our personal and cultural history.

The poet leads us back to the moment of the creation of the great gold-hall Heorot, the first (and the last) occasion on which Hrothgar's people feast in primal *dream* 'joy,' before the calamities brought by Grendel. The monster's uninvited visit by night begins a bloody war which can be alleviated by acts of great bravery but which nonetheless will continue until Heorot finally is consumed in flames. When the scene changes to Geatland fifty years later, King Beowulf's hall and gift-throne are abruptly destroyed by dragon-fire, leaving the hero to do two things: tell the story of his life and people, and kill the dragon. What is left after he has done these things, his parting gift, is a useless treasure; yes, but also the memory of a generous power that has spent itself, in the days of its life, rescuing humankind from the powers of death and destruction. All too often, we have been shown, the destruction is self-inflicted. After the last flames of Beowulf's burning have died away, there emerges a great memorial barrow, and beyond that poetry and history still unfolding.

Yet the world of myth – of Creation, fall, rescue, the ongoing war between heaven and hell, and Doomsday – is not yet passed. The most dangerous event since the beginning of time has been the monsters' discovery of us, their envious rage at our capacity for joy, at our ability to create gold-halls, to give and receive gifts, to delight in harp music and stories, and to be loyal to each other. The evil the monsters unleash goes far beyond their own attacks. It enters the very beings whose lives have been created for joy, and makes some of them into destroying sociopaths. The consequences of this demonic possession, countered by the power of the 'Helm of the heavens,' are the extraordinary events of the *Beowulf* poem – the devil worship, the emergence of the young hero with the strength of thirty men in his hand-grasp, the challenge by the brother-slayer Unferth, the prodigious battles with the monsters, the great banquets and gift-giving, the hoarding of treasure, the visions of vanished and vanishing dryhts, the endless feuding and bloodshed, and the prophecy of catastrophe for Geatland when the hero dies.

These hypnotic, deeply contradictory stories are what *Gold-Hall and Earth-Dragon* attempts to take us through. To a degree unusual perhaps among Anglo-Saxonists, I have spelled out in the preceding eight chapters the *ars poetica* by which I have proceeded, but always in ways that keep the poem itself in the foreground of the discussion. The scholarly apparatus has deliberately been kept uncomplicated, so that the poem and the theoretical construct together will do the main work of the book.

Beowulf is not only part of the memory of humankind in the remote past. In important ways it is our own hoarded and buried life. The study of it leads to recognition scenes, the discovery in the golden wine-cups, swords, and helmets, and in the ruined wind-swept halls, not just something of our past lives but part of the total cultural form of our present life. At the end of the poem the hero Beowulf dies, but the polysemous languages of modern and postmodern humankind and our atemporal sense of time and history have brought us closer than ever to the mythic conditions that gave rise to our earliest poetry. The myths and metaphors in *Beowulf* do not ask to be believed as history or turned into ideological doctrines. They ask to be experienced.

Notes

Chapter One

1 All quotations from *Beowulf* are from Klaeber's edition. Quotations from other Old English poems are from *The Anglo-Saxon Poetic Records*. Translations from the Old English are mine.
2 I do not translate this Old English word because there is no even approximately adequate Modern English equivalent. Swanton (1982) has shown that the Anglo-Saxons in general retained the continental Germanic concept of kingship (in which power derives from the people), a concept mirrored in such terms as *dryhten* (from *dryht*). But he has also shown that in *Beowulf* there is influence as well from the vertical Roman idea of kingship, in which the king is a divinely sanctioned ruler. Robinson 1985 sees in words like *dryhten* in *Beowulf* evidence of a dual vision of the pagan past; *dryhten*, he reasons, contains both the pre-Cædmonian meaning of lord of a comitatus and the post-Cædmonian meaning of the Christian God. For further discussion of *dryht* and *dryhten* see pages 64–71 of this book.
3 For judicious discussions of the poem's attitudes to the past, see Hanning 1974, Frank 1982, Robinson 1985, Howe 1989, Hill 1995, and Liuzza 1995.
4 Delasanta and Slevin begin the discussion by using Frye's modes thesis to characterize Beowulf as a 'romance hero' not a 'high mimetic' one. They also see him as a 'Christ-figure,' an attempt by the poet 'to perfect the pagan heroic ideal by submerged references to Christ' (1968, 410). For reasons that will become clear as this book proceeds, I do not agree with the Christ-figure identification.
5 For example, Robinson, using three episodes in the poem (the descent into Grendel's mere, the return from Frisia, the swimming feat with Breca), has argued that Beowulf is conceived as a heroic man and not as a romance hero. Taking these terms as mutually exclusive creates real problems for dealing with a poem like this one. Beowulf clearly is presented as heroic man but he also embodies elements of the marvellous.

His characterization and actions cannot be separated from the marked fictionality of the poem that he inhabits. Robinson finds characterization in heroic poetry embarrassing if it goes 'far beyond human dimensions' (1974/1995, 80). I am not sure what human dimensions are, but this hero stretches them well beyond what we usually think of as normal. Niles (1983), in the first chapter of his book, rejects attempts to explain away the marvellous, or to interpret Beowulf's actions in realistic terms.

6 Both discussed more fully later in this book. Earl, 'Beowulf's Rowing Match' (1979), sees Beowulf as a Germanic hero who, unlike Irish heroes, does not perform superhuman feats. He reads the contest with Breca as a rowing match, not as a demonstration of incredible swimming prowess. He also thinks Beowulf's dive into the mere and his swim from Frisia have been misread as superhuman feats. Robinson as well (1974/1995) gives a mimetic, non-romantic reading of the hero in which the episode with Breca is mainly a rowing, not a swimming, contest. He does not mention the first of the four sea adventures, in which there is no suggestion of rowing or of a boat or raft. Beowulf's allusive reference to his early monster-slaying does seem to be to an adventure separate from the one shared with Breca: the struggling in the waves and the killing of water-monsters could be part of the Breca episode, but the crushing of the five giants does not fit there. Frank brings to the now-controversial 'swimming' feats of the hero a fine blend of lexical knowledge and metaphorical insight, and so allows connotations of both swimming and rowing actions. She observes astutely: 'the *Beowulf* poet is rather good at making the impossible seem real' (1986, 160).

7 The manuscript reads *wundum*, which makes excellent metaphorical sense: 'hard with wounds,' or 'brave' or 'strong with wounds.'

8 The manuscript has *hlimbed* and this is retained by Klaeber, but he and others (Grein, Holthausen, Bosworth-Toller) read *hlinbed*, seeing in *hlimbed* the assimilation of *-n* before a labial. The verb form of the first half of the compound is *hleonian* (or *hlinian*) 'to lean.'

9 Writing his essay in the 1950s, Frye did not use female protagonists as examples, as I do here. There are female protagonists in all five fictional modes, including myth, although one has to go outside the more theistic, patriarchal Christian tradition to find goddesses.

10 Orchard (1995) has reexamined the monsters in *Beowulf* in the context of the other monsters in the manuscript, and has placed all these in the wider context of patristic and early medieval teratology. Unfortunately, in my view, in his relating of the traditional materials to *Beowulf* he accepts the Goldsmith (1970) and A.K. Brown (1980) characterization of Beowulf as a mighty monster-slaying heathen who is guilty of pride, and so is damned even while being given feigned praise.

11 When in this book there is reference to 'the *Beowulf* poet,' it is understood that this is a term cloaking profound ignorance, in a literary historical sense. 'The audience' is a

similarly slippery term, a stratagem based on the reasonable assumption that someone heard or read the poem or was meant to.

12 I realize that this translation, or non-translation, of *garsecg* is not generally accepted. I give reasons for accepting and using it on pages 74–5.

13 The poetic word *heoro, hioro* 'sword' is used in compounds. It appears several times in *Beowulf: heoroblac* 'sword-pale' (2488), *heorodreor* 'sword-blood' (487, 849), *heorodreorig* 'sword-bloody' (935, 1780, 2720), *heorogifre* 'sword-greedy' (1498), *heorogrim* 'sword-grim' (1564, 1847), *heorohocyhte* 'sword-hooked' (1438), *heorosweng* 'sword-stroke' (1590), *hiorodrync* 'sword-drink' (2358), *hioroserce* 'sword-sark' (2359), *hioroweallende* 'sword ('fierce'?) welling' (2781). Sometimes Klaeber translates *heoro* as 'battle,' but this abstracting translation attenuates the metaphorical force of the specific language.

14 Klaeber and other editors have *helle* at 588. Robinson (1995, 88–90) challenges this and suggests, but does not insist, that the word might be *healle*, so that Beowulf is saying of the fratricide Unferth, 'for that you must endure condemnation in the hall' rather than 'damnation in hell.'

15 The Norton Lectures at Harvard, published as *The Secular Scripture: A Study of the Structure of Romance* (1975), give a fuller sense of what that extensive reading included than can be gained from *Anatomy* (1957).

Chapter Two

1 This is a hazardous and difficult enterprise. It is well to remember in undertaking it that, as Frank has emphasized, 'the meaning of a word in Old English prose is a fallible guide to its meaning in poetry,' because the divergence between the meaning of a word in verse and its meaning in prose can be very wide (1986, 153). Robinson (1985) takes us a good distance in understanding the poetic language of *Beowulf*. He demonstrates how the appositive style of the poem emphasizes and revivifies meanings of traditional compounds and formulas, so that the audience's minds are invited to notice 'elemental meanings of words' and to recall etymological origins (66).

2 On the kenning as a verbal device see Marquardt 1938, Brodeur 1959, 1–38; 247–53, Gardner 1969–70, 1972, Greenfield and Calder 1986, 125, Brinton 1987, and Frank 1987.

3 Brady (1979) provides a discerning analysis of sixty-seven nominal compounds (including kennings) for weapons in *Beowulf*.

4 Frank mentions that the compound *herenet* is related to a skaldic kenning. She points out that when the *Beowulf* poet uses such kennings he usually clarifies the more obscure ones; also that 'His echoes of skaldic diction seem to be heard at a great distance from outside the tradition' (1987, 343).

5 In accepting the emendation *snedeþ* for the manuscript *sendeþ* I follow Imelmann,

Klaeber, and others. Granted, the change is conjectural, but it makes excellent figurative sense in the context.

6 The etymological meaning is 'sweaty,' though most translators prefer 'bloody.' Donaldson is an exception; he says 'the sword was sweating' (1975, 28). For reasons given in what follows, I think both meanings are at work in the passage.

7 Robinson (1974/1995, 86) points out that Beowulf, unlike Unferth, does not say it was winter. Robinson is opting for a non-marvellous reading of Beowulf and his role in the Breca episode, in which Beowulf's more credible version tells of a less imposing feat than Unferth's exaggerated one does. Beowulf does say, however, that it was 'the coldest of weathers' (*wedera cealdost,* 546b), and the waters in his account are storm-tossed by the battle-grim north wind, as well as being infested with whales, angry *merefixas*, and a fierce, cruel, monstrous sea-beast who drags him to the bottom. It sounds like a poetic and metaphorical winter to me.

8 Cassidy (1972) wonders if *garsecg* in *Beowulf* is a relic of a lost kenning, a mythical figure for the sea as a warrior who defends or attacks the land. He suggests Woden, who sometimes is associated with the sea and is husband to Nerthus 'Mother Earth.'

9 C.F. Brown (1940) sees it as a cup of death (*poculum mortis*) metaphor. Smithers (1951–2) reads it as a well-known medieval ironic metaphor for brewing or dispensing bitter drink. Splitter (1952) connects *ealuscerwen* with a Germanic ceremonial drinking ritual: the Danes are struck with awe, as in such a rite, when they hear the uproar inside the hall. Henry (1961) connects the second part of the compound *ealuscerwen (Beowulf,* 769) and *meoduscerwen (Andreas,* 1526) with Old Irish *seirbe* 'bitterness.' Rigby (1962) sees *ealuscerwen* as indicating a contrast between the heroic Beowulf struggling in the hall and the cowardly Danes who are having a beer. Irving (1966) reads the compound as 'ale-sharing' and links it with the analogous contexts of noisy drunkenness in *Andreas* and *Judith*. Trahern (1969) associates the *ealuscerwen* of the Danes with imagery in the biblical Book of Wisdom 11:5–9, thus comparing their experience to the Israelites' thirstiness of despair in the wilderness, followed by their terror, and then their receiving of the waters of grace. Klegraf (1971) explains *ealuscerwen* as a three-part compound: *ealu* 'ale,' *scearu* 'portion,' *wen* 'hope' – 'hope of beer-sharing.' Hanning (1973) reads *ealuscerwen* as 'sharing out of ale' and interprets it as part of an elaborate and ironic verbal pattern of sharing and separating in this part of the poem. Clark (1976) spoofs the mass of philological intensity focused on this one word by reading it as a kenning for urination, at once a deprivation and a pouring out of ale. But he does not stop the flow of scholarly glossing. Heinemann (1983) sees *ealuscerwen* as a prediction of disaster that does not come about and links it both with the belief that warriors arriving in Valhalla receive a welcoming drink and with the Christian 'cup of death' metaphor. Like several others, Glosecki (1987) interprets the word as 'dispensing of ale' in the 'cup of death' sense and as being an ironic reference to Grendel's death. Lehmann (1988)

Notes to pages 86–116   259

reads *ealu* as similar to ON *alu/öl* 'ale,' with connotations of 'beer,' 'good luck,' 'magic,' and 'protection'; she takes the whole compound as 'deprivation,' not 'pouring out.' Rowland (1990) associates *ealuscerwen* and *meoduscerwen* with passages in Welsh poetry where the taking of drink indicates acceptance of the lord's service and has symbolic overtones of bitterness and death.

Chapter Three

1 Henry (1981) identifies a West European tradition in which heroes in battle become distorted with fury. He says that in *Beowulf* such distortions are associated with -*bolgen*, with its root sense of 'to swell.' One form of the *furor heroicus* has the hero metamorphosing into a wolf or a bear. Is this the sense of Beowulf's fatal bear-hug of *Dæghrefn* (2501)?
2 Frye used this term in its root Greek sense of 'a looking at,' 'a viewing.'
3 Engberg (1984, 217) points out that Beowulf is recognized twice by Hrothgar as having *mod-mægen*, a balance of mental and physical strengths (1705b–6a, 1844). Robinson sees a duality of apposed meanings of *mægen* in *Beowulf*, a pre-Christian or pre-Cædmonian one of 'physical strength' and a Christian one of 'virtue' (1985, 53–5).
4 Bjork writes perceptively of the poet's sense of 'the creative energy of language' (1994, 997–8) and of the use of the *beot* in the poem.
5 I have heard it said of a confident and very able contemporary athlete, accused of boasting, 'It ain't braggin' if he can do it.' Nolan and Bloomfield's analysis (1980) of 'boast' speeches in *Beowulf* sees in them a ritualistic function similar to that of incantation. In their interpretation, with which I agree, the hero is not boasting in the usual Modern English sense of the word. Rather he is simultaneously announcing publicly his sense that he can carry out the heroic deed needed by the community and fortifying his will to do it. Bauschatz sees the *beot* speech, usually part of a *symbel* 'banquet' ritual, as a vow and a foreshadowing of what will be done (1982, 110). Robinson, in an astute analysis of drinking rituals in *Beowulf* (1985, 75–9), also emphasizes the ritualistic oath or vow character of the *beot*.
6 In chapter 12 of Bjork/Niles 1997, I discuss at some length the matter of historical allegoresis of *Beowulf*.

Chapter Four

1 Yates begins with the art of memory in antique Latin and Greek texts and, after a few well-chosen remarks on Martianus Cappella, Augustine, Jerome, Cassiodorus, Bede, Charlemagne, and Alcuin (1966, 63–7), moves to medieval scholasticism; then to the Renaissance, which is her main interest.

2 For discussion of these works, and of others concerned with possible thematic intentions and impacts of the poem, see Lee 1997.
3 See Klaeber's edition, Chambers 1967, and Garmonsway, Simpson, and Davidson 1980.
4 Or 'to his bright city.' The manuscript gives *here* not *þære*.
5 In addition to *ASPR* 3, see especially the five Malone editions of *Deor* (1933, 1949, 1961, 1966, revised by Swanton 1977), and Malone's edition of *Widsith* (1962). Also importantly for *Deor* see Klinck 1992, a critical edition of the poem with commentary and extensive bibliography. For both *Deor* and *Widsith* see Muir's comprehensive edition (1994) of all the poems of the Exeter Book 'as an anthology' (vol. 1, ix), including textual and critical commentary and bibliography for both *Deor* and *Widsith*.
6 I am indebted to Frank (1986, 157) for the translation of *biteran banum*.
7 While the Latin *intertexo* means to intermingle while weaving and has both a literal and a figurative sense, the term 'intertextuality' is historically a fairly recent creation by Kristeva, to elaborate a theory of the text as a network of sign systems located in relation to other systems of signifying practices in a particular culture: a textual *ensemble* in a social *ensemble*. See Kristeva 1980, 36–63. Exponents of general intertextuality, unlimited semiosis or dissemination, take the view that there is nothing outside of the text, following Derrida's statement 'il n'y a pas de hors-texte' 'there is no outside-text' (1967, 158).

Chapter Five

1 Some parts of the theoretical infrastructure of this chapter are taken from an earlier article on Old English poetry, medieval exegesis, and modern criticism (Lee 1975).
2 Many scholars and critics have tried to define the mix of Germanic and Christian elements in the poem, and I make no attempt here to recapitulate the story of the controversies involved. Robinson 1985, especially chapter 2, is a careful attempt to show how the poet verbally deploys both Germanic and Christian meanings.
3 The Bjork/Niles *Handbook* will assist this large, complex undertaking, as do *Anglo-Saxon England* and *The Old English Newsletter*. In chapter 12 of the *Handbook* I trace and discuss the history of allegorical interpretations of *Beowulf*; no attempt is made in this book to repeat the extensive bibliography involved there.
4 Many of the studies in the chapters on 'Digressions and Episodes,' 'Rhetoric and Style,' and 'Structure and Unity' in Bjork/Niles 1997 are involved (though not exclusively) with this phase of meaning.
5 Bolton (1978), for example, asks how Alcuin would have read *Beowulf* and provides an answer based on Alcuin's literary theory and practice.
6 Most editors take *gastlic* as *gæstlic* 'ready for guests, hospitable.' Doane, however,

says 'there is no reason not to take it as *gastlic* "spiritual," especially when the rest of the sentence is considered: "filled with the eternal benefits of grace(s)"' (1978, 238, n.209a).

7 This is the essential point about the newly created hall that I made earlier (1972, 178–81) when I characterized Heorot, prior to Grendel's attacks, as 'a place of communal joy,' 'a manifestation of the sacred in the world of men,' 'a sacred enclosure,' and 'paradisal' – and the Danes, its inhabitants, as 'innocent' and living in blessedness. Clearly it is Grendel's influence that causes the catastrophe for Heorot and makes it necessary for the hall to be 'cleansed.' Irving (1989, 8–11) seriously misreads what I wrote in 1972. He has me saying that it is the Danes, not Grendel, who cause the disaster and says, rather tendentiously, that I claim that Grendel (and his mother!) appear '*because* [italics mine] the Danes have taken up the worship of devils' (9). I neither say nor think any such thing, in *Guest-Hall* or here, though I do think the poem makes it clear that the Danes who engage in devil worship, *after* Grendel has possessed their hall, do not and cannot help their situation. I did say (1972, 190) that the Cain spirit is present in Heremod, but Heremod is not part of the Scylding dynasty and lived long before the new creation Heorot, in contrast to Unferth, who is also a brother-slayer and an integral part of the Scylding court during Grendel's ravages.

8 Taylor (1989) detects word-play by the poet in the use of *untydras* to mean both 'progeny' and 'misbegotten progeny,' to suggest an unnatural enemy.

Chapter Six

1 See Niles's perceptive account of ring composition and the structure of *Beowulf* (1983, 152–62).
2 The degrees of *conscious* choice actually available to him in these matters are impossible to measure.
3 In an incisive study of the necessity of evil in the moral vision of the poem, Earl (1979) recalls the theme of the learning of wisdom through calamity which is central in the Book of Job. He sees Hrothgar as Job-like in the way he understands his persecution of Grendel. Similarly, he continues, Beowulf learns a comparable wisdom from the exemplum of Hrothgar. To this I would add that only part of Beowulf's wisdom derives from the Scylding king. He learns a good deal from his own experiences, only some of which involve Hrothgar.

Chapter Seven

1 Among the detractors, with varying approaches and degrees of censoriousness towards Beowulf, are the following. Du Bois (1934) sees Beowulf as succumbing to

pride, sloth, and avarice. Leyerle (1965) thinks Beowulf exemplifies the 'fatal contradiction at the core of the heroic society' (89) by which the greater the hero's individual magnificence and bravery the more likely it is that he will be subject to pride, and so fail to exercise mature leadership. Goldsmith, by the time of her 1970 book, has developed a rigorous, anagogically inclined, judgmental perspective in relation to the heroic matter of the poem, including Beowulf. In her reading, Beowulf is 'wanting in the supernatural strength of the *miles Christi*' (239). Huppé (1975, 1984), from an Augustinian perspective, thinks that Beowulf is 'a hero without Christ and reveals that the heroic in itself is an empty ideal' (1984, 40). Bandy (1973) sees Beowulf as a culpable member of the society of Cain's descendants. A.K. Brown (1980) thinks Beowulf fails and is damned and that the dragon and the flames that consume him are God's judgment on him as one of the wicked. I discuss all these and other allegorizing interpretations in chapter 12 of Bjork/Niles (1997, 251–74).

2 For a useful selection of studies of the role and meaning of Unferth see Bloomfield 1949–51, Rosier 1962, Eliason 1963, Nicholson 1975, Robinson 1970; 1974/1995, Vaughan 1976, Clover 1980, and Hill 1995, 77–9; 177–8, notes 34–6.

3 Interestingly, Beowulf himself uses the word *gumcystum* (1486) to indicate what it is he hopes to be known for should he die in the mere. Much later the narrator, approving of Beowulf's decision to go alone to fight the dragon, also uses this word about him (2543).

4 These are described in Frye 1957, 198–203.

5 The fable is best known as told by Xenophon in his *Memoirs of Socrates* II i, 21–34 (pages 76–80 in the Penguin edition).

6 Robinson says that it seems that 'the only reasonable interpretation' of the line and a half ðа wæs hwil dæges, / ær he þone grundwong ongytan mehte is 'Then it was daytime before he could get to the bottom' (1995, 82–4). The argument for the meaning of *dæges hwil* is almost persuasive, but it seems unnecessary to translate *ær he þone grundwong ongytan meahte* as 'before he could get to the bottom.' That is not what the words say. The larger problem in Robinson's argument is that the extraordinary character of this adventure into the unknown cannot be rationalized away.

7 In a more psychological reading, Crépin (1983) explores the theme of the consciousness of the heroic self in Beowulf. He sees the hero's battles with the monsters as an odyssey of the conscious mind against the forces of the unconscious.

Bibliography

Aristotle. *On the Art of Poetry*. In Nahm, ed. 1948, 3–40.
Auerbach, Erich. 1953. *Mimesis: The Representation of Reality in Western Literature.* Translated by Willard Trask. Princeton.
Augustine, Saint. *Confessions.* In Outler, ed. 1955, 31–333.
Baker, Peter S., ed. 1995. *Beowulf: Basic Readings.* New York and London.
Bandy, Stephen. 1973. 'Cain, Grendel, and the Giants of *Beowulf.*' *Papers on Language and Literature* 9: 235–49.
Bauschatz, Paul C. 1982. *The Well and the Tree: World and Time in Early Germanic Culture.* Amherst.
Bede, The Venerable. *Ecclesiastical History of the English People.* In Colgrave and Mynors, eds. 1991.
Beer, Gillian. 1970. *Romance.* London.
Benson, Larry D., and Siegfried Wenzel, eds. 1982. *The Wisdom of Poetry: Essays in Early English Literature in Honor of Morton W. Bloomfield.* Kalamazoo.
Bergin, Thomas Goddard, and Max Harold Fisch, eds. and trans. 1984. *The New Science of Giambattista Vico.* Unabridged translation of the third edition (1744). Ithaca and London.
Bessinger, Jess B., and Philip H. Smith. 1978. *A Concordance to the Anglo-Saxon Poetic Records.* Ithaca and London.
Bjork, Robert. 1994. 'Speech as Gift in *Beowulf.*' *Speculum* 69: 993–1022.
Bjork, Robert, and John Niles, eds. 1997. *A 'Beowulf' Handbook.* Lincoln and London.
Bloomfield, Morton W. 1949–51. 'Beowulf and Christian Allegory: An Interpretation of Unferth.' *Traditio* 7: 410–15.
Bolton, Whitney F. 1978. *Alcuin and Beowulf: An Eighth-Century View.* New Brunswick, NJ.
Bond, George. 1943. 'Links between *Beowulf* and Mercian History.' *Studies in Philology* 40: 481–93.

Bosworth, Joseph, and T. Northcote Toller. 1898. *An Anglo-Saxon Dictionary*. London.

Brady, Caroline. 1979. 'Weapons in *Beowulf*: An Analysis of the Nominal Compounds and an Evaluation of the Poet's Use of Them.' *Anglo-Saxon England* 8: 79–141.

Brinton, Laurel J. 1987. 'A Linguistic Approach to Certain Old English Stylistic Devices.' *Studia Neophilologica* 59: 177–85.

Brodeur, Arthur G. 1959. *The Art of Beowulf*. Berkeley and Los Angeles.

Brown, Alan K. 1980. 'The Firedrake in *Beowulf*.' *Neophilologus* 64: 439–60.

Brown, Carleton F. 1940. '*Poculum Mortis* in Old English.' *Speculum* 15: 389–99.

Brown, Phyllis Rugg, Georgia Ronan Crampton, and Fred C. Robinson, eds. 1986. *Modes of Interpretation in Old English Literature: Essays in Honour of Stanley B. Greenfield*. Toronto.

Burlin, Robert, and Edward B. Irving Jr, eds. 1974. *Old English Studies in Honour of John C. Pope*. Toronto.

Burns, Norman T., and Christopher R. Regan, eds. 1975. *Concepts of the Hero in the Middle Ages and the Renaissance*. Albany.

Byron, Lord George Gordon. *The Vision of Judgment*. In McGann and Weller, eds. 1991.

Cassidy, Frederic. 1972. 'Old English *garsecg* – an Eke-name?' *Names* 20: 95–100.

Caudwell, Christopher. 1970. *Romance and Realism: A Study in English Bourgeois Literature*. Ed. Samuel Hynes. Princeton.

Chambers, R.W. 1967. *Beowulf: An Introduction to the Poem*. 3rd ed. Revised by C.L. Wrenn. Cambridge.

Chambers, R.W., ed. 1912. *Widsith: A Study in Old English Heroic Legend*. Cambridge.

Chase, Colin, ed. 1981. *The Dating of Beowulf*. Toronto.

Clark, Roy P. 1976. 'A New Kenning in *Beowulf*: ealuscerwen.' *Scholia Satyrica* 2: 35–6.

Clover, Carol J. 1980. 'The Germanic Context of the Unferth Episode.' *Speculum* 55: 444–68. Reprinted in Baker 1995.

Colgrave, Bertram, and R.A.B. Mynors, eds. 1991. *Bede's Ecclesiastical History of the English People*. Oxford.

Creed, Howard, ed. 1970. *Essays in Honor of Richebourg Gaillard McWilliams*. Birmingham, Alabama.

Crépin, André. 1983. 'La Conscience de soi héroique: L'exemple de Beowulf.' [Heroic Self-Consciousness: The Example of Beowulf]. In *Genèse de la conscience moderne: Etudes sur le développement de la conscience de soi dans les littératures du monde occidentale*. Ed. Robert Ellrodt. Publications de la Sorbonne, Série Littérature, no. 14. Paris.

Delasanta, Rodney, and James Slevin. 1968. 'Beowulf and the Hypostatic Union.' *Neophilologus* 52: 409–16.

de Lubac, Henri. 1959–64. *Exégèse Médiévale: Les Quatre Sens de l'Ecriture.* 4 vols. Paris.
de Man, Paul. 1979. *Allegories of Reading: Figural Language in Rousseau, Nietzsche, Rilke, and Proust.* New Haven and London.
– 1983. *Blindness and Insight: Essays in the Rhetoric of Contemporary Criticism.* Minneapolis.
– 1984. *The Rhetoric of Romanticism.* New York.
– 1986. *The Resistance to Theory.* Minneapolis.
– 1989. *Critical Writings 1953–1978.* Ed. Lindsay Waters. Minneapolis.
DeRoo, Harvey. 1979. 'Two Old English Fatal Feast Metaphors: *Ealuscerwen* and *Meoduscerwen.*' *English Studies in Canada* 5: 249–61.
Derrida, Jacques. 1967a. *Of Grammatology.* Trans. Gayatri Chakravorty Spivak. Baltimore, 1976.
– 1967b. *Writing and Difference.* Trans. Alan Bass. London, 1978.
– 1972a. *Spurs: Nietzsche's Styles.* Trans. Barbara Harlow. Chicago, 1979.
– 1972b. Dissemination. Trans. Barbara Johnson, London, 1981.
– 1984. *Otobiographies: l'enseignement de Nietzsche et la politique du nom propre.* Paris.
de Selincourt, E., ed. *The Poetical Works of William Wordsworth.* 2 vols. Oxford, 1944.
Doane, A.N., ed. 1978. *Genesis: A New Edition.* Madison.
Dobbie, Elliott Van Kirk, ed. 1953. *Beowulf and Judith.* New York.
Dodds, E.R., ed. 1959. *Plato: Gorgias. A Revised Text with Introduction and Commentary.* Oxford.
Donaldson, E. Talbot, trans. 1975. *Beowulf: The Donaldson Translation, Backgrounds and Sources, Criticism.* Ed. Joseph F. Tuso. A Norton Critical Edition. New York.
Du Bois, Arthur E. 1934. 'The Unity of *Beowulf.*' *PMLA* 49: 374–405.
Earl, James W. 1979a. 'Beowulf's Rowing Match.' *Neophilologus* 63: 285–90.
– 1979b. 'The Necessity of Evil in *Beowulf.*' *South Atlantic Bulletin* 44: 81–98.
– 1983. 'The Role of the Men's Hall in the Development of the Anglo-Saxon Superego.' *Psychiatry* 46: 139–60.
– 1987. 'Transformation of Chaos: Immanence and Transcendence in *Beowulf* and Other Old English Poetry.' *Ultimate Reality and Meaning* 10 (1987): 164–85.
– 1991. '*Beowulf* and the Origins of Civilization.' In *Speaking Two Languages: Traditional Disciplines and Contemporary Theory in Medieval Studies.* Ed. Allen J. Frantzen. Albany.
– 1994. *Thinking about 'Beowulf.'* Stanford.
Earle, John. 1982. *The Deeds of Beowulf: An English Epic of the Eighth Century, Done into Modern Prose.* Oxford.
Eliason, Norman E. 1963. 'The Þyle and Scop in *Beowulf.*' *Speculum* 38: 267–84.

Engberg, Norma J. 1984. "*Mod-Mægen* Balance in *Elene, The Battle of Maldon*, and *The Wanderer*." *Neuphilologische Mitteilungen* 85: 212–26.

Farrell, Robert T., ed. 1978. *Bede and Anglo-Saxon England*. Oxford.

Frank, Roberta. 1981. 'Skaldic Verse and the Date of *Beowulf*.' In Chase, ed. 123–39.

– 1982. 'The *Beowulf* Poet's Sense of History.' In Benson and Wenzel, eds. 1982, 53–65.

– '"*Mere*" and "*Sund*": Two Sea-Changes in *Beowulf*.' In Brown, Crampton, and Robinson, eds. 153–72.

– 1987. 'Did Anglo-Saxon Audiences Have a Skaldic Tooth?' *Scandinavian Studies* 59: 338–55.

Frye, Northrop. 1957. *Anatomy of Criticism: Four Essays*. Princeton.

– 1976. *The Secular Scripture: A Study of the Structure of Romance*. Cambridge, Mass.

– 1982. *The Great Code: The Bible and Literature*. New York and Toronto.

– 1990. *Words with Power, Being a Second Study of the Bible and Literature*. Markham and Harmondsworth.

Gallacher, Patrick J., and Helen Damico. 1989. *Hermeneutics and Medieval Culture*. Albany.

Gardner, Thomas. 1969–70. 'The OE Kenning: A Characteristic Feature of Germanic Poetical Diction?' *Modern Philology* 67: 109–17.

– 'The Application of the Term "Kenning."' 1972. *Neophilologus* 56: 464–8.

Garmonsway, G.N., Jacqueline Simpson, and Hilda Ellis Davidson, eds. 1980. *Beowulf and Its Analogues*. Revised ed. London.

Glosecki, Stephen O. 1987. '*Beowulf* 769: Grendel's Ale-Share.' *English Language Notes* 21: 1–9.

Goldsmith, Margaret. 1970. *The Mode and Meaning of Beowulf*. London.

Greenfield, Stanley B., and Daniel Calder. 1986. *A New Critical History of Old English Literature*. New York and London.

Grein, C.W.M. 1912. *Sprachschatz der Angelsächsischen Dichter*. Heidelberg.

Hanning, Robert W. 1966. *The Vision of History in Early Britain from Gildas to Geoffrey of Monmouth*. New York.

– 1973. 'Sharing, Dividing, Depriving – The Verbal Ironies of Grendel's Last Visit to Heorot.' *Texas Studies in Literature and Language* 15: 203–13.

– 1974. 'Beowulf as Heroic History.' *Medievalia et Humanistica* 5: 77–102.

Hasenfratz, Robert J. 1993. *Beowulf Scholarship: An Annotated Bibliography, 1979–1990*. New York and London.

Healey, Antonette diPaolo, and Richard Venezky. 1980. *A Microfiche Concordance to Old English*. Toronto.

Heinemann, Fredrik J. 1983. '*Ealuscerwen-Meoduscerwen*, the Cup of Death, and *Bauldrs Draumar*.' *Studia Neophilologica* 55: 3–10.

Henry, P.L. 1961. '*Beowulf* Cruces.' *Zeitschrift für vergleichende Sprachforschung* 77: 140–59.
- 1981. 'Furor Heroicus.' *Occasional Papers in Linguistics and Language Learning* 8: 53–61.

Hill, John M. 1995. *The Cultural World in 'Beowulf.'* Toronto.

Holthausen, F. 1934. *Altenglisches Etymologisches Wörterbuch*. Heidelberg.

Howe, Nicholas. 1989. *Migration and Mythmaking in Anglo-Saxon England*. New Haven and London.

Huppé, Bernard F. 1975. 'The Concept of the Hero in the Early Middle Ages.' In Burns and Reagan, eds. 1975, 1–26.
- 1984. *The Hero in the Earthly City: A Reading of Beowulf*. Binghamton.

Irving, Edward B., Jr. 1966. '*Ealuscerwen*: Wild Party at Heorot.' *Texas Studies in Literature and Language* 11: 161–8.
- 1989. *Rereading Beowulf*. Philadelphia.

Jazayery, Mohammed Ali, and Werner Winter, eds. 1988. *Languages and Cultures: Studies in Honour of Edgar C. Polomé*. Berlin.

Joyce, James. 1934. *Ulysses*. New York.

Kaske, Robert E. 1958. '*Sapientia et Fortitudo* as the Controlling Theme in *Beowulf*.' *Studies in Philology* 55: 423–56.

Keenan, Hugh T., ed. 1975. *Studies in the Literary Imagination*, vol. 8. Atlanta.

Keenan, Hugh T., ed. 1992. *Typology and English Medieval Literature*. New York.

Ker, W.P. 1897. *The Dark Ages*. Edinburgh and London.
- 1908. *Epic and Romance: Essays on Medieval Literature*. 2nd ed. London.
- 1912. *Medieval English Literature*. Oxford.

Klaeber, Friedrich, ed. 1950. *Beowulf and the Fight at Finnsburg*. 3rd ed. Boston.

Klegraf, Josef. 1971. '*Beowulf* 769: ealuscerwen.' *Archiv* 208: 108–12.

Klinck, Anne L. 1992. *The Old English Elegies. A Critical Edition and Genre Study*. Montreal and Kingston.

Krapp, G.P., and E.V.K. Dobbie, eds. 1931–53. *The Anglo-Saxon Poetic Records*. 6 vols. New York.

Kristeva, Julia. 1980. 'The Bounded Text.' In *Desire in Language: A Semiotic Approach to Literature and Art*. Trans. by Thomas Gora, Alice Jardine, and Leon S. Roudiez. New York. 36–63.

Lee, Alvin A. 1972. *The Guest-Hall of Eden: Four Essays on the Design of Old English Poetry*. New Haven and London.
- 1975. 'Old English Poetry, Mediaeval Exegesis, and Modern Criticism.' In Keenan, ed. 47–73. Reprinted in Keenan, ed. 43–70.
- 1997. 'Symbolism and Allegory.' In Bjork and Niles, eds. 251–74.

Lee, Alvin A., and Robert D. Denham, eds. 1994. *The Legacy of Northrop Frye*. Toronto.

Lehmann, Ruth. 1988. 'Some Problems in the Translation of *Beowulf*.' In Jazayery and Winter, eds. 365–71.
Leyerle, John. 1965. 'Beowulf the Hero and King.' *Medium Ævum* 34: 89–102.
Liuzza, Roy M. 1995. 'The Year's Work in Old English Studies: *Beowulf*.' *Old English Newsletter* 28.2: 41–51.
Lyotard, Jean-François. 1979. *La condition postmoderne*. Paris.
Macpherson, Jay. 1982. *The Spirit of Solitude: Conventions and Continuities in Late Romance*. New Haven and London.
Malone, Kemp, ed. 1962. *Widsith*. 2nd ed. Copenhagen.
– 1977. ed. *Deor*. Revised by M.J. Swanton. Exeter.
Marquardt, Hertha. 1938. *Die Altenglische Kenningar*. Halle.
McGann, Jerome J., and Barry Weller, eds. 1991. *Lord Byron: The Complete Poetical Works, Volume VI*. Oxford.
Muir, Bernard J., ed. 1994. *The Exeter Anthology of Old English Poetry. An Edition of Exeter Dean and Chapter MS 3501*. 2 vols. Exeter.
Müllenhoff, Karl. 1889. *Beovulf: Untersuchungen über das Angelsächsische Epos und die Älteste Geschichte der Germanischen Seevölker*. Berlin.
Murray, Alexander Callander. 1981. '*Beowulf*, the Danish Invasions, and Royal Genealogy.' In Chase, ed. 1981, 101–11.
Nahm, Milton C., ed. 1948. *Aristotle on Poetry and Music*. Trans. by S.H. Butcher. The Library of Liberal Arts 6. New York.
Nicholson, Lewis, ed. 1963. *An Anthology of Beowulf Criticism*. Notre Dame.
Nicholson, Lewis E. 1975. 'Hunlafing and the Point of the Sword.' In Nicholson and Frese, eds. 50–61.
Nicholson, Lewis E., and Dolores Frese, eds. 1975. *Essays in Appreciation for John C. McGalliard*. Notre Dame.
Niles, John D. 1979. 'Ring Composition and the Structure of *Beowulf*.' *PMLA* 94: 924–35.
– 1983. *Beowulf: The Poem and Its Tradition*. Cambridge, Mass., and London.
– 1993. 'Locating *Beowulf* in Literary History.' *Exemplaria* 5: 79–109.
Niven, Larry, Jerry Pournelle, and Steven Barnes. 1987. *The Legacy of Heorot*. New York.
Nolan, Barbara, and Morton Bloomfield. 1980. '*Beotword, Gilpcwidas*, and the *Gilphlæden* Scop of *Beowulf*.' *Journal of English and Germanic Philology* 79: 499–516.
O'Hara, Daniel T. 1985. *The Romance of Interpretation: Visionary Criticism from Pater to de Man*. New York.
Ong, Walter J. 1982. *Orality and Literacy: The Technologizing of the Word*. London and New York.
Orchard, Andy. 1995. *Pride and Prodigies: Studies in the Monsters of the Beowulf-Manuscript*. Cambridge.

Outler, Albert C., ed. 1955. *Augustine: Confessions and Enchiridion.* Library of Christian Classics 7. London.
Parker, Patricia A. 1979. *Inescapable Romance: Studies in the Poetics of a Mode.* Princeton.
Plato. *Gorgias.* In Dodds, ed. 1959.
Ricœur, Paul. 1975. *The Rule of Metaphor: Multidisciplinary Studies of the Creation of Meaning in Language.* Trans. Robert Czerny. Toronto.
Rigby, Marjory. 1962. 'The Seafarer, Beowulf l. 769, and a Germanic Conceit.' *Notes and Queries* n.s. 9: 246.
Robinson, Fred C. 1970. 'Personal Names in Medieval Narrative and the Name of Unferth in *Beowulf*.' In Creed, ed. 43–48.
– 1974/1995. 'Elements of the Marvellous in the Characterization of Beowulf: A Reconsideration of the Textual Evidence.' In Baker, ed. 77–96. A reprint (somewhat revised) of the article with the same title in Burlin and Irving, eds., 119–37.
– 1985. *Beowulf and the Appositive Style.* Knoxville.
Rosier, James L. 1962. 'Design for Treachery: The Unferth Intrigue.' *PMLA* 77: 1–7.
Rousseau, Jean-Jacques. 1740s or 1750s. *Essai sur l'origine des langues.* Ed. Angèle Kermier-Marietti. Paris.
Rowland, Jenny. 1990. 'Old English *ealuscerwen/meoduscerwen* and the Concept of "Paying for Mead."' *Leeds Studies in English* n.s. 21: 1–12.
Ryding, William W. 1971. *Structure in Medieval Romance.* The Hague.
Short, Douglas D. 1980. *Beowulf Scholarship: An Annotated Bibliography.* New York and London.
Smithers, George V. 1951–2. 'Five Notes on Old English Texts.' *English and Germanic Studies* 4: 65–85.
Splitter, Henry W. 1952. 'The Relation of Germanic Folk Custom and Ritual to *Ealuscerwen* (*Beowulf* 769).' *Modern Language Notes* 67: 255–8.
Stevens, John. 1973. *Medieval Romance.* New York.
Swanton, Michael J. 1982. *Crisis and Development in Germanic Society 700–800: Beowulf and the Burden of Kingship.* Goppingen.
Taylor, Paul Beekman. 1989. 'Some Uses of Etymology in the Reading of Medieval Germanic Texts.' In Gallacher and Damico, eds. 1989, 109–20.
Tolkien, J.R.R. 1936. '*Beowulf*: The Monsters and the Critics.' *Proceedings of the British Academy* 22: 245–95. Reprinted in Nicholson, ed. 1963.
Trahern, Joseph B., Jr. 1969. 'A *Defectione Potus Sui*: A Sapiential Basis for *ealuscerwen* and *meoduscerwen*.' *Neuphilologische Mitteilungen* 70 (1969): 62–9.
Tuve, Rosemond. 1966. *Allegorical Imagery: Some Medieval Books and Their Posterity.* Princeton.
Vaughan, M.F. 1976. 'A Reconsideration of "Unferð."' *Neuphilologische Mitteilungen* 77: 32–48.

Vico, Giambattista. *The New Science*. In Bergin and Fisch, eds. 1984.
Vinaver, Eugene. 1971. *The Rise of Romance*.
Whitelock, Dorothy. 1951. *The Audience of Beowulf*. Oxford.
Whitelock, Dorothy, ed. 1955. *English Historical Documents, Volume I, c. 500–1042*. London and New York.
Wordsworth, William. In de Selincourt, ed. 1944.
Wormald, Patrick. 1978. 'Bede, *Beowulf* and the Conversion of the Anglo-Saxon Aristocracy.' In Farrell, ed. 32–95.
Wrenn, Charles L., ed. 1973. *Beowulf with the Finnesburh Fragment*. 3rd ed., revised by Whitney F. Bolton. New York.
Xenophon. *Memoirs of Socrates and the Symposium*. Trans. Hugh Tredennick. Harmondsworth.
Yates, Frances. 1966. *The Art of Memory*. London.
Zumthor, Paul. 1972. *Essai de poétique médiévale*. Paris.

Index

Abel 135, 173, 174, 175, 179, 188, 190, 198, 217
Abraham 198, 209
Adam 44, 46, 168, 169, 172, 187, 188, 206, 242
Aeneas 230
Aeneid 211
Æschere 86, 165, 185, 218, 226
Alcuin 259, 260
Almighty. *See* God
Ambrose 144, 160
Andreas 27, 28, 73, 80, 82, 197, 209, 212, 258
Andrew 28, 212
Anglo-Saxon 22, 24, 31, 32, 42, 84, 89, 114, 119, 246, 253, 255; culture 21, 112, 157, 173, 207, 226; England 3, 4, 21, 49, 117, 144, 150, 161, 193, 194, 203, 204, 209; history 94; language 6; people 74, 116, 145, 148, 151, 157, 158, 160, 161, 196, 197; period 4, 14, 23, 93, 107, 111, 118, 163, 196; poetry 21, 24, 25, 27, 46, 59, 94, 110, 111, 151, 163, 169, 171, 242
Aristotle 13–14, 19, 89
Auerbach, Eric 25
Augustine, St 117–18, 144, 160, 259

Bacon, Francis 92, 108
Bandy, Stephen 262
Barnes, Julian 22
Barnes, Steven 22
Battle of Brunanburh 197
Battle of Maldon 41, 197
Baudelaire, Charles 20
Beckett, Samuel 170
Bede 4, 24, 144, 160, 191, 209, 259
Beer, Gillian 25
Beornwolf 110
Beowulf: association with light 96; battle with dragon 60, 82, 137, 143, 200–1, 213, 222, 225, 231, 240, 242; battle with Grendel 39, 61, 68, 70, 78, 105, 118, 128, 154, 181–5, 191, 198, 210, 216, 248; battle with Grendel's mother 28, 61, 68, 71–2, 172, 185–6, 210, 216, 227–30; boasts 98, 259; contest with Breca and struggle with sea-monsters 14–15, 50, 70, 214, 258; death of 18, 48, 80–1, 101, 110, 130, 131, 135, 207, 210, 213, 220, 231, 232–3, 242, 246, 249–51, 252, 253; extraordinary powers of 15, 36, 74, 86, 96, 135, 253; funeral of 59, 200, 208, 210, 239, 250, 253; and God, Christ, heaven 27, 38,

44, 49, 100, 198, 212, 214; as hero 10, 11, 32, 35, 226, 255, 256; and hoard 234; and Hrothgar 37, 45, 165, 166, 168, 173, 180, 181, 183, 218, 220–2, 238, 261; and Job 202; and kingship 218–21; and memory, mindfulness 128–9, 132–5, 201; mighty hand-grip of 17, 20, 28, 35, 36, 39, 47, 67, 86, 105, 111, 118, 129, 183–4, 232, 253; mythological dimensions 96, 110; and necklace 121–2, 124, 136; pattern of life 209–10, 213, 232, 233; perceptiveness of 240–1; and romance 35, 223–6; and Sigmund 119; as spiritual warrior 197; and tragedy 242–3; as typical, exemplary 162; and Unferth 75–6, 80, 215–17; and *wyrd* 248; youth of 14, 134, 223, 224, 239. *See also* hero.

Beowulf: as act of *anagnorisis* 51; and Anglo-Saxon Chronicle 188; beginning and end of 29, 32, 33; circularity of 189; lack of closure in 116, 135–6; concrete imagery in 4, 5, 85, 143; contemporary audience of 130, 135, 157, 196–7; criticisms of 147–8; defined 3; as definitive composition for poet 193–4; and *The Dream of the Rood* 242; and Germanic literature 124, 203–4; and high mimetic 19, 36–7; and history 11, 110, 117, 122–3, 152; and irony 20, 104; and *The Legacy of Heorot* 22; manuscript of 93; and memory 114, 117–18, 130; metaphor in 5, 21, 56–8, 61, 66, 68, 73, 90, 136, 137, 144, 150, 152, 190; metaphorical power of 4, 55; and monotheism 99–100; and Old English corpus 41–6, 94, 107, 112, 120, 145, 151, 163, 209, 212; and Old English *Genesis* 169; phases of meaning 4, 157; poetic language in 4, 56, 83, 84, 89, 95, 105, 144; as product of pre-technological culture 85; primal language in 87–8; and romance 19, 28, 47, 49, 51–2, 209, 212; structure of 6, 102, 210, 213; voice in 97

Bible 24, 25, 27, 46, 54, 100, 106, 107, 109, 115, 145, 160, 161, 162, 163, 167, 168, 171, 172, 186, 187, 191, 193, 197, 203, 209, 258; Christian mythology 4, 19, 21, 24, 27, 72, 85, 90, 91, 94, 162, 170, 177–204, 209; concrete imagery in 5; figurative language in 5
Bjork, Robert 259, 260, 262
Blake, William 193
Bloomfield, Morton W. 259, 262
Bolton, Whitney F. 260
Bond, George 110
Bosworth, Joseph 5, 256
Brady, Caroline 257
Breca 14, 15, 50, 62, 63, 70, 74, 76, 77, 80, 98, 214, 215, 216, 225, 233, 255, 256, 258
Brinton, Laurel J. 257
Brodeur, Arthur G. 257
Brown, A.K. 256, 262
Brown, C.F. 258
Byron, Lord 20

Cædmon 21, 24, 43, 45, 46, 111, 168, 169, 170, 171, 172, 203, 255
Cain 135, 137, 159, 162, 169, 173, 174, 175, 177, 179, 180, 181, 182, 185, 187, 189, 190, 192, 198, 215, 216, 217, 229, 261. *See also* Grendel.
Calder, Daniel 91, 257
Cassidy, Frederic 258
Cassiodorus 259
Caudwell, Christopher 25

Chambers, R.W. 123, 260
Charlemagne 259
Christ. *See* Jesus
Christ I 24, 46, 47, 94; *Christ II* 24, 46, 47, 94, 110; *Christ III* 24, 46, 47, 94
Christ and Satan 24, 41, 43, 44, 45, 46, 94, 171
Clark, Roy P. 258
Clover, Carol J. 262
coast-guard 10, 34, 101, 103, 134, 186
comedy 13, 20, 211–12
Corneille, Pierre 19
Creation, the 44, 46, 61, 71, 96, 135, 141–76, 179, 181, 184, 187, 188–9, 191, 196, 197, 198, 200, 202, 208, 209, 210, 212, 215, 216, 217, 229, 230, 231, 240, 241, 242, 246, 248, 249, 253
Creator, the 27, 46, 174, 177, 185, 224, 229. *See also* God
Crépin, André 262
Cynewulf 21, 204

Daniel 24, 80, 161
Daniel 198, 209
Danes 9, 15, 16, 31, 33, 34, 35, 36, 37, 38, 44, 48, 61, 63, 64, 67, 68, 75, 81, 86, 97, 98, 115, 119, 120, 121, 122, 124, 125, 126, 127, 130, 132, 134, 135, 136, 144, 150, 152, 153, 155, 156, 164, 165, 166, 167, 169, 170, 172, 173, 175, 176, 178, 180, 184, 185, 186, 187, 188, 189, 191, 192, 195, 198, 205, 215, 216, 217, 218, 219, 221, 225, 226, 229, 237, 249, 258, 261; Danish court 9, 17, 35, 37, 222; Ring-Danes 166, 218; Spear-Danes 29, 32, 37, 96, 164, 215
Dante 205

David 209
Davidson, Hilda Ellis 260
Deborah 209
deity. *See* God
Delasanta, Rodney 255
de Lubac, Henri 160
de Man, Paul 25, 54, 55
Denham, Robert D. 146
Denmark 10, 11, 18, 34, 35, 38, 40, 44, 45, 49, 51, 52, 64, 67, 71, 75, 80, 97, 125, 127, 130, 132, 134, 135, 150, 156, 166, 167, 183, 186, 205, 206, 207, 209, 211, 214, 217, 219, 221, 222, 223, 225, 229, 230, 238, 247, 252
Derrida, Jacques 54, 116, 260
Descent into Hell 24, 46–7, 94, 179
devil 9, 72, 105, 182, 229; devil worship 44, 169, 170, 217, 225, 261
Doane, A.N. 260
Donaldson, E. Talbot 103, 258
dragon 16, 17, 18, 20, 26, 32, 33, 40, 86–7, 88, 98, 105, 110, 111, 113, 115, 117, 119, 129, 133, 135, 143, 149, 152, 158, 159, 172, 177, 186, 200, 201, 202, 208, 213, 219, 230, 236, 243, 246, 248, 249, 250, 252–3, 262; battle with Beowulf 60, 62, 81, 120, 137, 206–7, 210, 213, 214, 222, 225, 233, 240, 242; earth-dragon 82, 203, 216, 222, 235, 241; fire-dragon 15, 18, 20, 43, 51, 62, 99, 107, 118, 129, 141, 142, 148, 201, 205, 219, 222, 228, 234, 241, 242, 248; sea-dragon 18, 81, 86, 186
Dream of the Rood 24, 41, 46, 94, 109, 163, 197, 242–3
Du Bois, Arthur E. 261

Eadgils 120, 128
Eagles' Ness 18, 88

274   Index

Eanmund 120, 128
Earl, James W. 117, 256, 261
Earle, John 110
Ecgferth 110
Ecgtheow 34, 35, 75, 78, 99, 120, 134, 166, 167, 168, 183, 224, 225
Ecgwela 165
Eco, Umberto 22
Eden 44, 46, 89, 168, 189, 230, 236
Einstein, Albert 92
Elene 27, 197, 204, 209
Eliason, Norman E. 262
Engberg, Norma J. 259
Eormenric 120, 123
Epic of Gilgamesh 103
Eve 44, 46, 168, 169, 172, 206
Exodus 24, 82, 94, 161, 167

Fates of the Apostles 24, 197, 209
fiction 3, 11, 13, 14, 19, 20, 21, 22, 27, 32, 40, 41, 47, 55, 133, 150, 159, 178, 184, 190, 212, 216, 223, 247; science fiction 22–3
Fight at Finnsburg 197
Finn 60, 61, 120, 125, 126
Finnsburg 61, 78, 87, 124, 125, 126, 127, 132, 165, 192, 206
Fitela 120, 135
foreshadowing 50, 64, 115, 116, 121, 132, 133, 141, 146, 206, 208, 221, 225, 238, 239
Fowles, John 22
Frank, Roberta 110, 117, 119, 255, 256, 257, 260
Freawaru 20, 64, 80, 165, 197, 208, 237, 238, 239, 240
Froda 120, 239
Frye, Northrop 4, 5, 6, 11, 13, 14, 16, 19, 20, 21, 22, 23, 25, 26, 28, 46, 49, 50, 54, 89–93, 95, 99, 102, 104, 105–6, 107, 108, 146, 157, 193, 255, 256; *Anatomy of Criticism* 25, 94, 146, 257; *Great Code* 54, 90, 146; *Secular Scripture* 25; theory of polysemous meaning 161–2, 192; *Words with Power* 54, 90, 146

García Márquez, Gabriel 22
Gardner, John 22
Gardner, Thomas 257
Garmonsway, G.N. 120, 123, 260
Geatland 9, 15, 17, 34, 36, 39, 40, 47, 48, 49, 51, 71, 80, 98, 100, 115, 128, 141, 181, 190, 199, 200, 205, 206, 207, 208, 210, 211, 213, 216, 221, 222, 223, 225, 236, 241, 243, 244, 247, 248, 250, 252, 253
Geats 9, 10, 11, 15, 16, 18, 19, 34, 35, 37, 38, 47, 50, 61, 63, 64, 68, 75, 81, 82, 83, 86, 87, 88, 96, 97, 99, 115, 116, 121, 122, 127, 128, 130, 133, 134, 135, 136, 141, 148, 149, 154, 155, 156, 158, 163, 166, 170, 172, 173, 181, 182, 195, 198, 200, 205, 206, 208, 213, 216, 219, 221, 223, 224–5, 226, 234, 237, 241, 246, 247, 249, 250, 252; Weather-Geats (Weather-Men) 18, 62, 71, 75, 98, 103, 105, 203, 228, 233, 250
Genesis 21, 45, 107, 161, 167, 168, 169, 217; *Genesis A* 24, 41, 42, 44, 46, 94, 169, 171, 172; *Genesis B* 24, 41, 42, 44, 46, 94, 169, 170
giants 14, 36, 38, 39, 67, 72, 119, 120, 172, 184, 185, 187, 198, 217, 225, 229, 231, 256
Gideon 209
gift-giving 17, 31, 32, 39, 46, 64, 96, 153, 155, 165, 192, 205, 211, 222, 225, 237–8, 240, 245, 253
Glosecki, Stephen O. 258

Index 275

God 10, 14, 15, 16, 18, 24, 27, 28, 30, 33, 35, 36, 38, 39, 41, 44, 46, 47, 48, 49, 51, 58, 63, 67, 68, 69, 70, 71, 72, 76, 85, 86, 87, 96, 98, 99, 100, 103, 107, 108, 111, 120, 128, 133, 135, 142, 143, 152, 153, 155, 165, 166, 168, 169, 170, 171, 172, 173, 174, 175, 177, 178, 179, 181, 182, 184, 188, 191, 198, 199, 200, 201, 202, 214, 217, 218, 219, 220, 221, 229, 233, 234, 241, 244, 245, 246, 247, 248, 252, 255, 262
Goldsmith, Margaret 256, 262
Goya, Francesco 20
Grass, Günter 22
Greenfield, Stanley B. 91, 257
Gregory of Tours 120
Gregory the Great 111, 144, 160
Grein, C.W.M. 256
Grendel 9, 10, 11, 14, 15, 16, 20, 35, 36, 37, 38, 39, 43, 45, 48, 50, 51, 60, 63, 64, 66, 70, 71, 75, 76, 78, 79, 85, 86, 88, 95, 98, 105, 110, 111, 121, 127, 138, 132, 137, 144, 156, 165, 166, 167, 168, 169, 170, 171, 172, 173–6, 177, 179, 180, 186, 187, 191, 198, 210, 211, 214, 217–18, 219, 220, 221, 222, 225, 227, 228, 229, 233, 236, 237, 239, 240, 246, 252, 255, 261; battle with Beowulf 61, 124, 154, 181–5, 199, 248; defeat and death 38–9, 40, 47, 64, 67–8, 69, 70, 71, 124, 125, 131, 155, 165, 183–5, 191–2, 210, 211, 216, 258; dual identity 174; Grendel kin 28, 66, 67, 71, 72, 115, 149, 153, 158–9, 173, 188, 198, 201, 214, 216, 218, 221–2, 223, 236, 245, 247; hand of 16, 17, 38–9, 81, 86, 154, 181, 183–4, 192, 216, 245; of race of Cain 137, 159, 162, 174, 215. *See also* monsters.
Grendel's mother 15, 28, 47, 50, 51, 64, 66, 67, 79, 81, 87, 95, 110, 128, 132, 165, 173, 175, 183, 185, 186, 187, 216, 228, 229, 233, 237, 239, 246, 261; battle with Beowulf 61, 62, 66, 67, 69, 86, 185–6, 210, 211, 218, 220, 226. *See also* mere; monsters.
Guest-Hall of Eden 24, 106, 261
Guthlac 28, 43, 170, 212, 230
Guthlac A 27, 80, 197, 209, 212; *Guthlac B* 27, 82, 197, 209, 212

Hæthcyn 134, 224
Halga 120
Hama 120, 123, 217
Hanning, Robert W. 255, 258
Hardy, Thomas 20
Hartman, Geoffrey 25
Healfdene 120, 208, 234
Heardred 99, 128, 173, 208, 219, 222
Heathobards 20, 64, 120, 132–3, 157, 206, 208, 238
heaven 14, 15, 23, 24, 27, 28, 30, 39, 40, 41, 42, 43, 44, 48, 49, 63, 66, 67, 70, 76, 85, 96, 105, 117, 155, 161, 171, 172, 181, 182, 189, 193, 198, 203, 206, 209, 212, 214, 215, 217, 226, 228, 234, 235, 242, 251, 253
Heinemann, Fredrik J. 258
Heliand 107
hell 23, 24, 27, 28, 39, 40, 41, 42, 43, 44, 45, 47, 48, 49, 66, 68, 85, 87, 97, 105, 111, 120, 135, 137, 144, 153, 155, 156, 161, 168, 169, 170, 171, 172, 174, 178, 179, 180, 181, 182, 186, 188, 189, 190, 193, 197, 198, 203, 215, 217, 218, 225, 226, 229, 230, 235, 237, 253
Hengest 60, 61, 126, 132
Henry, P.L. 258, 259
Heorot 9, 11, 16–17, 20, 28, 34–5, 36, 37, 39, 45, 46, 48, 60, 61, 63, 66, 68,

70, 71, 72, 75, 78, 80, 81, 86, 88, 96, 98, 105, 109, 111, 113, 115, 117, 120, 124, 125, 127, 128, 131, 133, 134, 137, 141–4, 148, 149, 150, 151, 152–7, 158, 163, 164, 167, 168, 169, 172, 173, 174, 175, 176, 179, 180, 181–5, 186, 187, 188, 189, 190, 191, 196, 198, 199, 205, 207, 208, 210, 211, 213, 215, 216, 217, 218, 219, 221, 224, 225, 226, 227, 228, 229, 230, 233, 236, 237, 238, 239, 240, 243, 245, 246, 252, 261; battle at 181–5; description of 64, 153–7; end of 87, 169, 173; meaning of 95, 187

Heoroward 120

Hercules 19, 225

Herebeald 134, 170, 224

Heremod 64, 80–1, 86, 119, 120, 164, 189, 205, 219, 261

hero 9–10, 11, 14, 15, 16, 18, 20, 22, 26, 30, 33, 34, 35, 36, 37, 38, 39, 40, 48, 49, 52, 60, 67, 72, 74, 77, 79, 86, 92, 96, 100, 113, 115, 130, 132, 137, 148, 153, 156, 158, 166, 183, 184, 186, 187, 192, 195, 197, 198, 199, 202, 205, 206, 207, 212, 215, 216, 218, 219, 220, 221, 222, 223, 224, 225, 226, 227, 228, 230, 231, 234, 235, 236, 237, 244, 247, 249, 250, 252, 259, 262; emergence of Beowulf as 17. *See also* Beowulf.

Hesiod 94, 107

Hildeburh 61, 78, 120, 125, 126, 127, 186, 238, 239

Hill, John M. 117, 255, 262

Hnæf 61, 125, 165

Holthausen, F. 256

Homer 13, 56, 85, 91, 92, 93, 94, 103, 107, 205, 237

Hondscio 38, 779, 183

Howe, Nicholas 117, 255

Hrabanus Maurus 160

Hrethel 35, 37, 99, 120, 134, 217, 221, 224, 225, 248; son's death 66

Hrethric 120, 173, 208, 221, 237, 238

Hronesness. *See* Whale's Ness

Hrothgar 16, 17, 18, 21, 32, 34, 35, 36, 37, 38, 44, 45, 48, 64–5, 67, 68, 69, 70, 71, 72, 74, 78, 80, 85, 88, 96, 97, 98, 99, 101, 104, 105, 109, 120, 124, 127, 128, 130, 131, 132, 134, 141–2, 143, 152, 153, 155, 156, 164, 165, 167, 168, 169, 173, 176, 178, 179, 180, 181, 183, 184, 185, 186, 187, 188, 189, 190, 197, 198, 199, 201, 207, 208, 214, 215, 218, 219, 220–1, 222, 224, 225, 227, 229, 230, 231, 234, 236, 237, 238, 239, 240, 243, 245, 246, 248, 249, 252, 259, 261; early life 166

Hrothmund 173, 208, 237, 238

Hrothulf 32, 120, 127, 128, 137, 169, 173, 237, 238, 240

Hrunting. *See* sword

Huppé, Bernard F. 262

Hygd 17, 80, 122, 124, 197, 222, 232, 239, 240

Hygelac 9, 10, 15, 17, 20, 34, 36, 48, 51, 61, 71, 80, 82, 99, 101, 103, 105, 115, 120, 121, 124, 131, 132, 133, 134, 165, 184, 208, 219, 221, 222, 223, 224, 230, 239, 240, 248, 249; death of 15, 60, 66, 122

Hynes, Samuel 25

imagery 51, 52, 77

Imelmann, Rudolph 257

Ingeld 64, 120, 157, 189

irony 20, 21, 23, 32, 38, 50, 61, 78, 87, 111, 158, 170, 185, 194, 216, 230, 258

Irving, Edward B, Jr 258, 261

Isaac 209

Isidore 144, 160

Jacob 209
Jerome 144, 160, 191, 259
Jesus 19, 41, 49, 111, 163, 209, 230
Joseph 209
Joshua 209
Joyce, James 20, 109, 151
Judgment Day I 24, 47, 94; *Judgment Day II* 24, 47, 94
Judges 103
Judith 24, 27, 197, 209, 258
Judith 209
Juliana 27, 170, 197, 204, 209, 212
Juliana 28, 43, 212
Junius manuscript 21, 45, 120, 169, 198

Kafka, Franz 20, 170
Kant, Immanuel 108, 109
kend heiti 58–9, 67, 69, 70, 73, 74, 82, 137
kennings 5, 53–83, 116, 136, 137, 144, 150, 151, 152, 179, 257, 258; for bodies 78–82, 125; categories of 59; distinct from *kend heiti* 58; as metaphors 82; for sea 73–8; for sword 61–73
Ker, W.P. 25, 26
Klaeber, Friedrich 5, 20, 56, 57, 58, 64, 65, 122, 123, 178, 201, 208, 222, 255, 256, 257, 258, 260; Glossary 5, 71, 86
Klegraf, Josef 258
Klinck, Anne L. 260
Kristeva, Julia 136, 260

Lee, Alvin A. 146, 260
Legacy of Heorot 22–3
Lehmann, Ruth 258–9
Leyerle, John 262
Liuzza, Roy M. 255
Locke, John 92, 108

Lucifer 15, 43
Lycidas 206
Lyotard, Jean-François 95

Maccabees 209
Macpherson, Jay 25
Malone, Kemp 260
Marlowe, Christopher 19, 207
Marquardt, Hertha 257
Martianus Cappella 259
mere 15, 17, 18, 20, 28, 39, 43, 45, 46, 47, 48, 50, 60, 61, 62, 66, 68, 70, 71, 79, 81, 86, 87, 88, 97, 99, 113, 115, 117, 120, 121, 150, 152, 153, 154, 158, 167, 171, 172, 173, 179, 186, 187, 188, 198, 199, 202, 210, 211, 217, 221, 225, 226, 227, 228, 229, 230, 236, 237, 240, 242–3, 255, 256, 262
metaphor 24, 30, 34, 40, 41, 46, 48, 49, 51, 56, 57, 60, 65–6, 67, 69, 72, 73, 74, 75, 78, 82–113, 116, 124, 137, 143, 151, 155, 165, 192, 203, 204, 215, 223, 224, 234, 235, 241, 242, 244, 247, 249, 252, 253, 256, 257, 258; concrete 86, 88, 104; diluted 56, 57; explicit and implicit 57; metaphorical force 3; metaphorical images 46; metaphorical language 5, 76, 114–15, 144, 150, 152, 159, 179, 184, 185, 187, 190; metaphorical processes 46
middangeard. *See* middle earth
middle earth 14, 27, 41, 43, 44, 68, 105, 114, 117, 157, 170, 189, 197, 208, 212, 226, 231, 249; middle dwelling 44, 46, 47, 66, 80, 85, 87, 89, 96, 99, 113, 114, 142, 157, 164, 166, 169, 172, 181, 185, 203, 205, 212, 222, 223, 236, 239, 241, 245, 246, 248
Milton, John 170, 205, 206, 215
mimesis 4, 5, 19, 21, 40, 41, 50, 53, 79,

89, 92, 151, 256; high 28, 33, 36, 37, 255; low 56, 78, 109
modern and postmodern 15, 22, 23, 24, 29, 76, 88, 95, 102, 111, 147–9, 150, 151, 156, 157, 158, 160, 181, 190, 192, 193, 214, 215, 246, 253
Modthryth 80, 197, 239
monsters 14, 15, 16, 21, 22, 23, 26, 28, 32, 35, 37, 38, 48, 59, 62, 67, 68, 70, 71, 72, 78, 79, 81, 85, 86, 87, 95–6, 98, 99, 105, 111, 115, 117, 119, 120, 134, 137, 148, 153, 154, 156, 157, 158, 171, 172, 173, 174, 181, 182, 183, 184, 185, 186, 188, 191, 192, 193, 198, 202, 204, 207, 215, 217, 221, 223, 226, 227, 228, 229, 231, 232, 235–6, 237, 238, 239, 240, 243, 244, 247, 248, 252, 253, 256; sea-monsters 39, 50, 62, 63, 76, 78, 96, 99, 137, 225; water-monsters 36, 67, 86, 226
Morris, William 5
Moses 198, 209
Muir, Bernard J. 123, 260
Müllenhof, Karl 110
Murray, Alexander Callander 119
myth 5, 14, 20, 21, 23, 24, 25, 26, 28, 33, 42, 43, 44, 46, 47, 49, 55, 56, 69, 72, 84–113, 116, 124, 129, 135, 144, 145, 158, 162, 163, 170, 171, 172, 203, 204, 208–9, 215, 235, 241, 244, 247, 250, 253; Christian mythology 4, 19, 21, 24, 27, 72, 85, 90, 91, 94, 162, 170, 177–204, 209

Nægling. *See* sword
narrator 10, 16, 39, 96, 104, 113, 121, 127, 130, 131, 133, 134, 137, 141, 142, 151, 152, 153, 155, 162, 165, 169, 173, 174, 175, 179, 180, 181, 182, 184, 185, 186, 187, 188, 189, 190, 191, 192, 194, 200, 207, 219, 224, 225, 226, 227, 228, 230, 233, 235–6, 238, 240, 247, 252
New Testament 5, 161, 163, 247
Nicholson, Lewis E. 262
Nietzsche, Friedrich 25
Niles, John D. 110, 117, 256, 260, 261, 262
Niven, Larry 22
Noah 19, 188, 189, 190, 198, 209
Nolan, Barbara 259, 262
Norton Lectures 257

Odysseus 19
Odyssey 211
Offa 110, 120, 239
O'Hara, Daniel T. 25
Ohthere 120, 128
Old English 22, 26, 36, 63, 103, 143, 144; language 13, 107, 172, 257; literature 23, 91, 93, 145, 160; poetry 3, 4, 21, 23, 24, 25, 30, 41–2, 43, 44, 46, 48, 49, 53, 54, 55, 57, 59, 69, 74, 77, 80, 84, 90, 94, 99, 100, 106, 111, 112, 114, 120, 123, 145, 146, 149, 150, 151, 155, 157, 159, 161, 167, 170, 186, 193, 194, 196, 197, 206, 209, 212, 217, 250, 255, 260; poets 27, 226; text of *Beowulf* 4, 5; words 5, 9, 29, 63, 74, 251, 255
Old Testament 5, 21, 91, 161, 162, 163, 200, 202, 234, 243
Ong, Walter J. 4, 11–13, 26, 136
Ongentheow 120
Onela 120, 128
Orchard, Andy 256

Parker, Patricia 25
Pater, Walter 25
Phoenix 94
Physiologus 107, 186
Piers Plowman 163, 206

Plato 91, 92, 104–5
postmodern. *See* modern
Pournelle, Jerry 22
Prince of Life 31, 33, 40, 100, 206, 245. *See also* God.
Prodicus 225

Racine, Jean 19
Ricœur, Paul 4
Rigby, Marjory 258
Robinson, Fred C. 255, 256, 257, 258, 259, 260, 262
romance 5, 6, 12–13, 14, 15, 16, 19, 20, 22, 23, 25, 26, 27, 28, 32, 33, 35, 36, 40, 41, 43, 44, 47, 49–50, 51, 52, 69, 89, 94, 100, 113, 124, 129, 178, 185, 195, 207, 209, 211, 212, 214, 223, 224, 225, 230, 231, 235, 239, 240, 255; structure of 50; heroic romance 27, 212, 216, 223
Rosier, James L. 262
Rousseau, Jean-Jacques 87, 90
Rowland, Jenny 258
Rushdie, Salman 22
Ryding, William W. 25

Samson 209
Samuel 103, 209
Satan 24, 43, 135, 169, 171, 201, 215, 217, 250
Saul 209
Sceaf 120, 188, 189, 231
Scyld Scefing 10, 15, 29–31, 32, 33, 34, 47, 74, 95, 96, 119, 120, 152, 156, 187, 188, 189, 205, 208, 210, 217, 219, 222, 231, 234, 236; sea-burial of 16, 75, 131, 164, 210, 240
Scyldings 9, 18, 20, 28, 29–30, 31, 32, 33, 35, 36, 37, 38, 47, 61, 63, 68, 70, 88, 96, 113, 115, 116, 119, 121, 122, 127, 131, 132, 133, 141, 142, 148, 149, 150, 151, 152, 153, 155, 156, 158, 163, 164, 165, 166, 167, 168, 169, 170, 173, 175, 176, 177, 179, 180, 185, 187, 188, 189, 198, 199, 205, 206, 207, 208, 210, 215, 217, 223, 224, 225, 226, 230, 231, 236, 237, 238, 239, 240, 243, 246, 247, 252, 261
serpents 18, 60, 86, 172, 186, 226
Seth 187
Shakespeare, William 19, 84, 170
Sheaf. *See* Sceaf
shield 9, 37, 59, 82, 85; -bearer 39; -warrior 129
Shield. *See* Scyld
spear 60; 'Glory Spear' 31; 'Sword Spear' 31; spear-man (kenning for 'ocean') 74–5
Spenser, Edmund 206
Splitter, Henry W. 258
Stevens, John 25
Swanton, Michael J. 255, 260
Sweden 97, 128; Swedes 120, 135, 208, 250
sword 15, 28, 37, 47, 50, 69, 70, 77, 79, 82, 84, 85, 126, 132, 143, 167, 187, 199, 202, 204, 215–17, 222, 227, 229, 257; embodiment of hatred 64; Hrunting 60, 61, 62, 67, 71, 72, 86, 87, 121, 216, 221, 226, 228, 236; kennings associated with 61–73; Nægling 15, 17, 62, 129, 233; 'Sword-Wealth' 165

Taylor, Paul Beekman 261
Theseus 230
Tolkien, J. R. R. 26, 137, 222–3
Toller, T. Northcote 5, 256
tragedy 6, 13, 19, 33, 52, 100, 114, 170, 195, 207, 211, 212, 216, 230, 232–51
Trask, Willard 25

Tuve, Rosemond 25

Unferth 50, 61, 62, 63, 75, 76, 77, 78, 79–80, 98, 103, 127, 137, 165, 169, 192, 215–17, 221, 226, 236, 237, 240, 248, 253, 257, 258, 261, 262

Vaughan, M.F. 262
Vico, Giambattista 89–91, 93, 94, 95, 107, 108, 109
Vinaver, Eugene 25
Virgil 205

Wægmunding 130
Wanderer 97
Wealhtheow 17, 80, 103, 104, 120, 127, 128, 130, 134, 153, 156, 165, 186, 192, 197, 230, 232, 237–40, 249; gives necklace to Beowulf 121–2, 124, 136
Weather-Men. *See* Geats
Webster, John 19

Wielder 87, 96, 233. *See also* God.
Weland 135, 248
Whale's Ness 81, 116, 206, 219, 223
Whitelock, Dorothy 157, 188
Wiglaf 16, 17, 32, 59–60, 81, 99, 100, 101, 103, 110, 129, 130, 132, 135, 148, 207, 213, 219, 220, 232, 233, 234, 249, 250
wonder 9, 16, 17, 19, 68, 72, 81, 127, 154, 185, 199
Wordsworth, William 89, 109
Wormald, Patrick 110, 117
Wrenn, C.L. 123, 175
Wulfgar 103, 166

Xenophon 262

Yates, Frances 116, 117, 118, 159

Zumthor, Paul 25

www.ingramcontent.com/pod-product-compliance
Lightning Source LLC
Chambersburg PA
CBHW052015070526
44584CB00016B/1758